MW01591531

IRAQ

THE WAR THAT SHOULDN'T BE

YOU DECIDE

M. M. Chantiloupe

ISBN 0-7414-3018-5

God of Every Nation by William W. Reid, Jr. 1958, Ren. 1986 The
Hymn society. Admin. by Hope Publishing Co., Carol Stream,
Il 60188. All rights reserved. Used by permission.

Published by:

INFINITY
PUBLISHING.COM

1094 New DeHaven Street, Suite 100
West Conshohocken, PA 19428-2713
Info@buybooksontheweb.com
www.buybooksontheweb.com
Toll-free (877) BUY BOOK
Local Phone (610) 941-9999
Fax (610) 941-9959

Printed in the United States of America

Printed on Recycled Paper

Published July 2006

CONTENTS

IRAQ:

THE WAR THAT SHOULDN'T BE YOU DECIDE

FOREWORD

Was the Iraqi War that started in March 2003 based on deception contrived by the Bush administration in order to achieve its goals to invade a foreign country?

Did the Bush administration mislead the American people into thinking that they were in imminent danger of being attacked by Saddam Hussein with weapons of mass destruction?

Was the purported claim a deliberate deception by the Bush administration to deceive the American people and to shock them into believing that they were in grave danger of another attack even worse than the September 11, 2001, attacks because Saddam Hussein was affiliated with Osama bin Laden?

Was it concocted by a number of the Bush administration team or cohorts to start an imperialistic government?

Was it Blood for Oil?

Was George W. Bush continuing his father's war of 1991 to complete the job his father did not finish by overthrowing Saddam? Or, was George W. Bush avenging the assassination threat made against his father for the 1991 Gulf War?

President Bush told the American people in no uncertain terms that the U.S. was in imminent danger of being attacked with chemical and biological warfare by both Saddam Hussein and Osama bin Laden. So much so, that it planned the attack against Iraq without the blessing of the American people or the United Nations. To be sure that the American people were convinced that these chemical and biological weapons existed, the U.S. started an inoculation program in 2002 to vaccinate more than 500,000 servicemen and women. They were ordered to take anthrax pills and smallpox vaccine to guard against purported chemical and biological attacks from Saddam Hussein. Since the Bush administration was so sure that Saddam Hussein had weapons of mass destruction and would use them on U.S. military forces, why then did it risk the lives of more than 250,000 American troops? They were placed in harm's way at the risk of losing their lives or contracting long-term or even lifetime illnesses from such exposures, (if in fact there were such chemical and biological programs).

Also, was the threat to the American people so imminent that the Bush administration could not delay the war until the bad weather abated instead of sending the troops to fight under extremely difficult conditions? Was there no regard for the well being of the American servicemen and women by subjecting them to such grave dangers?

The Iraqi people are no stranger to oppression and invasions. If the Bush administration were going to war to liberate the Iraqi people, waiting another six months or even a year for that matter would not have made a significant difference. After all, the Iraqi people have been suffering under Saddam Hussein's rule for more than a decade. Subjecting the U.S. troops unnecessarily should have been of great concern to the Bush administration.

Should the United Nations' inspectors have been given the time and manpower required to search-and-destroy Saddam Hussein's purported weapons of mass destruction? The majority of the people worldwide felt that way. So why then, was the Bush administration so impetuous to attack Iraq? Was it aware that such weapons might not have been found because there was no conclusive evidence of weapons of mass destruction in Iraq, therefore, giving the inspectors more time and manpower would not result in discovery of any weapons of mass destruction, thereby negating their argument to go to war?

On April 26, 2006, CNN reported that the U.S. had an insider in Iraq before the war. This means that the Bush administration must have been receiving information on Iraq's weapons of mass destruction or lack thereof.

For the most part, the majority of the American people agreed that Saddam Hussein should not be allowed to continue as the head of Iraq and continue to massacre its people. However, most people also agreed that war should have been a last resort. Why then did the Bush administration rush to war? Was this war planned years ago and was going to take place no matter what? You decide.

ONE

DECEPTION CONTRIVED ON BOTH SIDES OF THE OCEAN

It appears that the Bush administration had long planned an invasion of Iraq prior to the September 11, 2001, attacks on the United States, but not because it believed that Saddam Hussein had chemical and biological weapons and was affiliated with Osama bin Laden.

Maybe it was to finish the 1991 Gulf War and kill Saddam Hussein for his assassination threat against George Bush Sr., or could it have been truly blood for oil as many people have speculated?

Iraq is a small country the size of California with 23 million people. However, it is the second largest oil-producing country in the world. There was a news report on one of the major television stations well before the September 11 attacks, indicating that as far back as 1995 Dick Cheney, Donald Rumsfeld, Paul Wolfowitz and Richard Pearle had drawn up a road map on how to remove Saddam Hussein once the Republicans took over the White House.

The Bush administration sent out its heavy hitters, Vice President Dick Cheney, National Security Adviser Condoleezza Rice, Secretary of State Colin Powell, Deputy Secretary of State Richard Armitage, Secretary of Defense Donald Rumsfield and Deputy Secretary of Defense Paul Wolfowitz, to convince the American people that the U.S. needed to take out Saddam Hussein.

On January 23, 2003, Deputy Defense Secretary Paul Wolfowitz said three countries have disarmed with international help in recent years, and Iraq's actions are not consistent with the cooperative disarmament. On January 28 Defense Secretary Donald Rumsfeld said Iraqi dictator Saddam Hussein is in a league of his own as a threat to world peace. Also, on January 28 President Bush said, "Trusting in the sanity and restraint of Saddam Hussein is not a strategy, and it is not an option. And on January 30 Vice President Dick Cheney said, "Saddam Hussein's pursuit of weapons of mass destruction poses a grave danger not only to his neighbors, but also to the United States." In order to further cement the fear of terrorism in the minds of the general public, President George Bush and British Prime Minister Tony Blair on January 31, 2003, after a poison plot was uncovered in England and a terror cell in Italy, said that these two key threats must not be allowed to come together. Yet the potential for that to happen lies with Saddam Hussein. They all played the same tune that the American people were in imminent danger of being attacked with biological and chemical weapons and that Saddam would supply other terrorist organizations such as al-Qaeda with these biological and chemical weapons and that he was affiliated with Osama bin Laden.

The Bush administration had no concrete proof that Saddam Hussein had biological and chemical weapons and could not prove it to the American people. When the question arose that the administration showed proof, it claimed that it could not divulge its sources because that would compromise them. The administration said it needed to keep intelligence sources secret. Secretary of Defense Donald Rumsfeld, when pressured to provide proof, avoided the question and said if the U.S. releases intelligence on where something nasty is located in Iraq, the evidence is likely to be gone the next day. Furthermore, the Bush administration said it was up to Saddam Hussein to prove that he has disarmed and not for the U.S. to find the weapons of mass destruction.

The Bush administration has changed the U.S. doctrine from the Cold War's containment of enemies to Iraq's pre-emption. Is this the kind of message the United States should be sending to the rest of the world, that if other countries do not adhere to the wishes of the U.S., they too would be forcefully attacked by U.S. troops? As a matter of fact, North Korea threatened pre-emptive strikes against its neighbors after the Bush administration attacked Iraq, saying they too can use pre-emptive strikes. Bush and his top advisers have made it clear that their ambitions to use war in Iraq will reshape the entire Middle East. In a speech in early March 2003 Bush declared that removing Saddam Hussein would unleash latent democratic movements and make Israel-Pakistan peace more likely.

The Bush administration used the September 11 attacks at every opportunity to remind the American people of the tragedy of that day and to persuade them that they have to go to war with Iraq, knowing there was no proof that Saddam Hussein had any link to bin Laden. Bush said in the wake of the September 11 attacks, the U.S. has no choice but to strike Saddam Hussein before he could supply weapons of mass destruction to al-Qaeda or other terrorists. Vice President Dick Cheney echoed Bush's warning by saying that the September 11 attacks changed all the rules of how the U.S. would defend itself. He said, "If we simply sit back and operate by 20th-century standards …we say wait until we're hit by an identifiable attack from Iraq, the consequences could be devastating." Of course, when the American people hear words like these, they reflect back on those horrible memories, just as the Bush administration intended.

Poll after poll showed that the American people did not want the U.S. to go to war unless they were in danger of being attacked by Saddam Hussein. So the Bush administration used the argument to convince them that they were sure Saddam Hussein had weapons of mass destruction and would not hesitate to use them on the American people. It appears that the Bush administration's modus operandi all along was to take over Iraq so that Bush's special interest groups would not only take over the oil fields, but would benefit from the lucrative contracts to rebuild Iraq's infrastructure after the war.

There was an article in the March 2002 issue of Time magazine which stated that National Security Adviser Condoleezza Rice was meeting with three U.S. Senators to discuss how to deal with Iraq through the United Nations, or perhaps in a coalition with America's Middle East allies. Bush was not interested and said "F___Saddam, we're taking him out."

To further deceive the American people, Bush's cohort, British Prime Minister Tony Blair, also drummed the same information to the British people, as well as gave press conferences alongside Bush condemning Saddam Hussein and confirming Bush's argument that Saddam Hussein had weapons of mass destruction and would use them on his own people as he had done in the past. Both Bush administration officials and British government officials used scare tactics by saying that Saddam Hussein could release weapons of mass destruction with 45 minutes. Tony Blair led the American people and the British people to believe that he had seen intelligence which showed that Saddam Hussein had weapons of mass destruction. We later learned that the dossier on Iraq's weapons of mass destruction as reported by Tony Blair was partially plagiarized from a college student's thesis.

Jack Straw, the British Foreign Secretary, was also beating the war drum against Iraq, citing Saddam Hussein's weapons of mass destruction and immediate and imminent threat not only to Saddam's neighbors but to other countries as well. Straw later concurred that the dossier was in fact plagiarized from an Iraqi student's thesis and that it had proved an embarrassment to the British government and should not have happened. Straw also apologized to the author of the thesis, and said a "very substantial error" was made with its compilation. In fact, he said, "This episode has been a very great embarrassment to the government."

Straw also said "We did not use the words 'immediate' or 'imminent'... we did not use that because plainly the evidence did not justify that. We did say there was a 'current and serious' threat and I stand by that completely."

A Wall Street Journal article dated March 17, 2003, by Jeanne Cummings and Greg Hitt, headlined: "In Iraq Drama, Cheney Emerges as President's War Counselor. As Bush Pursued Diplomacy, Vice President Made Sure Invasion Remained on the Table," stated:

On September 12, 2002, the president stood before the United Nations and asked for new Security Council resolutions calling on Iraq to peacefully disarm. Two days earlier, Mr. Bush had received a proposal to deal with Iraq in a manner more favored by his influential vice president, Dick Cheney: An updated plan for invasion.

The divergence of the two paths was fully apparent when Mr. Bush joined his two closest allies on the Azores Islands and called on the United Nations to immediately fall in line behind the unconditional disarmament of Saddam Hussein, by force if necessary.

"Tomorrow is a moment of truth for the world," declared Mr. Bush, flanked by British Prime Minister Tony Blair and Spanish Prime Minister Jose Maria Aznar. Their joint news conference made clear that without U.N. action in the next 24 hours, the military option would become the only one left on the table.

While much attention in the move toward war with Iraq has been focused on the roles played by Defense Secretary Donald Rumsfeld, Secretary of State Colin Powell and National Security Adviser Condoleezza Rice, the vice president has played the largest role of all. That dynamic was clear as the Iraq drama reached its final act. The two most overpowering pictures were of Mr. Bush at a summit meeting and Mr. Cheney, after nearly a month out of the public view, emerging to make the case for war with lengthy interviews on national television.

Many heads of state and the general public wanted Saddam Hussein disarmed peacefully and that could have been accomplished if the Bush administration wanted to disarm him peacefully. However, it was apparent from the offset that the Bush administration had no intention of disarming him peacefully, as that would negate the plans of the warmongers. Saddam Hussein and his cabinet members were right when they said no matter what they did to comply with the demands of the United Nations and the U.S. their country would be attacked by the U.S.

On September 9, 2003, Former Defense Secretary William Cohen said on C-Span that over the past 10 to 12 years, the U.S. has decimated Saddam Hussein's defense capabilities, and that is why the U.S. was able to go into Baghdad within three weeks. Containment was working because of the no-fly zone to the North and to the South. In 1998, when the Clinton administration got information that Saddam was building chemical weapons, the administration launched Desert Fox and took out the facilities. "He was being contained," Mr. Cohen said. He also used the old adage, you make your friends before you need them; if not the price of your friendship goes up, referring to the price the Bush administration was paying to get other countries to join the coalition in Iraq.

Just about everyone agrees that Saddam Hussein should not have been allowed to continue to commit atrocities against the Iraqi people while other nations stood by idly and watched such human suffering. Conversely, the U.S. should not have furthered the demise of the Iraqi people by invading their country for no good reason. War is not a pretty picture and should be a last resort. Only the people who are caught up in war can appreciate the destruction that war brings not only to human lives, but also on the infrastructure, many of them experiencing a "living hell" day in and day out, not knowing if they would live to see another day, or how mangled their bodies would be even if they survived the vicious attacks from firebombs. Children and women would be killed, parents separated from their children, spouses would lose loved ones, and mothers and fathers would lose their children. When a soldier gives up his life in a war it should be for a very, very good cause. It should not be because some warmongers want to have a war for their own selfish reasons.

And, since only the oilfields were protected during the war in Iraq, some of the injured could not get medical help because the hospitals were no longer operative due either to damage or lack of medical staff. Food supplies diminished, water supplies interrupted, electricity cut off, and sewage systems demolished. People were suffering from starvation because they were afraid to leave their homes to seek food for fear they would be caught in the bomb raids.

Liberating the Iraqi people from Saddam should be a foregone conclusion. However, it should not have to be at such a grave price. The fact that many of the 23 million people were uprooted from their homes and businesses and reduced to impoverishment was unjust and unwarranted. The American people were not in imminent danger from Saddam, and the proverbial wisdom should have been to allow the inspectors to complete and destroy any weapons of mass destruction.

So, was this war really about weapons of mass destruction and the imminent danger to the American people or was it about controlling the oil and the country's infrastructure? Is this the message the U.S. wants to send to the rest of world? The message is that the U.S. can invade other countries, overthrow their leaders and take control of their commodities and infrastructure. How much better then is the U.S. than those heads of states whom the U.S. condemns, from time to time, who rule with iron fists. It is a sad day when the world sees the United States as an aggressor and invader rather than a compassionate country that seeks to deliver other nations from their oppressors.

The Bush administration claimed it was liberating the Iraqi people from Saddam Hussein. If the United States is so concerned about liberating oppressed people from tyrants and dictators, why hasn't it liberated other oppressed people like those under oppression in countries such as the Congo and Sudan? One would think that if the U.S. were such a liberator, it would seek to liberate and/or defend not just the people of oil-rich countries such as Kuwait and Iraq, but also the less fortunate countries.

Liberating the Iraqi people from Saddam Hussein is a good thing, but it should not be at such a high human cost for the Iraqis, American military and their families. And of course, not to mention the financial cost involved in reconstructing an entire country of 23 million people. There should not have been such a rush to remove Saddam Hussein from Iraq because he was being contained since the1991 Gulf War. If the United Nations were given the time needed to complete the inspection, this war would not have taken place. Moreover; information provided by the United Nations' inspectors on their findings were indicative of the fact that Iraq did not have a weapons program.

Of course, it was not long before the truth came out that both the Bush administration and the British government deceived the American people, the British people, and the rest of the world about Saddam Hussein's weapons of mass destruction, and the very reason they went to war against Iraq. Now the credibility of both the United States and British government is questionable. When a report came out that Saddam Hussein did not have weapons of mass destruction, the White House said that Bush's claim on Iraq had flawed origins. On July 7, 2003, the White House said that President Bush was relying on incomplete and perhaps inaccurate information from American intelligence agencies when he declared in his State of the Union speech that Saddam Hussein had tried to purchase uranium from Africa. But the Bush administration was emphatic that Saddam Hussein was reconstituting his nuclear weapons program, which added urgency to its case for military action against him.

The British Prime Minister's credibility was also damaged from this misinformation and misleading the country on Iraq's weapons of mass destruction in order to attack Iraq. He made reference to another dossier in September 2002 that claimed that Iraq's weapons of mass destruction could be deployed within 45 minutes of an order to do so. An unidentified intelligence source told the BBC that Blair's director of communication, Alastair Campbell, had insisted on the insertion of the 45-minute claim to add a touch of drama.

Is this the kind of government people should rely on to do the right thing? How can they deceive the people so blatantly to go to war without any regard for the human lives that would be lost? Mr. Straw said they never used the words "immediate' or "imminent" because the evidence did not justify that. However, they kept emphasizing that Saddam Hussein was a danger to his neighbors and others.

A BBC News article dated June 24, 2003, said:

BBC defense correspondent Andrew Giligan reported in May that a senior British official had told him that the government's dossier on Iraq's weapons program had been "sexed up" at Downing Street's request. Mr. Straw denied that a request was made from 10 Downing Street for the so-called "sexing up" dossier.

Mr. Straw also said that British sources had not been involved in information as reported in the news that Iraq was trying to buy uranium in Africa, which was later found to be based on forged documents.

Two British cabinet members, Foreign Secretary Robin Cook and British International Development Secretary Clare Short, resigned their cabinet posts under protest against the war on Iraq. Secretary Cook resigned when Tony Blair decided to back the U.S. to go to war with Iraq although security sources prior to the war said that Saddam Hussein did not pose an immediate threat with weapons of mass destruction. Later Secretary Short resigned after she realized that Tony Blair lied to the members of Parliament about Saddam Hussein having weapons of mass destruction. Short indicated that Blair used honorary deception to back the U.S. and to get the members of parliament to agree with him. Short also said that Blair had agreed with Bush to go to war with Iraq as early as September 2002, and she believed that the Bush administration was not fully prepared to govern Iraq, which results in a lot of chaos.

British Prime Minister Tony Blair claimed he had secret proof that weapons of mass destruction would be found in Iraq, but that he was waiting to publish a complete picture of intelligence gained before the war with a summary of the findings after the war. However, as of 2006 there was no published report on his findings on the pre-war process. During the interim, he changed his position to say that even if in fact weapons of mass destruction were not found, it was sufficient grounds to attack Iraq because of the way Saddam Hussein ruled his people. But that was not what they sold either the American people or the British people as to why they went to war against Iraq.

A June 2003 Guardian Unlimited article by Gaby Hinsliff, Nick Paton Walsh in St. Peterburg and Peter Beaumont in London said:

> Prime Minister Tony Blair insisted he had secret proof that weapons of mass destruction would be found in Iraq in his strongest signal yet that coalition forces believe they may have begun to uncover leads to Iraq's deadly arms cache.
>
> Stung by claims that the government exaggerated the threat from Saddam, Blair said he was waiting to publish a 'complete picture' of both

intelligence gained before the war and 'what we've actually found.' ...

According to intelligence sources, the new leads have been provided by Iraqi scientists and a member of the State Security Organization who was debriefed by MI6 and the CIA. This followed a week in which Government and intelligence sources appeared to have changed their story on the likelihood of finding weapons of mass destruction on an almost daily basis.

One source claimed that British intelligence suggested that Saddam Hussein had destroyed his weapons of mass destruction even before the United Nations' inspectors visited Iraq, a version of events that had been changed the day before to claim that chemical weapons may actually have been deployed in the field and then destroyed as American troops advanced. ...

Blair said in an interview that claims that the existence of weapons of mass destruction was "a great big fib got out by the security services" would be proved wrong. He said he had "absolutely no knowledge" of an alleged meeting between Foreign Secretary Jack Straw and his U.S. counterpart, Colin Powell, in a New York hotel to discuss concerns over whether the evidence of weapons of mass destruction would be strong enough. Leaked transcripts suggested Straw had warned the issue could 'explode in our faces.' The Foreign Office insisted the two men had not met on the date given in February.

Downing Street had been hampered in its argument by repeated suggestions from the Bush administration that weapons of mass destruction may never be found. Paul Wolfowitz, deputy to U.S. Defense Secretary Donald Rumsfeld, suggested in an interview that weapons of mass destruction were a bureaucratic pretext to start a war.

Blair said that weapons of mass destruction were the basis in law for taking action -- but "that's not the same as saying it's a bureaucratic pretext."

Hans Blix, the United Nations chief inspector, reported in 2003 that there was no evidence that Saddam had or had restarted his weapons of mass destruction program. Yet, the Bush administration continued its rhetoric that weapons would be found. Each time the United States' inspectors claimed that they found a "smoking gun" it turned out to be nothing. The so-called mobile trucks found near a farm with equipment to manufacture weapons of mass destruction turned out to be used for nothing but fertilizers. In April 2003, Hans Blix challenged the United States' weapons hunt when the Bush administration planned to send a 1,000-strong team to look for weapons of mass destruction in Iraq.

According to reports, the Pentagon wanted its own "Iraqi Survey Group" of military personnel, United States government analysts, civilian scientists and private contractors to look for any illegal weapons sites. However, Blix wanted his team to return, saying it would increase the credibility of any weapons discoveries. Blix told the British Broadcasting Corporation that they would receive the reports of the Americans and the British and would be able to corroborate it independently. He said that the world would like to have a credible report on the absence or eradication of the program of weapons of mass destruction.

On June 26, 2003, the Bush administration said that the CIA's procurement of centrifuge parts in Iraq were necessary in a nuclear weapons program. The CIA said it had critical parts and plans of a key piece of Iraqi nuclear technology, parts needed to develop a bomb program that was dug up in Baghdad. They claimed that an Iraqi scientist, Mahdi Obeidi, unearthed the parts in his back yard in Baghdad, where he had hidden them beneath a rose bush twelve years prior under orders from Saddam Hussein's son, Qusay, and Saddam's then son-in-law, Hussein Kamel.

Centrifuges are drums of cylinders that spin at high speeds to separate heavy and light molecules, allowing increasingly enriched uranium to be drawn off. National Security Council spokesman Sean McCormack said the equipment from Obeidi's back yard are "what might be needed to build a centrifuge, concealed over time as part of a plan to reconstitute a nuclear weapons program after the International Atomic Energy Agency inspectors were over." However, the International Atomic Energy Agency said the parts found in Baghdad were not "evidence of a smoking gun" proving Iraq has a current weapon of mass destruction program. In spite of this, the Bush administration would not allow the United Nations inspectors to accompany the CIA to verify any finds of weapons of mass destruction.

According to a CNN article dated June 26, 2003, by Mike Boettcher, David Ensor and Maria Fleet, Iraqi scientist Mahdi Obeidi said that the parts of a gas centrifuge system for enriching uranium were part of a highly sophisticated system he was ordered to hide to be ready to rebuild the bomb program. Obeidi said that he had very important things at his disposal that he was ordered to keep and would not want them to proliferate because of their potential consequences if they fall in the hands of tyrants, dictators or terrorists. Obeidi said he never worked on a nuclear program after 1991.

So if what Obeidi said is true, then it's obvious that Saddam did not have a weapons of mass destruction program as indicated by the Bush administration. This goes counter to what the Bush administration told the American people when it was making the case to go to war, namely, that Saddam would provide weapons of mass destruction to rogue states and terrorists. Moreover, if Obeidi was ordered to keep the information and some centrifuge components so that if he were given the order he could restart the centrifuge program and an order was never given, then in fact Saddam did not have a nuclear program.

Therefore, this would concur with the United Nations International Atomic Energy Agency report that Iraq had no nuclear weapons program after 1991. The Agency said the parts needed to develop a bomb program that the CIA says were found in Baghdad are not "evidence of a smoking gun" proving Iraq had a current weapons of mass destruction program. According to the agency spokesman, Mark Gwozdecky, "The findings refer to material and documents of the pre-1991 Iraqi nuclear weapons program that have been well-known to the agency."

Four months after the attack on Iraq, the Bush administration admitted that the intelligence information presented to the American people that Saddam Hussein had weapons of mass destruction was flawed.

Saddam Hussein was being contained since the 1991 Gulf War. He had destroyed his weapons of mass destruction programs and there was no evidence of his restarting those programs. The United States and Britain were bombing Iraq practically on a weekly basis in the "no fly zone". Iraq was constantly under the watchful eye of the U.S. and British intelligence. How then could Saddam restart his weapons program without the U.S. and Britain knowing about it?

TWO

WEAPONS OF MASS DESTRUCTION

President Bush, Dick Cheney, Donald Rumsfeld, et al, went to war under false pretenses, and when weapons of mass destruction were not found, they said Saddam Hussein is a bad man and should be overthrown anyway.

Despite the denial by the Iraqi government, and the lack of confirmation by the United Nations that Saddam Hussein could launch a missile attack within 45 minutes, the U.S. invaded Iraq.

Three weeks after Saddam Hussein's regime was toppled, Bush, speaking from his Crawford, Texas, ranch touted it was a matter of when – not if – weapons of mass destruction were found in Iraq. In a turn about face, Bush and other U.S. officials indicated that coalition troops may come up empty in their hunt, saying it is possible that weapons were destroyed before or during the U.S-led war.

A May 4, 2003, Associated Press article by Jennifer Loven said a senior Bush official said initial information suggested Iraq's weapons program was geared mostly toward just-in-time production.

In a joint appearance at his ranch with Australian Prime Minister John Howard, Bush said, "Saddam Hussein has weapons of mass destruction, it's well known." Bush said the search would be difficult and lengthy, but ultimately successful. He said, "Iraq's the size of the state of California. It's got tunnels, caves, all kinds of complexes."

After Tarig Aziz, one of Hussein's closest deputies was caught and in the U.S. coalition's custody, Bush complained that Aziz was not cooperating with U.S. forces. The U.S. wanted Aziz to tell them of the whereabouts of Iraq's purported weapons of mass destruction. But, it stands to reason that if there were no weapons of mass destruction, how could he provide them with that information? Bush then accused him of not telling the truth. Bush said "Tarig Aziz still doesn't know how to tell the truth. He didn't know how to tell the truth when he was in office. He doesn't know to tell the truth ...as a captive." The U.S. also expected that the captured scientists would give them the answer they seek regarding weapons of mass destruction. However, the scientists stuck to their argument – that Iraq had no weapons program in years.

Moreover, in 1993 the Clinton administration after bombing Iraq for four days halted the strike, saying "Operation is now complete." Clinton said, "I am confident we have achieved our mission. We have inflicted significant damage on Saddam's weapons of mass destruction programs, on the command structures that direct and protect that capability and on his military and security infrastructures." He said the United States would remain vigilant and monitor whether Iraq tried to rebuild its weapons program.

A May 4, 2004, Associated Press article by Jennifer Loven stated:

A military official involved with a small group of U.S.-led search teams in Iraq said they were under "intense pressure from Washington to come up with something." The official, who spoke on condition of anonymity, said the teams were overwhelmed with work and looking forward to planned reinforcements. The teams were visiting suspected sites and testing for the presence of any weapons or indications that ingredients may have been destroyed there, while some were sifting through documents and intelligence reports for clues.

According to a Wall Street Journal article by John J. Fialka, the Bush administration intensified the search for weapons of mass destruction by sending 1,000 scientists, technicians, intelligence analysts and other experts called the Survey Group to Baghdad. This team was equipped with mobile laboratories that could do tests in Iraq. It would also develop procedures for testing in laboratories in the United States and the United Kingdom. Meanwhile, the head of the United Nations' inspection team, Hans Blix, was preparing to brief the U.N. Security Council on his preparedness to send a U.N. inspection team to Baghdad. Under the existing Council resolutions, the U.N. Monitoring, Verification and Inspection Commission, which is called UNMOVIC, had the mandate to go back to Iraq. However, a U.S. official said, "We see no immediate role for UNMOVIC. We have other issues to deal with before we start bringing Blix back in. Nor are we convinced that Blix is the right person to lead any effort in Iraq."

An April 6, 2003 Chicago Tribune article by Howard Witt, stated:

A war President Bush launched a war expressly to rid Iraq of its weapons of mass destruction, which has yet to uncover any of them. ... Much of the political, diplomatic and legal justification for the U.S.-led war rests on the assertion that Hussein is hiding weapons of mass destruction and has defied repeated United Nations demands to surrender them. If that proves not to be true, the Bush administration's diplomatic credibility could be shaken, the Muslim world could be reinforced in its belief that Washington is waging war against Islam and U.S. leaders might even be vulnerable to legal challenges in international courts.

The Bush administration's mantra starts from the top down, namely, President George Bush, Vice President Dick Cheney, Secretary of Defense Donald Rumsfeld, Secretary of State Colin Powell, and so on. For example, Army Brig.

Gen. Vincent Brooks in Doha, Qatar, repeated the administration's mantra by saying, "Let's remember that this regime has been involved in a campaign of denial and deception for decades and has been very effective at it. And so, we don't expect that we're just going to walk up on any weapons of mass destruction. We'll have to do things that give us control of areas that let us then do deliberate work. Our first efforts are to destroy their regime and cause its removal. Secondary efforts will be related to weapons of mass destruction."

A July 2003 Wall Street Journal article by Dan Morse stated:

> Captain Stanton's 101st Airborne Division soldiers would spend 75% of their time going from house to house searching for weapons, ammunition and documents the first two months after the major conflict was over in Iraq. The troops found mortar systems, mortar rounds and AK-47 bullets, but no weapons of mass destruction. Although the 101st Airborne Division soldiers have been trained to helicopter into battle, they traveled mostly by land. They walked 70 miles through cities, often traversing longer distances aboard trucks or in hot-wired buses appropriated from Iraqis by other units according to Sgt. Ed Hawk.

As it became clear that there were no weapons of mass destruction in Iraq, the Bush administration became more adamant in not wanting the United Nations inspectors to accompany the U.S. team to verify the existence of any weapons of mass destruction. Instead, it wanted top Pentagon and White House staff to do the verification, assuming there was verification to be done. According to reports, these officials argued that international inspectors had been lax in the past, and if the hunt for chemical and biological weapons wasn't done quickly and securely, the weapons could leak out of a chaotic Iraq to terrorists or to some of Iraq's more unsavory neighbors. Many countries concurred that the United Nations should be the one to verify any weapons of mass destruction found in Iraq to legitimize the discovery.

An April 8, 2003, Wall Street Journal Article stated:

...Many outside experts stress the need for the U.S. to find a credible path for verifying any finds. The U.S. has "got to show" the world "independently verified evidence of the presence of these weapons," says David Kay, who led some of the early inspections teams into Iraq after the first Gulf War, and who has been a critic of the more recent U.N. efforts. He adds, "We have to communicate this credibility to places like the Middle East, where some people still think we or Israel's (intelligence services) staged the attack on the World Trade Center.

After the discovery of suspect barrels near Karbala, soldiers on the scene called in a mobile lab known as a Fox Nuclear, Biological and Chemical Reconnaissance System. The crew of the six-wheeled sealed laboratory could use the lab's probe to grab samples of air, water, soil and other substances without endangering the crew, immediately testing the samples for signs of weapons of mass destruction.

Even before specialized units could get to suspected sites, individual Army units could detect any nerve gas with hand-held electronic devices or chemically sensitive paper, which can signal a gas's presence.

In the months before the war, Pentagon officials working with the Defense Intelligence Agency and the Central Intelligence Agency developed their own detailed plans for the weapons hunt. These covered a host of operations: testing materials in the field, getting samples out of Iraq for more analysis, publicizing the finds and destroying the weapons on site.

As the months went by and there was no "Smoking gun," in other words, there were no weapons of mass destruction to be found anywhere in Iraq, the Bush administration hoped to take the pressure off by hiring David Kay to head the search in Iraq. According to a report, experts in the field of weapons inspection said that if anyone can get to the bottom of what weapons Saddam had and when he had them, it was David Kay.

An August 3, 2003, New York Times article by Dan Freeman, c.2003 Hearst Newspapers, said that David Kay, Texas Bulldog is Bush's Secret Weapon. The article said that the Bush administration has placed all its chips on veteran weapons inspector David Kay in the frustrating U.S. hunt for weapons of mass destruction in Iraq. In hiring Kay to direct the search, the administration has turned to an articulate pro-war hawk with previous high-profile experiences looking for weapons in Iraq. Kay was the chief U.N. inspector in 1991 when Saddam Hussein's soldiers kept him and his team surrounded in a Baghdad parking lot. The inspectors had just seized documents from Iraq's Atomic Energy Commission when their al fresco captivity began. ... He and his team walked away with 25,000 pages of documents detailing Iraq's nuclear weapons at that time. Before the war, Kay was in the vanguard of weapons experts arguing that continued U.N. inspectors would not work and that only Saddam's removal could end the threat posed by his reputed weapons.

So, if that was the case, it goes without saying that Saddam had no weapons of mass destruction because Kay and his team had not been able to locate any weapons once they arrived in Iraq. Yet, Bush continued his relentless accusation that there were weapons of mass destruction in Iraq and that they would be found in a matter of time. It is inexplicable that he was so confident that there were weapons in Iraq, yet he failed to take responsibility for the intelligence used to go to war. Moreover, the intelligence report was doctored to reflect information that the Bush administration could use to convince the world that the U.S. had to attack Iraq. One would think that before you send so many soldiers to face death and dismemberment, the information would be factual.

The Bush administration also said that it relied on information received from Ahmad Chalabi, who had his own agenda to see Saddam Hussein toppled. Chalabi fed the administration with the information that they wanted to hear. When Saddam kept saying there were no weapons of mass destruction in Iraq, President Bush, Cheney and others called him a liar. Now one wonders who was being disingenuous and who was telling the truth.

Even when the facts were known that the Bush administration manipulated intelligence information about Iraq nuclear weapons, the Bush administration passed the blame onto the British government's intelligence. In the State of the Union speech, Bush said they had learned that Saddam was buying significant quantities of uranium from Niger, when the only possible contact with Niger was in 1999. Bush also said that Saddam's nuclear weapons could be activated in 45 minutes. And the Bush administration, in no uncertain terms, told the American people that they were in imminent danger of being attacked by Saddam, given his nuclear capabilities.

In the final analysis, President Bush still has not taken responsibility. He has instead passed the buck onto the British government, CIA Director George Tenet and National Security Adviser Condoleezza Rise. He blamed George Tenet for not insisting that the famous 16 words were deleted from the statement so as not to have it in the final draft of the State of the Union message and blamed Rice for allowing them to remain.

According to reports, Tenet had concerns about the British information on Iraq's purchase of additional uranium ore from Niger because of doubts about its credibility, and to some insisted that that information not be included in the State of the Union message. In denying the impact those 16 words caused, Rice and Secretary of Defense Donald Rumsfeld said that the famous 16 words were "technically" accurate because of the attribution to the British.

A July 21, 2003, Boston Globe article by Thomas Oliphant stated:

...Even before Tenet issued his alleged declaration of responsibility on July 11, several of us were aware of a conflict between the CIA and the national security staff about their discussions that preceded the insertion of the 16 words about Africa in the speech. We were also aware of the identity of the negotiators: a senior CIA expert on unconventional weapons (Alan Foley) and the antiproliferation guy at the NSC (Robert Joseph).

Foley's basic account was that the CIA would have problems with the citation of British intelligence referring to a possible effort by Iraq to purchase additional uranium ore from Niger because of doubts about its credibility. He also said the CIA would have problems with specific reference to Niger or to alleged efforts to acquire a specific amount of nuclear bomb raw material. This dovetails with a successful effort in October by Tenet to get similar language out of another important presidential address.

...The other reason the inquiry proceeded relates to the preposterous assertions by Rice and Defense Secretary Donald Rumsfeld that the famous 16 words were "technically" accurate because of the attribution to the British. This is false.

In fact, the Bush speech hyped the claim by using the verb "learned" instead of simply using the word "said." It also fudged the significance of the allegation by saying the Iraqi effort had occurred "recently" when the only possible contact with Niger was 1999. And it was simply incorrect when it used the phrase "significant quantities of uranium" when in fact there was no credible claim relating to quantity at all.

The Bush administration's modus operandi is likened to that of a trial lawyer who makes a statement regarding a plaintiff or a defendant that should not be mentioned, knowing very well that the judge would strike it from the record. However, by then the damage is done. The jurors hear the information, which will stay in the back of their minds, and could ultimately have an impact in their decision. Once President Bush tells the American people that Saddam was trying to purchase additional uranium ore from Niger and that they were in imminent danger of being attacked by nuclear weapons, he accomplished his goal. That is, to instill fear and trepidation in the minds of the American people into believing that Saddam is a danger to the free world.

According to reports, both the CIA and the State Department had information as early as March 2002 casting doubt on British claims that Iraq was seeking uranium in Africa. Yet the Bush administration used the discredited British intelligence information as a justification for the war. A former diplomat hired by the CIA to check into the merits of the allegations said Vice President Dick Cheney's office knew in 2002 that the diplomat was unable to substantiate the intelligence.

White House spokesman Ari Fleischer said Cheney was not informed or aware of the CIA report casting doubt on the British allegations. But Wilson, the former envoy who helped the CIA write the report, said in an NBC-TV interview that Cheney's office requested and received from the CIA a report on Wilson's mission.

According to an Associated Press article of July 11, 2003, by Barry Schweid, in early March of 2002, the intelligence bureau at the State Department circulated a memorandum that described the British report as dubious. That report went to Powell and other department officials. Powell was also given comprehensive findings by the bureau that Iraq had not reconstituted its nuclear weapons program, said an official on the condition of anonymity. In making the U.S. case in February to the United Nations, Powell did not use the uranium allegation that Iraq possessed weapons of mass destruction. U.N. officials in New York said that the same day Powell briefed the Council his office gave U.N. weapons inspectors, documents trying to back up the discredited claim. The documents contained the caveat that the State Department had been unable to confirm the report.

In spite of the fact that the same information was circulated among these top officials, President Bush, Vice President Dick Cheney, National Security Adviser Condoleezza Rice and Secretary of Defense Donald Rumsfeld, they continued their never-ending persuasion that attacks on the U.S. by Saddam Hussein were imminent. On January 23, 2003, Rice wrote an article in the New York Times saying Iraq had tried to obtain uranium, and on January 29, 2003, Rumsfeld, appearing on CNN also said that Iraq was trying to purchase uranium from Niger. Rice also defended the 16 words in the speech, saying that the CIA had vetted the speech and that if Tenet had any misgivings about the sentence in the president's speech, "he did not make them known" to Bush or his staff. She said "the CIA cleared the speech in its entirety."

The Bush administration hoodwinked not only lawmakers who voted for the war, but also the American people who believed Bush when he said in the State of the Union message in January that Saddam was trying to buy uranium, and that he had the material to produce chemical weapons. The Bush administration also said that Congress had the same intelligence information. However, Richard Clarke, former counterterrorism coordinator said at a Miami Book Fair on November 20, 2005, that the Congress gets an analysis, a conclusion so to speak, not the raw intelligence material. So when the Bush administration said the Congress had the same information when they voted for the Iraq war that was not truly accurate.

Lawmakers such as Massachusetts Senator John Kerry demanded answers from the Bush administration regarding the forged documents on Saddam Hussein's purported purchase of uranium materials from Niger. He called for a full investigation into the issue, and said the "finger pointing" within the administration will "do nothing to make this country safer and will simply further erode the confidence of the American public and our allies around the world."

A letter signed by 16 Democratic house members asked Bush to back up other claims he made about Iraq in the speech, including whether Saddam Hussein had the materials needed to produce up to 500 tons of chemical weapons, and whether he had the munitions required to deliver them. The letter was signed by 16 democrats who voted for the House resolution authorizing the war.

White House officials admitted that the Iraqi uranium report should not have appeared in the January 28, 2002, speech. Bush's National Security Adviser Condoleezza Rice said no top officials in the White House knew of a report by a CIA emissary that said the report appeared to be bogus. How ironic! One would think that the top officials are exactly the people who would receive the reports, bogus or not. Senator Bob Graham, Democrat from Florida, on CBS's "Face the Nation," said the intelligence was available that should have made Bush realize the information in the uranium report was suspect. One source was Vice President Dick Cheney, he said. The vice president went to the CIA on several occasions, and asked specifically for additional information on the Niger-Iraq connection. The United States sent an experienced ambassador, Wilson, to investigate the validity of the claim. He came back after a full review with a report that these were fabricated documents.

Was this bogus information intentionally included to hoodwink Congress and the American people? On "Fox News Sunday," Rockefeller said Bush could make the controversy go away by coming clean whether the justification for war was exaggerated. Rockefeller told CNN that he requested the FBI involvement in the case after the International Atomic Energy Agency debunked the British report.

In May 2003, the Bush administration announced that it found two trailers in Iraq presumed to be production laboratories for biological weapons. It was later forced to retract the statement. According to an intelligence report, the trailers contained chemicals unrelated to making biological agents. U.S. officials said investigators found no traces of biological agents on the vehicles. According to a C-Span report of August 10, 2003, the so-called mobile laboratories were provided to Iraq by the British government for helium balloons. Since no stocks of biological weapons have been found in Iraq, the Bush administration has been forced to acknowledge that Iraq may not have possessed weapons of mass destruction immediately before the U.S. invasion.

If the U.S. had listened to the United Nations and Iraqi officials that there were no weapons of mass destruction in Iraq since they were destroyed after the 1991 Gulf War, there would never have been an invasion. But again, that would have thrown a monkey wrench in the Republicans' plans, since invading Iraq was a foregone conclusion long before the Bush administration took over the White House.

A Reuters article dated July 10, 2003, said four months after the war, a senior British official said it would be "extremely difficult" to find banned weapons to justify the war. Moreover, a diplomat to the United Nation's nuclear watchdog, (International Atomic Energy Agency) said that Britain has never provided evidence to back up its continued insistence that Iraq tried to buy uranium from Africa. The British Broadcasting Corporation said senior figures in London no longer believed banned missiles or chemical weapons would be found in Iraq.

The fact that Iraq did not use any weapons of mass destruction on the U.S. troops is evidence that Iraq did not have any weapons of mass destruction as purported by the Bush

26

administration. As a matter of fact, the Iraqi troops, for the most part, retreated when attacked by the U.S. and Britain.

The British government resorted to a smear campaign, just like the Bush administration regarding its "sexed up dossier" by smearing the dead scientist, David Kelley, a Ministry of Defense expert on chemical and biological weapons. His apparent suicide came shortly after he was named as the source for the BBC report alleging that the British government "sexed up" a September dossier on Iraqi weapons of mass destruction to make the case for war against Saddam Hussein more compelling.

According to an August 4, 2003, AFP news article, an official from the British Prime Minister's office referred to David Kelly as a Walter Mitty-style fantasist – a reference to a fictional character in literature who has delusions about his own importance. Also, a World AFP, August 20, 2003, article said the news regarding the British government's deception on weapons of mass destruction have caused some concern among the British people on the reliability of their government to be forthcoming with the truth. And, British Foreign Intelligence Chief Sir Richard Dearlove said he would leave his post in 2004. He said his decision was unrelated to the dossiers that allegedly exaggerated the threat posed by Saddam Hussein.

Meanwhile, back in the United States as White House officials try to control the latest fallout over President Bush's flawed suggestion in his State of the Union message, some White House officials suggested that National Security Adviser Condoleezza Rice resign. However, President Bush insisted that she would not leave her position.

CIA Director George Tenet took the blame for the flawed information in his report to the Congress. He said the false allegation about Iraq's nuclear deal rested squarely with him and his agency. He said the CIA should never have let Bush repeat a British allegation that Iraq was seeking uranium from the African country of Niger when U.S. intelligence analysts could not corroborate it. Tenet said officials reviewed portions of the draft speech and raised some concerns with national security aides at the White House that prompted changes in the language. But he said the CIA officials failed to stop the remark from being uttered despite the doubts about its validity. He said, "Officials who were reviewing the draft remarks on uranium raised several concerns about the fragmentary nature of the intelligence with National Security Council colleagues." But Bush and Rice, while on a trip to Africa, said Tenet's agency approved the language in the speech and never raised objections to them.

The Bush administration and the British government built a case to attack Iraq without any concrete evidence of either an imminent threat to the United States or its neighbors. They beat the war drum in unison day in and day out how Saddam must be taken out. But the fact that that there was no such danger to the American people and no weapons of mass destruction in Iraq, only serves to solidify beliefs that for all intents and purposes, the position taken by the Bush administration and the British government that Saddam Hussein was being overthrown to bring freedom and democracy to the Iraqi people was just a front so that special interests can control its oil and infrastructure.

According to a June 6, 2003, Reuters article, The Pentagon's intelligence service reported in September 2002, that it had no reliable evidence that Iraq had chemical agents in weaponized form. The timeframe is notable because it coincided with the Bush administration efforts to mount a public case for the urgency of disarming Iraq by force, if necessary.

George Bush, Dick Cheney, Donald Rumsfeld, Paul Wolfowitz, Colin Powell and Ari Fleisher insisted that Saddam Hussein possessed chemical, biological and other weapons and was hiding them. Colin Powell went before the United Nations and showed "purported" pictures and diagrams of mobile facilities to convince the United Nations, the American people and the rest of the world that Saddam possessed weapons of mass destruction. In making the case to attack Iraq, they argued that Iraq was seeking to develop nuclear weapons and might provide some of its mass-killing weapons to terrorists. Their refusal to allow the United Nations inspectors back in to verify the legitimacy of any found weapons cast a shadow over the reliability of weapons that would be found by the United States. Even the "so-called weapons" found under the "rose bush" was suspect.

On September 18, 2002, Secretary of Defense Donald Rumsfeld, speaking to the House Armed Services Committee, said, "We do know that the Iraqi regime currently has chemical and biological weapons of mass destruction." Still, on February 4, 2004, Rumsfeld defended the U.S.-led invasion of Iraq, even after Dr. Kay, the head of the search for weapons in Iraq, issued his report stating that there are no weapons in Iraq and resigned his position. There again, Rumsfeld continued the mantra saying, "I'm convinced that the president of the United States did the right thing in Iraq. Let there be no doubt. The world is a safer place today and the Iraqi people far better off for the action." But three years after the invasion, many Iraqis are not better off than during Saddam's regime. And, how was the world threatened by Iraq, a country the size of California with no major weaponry? Rumsfeld acknowledged the possibility that Iraq did not have weapons of mass destruction at the start of the war. His theories are:

Such weapons may have existed at the start of the war; Iraq had such weapons but they were "transferred in whole or in part to one or more other countries." Such weapons existed "dispersed and hidden throughout Iraq." These weapons were "destroyed at some moment prior" to the start of the war; Iraq possessed small quantities of biological or chemical agents, and had "a surge capability for a rapid build-up," evidence of which "we may eventually find in the months ahead."

On October 7, 2002, during a speech in Cincinnati that laid out how America was threatened by Saddam, Bush said, "If we know Saddam Hussein has dangerous weapons today

– and we do – does it make any sense for the world to wait to confront him as he grows even stronger and develops even more dangerous weapons? According to a report, many at the White House and on Capital Hill said that it was obvious that the intelligence reports about Iraq had been deeply flawed, and they doubted that President Bush would have the luxury of waiting to confront the issue.

On January 27, 2004, President Bush did not repeat his claims of Saddam's illicit weapons program. However, he said weapons would eventually be found in Iraq. He also insisted that the war was justified because Saddam posed "a grave and gathering threat to America and the world." When asked by reporters if he would repeat earlier expressions of confidence that the weapons would be found in light of statements by the former chief weapons inspector in Iraq, David Kay, that Hussein had gotten rid of them well before the war, Bush did not answer directly. He said, "I think it's very important for us to let the Iraq Survey Group do its work, so we can find out the facts and compare the facts to what was thought."

Even as the facts about Saddam WMD became well-known, Vice President Dick Cheney defended the U.S. decision to invade Iraq. In response to David Kay, who resigned January 23, 2004, as the chief U.S. arms inspector saying pre-war intelligence was wrong, Cheney said: "There's still work to be done to ascertain exactly what's there, and I am not prepared to make a final judgment until they have completed their work."

True to form, on January 31, 2004, U.S. Deputy Defense Secretary Paul Wolfowitz dismissed criticism of the U.S. decision to wage war on Iraq on the basis of faulty intelligence. He said "You have to make decisions based on the intelligence you have, not on the intelligence you're going to discover later."

Since it was obvious to so many U.S. officials that weapons were never there, why are so many lives being lost and billions of dollars being spent in Iraq? If this were a pipe dream of the Bush administration to justify the war it has finally come to an end. The American people should be asking the question now – who is incredulous? It is amazing that it took Rumsfeld almost two years to admit to the American people that there are no weapons of mass destruction in Iraq. He made this statement during a visit to Kuwait on November 7, 2004.

The Bush administration's policies have been aberrant, to say the least, from that of the usual U.S. policies that other administrations before him have adhered to for decades, such as its pre-emptive strikes. The Bush administration wants the American people to believe that these are different times, which call for different sets of rules, but in the end, many will suffer the consequences of these incongruous actions taken by this administration. Bush's policies also lack pacificatory tendencies with ultimate determinate fissures with the American people and the rest of the world.

It could be in the realm of possibility that the plan to go to war was in full gear from the start of the Bush administration, and their strategy all along was to use the weapons of mass destruction to justify the war and as a ploy to instill fear and win over the American people and the international community. Once they go to war, there wouldn't be anything that anyone could do but to see it to the end. In other words, tow the line or risk being called unpatriotic or having no regards for the soldiers who are risking their lives in Iraq, or other personal attacks such as having their tax returns audited. For example, for the first time in the history of the NAACP, it was audited by the IRS after someone made a remark about the war. Former Treasurer Secretary Paul O'Neil said in his book that the Bush administration planned to invade Iraq within months of taking office.

According to a Britain's daily tabloid newspaper, the Sun, in November 2003, President Bush in an interview said that the United States would wage war again, and alone if necessary, to ensure the long-term safety of the world. But was the Iraq invasion necessary for the safety of the world? Iraq's war was not a war. Two countries cannot have a war if only one country is fighting. Moreover, according to a report, the Iraq war was won before U.S. troops entered Iraq because the U.S. paid money to Saddam Hussein's loyalists to infiltrate Iraq's defense. They bribed and used psychological and propaganda techniques on the Iraqi people.

When Saddam Hussein invaded Kuwait in 1991 to take over its oil fields, the world was at odds with him. The United States then formed a coalition to drive him out of Kuwait. Ironically, 12 years later it appears that the United States invaded Iraq for the same reason according to consensus of opinion.

Wolfowitz said that the Iraqi regime was cheating on resolution 1441, but in fact they were cooperating with the United Nations. The Iraqi officials tried everything in their power to convince the Bush administration that they were telling the truth, but to no avail. They even allowed the U.N. inspectors to destroy the Al Samoud missiles that exceeded the range limits set by the U.N. I could see the frustration in the faces of the Iraqi officials as they told the world over and over again that they had no weapons of mass destruction. I, for one, believed the Iraqi officials were telling the truth. I base this on my professional experience and training. We use the phrase the "eyes are the windows of the soul." You can see through them like a pane of glass. In justifying the invasion, Wolfowitz said that intelligence was an imperfect exercise.

On February 5, 2003, Secretary of State Colin Powell, with the director of the Central Intelligence Agency, George J. Tenet, seated behind him at the United Nations in New York, told the United Nations Security Council that the evidence added up to "facts" and "not assertions," that Iraq had large stockpiles of chemical and biological weapons and that he was reconstituting his nuclear weapons program and building a fleet of advanced missiles. He also showed aerial pictures of supposedly mobile laboratories. According to reports, Powell's testimony was probably the most persuasive presentation of the Bush administration's case that Iraq had these weapons. It s believed that because of Powell's reputation as a cautious individual and well-respected by other nations, he added urgency to the Bush administration's claim to go to war against Iraq and that there was no time to wait for the United Nations to complete its inspection.

On October 15, 2003, CBS news reporter Scott Pelley stated:

Greg Thielmann, an ex-aide of Secretary of State Colin Powell, responsible for analyzing the Iraqi weapons threat says the Secretary misinformed Americans during his speech at the United Nations last winter. He said that at the time of Powell's speech, Iraq didn't pose an imminent threat to anyone – not even its own neighbors. ...He said, "I think my conclusion (about Mr. Powell's speech) now is that it's probably one of the low points in his long distinguished service to the nation." He also said he believes the decision to go to war was made first and then the intelligence was interpreted to fit that conclusion.

"...The main problem was that the senior administration officials have what I call faith-based intelligence," says Thielmann. "They knew what they wanted the intelligence to show. They were really blind and deaf to any kind of countervailing information the intelligence community would produce. I would assign some blame to the intelligence community and most of the blame to the senior administration officials," he said.

Steve Allinson and a dozen other U.N. inspectors in Iraq also watched Powell's speech. "Various people would laugh at various times (during Powell's speech, because the information he was presenting was just, you know, didn't mean anything – had no meaning," says Allinson.

... Allinson gave Pelley several examples of why he believes Iraq didn't have weapons of mass destruction. One time, he was sent to find decontamination vehicles that turned out to be fire trucks. Another time, a satellite spotted what they thought were trucks used for biological weapons. "We were told we were going to the site to look for refrigerated trucks specifically linked to biological agents," Allison tells Pelley. " … We found seven or eight (trucks), I think, in total, and they had cobwebs in them. Some samples were taken and nothing was found."

On September 14, 2004, Powell, like others, acknowledged that there are no WMD. He said, "I think it is unlikely that we will find any stockpiles." What did Powell know when he gave those confident speeches on Iraq's WMD. Because, a few days after his performance in 2003, a BBC reporter went to Iraq to the exact place shown by satellite photographs by Powell and found it not to be a chemical weapons site.

According to a January 31, 2004, article by Douglas Jehl and David E. Sanger of the New York Times, interviews conducted with current and former senior intelligence officials, a handful of Iraqi engineers, Congressional officials involved in investigations of the Central Intelligence Agency and current and former administration officials suggest that Powell's case was largely based on limited, fragmentary and mostly circumstantial evidence, with conclusions drawn on the basis of the little challenged assumption that Saddam Hussein would never dismantle old illicit weapons and would pursue new ones to the fullest extent possible.

The article said that the administration's argument that Iraq was producing biological weapons was based almost entirely on human intelligence of unknown reliability. When mobile trailers were found by American troops, the White House and the Central Intelligence Agency rushed out a white paper reporting that the vehicles were used to manufacture biological agents. But later, an overwhelming majority of intelligence and analysts concluded the vehicles were used to manufacture hydrogen for weather balloons or possibly to produce rocket fuel – a view shared by Dr. Kay. The original paper was still posted on the CIA's Web site on Saturday, January 31, 2004. Nor did they find evidence of anything but the most rudimentary nuclear program. United Nations sanctions had choked off the project, and the few parts saved from efforts to enrich uranium in the 1980s remained buried under a rose garden. While Hussein put money into reviving the program, scientists found themselves struggling to reproduce basic experiments they had conducted two decades before.

The administration's evidence, according to the interviews, was much more accurate in the arena of missiles and unmanned aerial vehicles: very active programs were under way for both. The missiles clearly violated range limits set by the United Nations, and Hussein was trying to buy better technology from North Korea. But the deal fell through, and he was left with missiles that his own scientists said were widely inaccurate. The aerial vehicles appear to have been designed mainly for surveillance, not the spread of anthrax or biological agents.

Powell told reporters that "Last year when I made my presentation, it was based on the best intelligence that we had at the time. Now, I think their best judgment was correct with respect to intention, with respect to capability to develop such weapons, with respect to programs."

A former senior intelligence official, who took part in the pre-war debates, said "They took every piece of information that proved their point and listed it," referring to the senior CIA officials whose analytical conclusions formed the basis of Powell's presentation. "They would disregard or make fun of any contrary evidence. They forgot they were making mere guesses, and even guesses have to be taken with caution. They didn't hedge or caveat. Instead they would say we're right and you're wrong and it's a matter of national security."

Powell's case at the United Nations was supposed to be bulletproof: he had thrown out President Bush's own assertions, since discredited, that Iraq sought uranium in Africa, and he tossed away pictures of Iraqi "nuclear mujahedeen" when he concluded that the CIA could not identify them. "There were a lot of cigars lit," Powell said last summer. "I didn't want any going off in my face or the president's face." Powell declared in his presentation to the United Nations that "Iraq today has a stockpile of between 100 and 500 tons of chemical weapons agent – enough to fill 16,000 battlefield rockets." To make the case, Powell unveiled before the Security Council an array of previously classified evidence on a scale not seen in that room since Adlai Stevenson appeared during the 1962 Cuban missile crisis, armed with photographs of Soviet missiles. ("This was my Adlai moment," Powell joked later.)

Some American intelligence agencies had resisted the conclusion and had voiced "very legitimate objections," including the possibility that the suspicious movements involved something far more benign: commercial chlorine-manufacturing activity. One former senior government official cited the episode as an example of an underlying flaw in the administration's working assumptions. Across the board, he said, the pre-war assessment was based on "an analysis of Saddam that if he didn't have something to hide, he wouldn't have been behaving the way he did. That's a dangerous assumption for any intelligence agency to make," he said, "but that's what we did," according to the NYT article.

The head of the U.N. inspection team, Dr. Hans Blix, made it clear in his final report that Iraq's weapons program was destroyed and that there was no sign that they were being restarted.

Former Ambassador Joseph C. Wilson IV was sent to Niger to investigate whether Iraq was trying to purchase uranium from Niger to restart its nuclear weapons program, but found the allegation to be false. Of course, that was not the information the Bush administration wanted from Wilson, because just after his report, some White House staff leaked the name of his wife as a CIA agent. Syndicated columnist Robert Novak wrote in a July 2003 column that two senior administration officials said that Ms. Valerie Plame, Wilson's wife, was an undercover operative for the Central Intelligence Agency, specializing in weapons of mass destruction. By releasing her name it ended her career as a CIA officer and put her life and others she worked with in danger. Revealing the identity of a CIA operative is like putting a gun to her head, in the words of Senator Schumer, Democrat from New York.

The White House said that Carl Rove was not behind the leak. It also ruled out I. Lewis Libby, Vice President Dick Cheney's chief of staff, and Elliot Abrams, director of Mideast Affairs at the National Security Council. If they were so sure who was not the leaker, then they must have known who the leaker was.

In keeping with the White House pattern of secrecy, no one came forward to admit who leaked the name, although Wilson accused Carl Rove, the president's chief political aide, of being involved in leaking the information to intimidate him into silence.

A September 29, 2003, New York Times article by David Stout indicated that the Washington Post reported that the Bush administration officials had contacted a half-dozen Washington reporters in an effort to publicly disclose Plame's identity, apparently in retaliation for Wilson's public assertion that President Bush had exaggerated the threat of any Iraqi weapons of mass destruction to help justify the war to topple Saddam Hussein.

According to an October 2005 Time Magazine article, In a White House where clout is often measured by how well you can keep a secret, few men are as furtive and powerful as I. Lewis Libby, Vice President Dick Cheney's chief of staff.

Wilson, said publicly that he suspects Rove of being behind the leak, which he theorized was intended to sound a warning to others who might challenge the White House on whether intelligence about Iraq was reshaped or ignored to fit a political agenda.

How ironic, the White House had said that Mr. Rove was not involved in the leak, I. Lewis Libby, Cheney's chief of staff, and Elliot Abrams, director of Mideast affairs at the National Council, were not involved. They were emphatic in their persuasion that these people were not involved, but now we know better. Bush said Washington is a city "where a lot of people leak."

On October 7, 2003, President Bush said that investigation may be unable to find out who disclosed the identity of the CIA agent. He said, "I have no idea whether we'll find out who the leaker is, partially because, in all due respect to your profession, you do a very good job of protecting the leakers."

However, in April 2006, it was reported that in 2003, President Bush told Vice President Dick Cheney to leak the CIA agent's name to counter the Iraq invasion criticism. The White House said that President Bush has also declassified the information. By declassifying the information, it prevented the leaker from being prosecuted for a crime, because the information about the CIA agent is no longer considered classified information..

There is a provision in the law that was signed by the first President Bush that could make it a crime for officials to intentionally disclose to non-officials the identity of a CIA operative who is working undercover. That provision is intended to protect the security of operatives whose lives might be jeopardized if their identities were known. Until Novak's column, Plame was known to friends as an energy industry analyst.

Retired General Wesley Clark told Reuters that "This administration has played politics with national security for a long time, but this is going too far." He suggested an independent commission to look into the accusations. And he said he doesn't think this administration's Department of Justice will have the credibility it needs to reassure American allies abroad, and people around the world about this matter.

38

Dean, former presidential candidate, told Reuters "We need to determine the facts in the highly sensitive matter free from any political taint." Tenet asked the Justice Department to look into whether one or more administration officials had leaked information to the news media disclosing Plame's identity as a covert agent. When asked if there would be a potential conflict of interest for Attorney General John Ashcroft to oversee an investigation that could have immense political implications for Bush, White House spokesman Scott McClellan said that there were "a lot of career professionals" at the Justice Department and that "they're the ones that, if something like this happened, should look into it."

The Associated Press reported on December 30, 2003, that Attorney General John Ashcroft would recuse himself from an investigation into who leaked the name of CIA operative Plame. According to the AP, the investigation will be headed by the U.S. attorney in Chicago, Patrick Fitzgerald, who will report to Ashcroft's new deputy, James Clomey.

One wonders if this was just a facade and that he would work behind the scenes.

New York Times reporter Judith Miller spent 85 days in jail because she refused to divulge her source to a grand jury. She was released after her informant, I. Lewis Libby, agreed for her to reveal him as her source.

It became apparent that Carl Rove and I. Lewis Libby are the leakers. However, when the leak came out in 2003, Bush had said he would fire anyone in his cabinet who leaked the CIA's agent's name. So what can one gather from this new information regarding Bush's previous remarks if Rove is not fired?

According to reports, after intense negotiations between Attorney General Patrick Fitzgerald and Carl Rove no decision was made on an indictment. Libby was indicted on October 29, 2005, not for a crime, which would carry a

39

harsher punishment, but for lying to federal investigators and obstructing justice, and resigned as Cheney's chief of staff.

On February 2, 2006, CNN reported that not all e-mail was archived in 2003, the year the Bush administration exposed the identity of undercover agent Valerie Plame. Could this be another "Watergate"? In November 2005, Bob Woodward said he received the name of the CIA agents but did not tell his boss because the information was given during a casual conversation for a book he was writing. Because of that, a new investigation has been ordered. Also, on December 16, 2005, Novak said that President Bush knew the name of the leaker. President Bush appearing on KPBS on December 16, 2005, was asked by Jim Lehrer about Novak's accusation, but he declined to confirm or deny it saying that he was advised by his lawyers not to discuss it.

In a report from the Council on Foreign Relations dated October 6, 2003, Daryl G. Kimball, the executive director of the Washington-based Arms Control Association, said that the report of the CIA's Iraq Survey Group headed by David Kay reinforces the view that senior administration officials were deliberately "misrepresenting" the facts to justify the war against Iraq. Kimball said the preliminary Kay report, which was submitted to Congress on October 2, 2003, "exaggerated the case in what we now know to be discredited, disputed, or entirely bogus intelligence information." Kay did not find any chemical weapons. He found a number of munitions facilities. A percentage of them have been searched but did not find any evidence of chemical weapons production post-1998 [the start of a four-year period when no U.N. inspectors were in Iraq].

In the progress report by the Iraq Survey Group (ISG) delivered to Congress, Kay said Saddam had taken no steps to revive his nuclear weapons plan since 1998. After three months of searching, the ISG found a single vial containing a possible strain of biological agent, botulinum, in the home of a scientist. In spite of Kay's report that Iraq had no chemical weapons program, President Bush said Kay's report in fact justified the Iraq invasion.

According to an October 6, 2003, New York Times article by Warren Hoge, on October 5, 2003, former foreign secretary to British Prime Minister Robin Cook said that Tony Blair conceded privately that Iraq did not have quickly deployable weapons of mass destruction as the British government was claiming as a justification for war. Cook resigned his post as leader of the House of Commons in March 2003, because of Britain's decision to join the United States in the invasion of Iraq. He said Blair also made it clear to him in a conversation two weeks before combat began that he did not believe Saddam Hussein's weapons posed a "real and present danger" to Britain.

Finally, the truth about Saddam's purported weapons of mass destruction has come to bare. Knowing that they would not find any weapons of mass destruction in Iraq, in May 2004, the Bush administration said they were changing their strategy from weapons of mass destruction in Iraq to intelligence developing, according to an MSNBC news report.

For two years, the Bush administration spent countless hours and millions of dollars in advertising convincing the American people that Saddam Hussein had weapons of mass destruction that could be unleashed on the United States within 45 minutes so that the United States was in imminent danger of being attacked; and that Saddam and Osama were working together, but it has been said that Osama does not like Saddam.

After spending over $300 million and requests for another $600 million to search for the purported weapons of mass destruction, in January 2004 the former chief American weapons inspector in Iraq, David Kay, said that there are, and there never were any weapons of mass destruction in Iraq. He has also called for an independent inquiry into the errors of the intelligence community. In his testimony before the Senate Armed Service Committee in Washington, David Kay said "It's quite clear we need capabilities that we do not have with regard to intelligence. We were almost all wrong, and I certainly include myself here." Dr. Kay said that "limited data" fed a widely held view among intelligence agencies and governments that Hussein had weapons of mass destruction. That view was seized upon by the White House in justifying its decision to invade Iraq.

Tens of thousands of people have been killed and mutilated, and there seems to be no sign of abating. Iraq's infrastructure has been demolished and now requires billions of dollars to put it back together. It would appear that the American people have gotten a double whammy. First from the attack on New York and Washington, and now they are burdened with billions of dollars of debt and a long term investment of keeping tens of thousands of troops in Iraq long after the war is over, not to mention the thousands of U.S. soldiers that will be killed in Iraq. Wouldn't it have been more prudent to have disarmed Saddam Hussein peacefully and save thousands of lives, and property from destruction? You decide.

Also in a turn about face, President Bush said he would consult with the former United States inspector in Iraq, Dr. David Kay, to get all the facts before naming an independent commission to examine intelligence shortcomings on Iraq and in the global war on terrorism. Here again, he juxtaposes Iraq and terrorism. On February 2, 2004, he announced that he would establish a bipartisan commission to examine American intelligence operations, including a study of possible misjudgments about Iraq's unconventional weapons. Bear in mind the March 31, 2003, Time article about a discussion with National Security Adviser Condoleezza Rice and three senators discussing how to deal with Iraq through the United Nations, when President Bush said "F___ Saddam we're taking him out."

According to a February 2, 2004, New York Times article by David Sanger, Bush intend to put the study into a broader context by retooling the American intelligence-gathering for a new era of terrorism and nuclear proliferation by rogue scientists and countries that might pass weapons into the hands of groups like al-Qaeda. But it is far from clear that those steps will insulate him from Democrats' charges that the White House tried to manipulate the Iraq intelligence to justify the March invasion. Republicans contend that Bush was the victim of bad intelligence, but many democratic candidates believe he would cherry-pick the evidence that would justify the decision to go to war instead of investigating the intelligence that supposedly led to the invasion of Iraq. Or, they could hide the information in a lengthy report.

This decision to appoint a commission came after pressure from both Democrats and Republicans for the White House to deal with what the head of the Senate Intelligence Committee called "egregious" errors that overstated Iraq's stockpile of chemical and biological weapons, and made the country appear far closer to developing nuclear weapons than it actually was, according to the article.

But how bipartisan is this panel going to be if the president will be the one appointing the members to the panel? It would be naïve of the public to believe he would be choosing those who are not biased toward him. Invariably the investigation would not put any emphasis on any flawed reports but would seek to minimize it. Furthermore, the commission would not report back until after the November 2004 elections. Do we see a pattern here – convince the American people that they had to go to war against Iraq to protect them, knowing quite well that they were being misled. Once the war started, everyone falls into line with their plan. The commission appointed by Bush will also fall into line. By the time the results comes out Bush would have already been re-elected.

According to a February 5, 2004, New York Times article by Douglas Jehl, before a number of students and faculty at Georgetown University, George J. Tenet, the director of the CIA, said that American spy agencies may have overestimated Iraq's illicit weapons capabilities, in part because of a failure to penetrate the inner workings of the Iraqi government. He also presented an impressionable defense of American spy agencies and their integrities. He went on to say "When the facts on Iraq are all in, we will be neither completely right nor completely wrong."

Tenet said that intelligence analysts had never portrayed Iraq as presenting an imminent threat to the United States before the American invasion in March 2003. He also said that intelligence agencies "may have overestimated the progress" that Iraq was making toward development of nuclear weapons and that the prewar assessment that Iraq possessed stockpiles of chemical and biological weapons, was based in large part on reports relayed by a friendly foreign government from human sources whose information the United States had not been able to corroborate. "We did not ourselves penetrate the inner sanctum," Tenet acknowledged, saying that American agents remained "on the periphery" of Iraq's illicit weapons activities. But a year prior in his testimony before Congress Tenet spoke of a "solid foundation of intelligence" on illicit weapons programs in Iraq. Tenet said his current view was that Iraq "intended to reconstitute a nuclear program at some point." This is contrary to the National Intelligence Estimate of October 2002, which said Iraq was reconstituting its nuclear program, according to the article.

Dr. David Kay said "We were all wrong." But not everyone was wrong. The U.N. inspections pre-war estimates of Iraqi nuclear, chemical and biological capabilities have turned out to be true. Consider Dr. Mohamed ElBaradei, head of the U.N. nuclear agency, whose report to the Security Council dated March 7, 2003, after his team had completed 247 inspections at 147 sites, said, "No evidence of resumed nuclear activities nor any indication of nuclear-related prohibited activities at any related sites." And, regarding chemical and biological weapons, the U.N. inspec-

44

tors headed by Dr. Hans Blix conducted 731 inspections between November 2002 and March 2003. Despite claims by the Bush administration of the existence of specific stockpiles of weapons and active weapons programs, they found no evidence of either. U.N. officials even asked the U.S. to provide them with specific sites, but to no avail.

Nevada Congresswoman Shelly Berkerly said she voted for the Iraq invasion because in the intelligence meeting, the Bush administration showed maps where the weapons of mass destruction were and was told that Iraq's nuclear program would be ready within six months and that al-Qaeda and Saddam were working together. She said she is now embarrassed and ashamed because she spoke on television and radios in her constituency selling the war to her people.

According to a January 28, 2004, Newsweek article by Michael Isikoff, Senator Jay Rockefeller ranking Democrat on the Intelligence Committee said that administration policymakers as well as the intelligence establishment itself owes an enormous apology to the American people and most particularly to the families of those who have been killed. Also, one of his aides said the senator and other Senate Democrats want to continue the committee's probe in order to pursue instances where the White House hyped evidence about Iraqi weapons of mass destruction and shunned dissenters within the intelligence community. The aide also noted that in many instances dissidents within the intelligence community were simply ignored or not invited back to meetings where their views could be aired, and that there were clear-cut cases where the administration exaggerated the intelligence.

Dr. Kay has publicly acknowledged that the weapons he has been looking for simply didn't exist. He also told NBC's Tom Brokaw that "clearly, the intelligence we went to war on was inaccurate, wrong." This means that the White House consistent argument that the threat posed by Saddam Hussein was "grave and gathering" was just their way of keeping the fear of September 11 fresh in the minds of the American people. And, let's not forget, the Bush administration has been persuasive enough to convince the American people that Saddam Hussein was involved in the September 11 attacks on the United States.

An Associated Press article dated January 8, 2004, stated that the U.S. overstated Iraqi Threat. Iraq posed no imminent threat to the United States and there was no solid evidence that President Saddam Hussein was cooperating with the al-Qaeda terror network, a private think tank maintained. The administration systematically misrepresented a weapons threat from Iraq, and U.S. strategy should be revised to eliminate the policy of unilateral pre-emptive war, said Jessica T. Mathews, Joseph Cirincione and George Perkovic of the Carnegie Endowment for International Peace.

While the Bush administration was saying publicly that weapons could still be found, a January 7, 2004, New York Times article said that the Bush administration quietly withdrew from Iraq a 400-member military team whose job was to scour the country for military equipment. Also, a report published in the Washington Post on January 7, 2004, cited a previously undisclosed document that suggested that Iraq might have destroyed its biological weapons as early as 1991. The report said investigators had otherwise found no evidence to support American beliefs that Iraq had maintained illicit weapons dating from the Persian Gulf War of 1991 or that it had advanced programs to build new ones.

Also, a January 7, 2004, Washington Post article by Barton Gellman, said that Iraq's arsenal was only on paper, and of all Iraq's rocket scientists, none drew warier scrutiny abroad than Modher Sadeq-Saba Tamimi, a 47-year-old engineering Ph.D. who designed and built a new short-range missile during Iraq's four-year hiatus from the United Nations arms inspectors. The inspectors, who returned in late 2002, enforcing Security Council limits, ruled that the Al Samoud missile's range was not short enough. The U.N. team crushed the missiles, bulldozed them into a pit and entombed the wreckage in concrete.

Secretary of Defense Donald Rumsfeld, on the other hand, said the uranium claim was a small part of the evidence for war "one scrap" of a larger picture." In his attempt to downplay the significance of the forged document, Rumsfeld told the Senate Armed Services Committee that "The United States did not choose war. Saddam Hussein did. The Iraqi government had an international obligation to destroy its weapons of mass destruction and to prove to the world that they had done so. He refused to do so." When asked by Mark Pryor, Democrat from Arkansas, if he had ever received any communication saying the intelligence was flawed, he replied, "I see hundreds of pieces of paper a day. Is it conceivable that something was in a document? It's conceivable. Do I recall hearing anything, or reading anything like that? The answer is no." When it comes to manipulating the English language to justify an action, Rumsfeld is excellent at it.

Senator Hillary Clinton, Democrat from New York, said that regarding the intelligence and the discredited claims of an Africa-Iraq link, "In this new threat environment in which we find ourselves, we are increasingly reliant on intelligence. Of the lessons to be learned, that I hope we have learned, the thorough scrubbing and very careful analysis of intelligence has to be at the top of the list."

A New York Times July 9, 2003, article by David E. Sanger and Carl Hulse stated:

In sidestepping the issue of faulty intelligence, Bush said he had "no doubt" that the United States was right to invade Iraq. "I am confident that Saddam Hussein had a weapon of mass destruction program," Mr. Bush said during a news conference in Pretoria, South Africa. When asked about his administration's use of fraudulent information to press its case against Hussein, Bush instead emphasized the ends rather than the means, and sidestepped the question by saying that "the world is a much more peaceful and secure place as a result of the actions. "There is no doubt in my mind that Saddam Hussein was a threat to world peace. And there's no doubt in my mind that the United States, along with allies and friends, did the right thing in removing him from power."

An August 18, 2003, Reuters article by Dominic Evans stated:

Blair's top aide, Jonathan Powell, wrote to a senior intelligence official, "The document does nothing to demonstrate threat, let alone an imminent threat from (Iraq President) Saddam Hussein. It shows he has the means but it does not demonstrate he has the motive to attack his neighbors, let alone the West." Powell wrote in an e-mail weeks before the controversial dossier that was published on September 24, 2002, six months prior to the U.S.-led invasion of Iraq.

Powell's comments were revealed in an inquiry into the apparent suicide of weapons expert David Kelly. He had supposedly slashed his wrist after being named as the source for the BBC reporter who accused Blair's communications chief Alastair Campbell of "sexing up" the dossier by inserting claims that Saddam could deploy banned weapons within 45 minutes notice. Another dossier detailing Iraq's efforts to deceive U.N. weapons inspectors included large chunks lifted from a student thesis. And, another dossier on human rights was filled with cases that had been ignored when Saddam Hussein was an ally of the United States and Britain.

Powell, in his note to the Joint Intelligence Committee chief John Scarlet, said the government should make it clear that "we do not claim that we have evidence that (Saddam) is an imminent threat" when it published the September dossier.

But if the Bush administration and the British government had used such a caveat, that would have defeated their purpose as they were using the "fear factor" on the American and British people to invade Iraq.

According to a July 21, 2003, Reuters report by Dominic Evans and Peter Griffiths:

A British government document released on August 20, 2002, showed top British officials tried to stop the scientist, David Kelly, from airing doubts on Iraqi weapons dossier. The document emerged in an inquiry into the apparent suicide of David Kelly.

An official note, written on July 14, 2003, the day before Kelly was due to testify to a parliamentary committee, made clear that Kelly would be told to keep his views to himself. The note said Kelly was due to be briefed later that day by the deputy chief of defense intelligence about his appearances in front of the foreign affairs committee, and intelligence and security committee on July 15 and 16.

Top civil servants at Britain's Ministry of Defense said at a meeting in Blair's office one week before Dr. Kelly was to be briefed that "if he was summoned to give evidence, some of it might be uncomfortable on specifics such as the likelihood of there being weapons systems ready for use within 45 minutes."

The inquiry heard how Blair's official spokesmen proposed ways to tighten the draft dossier's evidence on Saddam Hussein's intent to use banned weapons. Tom Kelly said in one of many e-mails written by Downing Street staff and shown to the inquiry that "The weakness obviously is our inability to say that he (Saddam) could pull the nuclear trigger any time soon. "We need that to counter the argument that Saddam is bad, not mad."

A second BBC reporter, Susan Watts testified that the late David Kelly told them the British government had included uncorroborated intelligence in its dossier setting out the case for war against Iraq. She said that Kelly told her it was "a mistake" to put in a claim that ousted Iraqi President Saddam Hussein had weapons of mass destruction ready to be deployed at 45 minutes notice. Andrew Giligan was the first BBC reporter who provided the information on the "sexed up dossier."

An article appearing in the Associated Press on September 8, 2003, stated that the U.N. inspectors had indicated that there were gaps in Iraq's accountability on nerve agents. Since no weapons of mass destruction had been found, ex-inspectors believed that the unaccountables may have been no more than paperwork glitches left behind when Iraq destroyed banned chemical and biological weapons years ago. Some may represent miscounts, and some may stem from Iraqi underlings' efforts to satisfy the boss by exaggerating reports on arms output in the 1980s.

Ron G. Manley of Britain, a former chief U.N. adviser on chemical weapons said "under that sort of regime, you don't admit you got it wrong. And, an American ex-inspector Scott Ritter said he too, was sure Baghdad's "WMD" accounts were at times overstated. He said there was so much pressure put on scientists to produce world-class systems they would exaggerate their reports to their authorities.

After the first three months of fruitless searches, U.S. military seven Site Survey units assigned to track down Iraqi weapons of mass destruction ran out of places to look and got time off or were assigned to other duties. A large team of Pentagon intelligence experts took over the search efforts, relying more on leads from interviews and documents. Lt. Col. Keith Harrington's team, along with several others, were taken off assignments completely after searching over

230 sites without finding any trace of weapons of mass destruction.

The United Nations inspectors spent years learning the names and faces of the Iraqi weapons programs scientists. But in postwar Iraq, the Bush administration cut the organization out of the hunt because of assessments that conflicted with Washington's portrayal of Saddam's weapons. Relations soured further amid reports that U.S. troops failed to secure Iraq's largest nuclear facility from looters. A U.N. nuclear team returned to Iraq to survey the damage at Tuwaitha, where 2 tons of uranium had been stored for more than a decade. One weapons team, specializing in nuclear materials, had been assigned to accompany the U.N. experts until they left on June 25, 2003, according to the AP article.

A Reuters September 16, 2003, article stated:

> Former U.N. chief weapons inspector Hans Blix believes that Iraq destroyed its weapons of mass destruction 10 years ago and that intelligence agencies were wrong in their weapons assessment that led to war.
>
> In an interview with Australian radio from Sweden, Blix said the search for evidence of biological, chemical or nuclear weapons would probably only uncover documents at best. "The more time that passed, the more I think it's unlikely that anything will be found," Blix said in the interview. "I'm certainly more and more to the conclusion that Iraq has, as they maintained, destroyed almost all of what they had in the summer of 1991," Blix said.
>
> In 1991, the United Nations International Atomic Energy Agency found what it called a secret nuclear weapons program in Iraq. It spent the next seven years dismantling Baghdad's nuclear capability, until its inspectors were thrown out of Iraq.
>
> Blix spent three years searching for Iraqi chemical, biological and ballistic missiles as head of

the United Nations Monitoring, Verification and Inspection Commission.

With all the top American scientists assigned to the hunt for Iraq's so-called weapons of mass destruction, they did not find any evidence of Saddam Hussein's stockpiling of smallpox. The three-month search by "Team Pox" showed only signs to the contrary. In fact, what they found was disabled equipment that had been rendered harmless by the U.N. inspectors. Because the Bush administration said smallpox could be used as a weapon, it launched a vaccination campaign for some 500,000 U.S. soldiers. Smallpox was declared eradicated worldwide in 1980.

A September 18, 2003, Mideast – Associated Press article by Dafna Linzer stated:

All samples of the smallpox virus were to have been destroyed except those held by special laboratories in Atlanta and Russia. In September 2003 two of the six-member of Team Pox left Iraq while the others were assigned to other aspects of the weapons hunt. One of the military officers said, "We found no physical or new anecdotal evidence to suggest Iraq was producing smallpox or had stocks of it in its possession." When Team Pox searched key locations in Iraq, such as the defunct Darwah foot-and-mouth disease center, they found the facility in the same condition U.N. inspectors left it in seven years prior.

In 1996, inspectors destroyed one fermenter, a storage tank and an inactivation tank at Darwah and poured concrete into the air conditioners while other equipment, including filter pressers and centrifuges, were tagged for monitoring purposes. The smallpox team found cobwebs covering much of the inside. The trucks the U.S. said its satellite images spotted pulling up to the site, indicating renewal of activity, were revealed by investigators to belong to black marketers stealing scrap metal and other parts.

Despite the lack of evidence of a smallpox program, Dick Cheney said two trailers discovered in Iraq could have been used to make smallpox. He referred to the trailers as "mobile biological facilities" a characterization that has been disputed by intelligence analysts within the U.S. government agencies that believe the trailers were used to fill weather balloons.

Former leader of the British House of Commons, Robin Cook, said he and other cabinet members worried that Blair's decision was motivated by his desire to maintain Britain's influence in Washington rather than to protect British interests against possible terrorist attacks. Cook wrote, "I am certain the real reason he went to war was that he found it easier to resist the public opinion of Britain than the request of the president of the United States." He also said, a year earlier Blair had instructed the cabinet, "We must steer close to America. If we don't, we will lose our influence to shape what they do."

A September 28, 2003, New York Times article by Douglas Jehl stated:

Defense Intelligence Agency's internal assessment concluded that most of the information provided by Iraqi defectors who were made available by the Iraqi National Congress was of little or no value. In addition, several Iraqi defectors introduced to American intelligence agents by the exile organization and its leader, Ahmad Chalabi, invented or exaggerated their credentials as people with direct knowledge of the Iraqi government and its suspected unconventional weapons programs. The arrangement between Chalabi and the U.S.

government cost the U.S. taxpayers more than $1 million. This prompted some federal government officials to question the credibility of Chalabi and the Iraqi National Congress. Both have enjoyed powerful backing from civilian officials at the Pentagon and have been playing a significant role in the provisional government in Baghdad.

Among the intelligence information provided by the defectors that could not be substantiated was information about Iraq's suspected program for nuclear, chemical and biological weapons, as well as other information about the Iraqi government.

A House Intelligence committee's interim assessments on how intelligence concluded that Iraq had forbidden weapons and ties to al-Qaeda said there were "too many uncertainties" in the outdated and inadequate information underlying a National Intelligence Estimate that the administration used to justify the war. This information was relayed to CIA Director George J. Tenet by senior Republican and the senior Democrat on the panel.

After resisting requests from the Senate Intelligence Committee to turn over intelligence documents on Iraq's weapons of mass destruction that were used to justify the U.S. invasion, the White House reversed its decision and said that all intelligence agencies would provide all the information sought by the committee. But if their cooperation is anything like the 9/11 investigation cooperation, it will be a long drawn-out investigation until the urgency dissipates from the minds of the American people and the international community.

The Democrats became frustrated and disgusted with the long delay in bringing to bare the conclusion of the intelligence investigation, so much so, that on November 1, 2005, without any warning, Senator Harry Reid, the Senate minority leader, invoked a little-used Rule 21 to force the Senate into a closed-door session to get the Republicans to promise to speed up the inquiry.

A report by Rory McCarthy in the October 3, 2003, issue of the Guardian stated:

Ibrahim Salim, 59, had worked for Iraqi Airways since he was 17. He has been unemployed since March when the airline was grounded. Like many in Baghdad, he knows nothing of the Iraq Survey Group, but he is bemused by Washington's continuing efforts to find the smoking gun that would justify its war. "It is well-known that the Americans came here for oil. There is no other reason. If America is such a great superpower, how can they not find the weapons they say exist in Iraq? They should start talking about unemployment and security here, rather than carrying on about weapons they know we don't have."

"I used to work hard, starting early in the morning. Now there is nothing to do," he said. "I can feel myself getting older sitting without any work."

Iraqi Airways has 24 aging aircraft, but none has flown since March 2003, and there appears to be no efforts under way to restart the airline.

The U.S.-led authority in Baghdad is paying the 2,300 airline staff monthly wages of $120 to $180. The airline building is now the U.S.'s biggest military base. Salim said, "The Americans turned our building into a hotel for soldiers. They call it the Florida Hotel."

Although there was no evidence that weapons of mass destruction would be found in Iraq, the Bush administration asked for another $600 million to extend the search for another six to nine months. The leading Democrat on the Senate intelligence committee, Jay Rockefeller, said, "To be where we are today, asking for another six to nine months and a good deal of money, leads me to believe we need to do some serious thinking about the doctrine of pre-emption, that we lead to some serious thinking about how did our intelligence allow us to get so that we could decide to go to war. "Did we misread it or did they mislead us or did they simply get it wrong? Whatever the answer is, it's not a good answer."

An Associated Press article published December 1, 2003, headlined: "Iraqi Scientists Lied About Nukes," reported:

> Abdel Mehdi, Baghdad University's Dean of Sciences, said the hope for an Iraqi atomic bomb was never realistic. "It was all like building sand Castles."
> And, Imad Khadduri writes in his book, "Iraqi's Nuclear Mirage." At best, it would have taken Iraq several years to build a nuclear weapon if the 1991 war and subsequent U.N. inspectors had not intervened. His self-published "Iraqi's Nuclear Mirage," a chronicle of years of secret weapons work and of a final escape into exile, is part of this senior scientist's emergence from a low profile in Canada – intended to refute what he calls a "massive deception" in Washington that led the United States into war.

One wonders about the mindset of Bush administration officials and their deception regarding the avoidance of an Iraq invasion. Case in point, according to a December 11, 2003, New York Times article by James Risen and Eric Lichtblau, U.S. Homeland Security informed Imad Hage that he was wanted on charges stemming from an incident in January when he tried to transport a handgun and four stun guns in his checked luggage on a flight from Washington to Beirut. A warrant was issued for his arrest. The notification to Hage came on the same day that an article appeared in The New York Times disclosing Hage's involvement in trying to deliver messages to the White House from Iraqi intelligence officials.

According to the article weeks before the war began in March, Hage, who holds both a United States and Lebanese citizenship, was drawn into an effort by top Iraqi intelligence officials to open a secret communications channel with the Bush administration. The Iraqi officials met with Hage in Beirut and Baghdad and told him they wanted Washington to know that Iraq no longer had any weapons of mass destruction. They said they were willing to make concessions in order to avoid war.

Hage met in early March in London with Richard Perle to pass on the Iraqi messages and Baghdad's interest in meeting with Perle or someone else close to the Pentagon. Mr. Perle said that he passed the message to officials at the CIA, but that he was told there was no interest in pursuing the contacts. After the meetings were disclosed in November, critics of the administration said Washington's refusal to pursue the Iraqi overture indicated that the White House was determined to go to war even if Iraq did offer concessions.

How ironic, the Bush administration said toppling Saddam Hussein would prevent weapons of mass destruction from falling into the hands of terrorists. While the U.S. is preaching weapons curtailment, it was planning to make it easier for U.S. companies to sell weapons to Britain and Australia.

Fortunately, a top Republican congressman, Henry Hyde, chairman of the House International Relations Committee was planning to block Bush's arms export. According to a November 3, 2003, Reuters article the U.S. said that the changes would not only strengthen two close allies of the United States, but also actually improve the monitoring of weapons exports. However, Hyde believes that terrorists could get access to these weapons.

The proposed changes would allow U.S. companies to export some non-classified weapons and arms-related technology to certain British and Australian companies without having to seek an export license. That license requirement is part of the Arms Control Act. Hyde said, "Lowering our country's standard for munitions and other arms-related transfer in part because it is advantageous to U.S. companies can only make more complicated the already difficult job you have" in persuading other nations to tighten export controls. "This is a moment in our nation's history when it behooves us to strengthen, not relax, international standards for nonproliferation and military controls."

But the U.S. has always supplied other countries with weapons, and Iraq was no exception. So it should be of no surprise that on April 28, 2004, an Iranian court ordered the U.S. to pay over $600 million to Iranian survivors of the gas attacks by Saddam Hussein during the Iraq-Iran war, because Saddam used chemical gas supplied by the U.S. in 1980-88.

Moreover, the U.S. also used chemical weapons when it invaded Iraq in March 2003. It used napalm bombs and white phosphorous. It also used spent uranium in its bombs. On April 10, 2004, it was learned that five soldiers returning from Iraq tested positive for uranium.

After nine months of searching hundreds of sites without any trace of weapons of mass destruction, David Kay, the head of the U.S. Iraq Survey Group, stepped down. U.S. government officials said Kay's departure would have little practical impact on the day-to-day work of the 1,400-member Iraq Survey Group. According to reports, it appeared that the Bush administration had drawn the conclusion that there were no weapons to be found; therefore, the search was over. Also, many of Kay's staff had been diverted from the weapons hunt to help search for Iraqi insurgents. It is hard to imagine that U.S. taxpayers' money went to pay these high salaries to search for insurgents.

The pre-emptive strike was culminated on the premise that Saddam possessed arsenals of banned weapons, or was pursuing weapons programs that might one day constitute a threat. However, on December 16, 2003, with Saddam Hussein being captured, and Bush's support rebounding, he said that he no longer saw much distinction between the possibilities. But when pressed on the topic by Diane Sawyer of ABC News, Bush said, "So what's the difference?"

But as far as the American public is concerned, there is a difference – it's a difference of not going to war at such a grave cost to human lives. Bush said removing Hussein from power was justified even without the recovery of any banned weapons. "If he were to acquire weapons, he would be the danger," Bush continued, referring to Hussein. "That's what I'm trying to explain to you. A gathering threat, after 9/11, is a threat that needed to be dealt with, and it was done after 12 long years of the world saying the man's a danger." Scott McClellan, the White House spokesman, said Bush was not backing away from his assertions about Hussein's possession of banned weapons, when pressed to explain the president's remarks. Even at that point the White House still contended that Saddam had a weapons program. McClellan said, "We continue to believe that he had weapons of mass destruction programs and weapons of mass destruction."

A December 18, 2003, Associated Press article headlined, Iraqi Scientist Now on U.S. Payroll:

Hundreds of Iraqi scientists and technicians whom the Bush administration said worked on nuclear, chemical and biological weapons programs for Saddam Hussein will be paid by the United States for their role in postwar projects, partly to keep the Iraqis from selling their expertise elsewhere. State Department spokesman Richard Boucher said the two-year program would begin with a $2 million U.S. contribution, and the United States may provide as much as $20 million more.

According to a December 8, 2003, Associated Press article, the U.S. intelligence is holding the following eight Iraqi scientists:

- Maj. Gen. Hossam Mohammed Amin, who oversaw the biological weapons program before taking over as head of he liaison unit to U.N. inspectors. He was among the 55 Most Wanted by the U.S. forces.

- Mahmoud Bilal, a chemist who worked with U.N. inspectors on both chemical and biological weaponization and was in charge of Iraq's chemical weapons facility.
- Sinan Abdul Hassan, who worked on Iraq's anthrax program and supervised the filling of biological weapons and bombs. In 1996 he was made head of the biological group established to work with U.N. inspectors.
- Amer Rashid, former Iraqi army general who was Saddam's point-man on weapons delivery systems and eventually rose to the post of minister.
- Thamer Abdul Rahman, headed Iraq's anthrax production groups before the 1991 Gulf War.
- Gen. Amer Al Saadi, Iraq's chief liaison to U.N. inspectors on chemical and biological weapons and Saddam Hussein's adviser on scientific affairs.
- Ismael Ahmed Saleh, who was on Iraq's botulinum production team before the 1991 Gulf War.
- Rihab Taha, a microbiologist who was in charge of the Iraqi facility that weaponized anthrax, botulinum toxin and aflotoxin. She was nicknamed "Dr. Germ" by U.N. inspectors and was among the 55 Most Wanted by U.S. forces.

At times it would appear that the U.S. is fighting a losing battle in Iraq for a number of reasons. One example is how Iraqis were able to loot dangerously radioactive capsules from Saddam Hussein's main battlefield testing site in the desert outside Baghdad. One 30-year-old Iraqi villager and a boy suffered from radiation sickness. American officers fear that more cases of the sickness may follow and that they would not be able to help because the villagers are afraid to come forth, according to a report.

By July 8, 2003, the only so-called weapons that the U.S. found were 40 anti-tank mines, dozens of mortars and hundreds of pounds of gunpowder buried in Saddam Hussein's hometown of Tikrit.

In a dramatic move over accusations that the Danish government also exaggerated the threat posed by Saddam Hussein to justify the U.S.-led war in Iraq, Danish defense minister Svend Aage Jensby resigned. According to an April 23, 2004, Associated Press article, Danish Defense Service Chief Rear Adm. Joern Olesen said the agency had always believed that Iraq probably had biological and chemical weapons, and said that the documents were based on information gathered by the U.N. and NATO. However, the Danish intelligence report dated March 7, 2003, concluded there was no certain information that Iraq had banned weapons. Denmark backed the invasion and contributed 500 troops and a submarine, saying force was needed because Saddam would not cooperate with U.N. inspectors.

On September 13, 2004, Secretary of State Colin Powell, testifying before the Senate Government Affairs Committee, said that it is unlikely that they will find any stockpiles in Iraq.

It is apparent that British Prime Minister Tony Blair is playing "follow the leader," because no sooner did Bush announce that he would appoint a commission to investigate the "faulty" Iraqi intelligence, did Blair say that he was preparing to announce an independent inquiry into the apparent failure of pre-war intelligence on Iraq's still-unfounded unconventional weapons. Robin Cook, the former foreign secretary who resigned over Blair's decision to join Bush to invade Iraq, said it was insulting for Blair to order an inquiry to mirror Bush's inquiry in the United States. Cook also said that it should not be difficult to reach conclusions quickly since so much intelligence information is in hand, and since the political judgments that were made from intelligence that was never as clear cut as political leaders made it out to be can be examined straightforwardly.

Dr. David Kelly was ridiculed by the British government when they found out that he told BBC reporter Andrew Giligan that the British government sexed up the information on Iraq's weapons of mass destruction and leaked his name to the press. A poll taken by YouGov for the Daily Telegraph newspaper, said 44 percent thought Blair was not telling the truth when he denied authorizing the leaking of Kelly's name to the press. He was later found dead, purportedly as a result of suicide.

According to a January 31, 2004, Reuters article in the investigation into Dr. Kelly's death and the misrepresentation by the British government, Judge Lord Hutton censured the BBC and granted near-total exoneration to the government on January 28, 2004. This decision infuriated hundreds of BBC employees who paid for a full-page ad to vent their feelings. They said Greg Dyke stood for brave, independent and rigorous BBC journalism that was fearless in its search for the truth," they said of the former director general who resigned a day after the inquiry was published. The chairman of the BBC board of governors Gavyn Davis, quit, and the investigative reporter Andrew Gilligan resigned a few days later. Some BBC staff walked out in protest at offices across the country the day after the inquiry was published. Some BBC staff said, "We are resolute that the BBC should not step back from its determination to investigate the facts in pursuit of the truth."

According to a February 25, 2004, Associated Press article by Patrick E. Tyler, a linguist, Katherine Gun who worked for the British General Communications headquarters, the intelligence agency that intercepts and deciphers communications around the world, was arrested in March 2003. Ms. Gun was charged under the Official Secrets Acts because she leaked a top secret e-mail message to The London Observer. Gun said she was horrified when she saw the top-secret request in January 2003 from the Americans to spy on United Nations diplomats to glean information that might sway the debate on the war in Iraq. Gun said she had acted out of conscience to expose what she regarded as an attempt by the United States to undermine the debate at the United Nations. The e-mail message was from Frank Koza, identified as the chief of staff for the regional targets division at the National Security Agency. He was seeking a "surge" in surveillance operations on the six nations – Angola, Chile, Cameroon, Bulgaria, Guinea and Pakistan – that were crucial to winning a majority of the 15 votes on the Security Council for a resolution authorizing war in Iraq. In a sudden reversal, on February 25, 2004, Britain said it would not prosecute Gun. A trial could have further intensified the debate over the war that has poisoned relations between Prime Minister Tony Blair and a large fraction of his Labor Party.

And, on February 25, 2004, former Minister for International Development Clare Short, who quit when Tony Blair decided to join the U.S. to attack Iraq, reported that British intelligence bugged U.N. Secretary-General Kofi Annan's telephone in New York just before they went to war in Iraq. Speaking on a BBC radio program, Short said British Intelligence officers were ordered to spy on Annan and other U.N. officials.

George McGovern wrote in "The Case of Liberalism – A defense of the future against the past" – Harpers Magazine December 2002:

I believe in the essential decency and fairness of the American people. This does not mean, however, that I believe our leaders and our voters always have sound judgment. Democracy does not guarantee wisdom or virtue; it guarantees only the principals of majority rule and freedom of choice. And freedom of choice includes, whether we like it or not, the right to be wrong. We can only hope that from time to time, our leaders will be right.

Now is not the time. President Bush and his team – Vice President Cheney, Secretary of Defense

Donald Rumsfeld, and National Security Adviser Condoleezza Rice – have claimed, on our behalf, the right to send the United States Armed Forces into Iraq, regardless of whether such a move would be acceptable to the international community. They have even implied a willingness to act without congressional approval if necessary. President Bush has already pushed past Congress, the press, and the American people an enormous addition to military spending on the grounds that our nation is "at war" – with Osama bin Laden and soon, possibly, with Iraq, Iran, and North Korea, the so-called axis of evil. Almost daily we hear or read an announcement from the White House, the Pentagon, or the Attorney General's Office of some new terrorist threat. If the aim of terrorists is to spread terror, I suggest that the Bush administration is doing their work for them.

How right George McGovern was, the Bush administration has attacked Iraq and was leaning toward attacking Libya. In December 2003, the leader of Libya, Moammar Gadhafi, announced that his country would abandon its pursuit of nuclear weapons program. The United Nations nuclear inspector's team led by Mohamed ElBaradei, who heads the International Atomic Energy Agency, visited the four nuclear sites in the capital Tripoli. ElBaradei said the North African country is years away from producing nuclear arms, and is largely dismantled. ElBaradei said "What we have seen is a program in the very initial stages of development. We haven't seen any industrial-scale facility to produce highly enriched uranium. We haven't seen any enriched uranium."

U.N. spokesman Mark Gwozdecky said some of the inspectors also met with Libyan officials on "technical matters concerning the history of (Libya's) entire program" related to weapons of mass destruction. ElBaradei will meet with Mohammed Matoug, a Libyan deputy Prime Minister and head of the country's nuclear program to develop a plan for future inspection. In spite of this latest information, the Bush administration started the rhetoric that Libya has weapons of mass destruction. One can only surmise that the rhetoric used to attack Iraq is unfolding again, only this time to attack Libya.

According to a report, Dr. ElBaradei's description of the Libyan nuclear program appeared more modest and less alarming than the descriptions given by Bush and Blair when they revealed that nine months of secret diplomacy had led to a breakthrough with Libya. Abdel-Rahman Shalqam reaffirmed that Libya is committed to full transparency and would sign a protocol allowing wide-ranging inspections on short notice, promises Gadhafi made during his announcement. Gadhafi said he hoped Libya's action would pressure Israel to disarm. Israel is the only Mideast nation believed to possess nuclear arms.

North Korea also folded temporarily under pressure and fear of being attacked. It has offered to freeze its nuclear power program, as well as to refrain from testing or making nuclear weapons. The Bush administration has now caved in on its previous decision not to negotiate directly with North Korea, and to allow negotiations only with Japan, South Korea, Russia and China. Now there appears that there will be a six-way talk with the United States participating directly.

Does the United States have two policies when it comes to weapons of mass destruction, one for the United States and Israel and one for the rest of the world? While America is telling other nations to destroy their weapons of mass destruction or the United States will do it for them, even if it means changing regimes in the process, the U.S. is increasing its arsenal. On December 11, 2003, America tested an Aegis cruiser in an undisclosed location in the Pacific.

According to reports, in December 2003, President Bush ordered the Pentagon to have ready for use within two years a bare-bones system for defending America's territory and that of its allies against attack by ballistic missiles. They call such action an essential step toward providing defense against threats such as missiles armed with chemical, biological or nuclear warheads. Under Bush's plan, 20 Standard Missile-3 interceptors would be placed aboard three Navy ships with improved versions of the Aegis system that uses radar to detect and track hostile missiles and cue on-board weapons to intercept them. However, sea-based system was outlawed under the 1972 Anti-Ballistic Treaty, but Bush gained the flexibility of testing it when the United States withdrew from the treaty in 2002. The plan also calls for the development of ground-based interceptors.

So why shouldn't other nations have a weapons program? They, too, should want to protect themselves from attacks – and why shouldn't they?

In view of the fact that the Bush administration is so adamant regarding the use of weapons of mass destruction by other countries, I find it hypocritical, to say the least, that the U.S. is trying to expand its weapons programs. The Bush administration requested more money to build a nuclear bunker buster, to research the feasibility of a low-yield "mini-nuke" warhead and for work on a new plant to produce plutonium triggers for the warheads. Everyone is well aware that the United States is the most feared nation in the world, not only because of its superpower defense capabilities, but also in terms of its financial strength. Some countries such as China said its troops were sent to Iraq as a humanitarian gesture. Thailand sent peacekeeping troops. South Korea, on the other hand, needs the U.S. superpower to protect it from being nuked by North Korea, so it too sent peacekeeping troops to Iraq. Japan, trying to appease the United States, also sent troops to Iraq, although its country had never sent troops to fight in another country since World War II.

Remaking Of The World: Bush And The Neoconservatives
By Joshua Micah Marshall
Excerpts from the November/December 2003 issue of Foreign Affairs:

Days before the United States launched Operation Iraqi Freedom a well-known intellectual close to the White House walked me through the necessity and promise of the coming invasion. Whatever rancor it caused in the short term, he said, would pale in comparison to the payoff that would follow. In the months and years to come, Iraqis who had suffered under Saddam Hussein's tyranny would write books and testify to the brutality of the regime, the bankruptcy of the Arab nationalism that stood idly by while they suffered, and the improvement of their lives. That testimony and the reality of an Iraqi state where basic human rights were respected would shatter the anti-Americanism that fills the Muslim Middle East and start a wave of change that would sweep over the region. It was a breathtaking vision, and one that was difficult to dismiss out of hand. But from the vantage point of late 2003, it seems little better than a fantasy. To be sure, the war did eliminate a dangerous and evil regime. But the Bush administration greatly exaggerated the scale and imminence of the danger Saddam posed, while dramatically underestimating the cost and burden of the postwar occupation. The prewar links between Iraq and terrorism proved to be as minimal as skeptics had charged. And the Iraqis' feelings toward their liberators turned out to be more ambivalent than Washington had assumed, the regional ripple effects less extensive, and the diplomatic damage of the whole episode worse and longer lasting.

Based on the fact that the U.S. and British arsenals are second to none, it was clear to see why Saddam Hussein never launched an attack against the U.S. and British superpowers. In the first day of fighting, the 173rd Airborne Brigade that consisted of 1,800 soldiers managed to kill over 1,200 Iraqi soldiers. Saddam Hussein going up against the United States was like David going up against Goliath. The Iraqi soldiers never had a chance. It is no wonder that the U.S. soldiers were able to slaughter the Iraqis so quickly and precisely.

Bush's position that the United States was in danger of being attacked by Saddam Hussein was such a farce and a moot point because Saddam Hussein did not have the weapons, the manpower or the capabilities to put the lives of the American people in danger. This was not a war. It was an assault on the Iraqis. It could not be a war if only one party was fighting. Many Iraqis suffered similar fates or atrocities such as those suffered by other family members under Saddam Hussein, when the U.S. dropped napalm bombs on them during the initial phases of the Iraq war.

President Bush in his January 2002 State of the Union address labeled Iraq, Iran and North Korea an "axis of evil." According to an April 24, 2005, Reuters article, North Korea's Vice Marshal Kim Yong-churn said the U.S. brought the six-party talks to a collapse and staged large-scale madcap war exercises targeted against North Korea after massively shipping ultra-modern war equipment and a nuclear strike group into South Korea in a bid to bring down its system. Yong-churn said his country would steadily bolster its nuclear capability to counter an invasion by the United States. He said "The army and the people of the Democratic People's Republic of Korea will never remain a passive on-looker to the U.S. moves to isolate and stifle its country, but steadily bolster its nuclear deterrent for self-defense to cope with the enemies' reckless moves for military aggression." North Korea has an active military force of 1.2 million.

When the Bush administration took over the White House, Colin Powell said that the administration would continue with the Clinton administration's policy on North Korea. However other officials immediately refuted Powell comments, and ridiculed Clinton's "appeasement" of North Korea. The administration later included Pyongyang in the "axis of evil." But after the North's clandestine uranium enrichment program was disclosed in late 2002, the administration slowly backtracked. The White House decided not only to negotiate with Kim Jong II and discuss a security guarantee, but it has even broached the possibility of granting him more aid before he dismantles his nuclear program. The result of the Bush team's tough approach is that North Korea now has two ongoing nuclear weapons programs, while U.S. relations with South Korea have deteriorated dramatically, according to reports.

It has been clear from the moment that the Bush administration took office that the plan was to take over Iraq. First, Bush said that Saddam Hussein tried to kill his father. Is that a reason to risk American and Iraqi lives to remove Saddam Hussein? Trying to kill someone and killing someone is definitely not one and the same thing, so why should the U.S. subject its servicemen and women to be slaughtered and physically and mentally impaired most likely for the rest of their lives, because someone made a threat to kill one person? We should be reminded that it was only a threat.

It also appears that the war plan was always in play because of the build-up of troops in the Gulf. On one hand the Bush administration gave the appearance that it was going along with the United Nations Security Council to carry out the search for chemical and biological weapons, while on the other hand it was working on a war plan.

These U.S. officials kept saying that no decision had been made to attack Iraq. But, as far back as November 2002, President Bush, Vice President Cheney, Secretary of Defense Rumsfeld and the U.S. commander in Iraq, Tommy

Frank, had decided that military action in Iraq would be carried out with large troop levels, according to reports.

President Bush said that no decision had been reached because he had not yet ordered the nation to war. Meanwhile, the Army was loading tugboats, forklifts and other cargo-handling equipment onto the Tern, a giant cargo ship in Hampton Roads, Virginia, that was bound for the Gulf to prepare ports for the arrival of tanks and other armored equipment. Heavy equipment was being deployed to the Gulf region while inspections were under way. Senior officials said the plan called for several Army and Marine divisions, aircraft carriers and Air Force wings. They also said that the only ally expected to contribute significant ground forces was Britain, with several thousand troops expected to participate.

According to one military officer, there were options within the plan, but there was only one plan. The plan was that the entire troop total would not necessarily be in the region when the offensive began. The bulk of the force would probably stand ready in case of battlefield setbacks and be poised to occupy parts of Iraq as soon as resistance ended. Under the plan, their campaign would be less than the 43 days of the first Gulf war, and probably under a month, according to reports.

The plan was that in the opening hours of the air campaign, Navy and Air Force jets, including B-2 bombers carrying 16 one-ton satellite-guided bombs and B-1 bombers carrying 24 of the same weapons, would attack a range of targets from military headquarters to air defenses. More than sixty percent of the weapons dropped in Iraq would be precision-guided, compared to the nine percent in the previous Gulf war.

The United States had taken the position of pre-emptive strike, even though there was no proof that the United States was being threatened or in any way in imminent danger of being attacked. In President Bush's address of March 17, 2002, he portrayed his confrontation with Saddam Hussein as a new fight for a new millennium. He said, "In the 20th century, some chose to appease murderous dictators whose threats were allowed to grow into genocide and global war." "In this century, when evil men plot chemical, biological and nuclear terror, a policy of appeasement could bring destruction of a kind never before seen on this earth." This was just another scare tactic to convince the American people that he really had a legitimate reason to attack Iraq.

Surely, the Bush administration knew that Saddam Hussein did not have a nuclear arsenal. In 1982, using United States F-16 Bombers, Israel blew up the nuclear facilities that Saddam Hussein was building.

Russian President Vladimir Putin denounced plans for an attack in unusually strong terms, saying a war would be fought with the gravest of consequences and that it would result in casualties and would destabilize the international situation in general.

The United States offered Turkey $30 billion to allow its troops to set up posts in Turkey for the launch into Baghdad, since that would be a more direct route into Iraq. However, the Turkey parliament voted against it because of outcries from the Turkish people.

Australian's Prime Minister John Howard agreed to send 2000 troops to Iraq in defiance of the Australians' wishes not to commit its soldiers to fight in an undeclared war. His response was similar to those who provided minimal symbolic support – because they need the United States.

British Prime Minister Tony Blair echoed President Bush's rhetoric that Saddam Hussein had weapons of mass destruction and that he used them on his people before and would use them again. He committed 40,000 troops to attack Iraq in spite of opposition from the British people and many cabinet members.

THREE

BLOOD FOR OIL

Just before the war in Iraq started, the U.S. Army Corps of Engineers awarded Halliburton, Dick Cheney's former company, an emergency contract to extinguish the fires in Iraq that would result from the destruction of the bombs and other materials, and to assess damages and other needs. No other company was given the opportunity to bid for the contract.

A December 29, 2003, New York Times article by Jeff Gerth and Don Van Natta Jr. stated:

> The contract to fix Iraq's oil industry was granted to Kellogg Brown & Root, a Halliburton subsidiary, by a secret Bush administration task force. The task force was formed in September 2002 to plan for Iraq's oil industry in the event of war. The task force was led by an aide to Douglas J. Feith, the undersecretary of defense for policy.
>
> Almost immediately, an alarm went off among members of the group. "I immediately understood there would be an issue raised about the vice president's former relationship with KBR," the official said, "so we took it up to the highest levels of the administration, and the answer we got was, 'Do what was best for the mission and we'll worry about the political' [fallout.]"
>
> The process began in November 2002 to plan the management of Iraq's postwar oil industry. "In the worst case scenario," said Lt. Gen. Robert B.

Flowers, the commander of the Army Corps of Engineers, "there would be massive oil spills and pollution resulting from the fires, extensive damage to associated infrastructure, including gas-oil separators, pipelines, pumping stations, refineries and import facilities."

Kellogg Brown & Root designed a plan for such an eventuality, and on March 8, as war loomed, the corps awarded Halliburton a no-bid contract to carry out the plan, officials said. The contract is labeled IDIQ, meaning indefinite delivery, indefinite quantity.

That is not the only contract Halliburton would receive from the Bush administration's demolition of Iraq's infrastructure. The contract given to Halliburton also includes the operation of facilities and distribution of products. Furthermore, the Halliburton emergency contract will be replaced with a long-term contract. The original authorization was for $7 billion. The corps later said that it did not have an estimate of how much the new contract would be worth.

According to a June 10, 2003, CNNMoney report, Corps officials said they gave the contract, which was worth up to $7 billion to the Halliburton subsidiary, KBR, to rehabilitate and operate Iraq's oil industry because it already has assets in the region and has the expertise to put out oil well fires and repair Iraq's oil facilities. Corps officials acknowledged that the contract, which has no set time limit or dollar amount, allows KBR to actually operate Iraq's oil fields and distribute its oil, rather than just putting out fires and making repairs.

This contract will allow KBR to cap oil blowouts, respond to oil spills, perform emergency repairs and assist Iraq's ministry in getting the oil system operating. They will be pumping and distributing Iraqi oil, contrary to the Bush administration's repeated statements that the oil is for the Iraqi people and its only intention is to rid the Iraqi people of

Saddam Hussein and to destroy his weapons of mass destruction. Rep. Henry Waxman, D- California, says, "It is simply remarkable that a single company could earn so much money from the war in Iraq."

Also, according to a CNNMoney report, the Halliburton Co. was given an "obscure and lucrative" contract in 2001 of nearly $500 million. This contract, called the Logistics Civil Augmentation Program (LOGCAP), is to provide logistic support to the Army "in wartime and other operations." Waxman said that one of the unique features of the LOGCAP contract is that it apparently allowed Halliburton to profit from virtually every phase of the conflict in Iraq. The work in Iraq under LOGCAP is in addition to the contract by the U.S. Army Corps of Engineers to repair and operate oil wells in Iraq, worth more that $70 million initially with a ceiling of about $7 billion, but even that ceiling has already been breached, because by July 2005, the contracts have passed the $10 billion mark. CNN reported on July 6, 2005, that the U.S. assigned Halliburton another $5 billion contract in addition to the $9.1 billion received so far.

Halliburton's subsidiary, KBR, also has a contract with the U.S. government to provide support services to the military including food supplies for the troops. It is estimated that the U.S. government is spending several billions of dollars per month on troop support, fuel, equipment and reconstruction. In addition to the monopoly no-bid contract, there is also a plus cost clause. One needs look no further to understand why Dick Cheney was gung-ho in making the point to convince the American people that the United States was in imminent danger of an attack by Saddam Hussein.

Moreover, Cheney has a vested interest in seeing that the Halliburton Company is profitable. According to reports he continues to receive $1million per year from Halliburton. The Halliburton Company showed a loss in 2002, but has shown a profit for the quarter ending June 30, 2003, due in part, to the lucrative Iraq contracts awarded by the United States. It should be agonizing to the American people that the Bush administration demolished Iraq's infrastructure and now the American taxpayers are footing the bill for billions of dollars to rebuild it and the check is payable to Halliburton and other cronies.

While the Bush administration made several requests for funds for Iraq, the U.S. was being fleeced by Halliburton. Rep.Waxman accused Halliburton, the Texas oil services company once run by Vice President Dick Cheney, of overcharging the U.S. government for gasoline the firm imports into Iraq. Halliburton subsidiary Kellogg Brown & Root defends its pricing as fair, has a contract with the U.S. Army Corps of Engineers to rebuild Iraq's oil sector. This includes importing gasoline products that are in short supply to the oil-rich nation. "Millions of Americans want to help Iraqis, but they don't want to be fleeced (by Halliburton)," Waxman told a news conference. Waxman said Army documents showed that as of September 18, 2003, the United States had paid Halliburton $300 million to import about 190 million gallons of gasoline into Iraq.

Halliburton billed the government an average price of $1.59 per gallon, excluding the company's fee of 2 percent to 7 percent. He said the average wholesale cost of gasoline during that period in the Middle East was about 71 cents a gallon, a figure an oil industry source told Reuters was accurate. That meant Halliburton is overcharging by more than 90 cents a gallon to transport fuel into Iraq from Kuwait.

"When we checked with independent experts to see if this fee was reasonable, they were stunned," said Waxman, adding a reasonable transport cost would be 10 to 25 cents per gallon, especially as the U.S. military was providing security. Waxman sent a letter to the White House Office of Management and Budget, complaining that KBR was overcharging for petroleum products. The overcharging by Halliburton is so extreme that one expert privately called it "highway robbery," he wrote. By this time, Halliburton has received more than $1.4 billion in work in Iraq to repair and restore the country's oil industry under a no-competition contract plus cost issued in March 2003. In another contract providing logistical support, more than $1.6 billion has been clocked so far, with more in the works. Sen. Frank Lautenberg, D-N.J., suggested an amendment to the $87 billion Iraq spending bill in Congress that would prevent firms with ties to senior administration officials from getting Iraq contracts.

In December 2003, auditors determined that Halliburton subsidiary Kellogg Brown and Root may have overcharged the military by $61 million for gasoline delivered to civilians in Iraq. The Pentagon has also raised concerns that the Halliburton Company has engaged in "substantial overcharging" on millions of overseas meals. After several months of accusation of overcharging, Pentagon officials said on February 23, 2004 that they have opened a criminal fraud investigation of Halliburton. The inquiry will examine potential overpricing of fuel taken into Iraq.

One report said that because of the spotlight on Halliburton, Dick Cheney's former company, and the fact that the election was fast approaching, to avoid this issue from becoming a part of the campaign debate, Halliburton said on February 26, 2004, that a team of company managers and auditors found deficiencies in its cost control system. This was after they have long contended that they were not overcharging. As a matter of fact, KBR President and Chief Executive Randy Harl had made the claim in January 2004, that the company had a "rigorous system of internal controls" for government contracts. Kellogg Brown & Root later said that its cost controls are "antiquated" and inadequate. The team's findings, contained in the 18-page internal document reviewed by The Wall Street Journal, call the company's procurement "disorganized" and marked by "weak internal controls." The memo acknowledges that KBR's paper-based, labor-intensive and bureaucratic" procurement system is not suitable for a fast-response situation like Iraq.

Many other companies are enjoying lucrative contracts for work in Iraq. Defense contractors such as Boeing received contracts and will receive another contract from the

U.S. Army for $14.8 billion for its Future Combat Systems program. Northrop-Grumman received lucrative contracts worth billions of dollars to lease refueling aircraft in the air at a cost that far exceeded the cost of purchasing the refueling aircraft by billions of dollars.

Of course, there are many other companies that are profiting from the fall of Iraq. For example, a February 17, 2004, Wall Street Journal article said the Bush administration and Citigroup Inc., are proposing a joint $200 million arrangement to finance Iraq's imports, with the bank's revenue from the project guaranteed by Iraq's oil sale. The proposal will call for a Baghdad bank to issue a letter of credit for a local company's imports. An international bank would confirm the letter, assuming the risk of non-payment. A separate institution, set up by Citigroup, would then guarantee that the international bank gets paid. Citigroup, and the Overseas Private Investment Corp., would guarantee that the separate institution gets paid. Finally, the coalition would pledge to use Iraqi oil revenue to cover any Citigroup and OPIC losses. All of the banks along the way would collect fees for their participation, and as long as the coalition runs Iraq, there is essentially no risk for any of them.

And, in January 2004, Nour USA, a privately held U.S.-led consortium, won a $327 million contract to supply Iraq's new armed forces and the Iraqi Civil Defense Corps with equipment. Nour, a Vienna, Virginia-based company, was set up specifically to bid for business in postwar Iraq and has previously won an $18 million contract to provide security in the country. Bechtel, which has ties to prominent Republicans like former Secretary of State George Shultz, who serves on the company's board, has been awarded a second lucrative contract to rebuild Iraq's infrastructure worth $1.8 billion.

The American taxpayers are paying billions of dollars in Iraq when some of the cost could have been borne by many other countries if the Bush administration had not rushed to war and instead waited for the United Nations inspectors to complete their job. For that matter, there might not have been an Iraqi invasion in 2003. Some of the money that is being spent in Iraq could be used to prop up the U.S. economy that is suffering from job losses, a poor education system and the need for infrastructure repairs, etc.

And, according to reports, one of the most influential persons who fed the Bush administration false information on Iraq, Ahmad Chalabi, receives approximately $350,000 per month from the U.S., and it was estimated that he could receive as much as $30 million. However, he has fallen from grace as it pertains to his relationship with the Bush administration. On May 20, 2004, Iraqi police backed by American soldiers raided his home and offices and confiscated computers and documents. Reporters said documents were scattered on the marble floors of the offices, cables ripped-off and furniture overturned. A portrait of Chalabi hanging on the wall in his home had a bullet hole in the forehead. U.S. officials deferred questions about the raid to the Iraqis, but said neither Chalabi nor his political organization, the Iraqi National Congress, was a target. State Department spokesman Richard Boucher said "clearly there were legal and investigative reasons, not political." On June 1, 2004, the Bush administration said Chalabi told Iran that the U.S. has broken their code. Chalabi, one of the members of the Iraqi Governing Council, was highly speculated to eventually take over as head of the Iraqi government.

And, as the U.S. pours money into Iraq, its deficit escalates and its infrastructure in need of repairs. On July 15, 2003, the Bush administration projected that the federal deficit will climb to a record $455 billion and surge to $475 billion in 2004. Of course, this estimate increased exponentially. There was also a report that the United States needed over $1.7 trillion to repair its own infrastructure.

One point needs considering: Will the American companies who will benefit from the lucrative contracts in rebuilding Iraq's oil industry and infrastructure be footing some of the cost by paying their fair share of the taxes? Or, will they be given some special tax breaks that would render their taxes negligible or nil? Will the middle class be burdened with this monstrous war cost?

On December 2, 2003, a CNN ticker tape said that the Pentagon would extend the time for awarding two contracts to rebuild Iraq. Delay in awarding these contracts to other bidders would only allow Halliburton more time with its no-bid contracts.

A December 10, 2003, New York Times article by Don Van Natta Jr. stated:

> The United States government is paying the Halliburton Company an average of $2.64 a gallon to import gasoline and other fuel to Iraq from Kuwait, more than twice what others are paying to truck in Kuwaiti fuel. Halliburton gets $2.64 for a gallon of fuel it imports from Kuwait and $1.24 per gallon for fuel from Turkey. Halliburton gets 26 cents a gallon for its overhead and fees.
>
> Gasoline imports are one of the largest costs of Iraq's reconstruction efforts as of December 2003, although Iraq sits on the third largest oil reserves in the world. More than $500 million has been spent to bring gas, benzene and other fuels into Iraq. And, as part of the $87 billion package for Iraq and Afghanistan that Congress approved in November, $18.6 billion will be spent on reconstruction projects, including $690 million for gasoline and other fuel imports in 2004. Independent experts who reviewed Halliburton's percentage of its gas importation contract said the company's 26-cent charge per gallon of gas from Kuwait appeared to be extremely high. Many other suppliers charge only a few cents a gallon. Phil Verleger, a California oil economist and the president of the consulting firm PK Verleger LLC said, "I have never seen anything like this in my life. That's a monopoly premium – that's the only term to describe it. Every logistical firm or

oil subsidiary in the United States would salivate to have that sort of contract."

Halliburton is paying $1.21 a gallon to transport the fuel an estimated 400 miles from Kuwait to Iraq and it is paying 22 cents a gallon to transport gas into Iraq from Turkey. Figures provided to Congressional investigators by the corps shows that Halliburton was charging as much as $3.06 a gallon for fuel from Kuwait in late November 2003. Also, if the corps concludes that Halliburton has successfully administered the gas contract, it could be paid an additional 5 percent of the total value of the gas it imported.

Isn't it also ironic that Iraq, being the second-largest oil-producing nation, had to purchase oil for its consumption?

On December 18, 2003, Halliburton denied overcharging for the fuel, and said it actually saved the Pentagon money. Meanwhile, Sen. Joe Lieberman, a Democratic presidential candidate, said a Pentagon official told him that Halliburton auditors also had warned the company about possible overcharging. The subsidiary, Kellogg Brown & Root, also submitted a proposal for cafeteria services that seemed to be inflated by $67 million.

According to a December 12, 2003, New York Times article by Douglas Jehl, another contract with the Army involved unacceptable delays by KBR in providing cost estimates for dozens of projects already under way in Iraq for work that includes food, housing, and other facilities for the military, which could also involve inflated costs. It estimated that Halliburton would refund $27.4 million to the Pentagon as a result of overcharges for meals that they provided to U.S. soldiers in Kuwait and Iraq. The two Halliburton contracts are the largest awarded by the Pentagon in Iraq. The Army Corps of Engineers awarded a contract for KBR to repair and restore Iraq's oil industry. The initial value of the work was set at $7 billion. A second contract with the Army for logistical support has a maximum value of $8.6 billion.

The article further stated that the audit agency was also concerned with KBR's delays in pricing elements of the logistics contract. Among the projects under way, the company has provided the government with cost estimates for just 12 orders, with 69 outstanding and overdue. Military officials said the delays raised the possibility that the company would eventually claim an unacceptably high cost for a project whose work was already largely completed.

These excessive charges are indicative that the Pentagon is being taken advantage of because of the relationship between Dick Cheney and the Halliburton Company. One needs only to look at what is going on with the contracts Halliburton is receiving from the Defense Department to understand why this is taking place. For example, according to reports, the Halliburton Company estimated that to overhaul the Qarmat Ali water treatment plant in southern Iraq it would cost $75.7 million, but within six weeks, the Bush administration asked Congress for $125 million to do the job – a 40 percent increase.

A spokesman for the corps, Richard V. Dowling, which oversees the contract, said the initial price was based on "drive-by estimating." Since when does the U.S. government award contracts based on such information? What happened to bids that are binding with regard to cost and completion? And what happened to "good faith contracts?" You would think that if a contractor gives an estimate, that contractor would have enough experience to be very close to the cost given. Moreover, according to the Bush administration, Halliburton has been given these lucrative contracts because that company is one of the most experienced companies in the oil industry. So that is all the more reason why the cost estimates should be pretty accurate.

A December 28, 2003, New York Times article by Jeff Gerth and Don Van Natta Jr., stated said that the Pentagon's contract with Halliburton's subsidiary, Kellogg Brown &

Root, conceived in secrecy before the war and signed in March, was meant as a stopgap deal to last no more than a few months. But it has been in effect since then and has grown to more than $2 billion. The scope of the contract includes myriad tasks, from importing fuels to repairing pipelines, and the costs have increased through task orders and subcontracts, some of which are carried out with limited documentation or disclosure.

After several complaints regarding Halliburton's unit Kellogg Brown and Root's exclusive contract to repair and rebuild Iraq oil fields, the Pentagon announced that it expected to formally solicit bids later in June 2003 for two potentially large contracts to help rebuild Iraqi's oil fields, which would end the government's controversial no-bid contract with Halliburton-Kellogg Brown and Root.

With chaos continuing to plague much of Iraq's petroleum industry, U.S. military engineers were unable to predict even the basic shape that the new contracts would take. Many heads of states and the general public wanted Saddam Hussein disarmed peacefully and that could have been accomplished if the Bush administration wanted to disarm him peacefully. However, it did not appear that way from the offset. Saddam Hussein and his ministers were right when they said no matter how they cooperate and no matter how many demands they met the Bush administration would attack their country.

A March 10, 2003, Wall Street Journal by Neil King Jr., said, prior to the beginning of the Iraqi war, the Bush administration planned to award a contract for as much as $900 million to begin the rebuilding of a post-war Iraq, in what would be the largest government reconstruction effort since Americans helped to rebuild Germany and Japan after World War II. The U.S. Agency for International Development quietly sent a detailed request for proposals to bid on the contract to five American infrastructure engineering companies. According to the Bush administration, the work would form the core plan to demonstrate its resolve to immediately improve the quality of life in Iraq. This contract was to restore essential water systems, roadways, ports, hospitals and schools immediately after the war ends. Planning envisions wrapping up the rebuilding in 18 months. The U.S. Agency for International Development also sought contractors for five other large tasks, one each to subsequently administer Iraq's main seaports, international airports, hospitals and health clinics, and primary and secondary schools, another for trucking in and warehousing water, electrical generators, and other crucial supplies.

Other industries also benefit from the Iraq invasion such as telephone communications, food suppliers, electrical engineers, water supply treatment systems, etc. Bechtel, one of the five companies that received bid proposals, was awarded a contract for $680 million. This was just the initial contract covering 18 months of reconstruction work. The whole reconstruction work was estimated to last for several years, eventually costing billions of dollars. Bechtel was one of the major Republican contributors to the Bush/Cheney 2000 campaign.

In addition to Halliburton, Bechtel also received a no-bid contract from the Department of Defense. Bechtel said it would also be interested in bidding for a U.S. Army Corps of Engineers contracts to restore Iraq's oil fields. Bechtel was also contracted to restore Kuwait oil fields after the first Gulf War. Bechtel's contract calls for them to repair and restore power facilities, city water and sanitation systems, airport, and the dredging and upgrading of Iraq's Umm Qasr seaport.

Moreover, these contractors are taking advantage of the situation. For example, Bechtel wanted $15 million for a job in Iraq, and an Iraqi contractor wanted only $80,000 to do the same job, according to Senator Waxman. Senator McCain said Boeing, on the other hand, was offered a sweetheart deal to lease refueling planes to the U.S. This contract would cost $2 billion more than if the U.S. bought the planes outright.

Since the Iraq war, several companies have returned to profitability. According to an April 28, 2004, Wall Street article by Jonathan Karp, Lockheed Martin's profit rose 16 percent in the first quarter of 2004 on the strength of combat-aircraft sales and information-technology services, and has raised its earnings outlook for 2004. The company delivered fifteen F-16 fighter jets, up from three a year before, and four C-130J transport planes, in addition to F-A-22 and F-35 Joint Strike Fighters. Additionally, Lockheed Martin has been awarded a contract to design and build the next-generation air-to-ground missile, a deal that is potentially valued at more than $5 billion and the first in a slew of big awards that were being reviewed as the Pentagon pushes to modernize the U.S. military. The Joint Common Missile will be used on Army, Navy and Marine Corps aircraft.

Defense contractor Boeing has also seen its bottom line increase considerably with profits of $623 million for the first quarter of 2004. According to an April 29, 2004, Wall Street article by J. Lynn Lunsford, Boeing is expected to earn between $2.05 and $2.25 a share in 2004, up from $1.95. For 2005, earnings-per-share guidance was lifted to between $2.20 and $2.45 up from $2.20 a share. Boeing's President and Chief Executive Officer Harry Stonecipher said the earnings-per-share guidance includes an assumption that the 767 tanker program for the U.S. Air force will go forward despite continued delays in the $23 billion deal for the Air Force to lease and purchase as many as 100 of the airplanes. U.S. Defense Department contracts brought in $7.42 billion in revenue up from $6.26 in 2003.

Originally, the Pentagon planned to offer the Boeing Company a contract valued at $18 billion for 100 Boeing 767 tankers. However, on December 1, 2003, in a letter to the Senate Armed Service Committee, Deputy Defense Secretary Paul Wolfowitz stated that he was ordering a "pause in the execution" of the Air Force contracts to lease and buy mid-air refueling tankers. The Pentagon told Congress it would postpone any action on the $18 billion contracts for the 100 Boeing 767 tankers until the deal is investigated following Boeing's firing of two officials for ethical violations.

First Energy is another of the Republicans' biggest campaign contributors who stands to gain from the war in Iraq. In 1999, First Energy met with Cheney and Bush when they were working on their campaign. Then in 2002, First Energy contributed $1.04 million, 70 percent of which went to the Republican Party.

In addition, contracts were awarded to other companies, such as General Electric and MCI/WorldCom, to participate in the rebuilding of Iraq's infrastructure. MCI/WorldCom was given the contract to build a wireless telephone system. MCI/Worldcom filed bankruptcy after an $11 billion accounting scandal and the biggest bankruptcy in the history of the United States of over $20 billion. This left thousands of employees without jobs. These employees not only lost their jobs, but their retirement savings as well. I know of an employee who rolled over her 401(K) from her previous employer to MCI. She lost not only the MCI portion of her 401(K), but also the funds rolled over from her previous employer. Yet in view of MCI's conduct, they were still awarded a contract to build a wireless phone system in Iraq.

Finally, some government official realized that to continue to award MCI government contracts was sending a negative message to the American people. On July 31, 2003, the General Services Administration announced that it was suspending federal business with the telecommunication giant because the company lacks necessary internal controls and ethics. MCI's government contracts are valued at more than $1 billion per year. This announcement to suspend federal business with MCI will not, however, affect MCI's existing contracts with state and federal government customers.

On September 9, 2003, the courts cleared the way for MCI/Worldcom to emerge from bankruptcy with a clean slate, relieving the company of its debts while the employees who lost their jobs and pensions were left out in the cold.

Yahoo News by Cynthia Johnston, July 31, 2003, stated:

Iraq's United States-led authority has barred partly state-owned companies from bidding on the three mobile phone licenses, a move that could give American firms an upper hand over Arab companies. Mobile phones were banned under Saddam Hussein. Now mobile phones have replaced satellite telephones as a major means of communicating abroad, at least for foreign journalists and businessmen.

The United States Army and development workers now use a network in Baghdad built by Worldcom/MCI, while this service is barred to ordinary Iraqis.

Consulting firms were formed in Washington and the Middle East to capture some of the monies that are being spent in Iraq by the U.S. government. Joe Allbaugh, the national campaign manager for President Bush in 2000, and Ed Rogers, a senior official in President Reagan and former President Bush White House, put together one such firm, New Bridge Strategies LLC.

According to a May 11, 2003, Wall Street Journal article, U.S. farmers are also vying for wheat contracts currently controlled by Australia. The Bush administration sent two ships with 56,000 metric tons of wheat to Umm Qsar. Australia supplies wheat to Iraq under the United Nations oil for food program and has warned Washington that any attempt to use food aid to break open the Iraq market might violate World Trade Organization rules. Companies such as Cargill Inc and Archer-Daniels- Midland could benefit from grain export to Iraq as well.

According to a London Times November 22, 2003, article, British firms will be getting contracts in Iraq valued at 11 billion pounds.

With so many lucrative contracts available for Iraq's reconstruction, many companies have been profiting from the demise of the Iraqi people. And with the U.S. economy in a slump, having these lucrative contracts will boost their profit margins over several years to come.

A Wall Street Journal April 25, 2003, article said the Bush administration plans to operate Iraq's oil industry like a corporation, using Americans as chief executive, a management team and board of advisers.

The chief executive will perform the same duties as the former oil minister and will represent Iraq at meetings of the Organization of Petroleum Exporting Countries. Philip J. Carroll, former chief executive of Shell Oil Co., the U.S. arm of Royal Dutch/Shell Group will be chairman of the board, working closely with an Iraqi vice chairman. The American-style structure and the appointments may rankle those who believe that the U.S. is wielding too much unilateral power over the occupied nation. It also could irk Iraqi oil-ministry officials who are already back at work trying to get the country's massive oil fields running again. Americans will control the top positions but rely on the expertise of the Iraqi officials to run the nuts and bolts of the oil operations.

The Pentagon's Office for Reconstruction and Humanitarian Assistance went back on their word when they said that top jobs at Iraqi agencies would on an interim basis be led by current Iraqi officials untainted by the Saddam Hussein regime. U.S. advisers had said Iraqi expatriates would be appointed only to advisory positions, and that the interim management team would be composed of current and former Iraqi oil officials constituting the executive leadership of the Iraq National Oil Co., with the chief executive also sitting on the advisory board. However, the position regarding the power of the advisory board was unclear. Would the board play an advisory role with little real authority or would it have the final say in all major strategic and investment decisions for Iraq's oil industry. The assumption is that Iraq could produce six million barrels of oil per day within the next five to six years. It is also estimated that Iraq has 115 billion barrels of proven reserves, and another 200 billion barrels of probable reserves. This means that Iraqi's oil reserve is second only to Saudi Arabia with the largest reserves in the world. Additionally, it is estimated that there are hundreds of unexplored petroleum structures in Iraq, according to the article.

According to an April 30, 2003, Wall Street Journal article, tensions mounted among the Iraq officials in the oil industry. The Iraqi engineers who operated the oilfields prior to the war want to maintain their management roles, but that is not what the United States wanted.

The United States needs the cooperation of the Iraqi engineers. But will the United States give them any kind of meaningful management roles? The U.S. Army Corps of Engineers and a group of Texas oil-field contractors are working to revive Iraq's petroleum industry. But the Iraqis are skeptical and hesitant to go back to work.

When the first call was made for Iraqi employees to return to work in the oil fields, of approximately 700 employees less than fifty engineers, maintenance men and firefighters turned up for work. The Iraqi people are leery of the United States' intention to bring them in to get the oil fields operating again without them being given any meaningful roles. Of course, problems arise such as no means of transportation for the employee to get to and from work. There is also the concern if and when they would be paid and by whom, according to the report.

The United States exerts it superpower by demolishing Iraq over a period of several weeks, and now they will put Iraq back together again by giving lucrative contracts to the Republican major campaign contributors and other cronies for several years to come. American bombs and missiles demolished the infrastructure, such as hospitals, schools, electrical plants, water and sewage systems, bridges and other facilities. The American taxpayers will have to foot the bill, for the most part, to rebuild the country.

There are no exact figures as to how much the war and the rebuilding efforts will cost. However, initial estimates ranged from $150 billion to $200 billion. Many lives have been shattered not only in the United States and Iraq, but also in Britain, Australia and other countries. The Bush administration refused to tell Congress or the American people how much the Iraq war would cost. Bush keeps saying that he'll do whatever it takes to free the Iraqi people, and continues to work behind closed doors to keep their plans a secret not only from the American people, but also from Congress.

By September 2003, the cost to the United States was between $40 billion and $50 billion dollars a year for the troops in Iraq, according to a CNBC September 3, 2003 report. Bremer, the United States' picked administrator in Iraq, said the reconstruction would cost tens of billions of dollars per year.

According to a Washington Post article of September 5, 2003, the White House informed congressional leaders that it was preparing a new budget request for between $60 billion and $70 billion to help cover the mounting costs of the reconstruction and military occupation of Iraq. Congressional budget analysts said the planned request would be nearly double what Congress expected. This reflects the increasing cost of the five-month-old U.S. occupation and serves as an acknowledgment by the administration that it vastly underestimated the price tag of restoring order in Iraq and rebuilding its infrastructure.

On September 7, 2003, Bush went before the American people to say that he would be asking Congress for $87 billion for the war in Iraq. This, of course, was in addition to the $79 billion that he requested and received from Congress in April 2003. Bush went before the American people to say he would be asking for $87 billion to fight terrorism in Iraq and Afghanistan and "engage the enemy where he lives." Deceptively for a greater impact and urgency, Bush chose four days before the anniversary of the 9/11 attacks to announce his request for $87 billion to fight terrorism.

In order to keep up his fear tactics and to get the Congress and the American people to acquiesce to his demands, Bush would equate 9/11 with Iraq. He said, "We are fighting that enemy in Iraq and Afghanistan today so that we do not meet him again on our own streets, in our own cities." Bush said the United States would not be intimidated into retreat by violence. "The terrorists have cited the examples of Beirut and Somalia, claiming that if you inflict harm on Americans, we will run from a challenge," Bush said, referring to U.S. withdrawals after the loss of American lives. "In this they are mistaken," he said.

True to form, in keeping with the Bush administration mantra to convince the American people that they are in constant danger of being attacked by terrorists, Secretary of Defense Donald Rumsfeld echoed Bush's statement saying, "We know for a fact that terrorists studied Somalia, and they studied instances that the United States was dealt a blow and tucked in, and persuaded themselves that they could in fact cause us to acquiesce in whatever it is they wanted to do." National Security Adviser Condoleezza Rice also echoed Bush's continued statement, and said on Sunday, September 7, 2003, on CNN's late Edition program: "We must remain resolute." She said the president believes that the freedom and cost of peace cannot be measured, and that it is important that we put adequate resources to this task.

Then, on September 14, 2003, Vice President Dick Cheney hinted that in 2004 the Bush administration would seek more money than the additional $87 billion already requested mainly to pay for postwar costs in Iraq. He further stated that the administration did not know when the U.S. military presence in Iraq would end. And, "I don't think anybody can say with absolute certainty at this point," he said. When asked on NBC's "Meet the Press" if that would be the final such request, Cheney replied. "I can't say that. It's all we think we'll need for the foreseeable future, for this year."

Secretary of Defense Donald Rumsfeld on CBS' "Face the Nation" said consultations were under way with lawmakers, and how long the $87 billion would last had not yet been determined. He said, "It's a process that was being handled by the president and the Office of Management and Budget. I think that after those consultations with Congress, we'll have the answer to your question. I think it's important to let the people who are engaging in that process define it."

This $87 billion request from the Bush administration was the second request in as little as five months, the first in April for $79 billion. When would the next request be forthcoming, and how much will it be, and how many more before Congress steps in to stop this runaway train? Is Congress going to approve every request made by the Bush administration? Well-thinking Americans should be asking the question, "When will this squandering of taxpayers' money end? It's obvious that the Bush administration and the Congress are mortgaging the wealth of future generations. In other words, they are being mortgaged out of house and home. I believe it was Senator McCain who said that Congress was spending money like a drunken sailor. At this point the current U.S. deficit was almost a half a trillion dollars and climbing.

While the Bush administration was beating the drum for war, it gave the American people every indication that the war would be executed expeditiously. At no time was there any indication that the Iraq war would be a protracted one. Every time the question was raised regarding the cost and the time period in which to expect the war to be over and the troops to return home, those questions were sidestepped and the same answers given: "For as long as it takes." Or "When the Iraqi soldiers stand up U.S. troops will stand down." The Bush administration keeps saying we need to stay the course in Iraq to fight terrorists, but are we there to fight terrorism, or to control the oil fields and the infrastructure?

It is mind boggling that the Bush administration was so reluctant to resolve the prescription drug problem being faced by the elderly. There were reports that many senior citizens are forced to take half of the prescribed medication because they cannot afford to buy the full amount needed. Yet, it has no qualms about requesting billions of dollars from Congress for Iraq. Shouldn't the U.S. take care of the needs of the American people while addressing the needs of the Iraqis? Why should the needs of American senior citizens be less important than the needs of the Iraqis? Why should the American children's education be compromised for the educational needs of the Iraqis?

The Pentagon is spending approximately $60 billion per year for the military in Iraq and Afghanistan up from the $40 billion to $50 billion previously estimated. The costs keep rising. And true to form on January 25, 2005, the Bush administration said it would ask Congress for another $80 billion for the war in Iraq and Afghanistan, bringing the total request to over $300 billion. These expenses do not include money being spent on rebuilding Iraq's electric grid, water supply and other infrastructure such as the oil fields. According to reports, Iraq has 80 oil fields that are second only to Saudi Arabia's. Iraq can produce oil for $1 per barrel cheaper than Saudi Arabia. With improvements to the oil refineries, Iraq could become the number one oil-producing country in the world. Furthermore, the Bush administration led the American people to believe that the cost for rebuilding Iraq's infrastructure after it was demolished would come from the sale of Iraq's oil. However, it appears that with the constant sabotage of the oil fields, there is not enough money forthcoming from the sale of Iraq's oil to defray the infrastructure cost, or that is the impression being given by the Bush administration. According to reports, the U.S.-appointed administrator, L. Paul Bremer, decided how the oil revenues would be spent.

When the United States attacked Iraq, the first thing they did was to secure the oil fields. According to a BBC news report, the oil fields were protected in the war more so than the hospitals. On August 16, 2003, a bomb was blamed for severing Iraq's newly reopened northern oil export pipeline, dealing a new blow to hopes of oil recovery. Thamir Ghadban, U.S.-appointed de facto oil minister, told a news conference in Baghdad, "We believe at this stage it was an explosive device planted on the pipeline."

The United States is now faced with a monumental task of rebuilding Iraq that the Bush administration never anticipated. Apparently they were under the illusion that all they had to do was to demolish Iraq's infrastructure and rebuild it. However, once Saddam Hussein's regime was toppled, chaos ensued. Stealing, robberies, murder and sabotage became the norm. On the one hand, while the American companies and soldiers were trying to get the oil fields operating, the Iraqis were trying to undo what the Americans accomplished. In addition, the pipelines that were damaged during the war have to be repaired. For example, Iraq's ability to export oil is impaired. A senior Iraqi oil executive said the country would be unable to repair a critical pipeline that links the country's southern and northern oil regions before the end of 2003.

According to a 2003 Wall Street Journal article by Keith Johnson, Adil al Qazzaz, the head of Iraq's North Oil Co., which manages the large Kirkuk oil field, said it is going to take a long time to repair K3, a crucial pumping station located near Hadithah in northwestern Iraq on the so-called Strategic Pipeline. The station was destroyed during the war in a U.S. bombing raid. The Strategic Pipeline is very important, according to Raad Alkadiri, an analyst at PFC Energy, Washington-based oil industry consultants. It gives Iraq flexibility in moving crude around the country.

The article also stated that the United States-led forces seized Iraq's main fields largely intact, but looting, sabotage and civil disorder set back efforts to restore output and exports. Iraq has two main export outlets: the Persian Gulf port of Mina al-Bakr, which before the war could handle about 1.2 million barrels a day, and the 800,000 barrel-a-day pipeline from Kirkuk to Turkey's Mediterranean port of Ceyhan.

The United States now has control and a monopoly over Iraq and its oil fields. Soon after the attack on Iraq, the United States announced that it would be withdrawing its troops from Saudi Arabia, the number one oil producing country in the world. I wonder if there is a correlation between the two. The U.S. has also pulled its troops out of Kuwait, saying its presence there is no longer needed now that Saddam Hussein has been toppled.

According to an October 21, 2003, Associated Press article, U.S. warplanes and helicopters had flown out of Ahmed Al Jaber, 50 miles west of Kuwait City, since 1991 Gulf war that forced Saddam to reverse his 1990 invasion of Kuwait. Among other missions, aircraft from the base helped monitor the zone over southern Iraq from which the United States had barred Iraqi fighter planes. The United States also has Camp Doha, an isolated Army base along the Gulf coast about 12 miles west of Kuwait City, and another air base, Ali Salem, about 40 miles northwest of Kuwait City. No mention was made of the fate of those installations.

The Bush administration would soon realize that getting the oil refineries up and running again would not be an easy feat as they first thought. Attacks by saboteurs on Iraq's decrepit infrastructure and oil industry have cost the economy billions of dollars, according to the U.S.-appointed administrator, L. Paul Bremer. The U.S. Army Corps of Engineers dropped water from helicopters to try to douse the flames on the main oil export pipeline to Turkey, a crucial economic lifeline which reopened on August 13, 2003, but was shut down two days later after saboteurs set it ablaze.

In addition to targeting the oil export pipeline, saboteurs mounted frequent attacks on the power grid, and stealing power cables which caused repeated electricity blackouts in the south of Iraq and badly hit exports from the country's southern oil fields, according to Bremer. On Sunday, August 17, 2003, a bomb attack on a major water pipeline in north Baghdad cut off water supplies to up to four million people for several hours. By Monday, more than 200,000 people were still without water supplies. The water supplies were restored on Monday afternoon by a team of United Nations agency, UNICEF.

A 2003 Wall Street Journal by Alexei Barrionuevo stated:

> The U.S. officials said they are relying on income from Iraq's vast oil reserves, the world's second largest oil-producing country, to offset some billions of dollars of the cost needed to rebuild the country. For example, Bremer said that Iraq will rely almost exclusively on oil revenues to finance its first public budget in more than three decades, but will fall short by $2 billion. He also said that Iraq's revenues are expected to total $3.88 billion over six months with $3.45 billion, 90% coming from oil, which it estimated to sell for $20 a barrel. Mr. Bremer said Iraq is "a rich country which is temporarily poor."
>
> The U.S. is spending more than Saddam Hussein did. In six months, the U.S. will increase Iraq's capital budget by 30% compared with the last half of 2002. Moreover, the U.S. will have to spend more than $1 billion to fix the oil facilities.

According to a June 24, 2003, Yahoo article the head of Baghdad's main Dura oil refinery, Dather al-Qassab said, an attack on a gas pipeline northwest of the capital on June 23, 2003, would hit power supplies. "It will affect electricity generators directly. People are already living in hell and it's only going to get worse. Some people do not want us to export oil and that will affect the recovery of Iraq," he said.

A senior oil ministry official said the number of armed guards patrolling the country's vulnerable fuel pipelines went from 3,000 to 6,000. According to U.S. figures, over 7,400 kilometers (4,500 miles) of fuel pipeline crosses Iraq. It will be extremely difficult if not impossible to guard the key ducts. Bremer warned at a meeting of the World Economic Forum in Jordan that a deteriorating security situation could upset oil exports. "We have had repeated acts of political sabotage against the pipelines and the refineries in the last month...We're going to have to deal with that; you could have some problems meeting production levels," he said. The U.S. pre-war plan was to use Iraq's oil to help fund the massive cost of rebuilding Iraq. With the constant attacks of oil fields, the U.S. started a house-to-house search looking for suspected saboteurs.

An Associated Press article dated October 21, 2003, stated:

Lack of security is just one of the hurdles that foreign companies who explore for oil in Iraq would have to overcome. It says, even as bullets fly in Baghdad, the price of holding back from at least analyzing data from Iraq's oil fields is to miss out on what one consultant calls the future "center of gravity" of the world's petroleum industry. "Iraq is it. Iraq is the oil province," the consultant, Mohamed Wafta, said at a meeting for potential investors in Iraq's oil industry. Wafta, a Dubai-based data manager for oil field services firm Schlumberger, was one of more than 100 participants at the conference, held in Geneva.

Some oil companies, particularly large, Western multi-nationals, are reluctant to send employees to Iraq to take a closer look at opportunities there until the U.S.-led coalition can stop or sharply curtail attacks by Iraqi militants. Royal Dutch/Shell Group of Cos. ConocoPhillips and Mitsubishi Corp. are among those waiting to see security improve before they take the plunge. "The first thing we need them to do is secure the safety so we can easily go in," said Tetsuro Imai, general manager for energy at Mitsubishi's European headquarters in London.

Safety concerns have led Iraq's Oil Ministry to delay by at least a month a meeting for oil executives planned for December 2003 in Baghdad. Some oil specialists doubt the meeting would happen at all, and suggest that Iraq oil officials would be better off continuing to woo investors at overseas gatherings such as this one. The stakes are high, both for Iraq and the oil companies. Iraq's official estimate of its proven crude reserves is 112 billion barrels, second only to those of Saudi Arabia. Schlumberger's Wafta claims this figure is long out of date and argues Iraq's true reserves are a staggering 300 billion barrels – the largest anywhere. "I think five years down the road, Iraq will be the center of gravity for the oil industry," he said.

Iraq is unusual for its large number of identified but untapped oil fields, and many analysts believe the operational risk of drilling for crude there is low. Although Wafta acknowledged Iraq's political uncertainty and security problems, he said they were temporary and advised would-be oil producers to get started with the time-consuming study of seismic data and other information from any of Iraq's 80 oil fields. However, Bremer and other American officials have repeatedly rejected such suggestions.

Before the war, Wallace and other military planners had counted on many large Iraqi military units staying in their barracks and surrendering. The Pentagon made clandestine contacts, radio broadcasts and leaflet drops encouraging Iraqi commanders and troops to do that. "There was a very detailed system of process by which a unit could capitulate and it was detailed well in advance of our starting the fight," Wallace told The Associated Press. "But as history would prove, no units actually took us up on that offer."

That same day, two top Pentagon officials in charge of Iraq's postwar reconstruction talked to reporters on condition that they not be named, elaborated on postwar plans to pay former Iraqi soldiers to help build roads and bridges, remove rubble and clear unexploded mines and bombs. "Using the army allows us not to demobilize it immediately and put a lot of unemployed people on the street," said the official, who is no longer part of the reconstruction process. Prior to the war, Rumsfeld said, "There's no doubt in my mind that there are elements of the Iraqi army that will end up in an army of Iraq at some point, in the event that Saddam Hussein's regime is gone."

According to an October 21, 2003, New York Times article, Sweden's Linden Petroleum AB has experience in Iraq, and like some other smaller, independent oil firms, is chasing fresh opportunities there. Iraq is "too big to ignore," said Ian Lundin, the firm's chairman. Lundin Petroleum had a contract in 1997 to explore for oil in Iraq's Western Desert, but it couldn't begin work because of U.N. economic sanctions in effect then. The new Iraqi government is likely to change the terms of this contract, so Lundin is resigned to seeking other projects in Iraq. "You don't just pack your bags and leave because there are a few bullets flying in different directions," he said. His big concern about Iraq is that its Oil Ministry has yet to decide what kind of commercial contracts to offer international oil companies that want to explore there. The ministry hopes to make its first formal contracts available in the spring of 2004. Mitsubishi's Imai said he'd have trouble signing any contract with an Oil Ministry that wasn't part of an elected government. The current administration has been appointed by the Americans, and he worries that any contract signed with it wouldn't be legally binding. "There is no political legitimacy in the country," he said.

On October 18, 2003, Iraq resumed pumping oil through its northern pipeline to Turkey, but a leak on the Iraqi side stopped the flow after two hours because of technical problems. This production was the first in two months after pumping crude oil through the northern pipeline to Turkey's Mediterranean port of Ceyhan in August when the flow was halted because of sabotage.

It appears that Bush administration officials have badly miscalculated the force and determination of the Iraqis in making it difficult for foreign occupiers to take over their oil industry. Apparently, they thought they could go into Iraq, secure the oil fields, destroy the infrastructure, disrupt the lives of the Iraqi people and take control of the country without any resistance. But, so far the oil fields are not producing as quickly as they expected or as much as they anticipated because of the constant sabotage and the disrepair of some of the facilities. Bremer said that the country is losing $7 million a day when the northern pipeline is not in service.

On November 17, 2003, saboteurs set another oil field in northern Iraq on fire as a new U.S.-led force was deployed to protect the area's infrastructure. According to a November 17, 2003, Reuters article, a bomb was placed near the Baiji refinery in the village of Burjwari along a northern pipeline section carrying oil. The northern oil infrastructure includes the export pipeline, which runs from its Kirkuk oilfields to Turkey's Mediterranean coast through the Baiji refinery. The pipeline has been closed since the Iraq war and hit by repeated sabotage. The U.S. Army has said that security would be strengthened by November 15, 2003, to restart the line. However, a senior Iraqi oil official said the pipeline was not secure enough to restart despite new U.S.-led forces deployed to guard it. The force, dubbed Task Force Shield, is made up of U.S. military personnel, a South African security contractor and local tribes.

According to Reuters, export revenues from oil sales are vital for U.S. hopes of helping to pay for Iraq's reconstruction. Iraq has been exporting approximately 1.4 million barrels per day over the first 10 days of November 2003, from its southern Basra oil terminal and hoped to increase export to 1.5 million barrels by December. Prior to the attack on Iraq by the United States, Iraq was exporting 2.2 million barrels. Iraq resumed the sale of oil in June, 2003 three months after the U.S invades Iraq. In the meantime, insurgents repeated targeting of pipelines, and sabotage of the oil infrastructure has become a major problem for the U.S.-run coalition. On Nov. 24, 2003, near the city of Kirkuk, an oil pipeline was set on fire. Adel al Qazzaz, manager of the Northern Oil Company, said he believed the cause was sabotage.

The following November 30, 2003, New York Times article by Jeff Gerth, headlined, "Oil Experts See Long-Term Risks to Iraq's Reserves," stated:

As the Bush administration spends hundreds of millions of dollars to repair the pipes and pumps above ground that carry Iraq's oil, it has not addressed serious problems with Iraq's underground oil reservoirs, which American and Iraqi experts say could severely limit the amount of oil those fields produce. In Northern Iraq, the large but aging Kirkuk field suffers from too much water seeping into its oil deposits, the expert say, and similar problems are evident in the sprawling oil fields in southern Iraq. Experts familiar with Iraq's oil industry have said that years of poor management have damaged the fields, and some warn that the current drive to rapidly return the fields to prewar capacity runs the risk of reducing their productivity in the long run. "We are losing a lot of oil," said Issam al-Chalabi, Iraq's former oil minister. He said it "is the consensus of all the petroleum engineers" involved in the Iraqi industry that maximizing oil production may be detrimental to the reservoirs.

A 2000 United Nations report on the Kirkuk field said "the possibility of irreversible damage to the reservoir of this supergiant field is now imminent."

American officials acknowledge the underground problems, but figuring out how to address them is a quandary for the United States. The Bush administration and the Iraqis are banking on oil reserves to help pay for Iraq's reconstruction, and American officials say that aggressively managing the reservoirs is crucial to keeping oil and revenue flowing. But so far, American officials have steered clear of developing below ground, partly, they say, out of fear of adding to suspicion in the Arab world that the United States invaded Iraq to control its oil. The above ground versus below ground debate also raises the question of whether the American-led reconstruction effort is intended just to repair damage from the war or improve conditions beyond what they were before the invasion. When Wayne Kelley, a Texas oil engineer, and other experts asked about attending to Iraq's oil reservoirs during a government conference for contractors in July 2003, Army Corps of Engineers officials said their mission was restoring war- damaged facilities, not "redeveloping the oil fields," according to a transcript of the meeting.

But in an interview, Rob McKee, a former top executive with ConocoPhillips who took over in October 2003 as senior oil adviser for the Coalition Provisional Authority in Baghdad, said that while some might overstate the underground problems, he believed that the reservoirs did demand attention. "It's bad," Mr. McKee said in a telephone interview, "but it will not be catastrophic and especially overnight." Still, he said, it is crucial to collect data, and do engineering on the problem. Wendy Hall, a spokeswoman for Halliburton, the Houston oil services and engineering company managing the Iraq's oil-repair job, said Iraq's present production levels and the administration's future oil goals "cannot be sustained without reservoir maintenance."

Thamir Ghadhban, a senior adviser to the Iraqi minister, Ibrahim Bahr al-Ulum, disputed this view and predicted that production would return to prewar capacity of three million barrels a day by the end of 2004; currently production is at slightly more than two million barrels a day. At the same time, he said in an interview, "we should do much more than we have in the past" to maintain the reservoirs. "We definitely have to put more money into it and bring in consultants," he said.

The Army Corps of Engineers has already set aside $1.7 billion for maintaining Iraq's oil supply, and the money has been split between paying for imported fuel and fixing the Iraqi pipes, pumps and transfer stations, officials say. Approximately $2 billion has been approved for oil infrastructure repairs in 2005, including about $40 million to begin the study of the reservoirs. But managing the reservoirs could be a long and expensive process involving complicated computer simulation and changes in the extraction techniques. This work is particularly important, oil experts say, because while Iraq sits on one of the world's largest deposits, most of its oil is being drawn from two older fields, Rumaila in the south and Kirkuk in the north. Pumping oil too quickly can upset the balance, leading to more gas and water migrating into the wells and ultimately making extraction of oil uneconomical. Oil experts said Saddam Hussein demanded high production, but United Nations economic sanctions precluded Iraq from acquiring the sophisticated computer modeling equipment and technology required to properly managing older reservoirs. As a result, despite the ingenuity of Iraq's engineers, the fields have suffered.

Oil experts working for the United Nations found that some reservoirs in the southern part of Iraq "may only have ultimate recoveries of between 5 percent to 25 percent of the total oil" in the field as compared to an industry norm of 35 percent to 60 percent.

Before the United States-led invasion, the Iraqis sought outside help in managing its reservoirs. "Kirkuk was of particular concern and particular urgency," said Maury Vasilev, senior vice president of PetrAlliance Services, a Russian oilfield company that held discussions with the Iraqi Oil Minister in 2003. He said that because of the water content in the wells "there was a question of how much oil they could recover." Several months after the invasion of Iraq, estimates of Kirkuk's oil refinery condition was still bleak. Fadhil Chalabi, a former top Iraqi oil executive now based in London, said Kirkuk's anticipated recovery rate had dropped to 15 percent from 30 percent. An American oil executive said Iraq engineers told him they were now expecting recovery rates of 9 percent in Kirkuk and 12 percent in Rumaila without more advanced technology.

Iraq's problems were well known to the United States before the war. The Energy Infrastructure Planning Group, set up by senior administration officials in September 2002 to plan for the oil industry in the event of war, learned that Iraq was reinjecting crude oil to maintain pressure in the Kirkuk field. The amount of oil being reinjected is 150,000 to 250,000 barrels a day, down from as much as 400,000 barrels a day in the summer of 2002, said Mr. McKee, but he added that he had never encountered such a practice in his lengthy career in the oil industry. The reinjection of oil was a clear sign of trouble in the underground reservoirs, but the energy planning task force decided not to address them, partly for political reasons, according to participants in the process. "We didn't want to give fuel to the fire of debate that was saying the U.S. was just doing this to steal the oil," one administration official said.

Task force participants said there was another potential political factor. The group had secretly decided without soliciting bids, that the contract for fixing Iraq's oil infrastructure would go to Kellogg Brown & Root, a unit of Halliburton, which had an existing Pentagon contract related to war planning.

"Everyone realized the selection of KBR was going to look bad," said one task force member. KBR and others made a case that reservoir management was necessary and the occupation authority asked Congress for the $40 million now set aside for reservoir management. But Ms. Hall, the Halliburton spokeswoman, said in November 2003 that those underground tasks had been "pulled and are not being funded" even though reservoir maintenance is critical to even present production. Mr. McKee, however, said the financing was not canceled, but just "pushed back for a short while." There is not yet a firm price tag of modernizing Iraq's oil industry, but it is clear it will be enormous.

Edward C. Chow, a former Chevron executive who is now a visiting scholar with the Carnegie Endowment for International peace, estimates it will cost $20 billion to restore Iraqi production to prewar levels, an amount that is more than double the administration's plan for oil reconstruction needs over the next four years.

Mr. McKee said he believed that Iraq could get back to the prewar production capacity of three million barrels a day under current budgets. But even he is cautious. "How sustainable that would be is a question," he said. "I think it would depend a lot on how long they could nurse their old infrastructure along without it cratering."

Just after Bush asked Congress for $87 billion in addition to the $79 billion dollars they had already received in 2003 for Iraq and Afghanistan, the Bush administration said it would ask for additional funds in 2004. In January the Bush administration said it would ask Congress in the coming months for up to $50 billion more for ongoing military operations in Iraq and Afghanistan. This $50 billion will be in addition to the $401.7 billion in defense spending that Bush included in the $2.4 trillion budget for 2005. In budget documents obtained by The Associated Press, the Defense Department said it expected to request extra money for Iraq and Afghanistan, but said it did not expect to do so this calendar year. That would push the next request until after the November presidential and congressional elections.

The costs to invade Iraq just keep mounting with no end in sight. According to a report, when the Bush administration took over the White House, Rumsfeld was told not to submit the defense budget until after the tax cut was passed. Now we know why. And, again in April 2004, the Bush administration said it would ask Congress for an additional $25 billion to continue to fight the war in Iraq and Afghanistan. The last request was on February 6, 2006 for $120 billion.

FOUR

UNITED NATIONS AND WEAPONS OF MASS DESTRUCTION

In minimizing the United Nations' status as it relates to the inspection in Iraq, Vice President Dick Cheney said the U.N. inspectors were useless at best. This was an attempt by Cheney, along with other Bush administration officials to mislead the American people and the rest of the world that Saddam Hussein had weapons of mass destruction and that the American people were in imminent danger of being attacked by him.

Two months after the war started and no weapons of mass destruction were found, Rumsfeld said, "Saddam Hussein has not been found either, does that mean that Saddam does not exist?"

Why did the Bush administration not want the U.N. inspectors to continue their search for the purported weapons of mass destruction? Is it because the Bush administration was aware that there were no weapons of mass destruction in Iraq?

Allowing the inspectors to search for and destroy any weapons of mass destruction would have saved the lives of thousands of U.S. soldiers and tens of thousands of Iraqis and preserved the country's infrastructure. The United Nations and many allied countries repeatedly asked the Bush administration to give the inspectors the necessary time to complete the inspection, and to provide them with specific sites to search, but the Bush administration declined. Some even asked that the number of inspectors be increased to expedite the process. However, the Bush administration continued to press for force against Iraq, saying that the inspectors would not be able to find any weapons of mass destruction because Saddam Hussein was playing a cat-and mouse game by hiding the weapons, and that he could not be trusted.

The following is an excerpt from a September 16, 2002, C-Span article in which former United Nations weapons inspector, Scott Ritter, addressed the Iraqi Parliament on September 8, 2002:

He said Iraq should allow the immediate and unconditional return of United Nations weapons inspectors. He also said the United States was using the "rhetoric of fear" to justify an attack on Iraq although there were no hard facts to substantiate its allegations that Iraq possessed weapons of mass destruction or supported terrorism.

He said Iraq should counter U.S. threats by adopting a "more welcome posture". He proposed a confidence-building mechanism based on the use of an honest broker to oversee the work of the inspectors and Iraq's compliance with their work, since Iraq had legitimate reasons to distrust inspectors after previous teams had been used by the United States and Britain's intelligence services to gather information on Iraq outside their mandate.

In a report to the National Assembly's Arab and Foreign Relations Committee, Mr. Ritter said that the United States was on the verge of making a historical mistake, one that would forever change the political dynamics which have governed the world since the end of the second World War; namely, the foundation of international law as set forth in the United Nations Charter, which calls for the peaceful resolution of problems between nations. He said the United States is set forth on a policy of unilateral intervention that runs contrary to the letter and intent of the United Nations Charter.

He said the consequences of such action are not only dire near-term as measured by death, destruction and lost opportunities, but also the long-term global destabilization that will result in the rejection of an international law by the world's most powerful nation. He said as someone who counts himself as a fervent patriot and a good citizen of the United States of America, he could not stand by idly while his country behaves in such a fashion.

He further stated that we are facing a crisis in America, where the politics of fear have clouded the collective judgment of the people of the United States to the point where we, unfortunately, are willing to accept at face value almost any allegation of wrongdoing on the part of Iraq without first demanding to know the factual basis of such allegation.

He went on to say that the United States would mark the one-year anniversary of an event that scarred the psychological persona of the country, the terrorist attacks of September 11 that killed nearly 3,000 innocent Americans in the span of 100 minutes. He said he knows that the Iraqis suffered much greater losses and withstood equally horrific suffering over the past decade through the combined effects of economic sanctions and war and that he was not trying to put a greater worth on the value of an American life over that of an Iraqi civilian. But he was trying to explain the phenomenon that is taking place inside the United States that allows war fever to catch on in such a rampant manner. Because of September 11, we are a nation fearful of the unknown and more easily prone to exploitation by those with agendas other than legitimate self-defense who play upon these fears.

Dr. Mohamed ElBaradei's report of March 7, 2003, just a few weeks before the U.S. invaded Iraq, said that he was convinced that Iraq's weapons of mass destruction program was non-existent. He said that the United Nations destroyed them after the 1991 Gulf War.

On October 7, 2005, Dr. Mohamed ElBaradei, head of the U.N. nuclear watchdog program and the International Atomic Energy Agency (IAEA), won the 2005 Nobel Peace Prize. The Norwegian Nobel Committee praised ElBaradei as an "unafraid advocate" of measures to strengthen non-proliferation efforts.

As the world pressed the U.S. to allow the completion of the inspection, the Bush administration became increasingly adamant, insisting that additional inspectors would not result in finding the weapons of mass destruction. Instead, the administration kept saying that Saddam was running out of time. Certainly there was no immediate urgency to locate the purported weapons. And certainly there was no immediate urgency for the U.S. to attack Iraq. The American people were not in any imminent danger from Saddam Hussein, neither were his neighbors. The United States was more a threat to Iraq than Iraq was to the U.S. Iraq did not have an army as such that could go up against the United States superpower. Moreover, the United Nations had contained Saddam Hussein since the 1991 Gulf War.

On February 5, 2003, Colin Powell went before the United Nations and the world and presented satellite images and other information to prove that Saddam Hussein lied about his weapons of mass destruction program. He showed an aerial view, which was purported to be an ammunition depot located nine miles north of Baghdad, and claimed that Iraq was manufacturing chemical and biological warfare there. However, not long after Powell showed the pictures, a BBC reporter disputed Powell's report. He went to Iraq at that exact site presented by Powell and verified that it was not an ammunition depot. Colin Powell, in making the administration's case to the U.N. Council for a pre-emptive strike against Iraq, also showed trucks that the administration claimed to be mobile chemical and biological laboratories.

Saddam Hussein had met every demand made by the United States. The United Nations inspectors carried out surprise, unannounced inspections and returned to many sites. However, they could not find any weapons of mass destruction. The U.S. even demanded that U.S. spy planes be used to monitor Iraq and to spy on their every move, and Iraq agreed to the demands. Yet, Bush continued to tell the American people that he was confident that Saddam Hussein had weapons of mass destruction and was playing a cat and mouse game, and that the only way to prove it was to disarm him.

International Atomic Energy Agency Director General Mohamed ElBaradei reported to the United Nations Security Council on March 7, 2003, that his report to the Council is an update on the status of the Agency's nuclear verification activities in Iraq pursuant to Security Council Resolution 1441 and other relevant resolutions. ElBaradei said that when he reported to the Council on February 14, he explained that the Agency's inspection activities moved well beyond the reconnaissance phase, re-establishing their knowledge base regarding Iraq's nuclear capabilities to revive or to attempt to revive its defunct nuclear weapons program over the last four years. Dr. ElBaradei said, "At the outset, let me state on general observation, namely that during the past four years at the majority of Iraqi sites, industrial capacity has deteriorated substantially due to the departure of the foreign support that was often present in the late 1980s, the departure of large numbers of skilled Iraqi personnel in the past decade and the lack of consistent maintenance by Iraq of sophisticated equipment.

At only a few inspected sites involved in industrial research, development and manufacturing have the facilities been improved and new personnel had been taken on. Dr. ElBaradei also stated that they have conducted a total of 218 nuclear inspections at 141 sites, including 21 that have not been inspected before. In addition, the agency experts have taken part in many joint UNMOVIC (U.N. Monitoring, Verification and Inspection Commission)-IAEA inspections.

Dr. ElBaradei stated that technical support for nuclear inspections continued to expand. Three operational air samplers collected weekly air particulate samples were sent to laboratories for analysis from key locations in Iraq. Additional results of water, sediment, vegetation and material sample analysis had been received from the relevant laboratories.

The inspectors' vehicle-borne radiation survey team covered some 2,000 kilometers over a three-week period.

110

Survey access had been gained to cover 75 facilities, including military garrisons and camps, weapons factories, truck parks and manufacturing facilities and residential areas.

Interviews were conducted with relevant Iraqi personnel, at times with individuals and groups in the workplace during the course of unannounced inspections, and on other occasions in pre-arranged meetings with key scientists and other specialists known to have been involved with Iraq's nuclear program.

The IAEA conducted interviews, even when the conditions were not in accordance with the IAEA-preferred modalities, with a view to gaining as much information as possible. That information could be cross-checked for validity with other sources and could be helpful in their assessment of areas under investigation.

The IAEA requested private unescorted interviews which were denied at first. The Iraqis wanted the interviewees to be escorted and taped. However, at the insistence of the IAEA, the Iraqis acquiesced and allowed people to be interviewed without being escorted or taped.

Iraq provided a considerable volume of documentation relevant to the issues that are of particular concern, including Iraq's efforts to procure aluminum tubes, and its attempt to import uranium. Dr. ElBaradei went on to say that Iraqis' decision-making process with regard to the design of these rockets was well-documented and that Iraq provided copies of design documents, procurement records, minutes of committee meetings and supporting data and samples.

A thorough analysis of this information, together with information gathered from interviews with Iraqi personnel, allowed the IAEA to develop a coherent picture of the attempted purchase and intended usage of the 81-millimeter aluminum tubes as well as the rationale behind the changes in the tolerance.

The IAEA also learned that the original tolerance for the 81-millimeter tubes were set prior to 1987 and were based on physical measurement taken from a small number of imported rockets in Iraq's possession. Based on the available evidence, the IAEA concluded that Iraq's efforts to import these aluminum tubes were not likely to have been related to the manufacture of centrifuge, and moreover, that it was highly unlikely that Iraq could have achieved the considerable redesign needed to use them in a revived centrifuge program.

Also, regarding reports about Iraq's efforts to import high-strength permanent magnets or to achieve the capability for producing such magnets for use in a centrifuge program, Dr. ElBaradei pointed out that Iraq has been purchasing high-strength magnets for various uses since 1998. The IAEA verified that previously acquired magnets have been used for missile guidance systems, industrial machinery, electricity meters and field telephones. Furthermore, through visits to research and production sites, review of engineering drawings and analysis of sample magnets, the IAEA experts familiar with the use of such magnets in centrifuge enrichment have verified that none of the magnets that Iraq had declared could be used directly for centrifuge magnetic bearings.

In June 2001, Iraq signed a contract for a new magnet production line for delivery and installation in 2003. The delivery was never made and Iraqi documentations and interviews of Iraqi personnel indicated that the contract would not be executed. The Iraqis concluded that the replacement of foreign procurement with domestic magnet production seems reasonable from an economic point of view.

The IAEA also concluded that the training acquired by Iraq in the pre-1991 period made it likely that Iraq possessed the expertise to manufacture high-strength permanent magnets suitable for use in enrichment centrifuges, and that the IAEA would continue to monitor and inspect equipment and materials that could be used to make magnets for enrichment centrifuge.

The primary technical focus of IAEA field activities in Iraq was on resolving several outstanding issues related to the possible resumption of efforts by Iraq to enrich uranium through the use of centrifuge. Therefore, the IAEA assembled a special qualified team of international centrifuge manufacturing experts to ascertain whether or not Iraq was trying to resume efforts to enrich uranium through the use of centrifuge. The IAEA conducted a thorough investigation of Iraq's purported attempt to purchase large quantities of high-strength aluminum tubes. Iraq maintained that these aluminum tubes were sold for rocket production. Extensive field investigation and document analysis failed to uncover any evidence that Iraq intended to use these 81-millimeter tubes for any project other than the reverse engineering of rockets.

With regard to uranium acquisition, the IAEA made progress in its investigation into reports that Iraq sought to buy uranium from Niger. The investigation was centered on documents provided by a number of states that pointed to an agreement between Niger and Iraq for the sale of uranium between 1999 and 2001. The IAEA discussed these reports with the government of Iraq and Israel, both of which have denied that any such activity took place.

Iraq provided the IAEA with a comprehensive explanation of its relations with Niger and described a visit by an Iraqi official to a number of African countries, including Niger in February of 1999, which Iraq thought might have given rise to the reports. The IAEA reviewed correspondence coming from various bodies of the government of Niger and compared the form, format, contents and signature of that correspondence with those of the alleged procurement-related documentation. Based on thorough analysis, the IAEA concluded with the concurrence of outside experts that these documents which formed the basis for the report of recent uranium transactions between Iraq and Niger were in fact not authentic. They then concluded that these specific allegations were unfounded. However, they would continue to follow up on any additional evidence that emerged that would be relevant to efforts by Iraq to illicitly import nuclear materials.

Many concerns regarding Iraq's possible intention to resume its nuclear program have arisen from Iraq's procurement efforts reported by a number of states. In addition, many of Iraq's efforts to procure commodities and products, including magnets and aluminum tubes, have been conducted in contravention of the sanctions specified under Security Council Resolution 661 and other relevant resolutions.

The report went on to say that the issue of procurement efforts remains under thorough investigation, and further verification would be forthcoming. An IAEA team of technical experts composed of custom investigators and computer forensics specialists would conduct a series of investigations through inspections of trading companies and commercial organizations aimed at understanding Iraq's pattern of procurement.

Dr. ElBaradei also pointed out that during the three months and particularly during the last three weeks of these inspection sites, the IAEA made important progress in identifying what nuclear-related capabilities remained in Iraq, and its assessment of whether Iraq had made any effort to revive its past nuclear program during the intervening four years since inspections were brought to a halt. Dr. ElBaradei stated that there was no indication of resumed nuclear activities in those buildings that were identified through the use of satellite imagery as being reconstructed or newly erected since 1998, nor any indication of nuclear-related prohibited activities at any inspected sites. There was no indication that Iraq had attempted to import uranium since 1990. There was no indication that Iraq had attempted to import uranium tubes for use in centrifuge enrichment. Moreover, even had Iraq pursued such a plan, it would have encountered practical difficulties in manufacturing centrifuges out of the aluminum tubes in question. Furthermore, there was no indication that Iraq imported magnets for use in the centrifuge-enrichment program.

Dr. ElBaradei said that after three months of intrusive inspections, they found no evidence of plausible indication of the revival of a nuclear weapons program in Iraq, and making use of all additional rights granted under Resolution

1441 and all additional tools that might be available to them, including reconnaissance platforms and other relative technologies, would continue their inspection activities.

Further, he stated that Iraq had been forthcoming in its cooperation, particularly with regard to the conduct of private interviews and in making available evidence that could have been contributed to the resolution of matters of IAEA concern. He went on to say that the detailed knowledge of Iraq capabilities that the IAEA experts have accumulated since 1991, combined with the extended rights provided by Resolution 1441, the active commitment by all states to help them fulfill their mandate and the recently increased level of Iraq's cooperation should have enabled them to provide the Security Council with an objective and thorough assessment of Iraq's nuclear related capabilities.

Dr. ElBaradei concluded that "however credible this assessment may be, they would endeavor, in view of the inherent uncertainties associated with any verification process, and particularly in the light of Iraq's past record of cooperation, to evaluate Iraq's capabilities on a continuous basis as part of their long-term monitoring and verification program in order to provide the international community with ongoing and real-time assurance."

The United States went to war against Iraq, in spite of the relative information provided by the U.N. that there was no evidence of a weapon of mass destruction program in Iraq. The U.N. also reported that there was no evidence of a smallpox stockpile anywhere in Iraq. However, Bush continued to defend the war against Saddam Hussein, repeating his rhetoric that "Saddam Hussein was a threat to America and the free world in 1991, in 1998, in 2003." Bush said that "Saddam continually ignored the demands of the free world, so the United States and friends and allies acted."

Although there was an overwhelming call not just from the American people, but from people all over the world asking the United States not to attack Iraq without the sanction of the United Nations, the Bush administration relentlessly pursued the attack. It used the same rhetoric of the imminent threat posed by Saddam Hussein to the American people, and the free world. Both the Bush administration and the British government insisted that Saddam would sell weapons of mass destruction to rogue nations and terrorists. But how could he sell weapons that did not exist? This further proves that the fear of threat was only a ploy to deceive.

A June 6, 2003, Reuters' article by Jim Wolf stated:

The CIA bowed to Bush administration pressure to hype the threat of Saddam Hussein's weapons programs ahead of the U.S.-led war in Iraq, a leading national security historian concluded in a detailed study of the spy agency's public pronouncements. "What is clear from intelligence reporting is that until about 1998 the CIA was fairly comfortable with its assessments on Iraq," John Prados wrote in an issue of the Bulletin of the Atomic Scientists. "But from that time on the agency gradually buckled under the weight of pressure to adopt alarmist views. After mid-2001, the rush to judgment on Iraq became a stampede."

On September 22, 2003, on TV channel WLIW 21, New York, former U.N. 1991ambassador to Iraq, Dr. Abdul Amir A. Al-Anbari, said that Iraq was trying to develop capabilities to defend itself, not to attack the U.S. He also said Iraq was not stockpiling chemical weapons. They were developing weapons to keep Iran at bay. He said Iraq's weapons were destroyed and they did not produce anything after 1991. He also said that Iraq had decided not to develop chemical weapons, but to develop the capabilities if they did need it. He disagreed with the 45-minute weapon statement. He said in 1995 that it was not plausible that Iraq had weapons of mass destruction.

Also, according to an October 6, 2004, report by the top American inspector for Iraq, Charles A. Duelfer, Iraq had destroyed its illicit weapons stockpiles within months after the Persian Gulf War of 1991, and its ability to produce such weapons had significantly eroded by the time of the American invasion of 2003.

In ignoring the millions of protesters all over the world to disarm Saddam Hussein peacefully, Bush said he does not pay any attention to protesters. Despite the objections of many nations not to attack Iraq and to let the U.N. inspectors do their work, the Bush administration was adamant that the U. S. must go to war to protect the American people. The U.S. pressured the United Nations Security Council to vote for a resolution for the U.S. to use force and went as far as to call the United Nations Security Council irrelevant. The U.S. even ordered eavesdropping on a number of countries whom it believed would vote against the resolution and also tapped Kofi Anan's telephone. The United States, Britain and Spain withdrew a Security Council resolution authorizing military action because it was bound to go down in defeat.

Bush uses the "Bully Pulpit" at every opportunity he can, and the U.S. media, for the most part, has been in compliance. For example, American journalists have shied away from asking President Bush or his cabinet members any of the hard questions. When a foreign journalist asked United Nations Secretary General Kofi Annan if it were true that at some point the Bush administration would tell the United Nations inspectors to step aside so the U.S. could attack Iraq, he could not, or did not want to answer the question. The U.S. attack is exactly what happened shortly thereafter. The U.N. was told to withdraw its inspection team from Iraq and within days the United States attacked Iraq.

The United Nations spent more than three months checking Iraq's weapons and did not find any weapons that were not in the United Nations' mandate. Moreover, three months after the United States attacked Iraq and sent in its own inspection team to search for these purported weapons of mass destruction, no weapons were located. Also, the U.S. refused to allow the U.N. to go alongside the U.S. team to verify the purported weapons of mass destruction in case any weapons were discovered.

The Bush administration was under pressure to deliver the purported weapons of mass destruction that prompted the pre-emptive attack. But despite the numerous searches conducted by U.S. specialists, weapons were not found. Yet the Bush administration continued to say that the weapons were there. After four months of saying that Saddam Hussein had weapons of mass destruction and that they were sure that these weapons would be found, the Bush administration said that the information used to make the case for war against Iraq had been flawed. However, this admittance only came about when several reports started floating about that the Bush administration and the British Prime Minister misled the world about their intelligence on Iraq's weapons program.

The Bush administration knew as early as February of 2002 when an envoy sent by the CIA to Africa to investigate allegations about Iraq's nuclear weapons program said that the Bush administration manipulated his findings, possibly to strengthen the case for war.

On July 8, 2003, the White House National Security Council said President Bush's claim in his State of the Union speech that Iraq tried to buy uranium from Africa was based on forged information. Michael Anton, a spokesman for the Security Council said, "At the time, the national intelligence estimate on Iraq's weapons of mass destruction referred to an attempt by Iraq to acquire uranium from several countries in Africa. We know now that documents alleging a transaction between Iraq and Niger had been forged."

The Bush administration said Italy's intelligence service circulated reports about the Niger documents – not the documents themselves to other Western intelligence services in early 2002, and that was apparently how the British and the United States intelligence services learned of them. How could the U.S. go to war based on such information, putting the lives of these servicemen and women in harm's way, knowing very well that many lives would be lost, and destroy the lives of many families. Moreover, it disrupted an entire country and the lives of its citizens.

An October 3, 2003, Guardian Unlimited news article by Julian Borger stated:

U.N. Inspectors Vindicated – at $300 million cost.

The conclusions from the Iraq Survey Group were, as U.S. officials repeatedly insisted, only an interim report. The search would continue with the help of a further $600 million. But long before the group arrived, Iraq was the most scrutinized country on the planet.

The process began on June 9, 1991, when the U.N. special commission on Iraq (UNSCOM) began its first chemical weapons inspection in the wake of the Gulf war. The impact of that work was confirmed in the small print of a June 8, 2003, report. Iraq's stockpile of weapons of mass destruction was largely, if not completely, eradicated during that period. By 1995, UNSCOM's biological team had dug up enough evidence to force Baghdad into admitting that it had a program to produce biological agents.

Meanwhile, the International Atomic Energy Agency discovered that Baghdad had been within six months of producing a nuclear weapon at the time of the Gulf War, but later satisfied itself that the program had been dismantled.

But much of Saddam Hussein's prewar arsenal could not be accounted for and the U.N. demanded proof from Baghdad that it had destroyed the outstanding weapons. UNSCOM and the IAEA were aware that Saddam Hussein retained the capacity to reconstitute his weapons program and installed sensors and cameras at key sites. That system broke down after UNSCOM's departure in December 1998, as tensions mounted between the U.N. and Baghdad. The exodus was followed by U.S. and British air strikes and the end of UNSCOM.

Its successor, the U.N. monitoring, verification and inspection commission (UNMOVIC), was born a year later as the international community grew uneasy over what Iraq might be up to. Baghdad relented and inspections resumed on November 27, 2002. There were 731 inspections over the next four months at 411 sites.

Once Baghdad had fallen, the U.S. military gave the job of looking for the elusive weapons to an almost-exclusively American unit, the 75th Exploitation Taskforce, known as the XTF. Without an Iraqi government with which to negotiate, the XTF would have free rein to ransack the country. The Pentagon thought the task would be easy. But the hunt was a debacle. They treated scientists who cooperated as criminals, locking them up and cutting them off from their families. Cooperation dried up.

Also, according to a report, despite the war and occupation, the U.N. International Atomic Energy Agency (IAEA) had been able with the support of Member States, to continue with some of its investigations outside of Iraq, and to follow up on previous inspections with subsequent analysis. IAEA also conducted inspections inside Iraq for a week in June. The agency had not found any evidence of a nuclear weapons program. The report by the IAEA to the U.N. dated Oct. 10, 2003, said, "Those post-inspections activity have revealed no evidence of a nuclear weapons program in Iraq."

This report further confirms Saddam Hussein and members of his cabinet's relentless denial of weapons of mass destruction. They argued that the Bush administration only wanted to invade their country and that they were not interested in the truth.

120

Under fire at home for making false arguments for war, the Bush administration asked David Kay, an American former U.N. inspector, to oversee a new unit, the Iraq Survey Group. It was assigned more than 1,200 staff, composed of experts and support workers from the U.S., Britain and Australia. Its budget of $300 million for its initial three months' work was about five times the annual Unmovic budget. For all that, the ISG had basically confirmed Unmovic's findings that Iraq had no chemical or biological weapons program.

The United Nations inspectors would have been able to keep Saddam in check. They could have monitored human rights, installed a permanent international peace-keeping force. Using diplomatic means the international community could change the country's direction from that of a dictatorship into a better form of government. Ultimately, the country would have developed a more civilized form of government and rid the Iraqis of the one-man-rule regime. Possibly, Hussein would have been exiled from Iraq just as they did in Haiti and other countries so that he would never have another opportunity to rule the country. Moreover, he could be charged for war crimes and put in jail for the rest of his life; thereby relieving the threat of him ever again being able to bring such atrocities to another human being. All this could have been achieved without the unnecessary loss of lives.

The Bush administration gave the impression that the United Nations was irrelevant and would no longer be needed in Iraq once it took over the country. However, on June 23, 2003, the United Nations appealed to donor countries to make up an outstanding $259 million in funding needed to carry out its humanitarian relief operations in Iraq through to the end of the year. The amount covers the remainder of the $2.2 billion flash appeal launched in March and the unpredicted requirements that emerged during and after the conflict in Iraq from widespread looting and destruction of hundreds of public facilities. At that time, about 88 percent of $2.2 billion had already been pledged.

"There is still much work to be done and more resources needed," according to the Deputy Secretary-General Louise Frechette at the formal launching of the appeal at U.N. Headquarters in New York, despite the dispatch of more than 800,000 tons of food, the daily provision of millions of litres of fresh water, the supply of medicine across the country, the distribution of school kits to 400,000 children and the repair of water, sewage and power facilities.

In planning the attack on Iraq, the Bush administration made concentrated efforts to develop a plan to secure the oil fields, but not to take care of the Iraqis' basic necessities. The first order of priority was to secure the oil fields and put out any fires that may occur. Were the oil fields more important than basic human needs?

The U.N. Humanitarian Affairs received more than $1 billion in resources from the Oil-for-Food program, under which the Saddam Hussein regime was allowed to sell oil for humanitarian supplies. However, this Oil-for Food program was terminated on November 21, 2003. Executive Director Benon V. Sevan said that the uncertain situation in Iraq had compelled the program to keep revising its options. "Most of our assumptions in developing our exit strategies have been constantly overtaken by events over which we have no control." He said the program needed a minimum of 115 international staff in the northern governorates to meet its objectives for an orderly closure and transfer of assets and responsibilities to the Coalition Provisional Authority (CPA).

Mr. Sevan said that in the absence of the minimum number of required international staff, the only alternative course of action could be the transfer of assets, ongoing operations and responsibility for the administration of any remaining activity under the program to the Coalition Provisional Authority (CPA) "as is", together with the relevant documentation.

The Security Council established the Oil-for-Food Program on April 14, 1995. Some 3.4 billion barrels of Iraqi oil valued at about $65 billion were exported under the program between December 1996 and March 20, 2003. Of this amount, 72 percent of the total was allocated towards humanitarian needs nationwide after December 2000. The balance went to Gulf War reparations through a Compensation Fund (25 % since December 2000); U.N. administration and operational costs for the program (2.2 %) and costs of the weapons inspection program (0.8%)

Almost $28 billion worth of humanitarian supplies and equipment were delivered to Iraq under the Oil-for-Food program between March 20, 1997 and March 20 2003, including $1.6 billion worth of oil industry spare parts and equipment. Additional goods and supplies from the Program's $10 billion humanitarian pipeline were delivered on a priority basis in consultation with the Coalition Provisional Authority, Iraqi representatives and U.N. agencies and programs. However, at the time, they still needed significant additional resources to allow agencies to respond to priority needs such as assistance to the basic health system and nutrition support, education, and mine clearing.

The U.N. Humanitarian Affairs were faced with great difficulties delivering the supplies to the Iraqi people, because the lack of security continued to inhibit relief efforts. Also repeated looting of rehabilitated infrastructures was creating a deep sense of frustration among the population and the humanitarian community.

On July 4, 2003, the U.N. said that every hour, the U.N. World Food Program (WFP) was delivering 1,000 tons of food to Iraq in what the agency called the largest such operation in its 40-year history. In June, WFP delivered over three quarters of a million tons of food to the war-ravaged country as part of its $1.5 billion bid to feed the entire Iraqi population through October. Yet the Bush administration officials called the U.N. irrelevant.

WFP Deputy Executive Director Jean Jacques Graisse pointed out that even before the war six out of every ten Iraqis relied on a food ration as their only source of income. "It is very likely that the food aid is even more important today in this post-conflict period, since many people have lost their jobs and have not received salaries, while at the same time they are seeing prices rise," he said.

A July 6, 2003, U.N. News Centre reported, "As Blix Leaves Office, Annan lauds U.N. Arms inspector's steadfast integrity." Hans Blix, the head of the United Nations weapons inspectors in Iraq, concluded his term of office, receiving expressions of "profound gratitude" from Secretary-General Kofi Annan, who voiced his admiration for Blix's ability to handle the intense demands of his tasks.

In a letter to Blix, who served as executive chairman of the U.N. Monitoring, Verification and Inspection Commission for Iraq, Kofi Annan said, "Few United Nations officials have demonstrated the calm, grace and professionalism that you have in the face of virtually unprecedented pressure and attention over the past several months." The letter went on to say, "Your steadfast integrity, objectivity and sound judgment were an asset to the organization and the international community as a whole."

A July 22, 2003, Associated Press article by Jessica Vascarello stated:

> United Nations – Delegates from Iraq's new Governing Council attended a U.N. Security Council session, welcomed by Secretary-General Kofi Annan as a first step toward restoring Iraqi control over the U.S.-administered nation.
>
> Four months after diplomacy fell apart inside the Security Council over war in Iraq, Annan, his special envoy to Iraq, and the Iraqi delegates addressed the Council and discussed the highs and lows of postwar life in Iraq.
>
> "Our collective goal remains an early end to the military occupation through the formation of an internationally recognized, representative government," Annan said. "It is vital that the Iraqi people should be able to see a clear timetable ... leading to

the full restoration of sovereignty as soon as possible."

The Iraqi delegates: Ahmed Chalabi – once favored by the Pentagon to be Iraq's next president – Adnan Pachachi, a former Iraqi foreign minister, and Aqila Hashimi of the Iraqi foreign ministry.

Before the meeting, Chalabi said the purpose of his visit was to brief the Security Council on the state of Iraq, not to seek any official U.N credential.

"We are talking about a briefing of Iraq to the United Nations," he told reporters at the Iraqi Embassy. "Part of the purpose of the Governing Council is to represent Iraq internationally and in international organizations."

The Governing Council will be able to pick ministers for a new administration and hold other powers, but U.S. administration will have the final say.

At the Security Council meeting, Annan delivered a warning to the United States that "democracy cannot be imposed from the outside."

"It is important that Iraqis are able to see a clear timetable leading to the full restoration of sovereignty," Annan wrote in his report, also noting concerns about the U.S. treatment of Iraqi detainees and the failure to improve security in Baghdad.

The critical tone of the report was unlikely to help U.S. efforts to win support for an international peacekeeping force that could relieve overburdened American troops in Iraq.

Richard Grenell, spokesman for the U.S. mission to the United Nations, said "We certainly agree that Iraqis should be in charge of their own country and we are working hard to do that and that's why the Governing Council is a good first step."

Annan's report offers U.N. help to Iraqis in defining the priorities and policies that will shape the future of the country. But throughout the report,

Annan emphasized the importance of Iraqi sovereignty. "There is an overwhelming demand for self-rule and democracy cannot be imposed from the outside."

Much of the report was based on observations and discussions that Annan's envoy to Iraq, led by Sergio Viera de Mello, had with U.S. officials in Baghdad, including L. Paul Bremer, the U.S. occupation governor for Iraq.

Annan wrote that Viera de Mello complained to Bremer about the "treatment of detainees and the conditions under which they were held in detention."

The report also expressed concerns about the living conditions and "precarious security situation" in the capital.

Annan also offered the United States assistance in a host of areas including de-mining and police training. But Annan ruled out the possibility of a U.N. police force working side-by-side with U.S. troops.

"Such an action would create a parallel system of law enforcement which would not be effective in promoting law and order," he said.

Since the attack on the U.N. building in Iraq on Aug. 19, 2003, killing 22 including the Chief U.N. Envoy, Sergio Virera de Mello and wounding over 100, the U.N. has reduced its staff from 600 to 50.

A September 5, 2003, Washington Post article by Dana Milbank and Thomas E. Ricks stated that:

Secretary of State Colin Powell told President Bush that they had to go to the U.N. with a resolution seeking a U.N.-sanctioned military force in Iraq. Something the administration had resisted for about five months. Bush and his national security adviser, Condoleezza Rice, whose office had been slow to embrace the U.N. resolution, agreed.

It appeared that Powell went to Bush after a meeting with U.N. Secretary-General Kofi Annan two days after the car bombing of the U.N. Headquarters in Baghdad. Annan made it clear that the best feasible option was a multinational force under U.S. command. On August 26, 2003, Deputy Secretary of State Armitage broached the idea of a U.S.-led multinational coalition with a U.N. mandate.

Secretary of Defense Donald Rumsfeld and his civilian aides had successfully resisted the wishes of the State Department and the British government for U.N. help, arguing that U.S. troops and foreign troops could get the job done. However, the wave of attacks at the Jordanian Embassy and the United Nations Headquarters convinced many officials that there were not enough U.S. troops in Iraq to maintain order. Nor were there enough foreign or American reserves to replace the 40,000 troops Rumsfeld planned to bring home.

According to reports, many in Congress felt that the United Nations was the appropriate agency to coordinate an international peacekeeping force, because they have the experience of doing it all over the world for so many years. Also, the U.S. troops are trained to fight and are not trained to act as peacekeepers. Furthermore, this would free up the soldiers' time so that they could do the work they were sent to Iraq to do.

During the U.N. General Assembly annual high-level debate on Feb. 10, 2003, the need for joint action was stressed concerning development, Iraqi reconstruction and weapons proliferation. During the two-week session, 19 speakers, including 77 heads of state and government, 4 vice presidents, 94 deputy prime ministers and foreign ministers reaffirmed multilateralism as the surest safeguard of global solidarity and collective security. And that only joint action could curb weapons proliferation and ensure the achievement of global development goals and the speedy recovery of Iraq.

Secretary-General Kofi Annan challenged the United Natitons' 191-member governing body to seriously consider drastic reform of the organization and its institutions, in order to enhance their authority by making them both open to more voices and more effective in taking action. The unilateralism of recent events had called into question the decades old tradition of global consensus on collective security and brought the international community to a fork in the road. Countries such as France and Germany argued against the U.S. having sole control over Iraq and that other countries should be allowed to have some say in the rebuilding of Iraq and the length of occupation by the United States.

FIVE

ATTACKS OF SEPTEMBER 11, 2001

Could the September 11, 2001, Attacks Have Been Avoided?
That is the million-dollar question that has been asked time and time again.
President Bush's former counterterrorism coordinator, Richard A. Clarke, said that the 9/11 attack may have been avoided if the Bush administration had paid more attention to the risk posed by the al-Qaeda network. Clarke said that President Bush's national security adviser, Condoleezza Rice, "looked skeptical" when she was warned early in 2001 about the threat from al-Qaeda and appeared to never have heard of the terrorist organization. He said her facial expression gave him the impression that she had never heard the term before. He said Rice, who previously worked for Bush's father, appeared not to recognize post-Cold War security issues and effectively demoted him within the National Security Council. I might add that Clarke was appointed as the anti-terrorism czar under the Clinton administration because it felt that the threat of terrorism by the al-Qaeda network was of such a high priority. Clarke said Rice has an unusually close relationship with Bush, which "should have given her some maneuver room, some margin for shaping the agenda."

Clarke said that within one week of the Bush inauguration, he "urgently" sought a meeting of senior Cabinet leaders to discuss "the imminent al-Qaeda threat." Months later, in April, Clarke met with deputy secretaries. During that meeting, Deputy Defense Secretary Paul Wolfowitz told him, "You give bin Laden too much credit," and sought to steer the discussion to Iraq. Clarke also said that Bush asked him directly almost immediately after the September 11 terror attacks to find whether Iraq was involved in the suicide hijackings. Clarke said: "One shudders to think what additional errors (Bush) will make in the next four years to strengthen the al-Qaeda follow-on: attacking Syria or Iran, undermining the Saudi regime without a plan for a successor state?"

National Security Adviser Condoleezza Rice told the American people in May of 2002 that the pre-Sept.11 intelligence briefing for the president on terrorism contained only a general warning of threats and largely historical information, not a specific plot to attack the United States. However, the converse is true. The authors of a congressional report stated that the briefing given to the president a month prior to the suicide hijackings included intelligence that al-Qaeda was planning to send operatives into the United States to coordinate an attack using high explosives. Plus, considering the fact that al-Qaeda attacked the World Trade Center in 1993 from the ground but failed to bring the buildings down, who was to say they would not attack from the air the next time?

Rice said that she didn't think anybody could have predicted that these people would take an airplane and slam it into the World Trade Center, take another one and slam it into the Pentagon and that they would use a hijacked airplane as a missile. But the President Daily Briefing on August 6, 2001, said exactly that. That al-Qaeda intended to attack the United States, using commercial passenger planes. This should have set off an alarm such as the warnings for the millennium. Furthermore, a congressional report stated that from at least 1994 and continuing into the summer of 2001, the intelligence community received information indicating that terrorists were contemplating, among other means of attack, the use of airplanes as weapons.

Also, prior to the September 11 attacks, Kenneth Williams, an FBI agent in the Phoenix, Ariz., office warned his superiors about a suspiciously large number of Arabs attending flight schools in the United States. And, before the Clinton administration left the White House, Sandy Berger gave the Bush administration officials a power point presentation on Osama bin Laden advising them of the danger he posed against the United States. In 1996, President Clinton signed an order to shut down bin Laden's network. And, in 1998, Clinton launched an attack on bin Laden's camp, but he escaped. The U.S. offered a $5 million reward for the capture of bin Laden. Bin Laden sent a message to Clinton saying the war has not yet started. And, in 1998 bin Laden called for holy war Jihad on Jews and American civilians anywhere in the world.

Why didn't the Bush administration prevent the September 11, 2001 attacks? U.S. intelligence can pinpoint where and when terrorists will strike Saudi Arabia or London, so why didn't they take the necessary precaution to prevent the attacks on the United States? National Security Adviser Condoleezza Rice said that it was luck that the Clinton administration was able to prevent the millennium attacks. But I beg to differ. It was taking immediate steps to engage other nations to find the root of the plots and, of course, some luck by the Border Patrol that thwarted the attacks. If these attacks were not thwarted, 9/11 might have been pale in comparison to the millennium attacks if they had been carried out. I believe the steps taken by the Clinton administration to thwart the millennium attacks are worth repeating here verbatim.

The following article by Neil King Jr. and David S. Cloud of the Wall Street Journal appeared in a March 8, 2000, issue:

On High Alert – Casting A Global Net, U.S. Security Forces Survive Terrorist Test:

A Rash of Millennial Plots Meant Calling on Allies from Ottawa to Amman – Bin Laden in Your Basement' Washington – Richard Clarke, President Clinton's antiterrorism chief, took the call on December 2. On the line was Cofer Black, the CIA's hulking chief of counterterrorism. His message was simple and chilling: "We're in deep trouble." That set off one of the most grueling months of counterterrorist activity in U.S. history. Within days, the U.S. had indications that operatives linked to Osama bin Laden could carry out as many as 15 violent attacks on American citizens around the world. Federal law-enforcement agencies scrambled to head off a disaster – or multiple disasters – which they feared would strike on the eve of the millennium.

As it turned out, New Year's Day came and went without incident. But as authorities congratulated themselves on a job well done, a question lingered: Were they really that good – or just lucky? A look at what happened in the weeks following Black's warning suggests that the answer is: probably both.

Muscle and Mishaps

George Tenet, director of the Central Intelligence Agency, credits an intense multifaceted effort for thwarting attacks and saving countless lives. Tapping extensive U.S. antiterrorism forces built in the wake of the 1993 World Trade Center bombing, Mr. Tenet says, the CIA, the Federal Bureau of Investigation and U.S. allies threw hundreds of potential terrorists off balance, chasing them underground or tossing them in jail. But the authorities often worked blind, and along the way they stumbled on problems in the U.S. counterterrorism machinery. Surprises cropped up almost daily, deepening their apprehension and making it increasingly difficult to distinguish genuine threats. Officials concede that the danger could re-emerge at any moment. But when? "That's what we keep asking ourselves," Mr. Clarke says.

Before December, some officials had fretted about possible terrorist attacks near the New Year. At millennium celebrations around the world, American and other Western tourists would be inviting targets for Islamic extremists. But hard evidence of foreign-based terrorism plots was scant. The FBI, for one, saw its chief year-end threat coming from home-grown extremists in the U.S. Then came Black's December 2 call to Clarke. The day before, Jordanian security agents had broken up a terrorist cell in Jordan that they believed had been planning attacks for around December 31. Evidence suggested that the 13 men in custody had hatched a detailed plot – "a real bell-ringer," as one U.S. intelligence official described it – that called for attacks on multiple targets.

Ties to bin Laden

The worst news was that many of the suspects had ties to Mr. bin Laden, the wealthy Saudi exile whom the U.S. has indicted for allegedly ordering the 1998 bombings of U.S. embassies in Tanzania and Kenya. Those two attacks had occurred within minutes of each other, killing 256 people, so the fear of millennial attacks occurring simultaneously around the world would haunt U.S. officials throughout December. FBI agents and U.S. prosecutors were on their way almost immediately to the Jordanian capital, Amman, where they began to sift evidence and question suspects. From Jordan came a jet carrying to the U.S. boxes of floppy disks copied from the suspects' computers. Dozens of Arabic linguists from the CIA, the FBI and the National Security Agency set about translating them.

The disks held files with instructions on building bombs and on terrorist training camps in Afghanistan. There was also a crude drawing of a building with a flag on top; authorities feared it represented a U.S. embassy. The sketch was faxed to U.S. posts in Europe and elsewhere in search of a match. No one ever figured out what it meant, but embassies in sensitive regions were put on high alert. On December 8, President Clinton's national security team gathered in the wood-paneled Situation Room in the White House basement for a briefing by Messrs. Tenet and Clarke.

Grim assessment

Mr. Tenet began with a grim assessment, according to a person at the meeting. The suspects in Jordan, he said, had planned to use AK-47 rifles to gun down tourists at holy sites on Mount Nebo, which is 25 miles from Amman, and along the Jordan River. "But this isn't the extent of it," Mr. Tenet said. "We have to assume there's more. And possibly a lot more." In addition to what had been uncovered in Jordan, the CIA now had evidence that Americans could face from five to 15 attacks by terrorists linked to Mr. bin Laden. The news rattled Mr. Tenet's audience. "We basically looked at each other and said, 'Holy s---, this is serious,'" another participant says. Then came Clarke, a dour veteran diplomat who keeps a gas mask and a mock anthrax vaccine in his office. Placed before each of the officials was a thick document titled, "Millennium Threats Plan." Clarke and his staff had spent the weekend drafting the secret plan, which would become the government's blueprint for action once President Clinton approved it. The core strategy couldn't have been more basic: Overseas, the U.S. would ask the intelligence services of friendly countries from South America to Southeast Asia to do the dirty work of questioning people, arresting some on petty charges, denying them visas, deporting them.

Coming out of the White House meeting, the Clinton administration faced a delicate decision: how and when to publicly disclose its concern without provoking panic, and without alerting any operatives who may have eluded capture in the Jordan sweep. State Department officials argued about it for days. At one heated session, the department's chief of diplomatic security, David Carpenter, said he wasn't convinced a global warning was warranted. "What specifics do we have? We need to know more," he said, according to one person present. The warning issued December 11 cautioned travelers that the government had "credible information" about possible terrorist attacks "specifically targeting

American citizens." But it was only for travelers abroad and it specified no country.

First U.S. Prize

Three days later, the U.S. antiterrorism effort bagged its first prize. At the behest of a top U.S. Marine general acquainted with Pakistan leader General Pervez Musharraf, Pakistan plainclothes agents swarmed into a two-story house on the edge of Peshawar and collared Khalil Deek, a pudgy computer engineer with a taste for wild honey and radical Islam.

U.S. intelligence officials had tracked the onetime California resident for years before they had tied him, just days before, to the alleged Jordan plot. From behind the high wall surrounding his rented, whitewashed villa, Deek ran a small computer school and exported drums of local honey to the Middle East, according to neighbors. U.S. authorities say his house near the Afghan border also served as a way station for recruits heading in and out of terrorist training camps in Afghanistan. Calendars with photographs of machine guns hung on the wall, and an Arabic paperback, "Thoughts on Judgment Day," sat on a windowsill. Computers hauled out of the house contained more bomb-making plans and a terrorist training video apparently shot in Afghanistan. Deek is now in custody in Amman, where he was flown two days after his arrest. Documents found on the men arrested in Amman linked Deek to their plot, U.S. officials say. He faces a possible death penalty on Jordanian charges that he plotted a terrorist attack. He has pleaded not guilty.

Target: An Amman Hotel

The arrest was good news because, by now authorities in Jordan had found a cache of ammonium nitrate, a chemical sometimes used in homemade bombs, and determined that the suspects may have planned to use a truck bomb to destroy the SAS Radisson, an Amman hotel popular with

Westerners. But the news wasn't all good. The U.S. also had wanted the Pakistanis to grab Abu Zubnaydah, a Palestinian whom the U.S. thinks worked as an organizer at terrorist training camps in Afghanistan and helped plan the Jordan plot. U.S. intelligence thought Zubaydah was in Pakistan, but efforts to track him down then have come to naught.

Later on the day of Deek's arrest, U.S. officials were blindsided by news from their own country. A U.S. customs agent, acting purely on a hunch, opened the trunk of a rented Chrysler at a sleepy border post north of Seattle. Inside he found a cache of circuit boards and high-powered explosives. The car's driver, Ahmed Ressam, was a 28-year-old man in baggy clothes who spoke little English and tried to flee when questioned. In his car's wheel well, authorities found other suspicious items, including powders and a syrupy liquid. Samples were hustled to a nearby crime lab, where analysts determined that Ressam had brought from Canada the makings of several bombs. He had ties to at least one militant Algerian group in Montreal, and investigators found evidence that he had spent time in an Afghan terrorist camp known for training Algerians.

Pressure on Afghanistan

Authorities were glad to have Ressam behind bars, but dismayed to realize that sheer luck had put him there. As far-reaching as the U.S. effort had been, no one had focused on the possibility of foreign militants infiltrating from Canada – expect, it seemed, bin Laden. So the U.S. moved to ratchet up the pressure on Afghanistan. Late that night, Michael Sheehan, the State Department's counterterrorism chief, picked up a secure phone in the kitchen of his home in Washington and called Afghanistan's foreign minister, Wakil Ahmed Muttawakil. The country's ruling Taliban militia had sheltered bin Laden since 1995, refusing to turn him over to the West while disavowing any responsibility for his actions. Sheehan told Muttawakil that the U.S. would no longer tolerate the Taliban's stance. Bin Laden, Sheehan recalls saying that bin Laden "is like a criminal who lives in your basement. It is no longer possible for you to act as if he's not your responsibility. He is your responsibility."

The implied threat was that, if terrorists linked to bin Laden struck, the U.S. might punish the Taliban – possibly with military force. The minister said he understood, and urged that the U.S. use restraint. The U.S. fearing the repercussions of an attack on Afghanistan quietly pulled its staff from consulate offices across the border in Pakistan. The U.S. closed its embassy in Afghanistan in 1989. At the same time, leads were pouring in to U.S. intelligence from around the world. Even sketchy reports, such as a tip about package bombs coming from Frankfurt, rocketed straight to the Clinton cabinet's attention.

Clean and Dirty Teams

With so much happening, FBI Director Louis Freeh drove to CIA headquarters in suburban Virginia for an impromptu meeting with his CIA counterpart. As Tenet chomped on an unlit cigar, the two men discussed the latest intelligence reports and sketched scenarios for possible year-end attacks. They agreed to send additional CIA and FBI agents to Europe, including a "clean team" trained in handling evidence to launch any formal investigations, and a "dirty team" with access to secret intelligence crucial to tracking down suspects in a hurry. To maintain a calm public face, the administration set up twice-daily conference calls among press secretaries at the White House, the Pentagon, the State Department, the CIA and the FBI. After the government announced on December 21 that it was tightening airport security and putting all U.S. military bases on "high alert," President Clinton tried to reassure citizens, telling them to "go about their holidays and enjoy themselves." The State Department's Mr. Sheehan vowed to spend New Year's Eve mingling in the crowd on the Washington Mall.

On December 30, while other nations continued to roust suspected troublemakers around the world, FBI agents made a sweep of Arab-Americans in the U.S. whom they suspected of being linked to the millennium plots and tried to squeeze information out of them. Eight FBI agents backed up by two police cruisers paid a visit to Tawfiq Deek, brother of Khalil Deek, at his garden apartment in Anaheim, California. Agents fanned out in the complex to interview neighbors while two agents asked Tawfiq Deek if he knew of Muslim groups planning something in the next few days. "No way," Deek says he told them.

On New Year's Eve, two dozen members of the U.S. terrorist-response team waited at an air base in southern Europe, ready to leave immediately for any site where an attack might occur. A fleet of response aircraft, poised for a domestic attack, waited to move in the U.S. The CIA, worried it might have missed something, ran the electronic files from Jordan through its computers again, using fresh search criteria. What they feared most was what they didn't know, an anxiety that plagues them.

Some Lessons Learned

Officials concede that they were blindsided by the threat of terrorism from Canada, and they have moved to tighten border controls and cooperation with Ottawa. The events of December have focused more attention on the threat of bin Laden-planned attacks within the U.S. But the larger lesson for some officials was that, by its sheer scale, the $7 billion-a-year U.S. counterterrorism effort seemed to be working – at least for the moment. As midnight and the new millennium neared, Mr. Freeh worked the FBI's strategic operations center. Mr. Sheehan ventured down to the celebration on the mall, keeping the promise he had made. Mr. Clarke and his White House team watched the festivities from a rooftop, lingering until midnight tolled in California. But the only explosions were the fireworks bursting over the Washington Monument. After the show, President Clinton's national security adviser Sandy Berger called Mr. Clarke on his mobile phone. "How's everything been?" Mr. Berger asked. "We've won this battle," Mr. Clarke told him, "But the war definitely isn't over."

It stands to reason that if the Clinton administration was able to root out the al-Qaeda cells that were planning a millennium attack on the United States and thwarted the attacks, the Bush administration could have done likewise. Why didn't it use the same approach that the Clinton administration used when it received intelligence reports on the frequency of chatter regarding the threats to the U.S? Grant it that the Bush administration didn't want to make al-Qaeda a top priority because it may not have believed the Clinton administration that Osama posed a great danger to the United States. But, Osama's record should speak for itself. Not only has Osama been a great threat to the United States, he had already attacked Americans in 1993 when he tried to blow up the World Trade Center from the underground parking lot, and bombed the U.S.S. Cole and the African embassy. These occurrences should be sufficient to warrant the appointment of a czar. Instead, National Security Adviser Condoleezza Rice demoted Richard Clarke, the czar under the Clinton administration, when Bush's staff took over the White House in 2001. Bear in mind that Richard Clarke was the anti-terrorism czar when the potential millennium attacks were thwarted. What other proof did they need to make this a top priority and go after Osama and his al-Qaeda network?

If terrorism had been a priority with the Bush administration, it would not have missed so many clues. If an intelligence report said al-Qaeda was planning to use commercial aircraft to attack buildings in the U.S., one would think that should be enough to send up a red flag. One cannot wait for information giving specific places and time. That is why you have intelligence analysts, and other experts to decipher information gathered from various means. When questioned why nothing was done about the intelligence information that he received on August 6, 2001, that al-Qaeda was planning to use commercial vehicles to blow up buildings in the U.S., Bush said the information was not specific. He said if he had information that a specific building would be attacked, he would have done something about it.

On August 4, 2002, the Bush administration said it moved as swiftly as possible to develop a plan on how to eliminate al-Qaeda – a process that took eight months and wasn't completed until one week before the September 11 attacks, according to an Associated Press article. But the Clinton administration had less than a month. The country was on an extremely high alert for the New Year celebrations. As the American people were told to go out and enjoy the holidays, the federal and state governments were busy working to stop the attacks and at the same time preparing for the worst. In New York, for example, Mayor Rudolph Giuliani sealed all the sewer manholes in the city, and took away all of the garbage cans from the streets. Thousands of police officers, both uniformed and plainclothes went through the crowds at Times Square with wands searching people for weapons. We also learned later that Mayor Giuliani had ordered three thousand body bags in case one of the expected attacks took place.

Moreover, the Clinton administration had handed over to the incoming Bush administration team detailed assessments of the threat, and offered ideas on how to counter al-Qaeda. But a senior Bush administration official said the Clinton White House offered the incoming Bush team ideas on how to roll back the threat over a three-to five-year period. The Bush administration said its review of its predecessor's briefing became bogged down in bureaucracy and denied receiving any firm plans for dealing with al-Qaeda. White House spokesman Sean McCormack said, "We were briefed on the al-Qaeda threat and what the Clinton administration was doing about it. These efforts against al-Qaeda were continued in the Bush administration."

According to Time magazine, Clinton's anti-terror czar, Richard Clarke, offered detailed proposals: arresting al-Qaeda personnel, choking off the group's financing, aiding nations fighting the organization and beefing up covert action in Afghanistan to deny al-Qaeda sanctuary. Clarke, who stayed on in the Bush administration, also called for a substantial increase in support for the Northern Alliance in Afghanistan and planning of air strikes on Afghan terror camps.

It is obvious that the Bush administration did not connect the dots, although so many pieces of information flowed into the various intelligence agencies well before 2001, and the new administration would have to be aware of Osama's network and activities. Furthermore, Bush administration counterterrorism official Richard Clarke said that President Bush ignored the threat of al-Qaeda for months and did too little to stop the September 11 attacks on the United States. Clarke said, "I find it outrageous that the president is running for re-election on the grounds that he's done such great things about terrorism. He ignored it. He ignored terrorism for months, when maybe we could have done something to stop 9/11."

Clarke also said that before the September 11 attacks, the Bush administration was focused on Iraq rather than on al-Qaeda and that immediately after the 9/11attacks it searched for a way to blame Saddam Hussein. Clarke said Bush took him aside the day after the 9/11 attacks and ordered him to "see if Saddam did this. See if he's linked in any way." Clarke said that he responded that al-Qaeda was responsible and that Iraq was not linked to the attacks. However, he agreed to look into Bush's request and again found no cooperation between Saddam and al-Qaeda. Clarke also said that the day after the 9/11 attacks, Defense Secretary Donald Rumsfeld suggested bombing Iraq, despite the lack of any evidence of Baghdad's involvement. When told al-Qaeda's bases were in Afghanistan, not Iraq, Clarke said Rumsfeld responded that there were no good bombing targets in Afghanistan, but there were plenty of such targets in Iraq. Clarke said he thought at first that Rumsfeld was joking, but quickly realized that he was serious. He also said that the Bush administration ignored intelligence "chatter" in 2001 about possible terror attacks.

The Bush administration played with words as it manipulated the facts so as to lead the American people into believing that Saddam Hussein and Osama bin Laden coordinated the attacks in the United States on September 11, 2001. Every time Bush administration officials mentioned 9/11 and Osama bin Laden terrorist activities, such as the U.S.S. Cole and the African embassy bombings, they linked Saddam Hussein in conjunction with the September 11, 2001, terrorist attacks. The Bush administration postulated that Saddam Hussein worked with Osama bin Laden's al-Qaeda terrorist network to attack the United States, in order to win over the American people against Saddam Hussein.

It appears that the mindset of Bush administration officials was to use fear tactics to convince the American people and the rest of the world that the United States must overthrow the Iraqi regime to prevent another terrorist attack like that of September 11, 2001, not only on U.S. soil, but also in other parts of the world. The Bush administration tried to tell other countries that they may be attacked next by terrorists and that Saddam Hussein would sell weapons of mass destruction to terrorists to be used on their people.

In just about every statement made by the heavy hitters of the Bush administration, they juxtaposed Saddam Hussein and Osama bin Laden in ways that linked the two as the bad guys that must be rooted out because they had a direct link to 9/11 and terrorism. On NBC's "Meet the "Press," Dick Cheney referred to a meeting that Czech officials said took place in Prague in April 2000 that connected Iraq to the September 11 attack. This allegation was echoed by many Bush administration officials, leading right up to the attack on Iraq. But a congressional report on the attacks said, "The CIA has been unable to establish that [Atta] left the United States or entered Europe in April under his true name or any known alias." Also, in a March speech leading up to the war about "weapons of terror" Bush said, "If the world fails to confront the threat posed by the Iraqi regime, refusing to use force, even as a last resort, free nations would assume immense and unacceptable risks. The attacks of September 11,

2001, showed what the enemies of America did with four airplanes. We will not wait to see what terrorists or terrorist states could do with weapons of mass destruction. Statements like these could send shivers through the American people as they were reminded of the terrible attacks on the United States.

And as Bush declared the end of major combat in Iraq, he reminded the American people of the attacks on the United States by linking Iraq and the September 11 attacks. He said, "The battle of Iraq is one victory in a war on terror that began on September 11, 2001, and still goes on. That terrible morning, 19 evil men – the shock troops of a hateful ideology – gave America and the civilized world a glimpse of their ambitions." He added, "The liberation of Iraq is a crucial advance in the campaign against terror. We've removed an ally of al-Qaeda, and cut off a source of terrorist funding. And this much is certain: No terrorist network will gain weapons of mass destruction from an Iraqi regime, because the regime is no more."

Bush said, in these 19 months that changed the world, our actions have been focused and deliberate and proportionate to the offense. We have not forgotten the victims of September the 11th – the last phone calls, the cold murder of children, the searches in the rubble. With those attacks, the terrorists and their supporters declared war on the United States. And war is what they got." But as we all now know, neither Saddam Hussein nor the Iraqi people had declared war on the United States, yet the Iraqis suffer the wrath of the U.S. superpower. The Bush administration exploited the misconception by linking the two. Many Americans do not have the time to read the news or to analyze the information being fed to them by the media. And many probably rely on their elected officials to be forthright with them and the media to provide accurate, fair and unbiased information. Therefore, it was not surprising when a poll taken just before the second anniversary of the 9/11 attacks showed that seven in 10 Americans continued to believe that Iraq's Saddam Hussein had a role in the attacks.

According to a September 6, 2003, Washington Post article by Dana Milbank and Claudia Deane, even after the Bush administration and congressional investigators said they have no evidence of this link, many people continue to believe that there is a link between the two. Sixty-nine percent of Americans said they thought it was at least likely that Hussein was involved in the attacks on the World Trade Center and the Pentagon, according to a Washington Post poll, despite the fact that the hijackers were mostly Saudi nationals acting for al-Qaeda.

According to the article, Bush's defenders said the administration's rhetoric was not responsible for the public perception of Hussein's involvement in the September 11, 2001, attacks. While Hussein and al-Qaeda come from different strains of Islam, and Hussein's secularism is incompatible with al-Qaeda fundamentalism, Americans instinctively lump both foes together as Middle Eastern enemies. Some administration officials abandoned any claim that Iraq was involved in the September 11, 2001 attacks. Deputy Defense Secretary Paul D. Wolfowitz, one of the war hawks, said on the Laura Ingraham radio show on August 1, 2003: "I'm not sure even now that I would say Iraq had something to do with it." A top White House official told the Washington Post on July 31, 2003: "I don't believe that the evidence was there to suggest that Iraq had played a direct role in 9/11."

In follow-up interviews, poll respondents were generally unsure why they believed Hussein was behind the September 11, 2001, attacks, often describing it as an instinct that came from news reports and their long-standing views of Hussein. One example is that the connection was fed to people in some public relations way.

Most people don't have the time to rationalize and to separate the rhetoric from the facts. And, if all they hear day in and day out is Saddam Hussein and terrorism, Saddam Hussein and Sept. 11, Saddam Hussein and Osama bin Laden, eventually the two become intertwined. Former Vice

President Al Gore in a speech on August 7, 2003, cited Hussein's culpability in the attacks as one of the "false impressions" given by the Bush administration making a "systematic effort to manipulate facts in service to a totalistic ideology."

It is a foregone conclusion that as long as the American people believe that Saddam Hussein attacked the United States on September 11, 2001, they would continue to support the war in Iraq. There was a report that a woman in Florida is determined to sew a quilt for the family of every American soldier killed in the Iraq war. She said, "We have to stay there as long as it takes and take care of it once and for all. No one wants another September 11."

If the same information is being repeated over and over again, eventually the subconscious accepts it as a fact, whether or not it is true. It is a form of autosuggestion. But regardless of which information the American people use to connect the dots between Saddam Hussein and Osama bin Laden, all comes down to one factor, the repeated deliberate linkage between Saddam Hussein and Osama bin Laden by the president, vice president and other administration officials. President Bush said, "Those deadly attacks on our country – we have carried the fight to the enemy. For America, there will be no going back to the era before Sept.11 – to false comfort in a dangerous world. We are fighting the enemy today so that we do not meet him again on our own streets in our own cities."

An Associated Press article dated September 14, 2003, by John Solomon stated that the Bush administration said it had evidence of some pre-war Iraqi contacts and training with al-Qaeda, based on prisoner interrogations, defector statements and documents collected in Iraq and Afghanistan, but no proof of joint terror operations, according to U.S. officials. Some U.S. officials who spoke on condition of anonymity said there was credible evidence of more than a half dozen high-level contacts between Iraqi intelligence agencies and leaders of bin Laden's organization, but no direct evidence of Iraqi government sponsorship of al-Qaeda attacks. U.S. officials said whatever the intelligence ultimately concludes about the prewar contacts between Iraq and bin Laden, there is little doubt that Saddam's fall has opened the door for al-Qaeda to operate more overtly inside Iraq, as evidenced by a wave of attacks on U.S. soldiers. Greg Thielmann, a retired State Department expert on chemical, biological and nuclear weapons, said, "The U.S. attack on Iraq has now made a terrorist connection a self-fulfilling prophecy. We really found the one formula that maximizes al-Qaeda's chances of increasing their operations in Iraq." In other words, if there were no connection before between Iraq and Afghanistan by the U.S. overthrow of Saddam Hussein, it is now possible for al-Qaeda to take a position in Iraq.

In several speeches Vice President Dick Cheney linked the major bombings in Iraq to the deadly strikes in Bali, Casablanca and Riyadh, although senior military, intelligence and law enforcement officials said there was no conclusive evidence pointing to a particular group as the mastermind behind any of the major attacks in Iraq. They repeatedly tried to show the war in Iraq and its aftermath as part of the broader campaign against terrorism.

Administration officials said that linking the bombings in Iraq to al-Qaeda and the broader war on terrorism puts the attacks in a better political light than if they are viewed as guerrilla strikes by Baathist die-hards. Bush and Cheney said the war in Iraq is a front for the campaign against terrorism. At fund-raising events in Houston and Austin, Texas, Cheney said that Hussein had "an established relationship with al-Qaeda," an assertion some intelligence said was overstated. "Freedom still has enemies in Iraq." Cheney added, "These terrorists are targeting the very success and the freedom that we're providing to the Iraqi people," according to the AP article.

In an address at the James A. Baker III Institute for Public Policy in Houston on October 17, 2003, Cheney reiterated, "Since September 11, the terrorists have continued their attacks in Ryadh, Casablanca, Mombassa, Bali, Jakarta,

Nijaf and Baghdad. Against that kind of determined, organized, ruthless enemy, America requires a new strategy – not merely to prosecute a series of crimes, but to conduct a global campaign against the terror network."

After the attack on the United States, many in Congress and families of the 9/11 attack victims called for the creation of a commission to look into how the Bush administration missed the various warning signs that a major attack was being planned against the United States using commercial aircraft. However, President Bush successfully opposed the creation of the commission for more than a year. When Pearl Harbor was attacked by Japan, a commission was created immediately to investigate what went wrong that allowed the Japanese to attack the U.S. without the U.S. having advance warning. Bush said that an independent investigation would distract leaders from his newly declared war on terrorism.

According to a Wall Street Journal report, after a joint House and Senate intelligence committee inquiry found that some information related to the Sept. 11 hijackers had been mishandled by the Federal Bureau of Investigation and Central Intelligence Agency, Congressional support for a commission mushroomed. The White House then reversed itself and on September 20, 2002, announced its support for a commission. A fight ensued over the bill creating the commission. Sen. McCain pushed for a 24-month deadline for the investigation. The White House demanded that the commission complete the investigation within 12 months, and won a compromise for 18 months. President Bush insisted on the right to name its chairman, former Secretary of State Henry Kissinger. However, Kissinger resigned because he did not want to disclose his consulting clients after questions arose about possible conflicts of interest.

A 10-member commission, headed by Chairman Thomas H. Kean and Vice Chairman Lee H. Hamilton, was established in November 2002 and was given a wide range of responsibilities by Congress, including looking into what information the White House had about terrorist threats in the months before the attacks, and what it did in response. To issue a subpoena, six of the 10 commissioners must vote to do so. A split along party lines would have blocked a subpoena.

According to the Wall Street Journal article, the administration also decided that the commission had to channel its requests to obtain documents and interview personnel from the executive branch through the Justice Department. Kean said that he intended to meet the May 2004 deadline, although it would be difficult. He ruled out asking for an extension because, he said, "the White House had made it known they didn't want it to go into the election period." After insisting that the president's briefing papers are sensitive and should not be released to the September 11 commission, Bush acceded. However, this decision to release the information to the commission came after some commission members threatened to seek a subpoena. The agreement allowed four members of the commission to review documents known as the President's Daily Briefs, including one from August 2001 that warned of the possibility of an al-Qaeda plot to hijack airplanes.

However, getting information from the Bush administration was no easy feat, because of the many roadblocks that the commission would encounter as it tried to gather pertinent information from the various departments to enable the commission to do a thorough and complete investigation of the facts.

The first official progress report from the 9/11 Commission was issued in July 2003. The report said that certain federal agencies were slow to turn over documents and had imposed conditions making interviews of government personnel difficult. The commission also raised the possibility that it may not finish its work by a May 2004 deadline.

According to the report, the commission was far behind in its work and that the White House had taken several steps that had handicapped it. Commissioners disagreed with a White House requirement that federal agency officials be present as observers when commission staff interview agency employees, and were especially critical of the Defense Department, which it said hadn't responded to requests for documents. It also cited problems in getting information and records from the Justice Department and Central Intelligence Agency, particularly CIA data relating to its activities "in the pre-9/11 war on terrorism." Claire Buchanan a White House spokeswoman said, "The president was committed to ensuring that the commission has the information it needs to do a thorough review of the circumstances surrounding the 9/11 attacks." However, she said she wouldn't speculate on whether Bush might eventually agree to extend its deadline.

Thomas H. Kean and Lee Hamilton said that they had intended to complete the work by May 27. But they warned that further resistance from government agencies could threaten their ability to meet the deadline.

Former Senator Bob Kerrey said the Bush administration would continue to use delay tactics by not providing the commission with the President's Daily Briefs showing the day Bush received the information on Osama bin Laden's terrorist threats.

The following is an excerpt from a Wall Street Journal report:

Adam G. Ciongoli, counselor to the attorney general who was assigned to take on this role, said he has merely acted as a facilitator. But Commissioner Max Cleland, a former Democratic senator from Georgia, said that Ciongoli was acting as a political gatekeeper, cherry picking the documents the White House wanted to withhold. "It's obvious that they're sifting the information to the 9/11 commission now," Cleland said. "We're way, way too late here. The picture is not encouraging." Bartlett said that the White House had been trying to dissuade the commission from pushing for access to daily briefing memos to the president from the CIA and minutes of meetings of the National Security Council. Ciongoli said that no category of documents had been ruled out for turning over to the commission. Bartlett agreed, and added, "That's a question of what is contained in the most highly classified information provided to the president personally and only seen by less than a handful of people. He noted that the underlying intelligence information on which the briefing memos were based was available to the congressional investigators and that the White House was encouraging the commission instead to go to those original sources.

One reason the commission had been delayed in conducting interviews was that talks with Ciongoli over ground rules for interviews had become bogged down, according to people with knowledge of the talks. Among the sticking points were whether the administration would require minders to be present when staffers are questioned, and whether investigators would be able to interview staffers from federal agency field offices without first notifying their Washington headquarters.

Several commissioners, including Tim Roemer, a former Democratic Congressman from Indiana, complained that they were initially denied access to the still-classified Congressional report on which by law, they were supposed to build their own investigation. In April 2003, Roemer tried to visit the secure room in a House office building where the report and supporting documents are kept, he said. He asked to review the transcripts of several closed-door hearings, which he had participated in while still a congressman. A congressional staffer told him that he couldn't review the material. He then learned that the White House had requested the right to review much of the material so that it could assert executive privilege, and that the commission's executive director Philip D. Zelikow, had agreed. After Roemer and others complained, the

White House agreed to let the commission have access to the documents in the room.

Zelikow, a historian and lawyer who spends a few days a week as the director of the University of Virginia's Miller Center of Public Affairs, has close ties to the White House. He was a senior staffer on the National Security Council under the first President Bush. In 1995 he co-wrote a book about Europe with Condoleezza Rice. He served on the Bush transition team, and afterward on the president's Foreign Intelligence Advisory Board until he took the commission's job. Zelikow was hired to work on the investigation after he was recommended by Commissioner Slade Gorton, a Republican who had served on the National Commission on Federal Election Reform. Zelikow was executive director of that and other commissions.

According to a March 24, 2004, New York Times article by Philip Shenon and Eric Schmitt, under an agreement with the White House in 2003, one member of the commission, Jamie Gorelick, former deputy attorney general in the Clinton administration, was allowed to read through a full library of the President's Daily Briefs, and two other commissioners were allowed a partial review. Gorelick said at the hearing on March 23, 2004 that information in the documents "would set your hair on fire, and not just George Tenet's hair on fire," referring to the director of central intelligence. While barred under secrecy regulations from discussing much of what was in the reports, she said that there had been "an extraordinary spike" of intelligence warning of an al-Qaeda attack cited in the Daily Briefs during 2001 and that "it plateaued at a spike level for months." In the meantime, the chairman, Thomas Kean, said that the White House had continued to withhold several highly classified intelligence documents from the panel, and that he was prepared to subpoena the documents if they were not turned over within weeks.

An October 26, 2003, New York Times article by Philip Shenon stated:

> The chairman, Thomas H. Kean, the former Republican governor of New Jersey, said in an interview that he believed the bipartisan 10-member commission would be forced to issue subpoenas to other executive branch agencies because of continuing delays by the Bush administration in providing documents and other evidence needed by the panel. "Anything that has to do with 9/11, we have to see it – anything. There are a lot of theories about 9/11, and as long as there is any document out there that bears on any of those theories, we're going to leave questions unanswered. And we cannot leave questions unanswered." While Mr. Kean said he was barred by an agreement with the White House from describing the Oval Office documents at issue in any detail – he said the White House was "quite nervous" about any public hint at their contents – other commission officials said they included the detailed daily intelligence reports that were provided to Bush in the weeks leading up to Sept.11.
>
> Despite the threat of a subpoena and his warning of the possibility of a court battle over the documents, Mr. Kean said he maintained a good relationship with Mr. Gonzales and others at the White House, and that he was hopeful that the White House would produce all of the classified material demanded by the panel without a subpoena. "We've been very successful in getting a lot of materials that I don't think anybody has ever seen before," he said of his earlier dealings with the White House. Within the legal constraints that they seem to have, they've been fully cooperative. But we're not going to be satisfied until we get every document that we need."

In 2002, the White House confirmed news reports that President Bush received a written intelligence report in August 2001, the month before the attacks, that al-Qaeda might hijack American passenger planes. Ms. Snee, the White House spokeswoman said, "The president has stated a clear policy of support for the commission's work and, at the direction of the president, the executive branch has dedicated tremendous resources to support the commission, including providing over two million pages of documents.

After months of stating that it believed subpoenas to the executive branch would not be necessary, the commission voted unanimously to issue its first subpoena to the Federal Aviation Administration after determining that the F.A.A. had withheld dozens of boxes of documents involving the September 11 attacks. The subpoena appeared to be a turning point for the commission and for Mr. Kean, a moderate Republican known for his independence. In a statement on October 15, 2003, the commission said it was re-examining "its general policy of relying on document requests rather than subpoenas" as a result of the issues with the F.A.A.

The deadline for the commission to complete its work was May of 2004. However, the commission members said that deadline may be impossible to meet because of the Bush administration's delays in turning over many documents.

Max Cleland, another member of the commission, accused the White House of withholding classified information from the panel for purely political reasons. He said "It's obvious that the White House wants to run out the clock here. It's Halloween, and we're still in negotiations with some assistant White House counsel about getting these documents – it's disgusting." He also said that the White House and President Bush's re-election campaign had reason to fear what the commission was uncovering in its investigation of intelligence and law enforcement failures before Sept.11. "As each day goes by, we learn that this government knew a whole lot more about these terrorists before Sept.11 than it has ever admitted."

Kean's concerns were widely shared on the panel, and that the concern was bipartisan. Slade Gorton, a Republican member of the panel who served in the Senate in Washington from 1982 to 2000, said that he was startled by the "indifference" of some executive branch agencies in making material available to the commission. He said, this lack of cooperation, if it extends anywhere else, was going to make it very difficult for the commission to finish its work by May 2004. Tim Roemer, President of the Center for National Policy in Washington and a former Democratic member of the House from Indiana, said that "our May deadline may, in fact, be jeopardized – many of us are frustrated that we're still dealing with questions about document access when we should be sinking our teeth into hearings and to making recommendations for the future."

Congress would need to approve an extension if the panel requested one, a potentially difficult proposition given the reluctance of the White House and many senior Republican lawmakers to see the commission created in the first place. Senator McCain, R-Ariz., one of the sponsors of the legislation creating the commission said, "If the families of the victims weighed in – and heavily as they did before, then they would have a chance of succeeding. He said that given the obfuscation of the administration in meeting document requests, he was ready to pursue an extension "if the commission feels it can't get its work done."

On November 7, 2003, the commission issued a subpoena to the Pentagon and was weighing a subpoena to the administration for Oval Office documents President Bush received in the days before September 11, 2001. According to a November 8, 2003, New York Times article by Philip Shenon the 10-member panel said in a statement that they encountered "serious delays" in obtaining information from the Defense Department. It voted to subpoena the Pentagon for documents, tapes and transcripts involving the actions of the North American Aerospace Defense Command, or NORAD, on the morning of September 11, as the suicide hijackings were being carried out. The Defense Command is responsible for protecting American airspace. "In several cases we were assured that all requested records had been produced but we then discovered through investigation, that these assurances were mistaken," the panel said. "We are especially dismayed by problems in the production of the records of activities of Norad and certain Air Force commands on September 11."

According to the article, commission members said they were trying to determine how NORAD responded to the first reports of the hijackings and whether the military could have done anything to prevent the attacks on the World Trade Center and the Pentagon, possibly by using fighter jets to shoot down the passenger planes. In its statement, the commission said it had alerted Defense Secretary Donald H. Rumsfeld about the panel's problems in obtaining documents related to the September 11 attacks, and that Rumsfeld had pledged to do everything in his power to address the commission's concern.

Although the Bush administration agreed to help the 9/11 Commission investigate the September 11 terrorist attacks, its cooperation was limited at best. But not just the Bush administration was trying to keep the panel at bay from getting access to pertinent information which would enable it to complete its investigation, the mayor of New York, Michael R. Bloomberg, also tried to prevent access to certain records. It was not until the panel issued a subpoena for the records of the emergency 9/11 calls and other materials that Bloomberg agreed to release the records. The commission issued a total of three subpoenas; the others were issued to the Federal Aviation Administration and the Defense Department.

The commission requested an extension from the May deadline, but for some time to no avail. However, it was not until February 2004, that the White House yielded to the commission's request, saying it would back a two-month extension to July 26, but the extension was held up in the Congress. House Speaker Dennis Hastert was opposed to an extension.

According to an Associated Press article dated November 27, 2003, victims' relatives who were influential in forming the commission said the panel risks being undercut by the government's failure to cooperate with it. The Family Steering Committee, a group of victim advocates, marked the anniversary by urging an extension of its May 27 deadline for submitting findings and recommendations. "Unfortunately, the production of a timely report was no longer possible, in large part because of the delays caused by the Bush administration and the agencies that report to it," the group said in a statement.

Kean said the commission ultimately got all of the documents it requested. But, he said, "Some of the negotiations with the White House have been long and somewhat tortured and have taken up a tremendous amount of time." The commission would not be able to provide a complete report unless they received the full cooperation of the Bush administration. Moreover, since most of the information given the commission is classified, the White House and Central Intelligence Agency will review its report to determine which parts cannot be made public. In other words, the final report would have to be vetted by the White House before it could be released.

And, on March 24, 2004, members of the 9/11 Commission said a series of intelligence reports sent to President Bush in 2001 warned of an imminent, possibly catastrophic attack by al-Qaeda. Both Secretary of Defense Donald Rumsfeld and Secretary of State Colin Powell acknowledged in their testimony before the 9/11 panel that they were aware of the intelligence reports in 2001 warning of the especially dire terrorist threat against the United States. In response to questions by the panel about why they had not done more to pre-empt a possible terrorist attack, Rumsfeld said, "There was a good deal of concern. It was certainly not business as usual." But, 9/11 Commissioner Jamie Gorelick told Rumsfeld that the spike in the spring and summer of 2001 should have raised his hair – it should not have been business as usual.

Senator Gordon said in December of 2000, the Clinton administration was working to get bin Laden and the al-Qaeda network because of the Cole bombing in October of 2000. However, the Bush administration did not follow through. When asked by a 9/11 commission member why didn't the Bush administration continue the plan to get bin Laden, Rumsfeld replied that the Cole attack was (stale), and firing a cruise missile in Afghanistan four months after the attack would make the U.S. appear to be weak.

Another warning sign was the August 2001 arrest of Zacarias Moussaoui on immigration charges in Minneapolis, where his behavior at a flight training school had aroused suspicions. He wanted to learn how to steer an airplane, not how to take off or land, and no one took action.

The 9/11 panel cites the CIA for failures to thwart terrorism, in that George J. Tenet and his deputies were presented in August 2001 with a briefing paper labeled "Islamic Extremist Learns to fly" about the arrest days earlier of Zacarias Moussaoui, but did not act on the information. Tenet testified that he had no contact at all with President Bush in the month of August, the month in which the president received a CIA report suggesting that terrorists of al-Qaeda were already in the United States and might be planning a domestic airplane hijacking. August 2001 was when President Bush took the entire month off and was at his Crawford ranch in Texas. Tenet insisted that the agency had provided "clear and direct' intelligence about the larger danger posed by al-Qaeda before September 11. "Warning was well understood, even if the timing and method of attacks was not."

Furthermore, former acting FBI Director Thomas Pickard from June 25 to September 4, 2001, told the 9/11 panel that he briefed Attorney General John Ashcroft twice about the al-Qaeda warnings and when he tried to talk to him again, Ashcroft told him in the summer of 2001 that he did not want to hear about it again. He said Ashcroft's interest in al-Qaeda was limited. He said Ashcroft ignored warnings about al-Qaeda. Former FBI Director Louis Freeh told the 9/11 panel that September 11 could have been prevented if the FBI had more agents overseas. According to an April 13, 2004, Reuters article, the FBI sought permission to hire almost 1900 counter-terror linguists, analysts and agents before the September 11 attacks to combat a growing threat but was allowed to add just 76.

Also, from 1998 to 2001, there were threats of using UAV (Unmanned Aerial Vehicles) to shoot down commercial flights and explosives-laden gliders to attack the U.S. Even with the spikes in intelligence in 2001 that something dramatic was going to happen, no one at the airports on the ground or FAA was notified about the threat.

On CNN with Wolf Blitzer on March 23, 2004, former Secretary of Defense William Cohen said the Clinton administration first used diplomacy to get the Talibans to turn over bin Laden, and when that did not work, the Clinton administration shut down the Taliban airport going into Afghanistan and froze their assets. Also, in 1998 the Clinton administration launched 60 Tomahawk missiles against bin Laden.

President Bush said "If my administration had any information that terrorists were going to attack New York City on September the 11th, we would have acted. We have been chasing down al-Qaeda ever since the attacks." Rice said the Bush administration was concerned with terrorism overseas. However, Bob Woodward said in his book that President Bush told him that he did not take al-Qaeda's threat seriously. Six out of 10 Americans say the Bush administration underestimated the threat of terrorism prior to September 11, 2001, and nearly two out of three are at least somewhat concerned Iraq could become another Vietnam, according to a Newsweek Poll released on April 10, 2004.

According to an April 11, 2004, Reuters article, on April 10, 2004, the White House released a secret memo. However, this was after being pressured to release the information that President Bush was told a month before September 11, 2001, that al-Qaeda members were in the United States and the FBI had detected suspicious activity "consistent with preparations for hijackings or other types of attacks." The President's Daily Briefs, included a report titled "Bin Laden Determined to Strike Inside the U.S." The report said it had not been able to corroborate some of the "more sensational threat reporting," such as one in 1998 that Osama bin Laden wanted to hijack a U.S. aircraft to gain the release of those responsible for the 1993 bombing at the World Trade Center. But the document said the FBI since then had detected "patterns of suspicious activity in this country consistent with preparations for hijackings or other types of attacks, including surveillance of federal buildings in New York."

National security adviser Condoleezza Rice insisted in her public appearance before the 9/11 commission that the memo contained mostly historical information and did not warn of any coming attacks inside the United States. But the brief included information from three months prior that al-Qaeda members were trying to enter the United States for an attack with explosives. The document stated "The FBI is conducting approximately 70 full field investigations throughout the U.S. that it considers bin Laden-related. CIA and FBI investigated a call to the U.S. Embassy in the UAE (United Arab Emirates) in May saying that a group of bin

Laden's supporters was in the U.S. planning attacks with explosives."

According to a March 24, 2004, article by Philip Shenon and Eric Schmitt, the commission released a staff report finding that Rumsfeld did not order the preparation of any new military plans against al-Qaeda or its Taliban sponsors during the seven months between his arrival at the Pentagon and the September 11 attacks. The report said that despite the intelligence alerts received throughout the year, there was an impression among specialists at the Pentagon that Rumsfeld and his new team were "not especially interested in the counterterrorism agenda." A separate staff report on the government's diplomatic response to the terrorist threat found that Condoleezza Rice, Bush's national security adviser, and her deputies rebuffed a staff proposal in early 2001 that the administration step up its support for anti-Taliban rebels in Afghanistan. Rice had instead spent more than seven months trying to formulate policies to deal with al-Qaeda and the Taliban, policies that were not in place by September 11 and, according to White House aides, might have taken as long as three years to implement.

Attorney General John Ashcroft, in his appearance before the 9/11 commission on April 13, 2004, blamed the refusal of the FBI and the CIA to work together during the Clinton administration for the failure to detect the plot for the September 11, 2001, terrorist attacks. Ashcroft also criticized inaction in the final months of the Clinton administration, saying a review of proposals to disrupt al-Qaeda by the National Security Council in March 2000 went unheeded, perhaps because Clinton officials did not have the stomach for the outcry and criticism which follows such tough tactics. "It is clear from the review that actions taken in the millennium period should not be the operating model for the U.S. government," Ashcroft said.

The commission staff statement said it had found inconsistencies in Ashcroft's strategy against domestic terrorism before the attacks. The commission staff said that on September 11, 2001, about 1,300 agents, or 6 percent of the FBI's total personnel, worked on counterterrorism.

According to an April 13, 2004, MSNBC.msn.com article, before the attacks, Ashcroft once testified that the Justice Department "had no higher priority" than preventing domestic terrorism, but the commission staff statement quoted a former FBI counterterrorism chief, Dale Watson, as saying he "almost fell out of his chair" when he saw a May 10, 2001, budget memo from Ashcroft listing seven priorities, including illegal drugs and gun violence, but not terrorism.

Former FBI Director Louis Freeh disputes Ashcroft's charges. He said, "We had a very effective program with respect to counterterrorism prior to September 11 given the resources that we had." In fact, he said the bureau performed heroically in dealing with terrorist threats for years despite an inadequate budget. And, Mr. Pickard said that in his three months as head of the FBI he repeatedly ordered his deputies to be ready for a possible domestic attack. Ashcroft suggested that the failings of the Justice Department and the FBI before September 11 were largely the fault of the Clinton administration.

Both Ashcroft and Pickard agreed that neither of them had been informed by the White House during the summer of 2001 that President Bush had taken an interest in the question of domestic threats posed by al-Qaeda and had received a special CIA briefing on the issue on August 6, after months of dire intelligence warnings that suggested an imminent, possibly catastrophic attack. They also testified that the White House had not provided them the written intelligence report that accompanied the briefing, even though the so-called Presidential Daily Brief outlined investigations by the FBI that summer into the possibility that al-Qaeda terrorist cells were present in the United States.

Former Attorney General Janet Reno said that in her briefing to Ashcroft in 2001, she emphasized that terrorism was one of the most important issues facing the Justice Department. However, she did not specifically remember discussing al-Qaeda or the possibility that members of the terrorist network were already in the United States.

With conspiracy theories circulating, during the commission hearing, Richard Ben-Veniste asked Attorney General John Ashcroft about reports that he stopped flying on commercial aircraft before the attacks. Ashcroft replied that he never ceased to use commercial aircraft for his personal travel.

Alerts from intelligence agencies were stark, with headlines like "bin Laden's threats are real" and "bin Laden planning high profile attacks." Other alerts warned that there was "a high probability of near term 'spectacular attacks'" that would result in numerous casualties and "cause the world to be in turmoil," the commission said. But Bush administration officials said the warnings were too vague to act on. Freeh pointed out in a Wall Street Journal article that the FBI relentlessly did its job pursuing terrorists before the September 11 attacks, but was hampered by lack of resources and political will. He said it took the attacks in New York City and Washington to make others see the danger posed by al-Qaeda. "The al-Qaeda threat was the same on September 10 and September 12. Nothing focuses a government quicker than a war," he wrote.

Freeh said during his tenure, which ended three months before September 11, 2001, the FBI had expanded its overseas legal attaché offices from 19 to 44 and increased the prominence of joint terrorism task forces that include personnel from other agencies. Freeh said terrorism and the war against al-Qaeda were not even an issue in the 2000 presidential campaign, and that more could have been done to protect the nation. He wrote, "As FBI director, I share in that responsibility."

The 9/11 panel said that both the Clinton and the Bush administrations relied too heavily on diplomacy instead of military action to curb al-Qaeda before September 11, 2001. But the Clinton administration was hampered in its efforts to curtail terrorism.

The following article, "First Blood" which appeared in Sidney Blumenthal's book, "The Clinton Wars" is indicative of the roadblocks the Clinton administration encountered in trying to get the Congress to work with him to catch bin Laden:

After the bombing of the World Trade Center in February 1993, President Clinton had included anti-terrorism measures in his proposed new crime bill: new deportation laws and a federal death penalty for terrorists. Parts of that bill had been passed, but the 104th Congress was not receptive to Clinton's new omnibus anti-terrorism bill, which contained what had not previously passed as well as new proposals: for roving wiretaps, already used against mobsters; taggants for explosives; new laws against money laundering; a ban on fund-raising by terrorist organizations; and even more stringent deportation powers.

It seems as if anything the Clinton administration attempted to accomplish for the American people was railroad by the opposition party and their special interest groups. The Republican right, supported by the NRA and the Gun Owners of America, opposed the bill, forging an alliance of convenience with liberals worried about civil liberties. Less than a month after the Oklahoma City carnage, Newt Gingrich defended this opposition by remarking that people living in the rural areas had a "justified fear" of the federal government. The anti-terrorism bill went down in defeat. It was not until April of 1996 before the antiterrorism bill was passed. However, the Republican Congress deleted crucial provisions advocated by the president: it forbade the FBI to use further powers to track suspected terrorists' hotel and transportation records, to install roving wiretaps so that separate warrants didn't have to be issued for each phone used by a suspect, including cell phones; and to put tags ["taggants"] in smokeless and black explosives so their source could be traced – this last measure was opposed as an insidious form of gun registration.

In spite of the Bush administration denial that it was not aware that al-Qaeda was planning to fly commercial planes into buildings in the United States, the chairman of the commission investigating the September 11, 2001, terrorist attacks said he believes that the strikes could have been prevented.

A December 19, 2003, Washington Post article by Dana Milbank stated:

> In an interview with CBS News broadcast on December 17, 2003, Tom Kean, the former Republican governor of New Jersey who was chosen by Bush to head the panel, said the attacks could have been avoided. "I do not believe it had to happen," he said in the interview. When asked whether people should have been fired, he replied: "There were people certainly, if I was doing the job who would certainly not be in the position that they were in at that time, because they failed. They simply failed." Al Felzenberg, spokesman for the commission headed by Kean, noted as others have previously, that some terrorists had expired visas, that all eluded aviation security and that there was miscommunication between intelligence agencies that may have kept authorities from following clues to the attacks. "If any of these things hadn't happened, it might have been a different story," he said.
>
> Kean is not the first public official to suggest that the attacks might have been prevented. Senator Bob Graham, Democrat of Florida and co-chairman of the joint panel of the House and Senate intelligence committees, concluded last summer that the

attacks of September 11 "could have been prevented if the right combination of skill, cooperation, creativity and some good luck had been brought to task."

New York Times columnist Maureen Dowd wrote in an Opinion Page article – If only Sandy Berger had told the incoming Bush officials that al-Qaeda was no big deal, they might have gotten alarmed about it. They were determined to disdain all things Clinton, including his overemphasis on terrorism.

The American people want to know if the Bush administration had information regarding impending terror attacks prior to September 11, 2001, and what did they do about it. They also want to know if these attacks could have been prevented. And why didn't the Bush administration want to get at the truth about the September 11 attacks on the United States? Could it be because 15 of the 19 terrorists came from Saudi Arabia and because Bush and Cheney have close and lucrative relationships with the Saudi government and the Bush administration does not want to rock the Saudis' boat?

Michael Moore, author of "Dude Where's My Country," stated that:

The Bush family has been doing business with the bin Laden family off and on for the past twenty-five years. Going back to 1977 Bush senior set up Bush junior with an oil company named Arbusto, financed by James R. Bath, who was hired by Salem bin Laden, Osama's brother, to invest the bin Ladens' money in various Texas ventures. Some $50,000, or five percent of control of Arbusto, came from Mr. Bath.

After leaving office, Bush senior became a consultant for the Carlyle Group, an investment firm with billions in defense holdings. The bin Laden family has invested a minimum of $2 million in the Carlyle Group. Frank Cartucci, secretary of defense under Reagan and now the head of Carlyle, sits on the board of directors of a think tank called Middle East Policy Council along with a representative of the bin Laden's family business.

There was a number of bin Laden family in the United States at the time of the attacks. The New York Times reported that they were quickly called together by officials from the Saudi Embassy, which feared that they might become the victims of American reprisals. With approval from the FBI, according to a Saudi official, the bin Ladens flew by private jet from Los Angeles to Orlando, then on to Washington, and finally to Boston. Once the FAA permitted overseas flights, the jet flew to Europe. United States officials apparently needed little persuasion from the Saudi ambassador in Washington, prince Bandar bin Sultan, that the extended bin Laden's family included no material witnesses." The New York Times states that "In the first days after the terror attacks on New York and Washington, Saudi Arabia supervised the urgent evacuation of twenty-four members of Osama bin Laden's extended family from the United States.

According to the Times of London "the departure of so many Saudis worried U.S. investigators, who feared that some might have information about the hijackers. FBI agents insisted on checking passports, including the royal family."

Jane Mayer wrote in the New Yorker that "When I asked a senior United States intelligence officer whether anyone had considered detaining members of the family, he replied, "That's called taking hostages. We don't do that."

It is strange that while Americans were unable to travel in or out of the United States, a private jet under the supervision of the Saudi government backed by Bush's approval were allowed to fly around the country picking up twenty-four members of the bin Laden extended family and taking them to Europe. The bureau, we understand, was furious because they were not allowed to keep the bin Ladens' family in the country to conduct a real investigation.

Prince Bandar, a close friend of the Bush family, attended Barbara Bush's seventy-fifth birthday-party. He donated $1 million to the George Bush presidential Library and Museum in Texas and arranged for $1 million more to be donated to Barbara Bush's literacy program, and also invested in the Carlyle Group. In other words, the relationship goes far beyond business. George Bush senior even has a name for the Saudi Prince – he calls him "Bandar Bush."

Additionally, the Saudis are major investors in the U.S. They have over $1 trillion invested in the stock market and another $1 trillion in U.S. banks.

Furthermore, The Bush administration refused to declassify 28 pages of a congressional report, which shows possible links between Saudi government officials and the September 11 hijackers, saying that "would help the enemy regarding the U.S. intelligence and methods. Saudi Arabia's Foreign Minister al-Faisal called the suggestions of such links an outrage and said his country had been wrongfully and morbidly accused of being linked to the September 11 attacks. The Saudi wanted the 28 missing pages to be put back into the report so that they can respond to the allegations. They vehemently denied supporting the hijackers.

The Bush administration said there is an ongoing investigation that could be compromised if those pages are kept in, i.e., that part of the 900-page document would reveal the sources and methods that would make it harder for the U.S. to win the war on terror. The Saudi government, some members of Congress and some presidential candidates have sought declassification of the 28-page section of the report.

Saudi Ambassador Prince Bandar bin Sultan issued a statement saying that the blanked-out pages are being used by some to malign their country and their people. Senator John Kerry, D-Massachusetts, called on Bush to make public the section at issue. Senator Bob Graham, D-Florida and co-chairman of a congressional committee investigating the September 11, 2001 attacks, also called for declassification. Senator Graham said releasing the pages would allow the Saudi Arabian government to deal with any questions in the currently censored pages and allow the American people to make their own judgment about who are our true friends and allies in the war against terrorism.

The top Republican senator on the 9/11 inquiry, Richard Shelby, said that these classified pages could be released without jeopardizing national security. But, White House spokesman Scott McClellan said that the material included in that section in question contains information about ongoing investigations, counterterrorism operations and sensitive sources and methods.

The following article by Glenn R. Simpson appeared in the Wall Street Journal on March 18, 2004: "White House's Saudi Policy goes full Circle since the 9/11 Attacks:"

> Immediately after the attacks of September 11, 2001, the Bush administration took a tough stance toward Saudi Arabia, publicly accusing prominent Saudi citizens and charities of funding terror. But within months, that position shifted to a strategy of working privately with the kingdom to cut off funding for terrorism, newly available documents show. The Treasury Department memos, and interviews with key figures in the drive to cut off funding for terror, show how the U.S. position evolved from public confrontation to private cooperation and back again in the year after September 11.
>
> The circular course followed by the Bush administration reflects its struggles to come up with an

effective Saudi policy that combats terror while protecting the kingdom's monarchy from internal challenges. Today, cooperation between the two countries is described by U.S. and Saudi officials as strong, in part because the Saudi capital was hit by al-Qaeda attacks last year.

The two treasury memos were made available to The Wall Street Journal by Ron Suskind, a former Wall Street Journal reporter who obtained 19,000 government documents from former Treasury Secretary Paul O'Neil for his book "The Price of Loyalty." The shifts in policy were also described by former U.S. Ambassador to Saudi Arabia Robert Jordon and a former top aide to the National Security Council.

Right after September 11, the Treasury Department and National Security Council launched a frontal attack on Saudis suspected of funding terrorism, publicly designating a prominent Saudi businessman and a government-backed welfare group as sponsors of terror. But that provoked a backlash within Saudi Arabia, where many officials denied that Saudi citizens were complicit in the attacks and minimized the support for al-Qaeda leader Osama bin Laden, a Saudi exile.

The Saudi attitude is reflected in a September 26, 2001, memo in which then-Treasury Undersecretary Kenneth Dam recounted a series of calls to finance ministers around the globe. When Mr. Dam asked Jobarah al-Suraisry, the Saudi vice minister of finance, for help fighting al-Qaeda, Mr. Suraisry said he "didn't think they had any accounts that might help terrorism," Mr. Dam wrote. Treasury's top lawyer at the time has since referred to Saudi Arabia as the "epicenter" of financial support for terrorism.

A month after the call to Mr. Suraisry, Treasury staff members met with their counterparts at the

State Department and the National Security Council to discuss Saudi cooperation on combating terror financing. In an October 29, 2001, memo to Mr. O'Neil, Treasury Undersecretary John B. Taylor wrote, "the group generally agreed that due to domestic Saudi political sensitivities, a more private and consultative approach was needed on achieving specific actions."

"I do recall a decision was made that working with the Saudis in this initial phase could best be done on a private basis in which we should try to share intelligence and gather evidence, relying mostly on the Saudis to work these cases," said Mr. Jordan, then U.S. ambassador to Saudi Arabia, in an interview. He said the Saudis Understood that "if this private efforts wasn't successful, we would move to a more public and confrontational phase and do it ourselves."

In December 2001, U.S. officials, including Richard Newcomb, Treasury's frontline warrior against terror financing, traveled to Riyadh to provide their Saudi counterparts with information about suspected terror financiers, former U.S. officials said. But the policy of private consultations was never formalized by top deputies to Bush cabinet members, said Joseph Myers, former NSC terror-financing chief.

In November 2002, after revelations of possible Saudi funding for the attacks of September 11, the decision was made by the Bush administration to become more aggressive with the Saudis, and the two governments began sharing more information and set up joint task forces. Cooperation had accelerated after al-Qaeda attacked the Saudi capital of Riyadh.

"They have dramatically stepped up their cooperation, particularly since the May 12 bombings of

Riyadh," said Mr. Jordan, a respected Texas lawyer and longtime confidant of President Bush.

Some of the private discussions between the U.S. and Saudi governments concern the billionaire Al Rajhi family and the bank they founded, Al Rajah Banking & Investment Corp., where most of Saudi Arabia's top charities keep accounts. Mr. Jordan said some were concerned "the way Al Rajah bank operates, which is large cash transactions. It was the bank of choice for people to engage in cash; you could get a big cash withdrawal." A lawyer for the bank couldn't be reached to comment.

The Al Rajhi family is pursuing a libel case in the United Kingdom against The Wall Street Journal Europe, contending that a February 2002 article reporting that accounts at Al Rajhi bank were under scrutiny by U.S. and Saudi officials was false. Dow Jones & co., publisher of The Wall Street Journal Europe, stands behind the accuracy of the report.

The following is an excerpt from a July 25, 2003, New York Times article about a report by Congressional intelligence committees on the actions of the FBI and the CIA before and after the attacks of Sept. 11. The committees' deletions of classified materials, or changes in wording for national security reasons, are indicated by brackets:

Intelligence About Bin Laden's Intentions:

Central to the Sept. 11 plot was bin Laden's determination to carry out a terrorist operation inside the United States. The Joint Inquiry reviewed information in the intelligence community held before September 11 that suggested that an attack within the United States was a possibility. The review confirmed that shortly after bin Laden's May 1998 press conference, the community began to acquire intelligence that bin Laden's network intended to strike within the United

States. Many of these reports were disseminated throughout the community and to senior U.S. policy makers.

The intelligence reports did not contain specific information as to where, when and how a terrorist attack might occur, and generally, they were not corroborated. These reports represented a small percentage of the threat information that the intelligence community obtained during this period, most of which pointed to the possibility of attacks against U.S. interests overseas. Nonetheless, there was a modest, but relatively steady stream of intelligence indicating the possibility of terrorist attacks inside the United States. And, the credibility of the sources providing this information was sometimes questionable.

While one could not, as a result, give too much credence to some of the individual reports, the totality of the information in this body of reporting clearly reiterated a consistent and critically important theme: bin Laden's intent to launch terrorist attacks within the United States. In the spring of 1999, the intelligence community obtained information about bin Laden's planned attack on a government facility in Washington, D.C. In August 1999, the community obtained information that bin Laden's organization had decided to target the U.S. secretary of state, secretary of defense, and Director of Central Intelligence. "Target was interpreted by community analysts to mean "assassinate."

In September 1999, the community obtained information that bin Laden and others were planning a terrorist act in the United States, possibly against specific landmarks in California and New York City. In Late 1999, the community obtained information regarding the possibility that the bin Laden network plans to attack targets in Washington, D.C., and New York City during the millennium celebrations. On December 14, 1999, Ahmed Ressam was arrested as he attempted to enter the United States from Canada, and chemicals and detonator materials were found in his car. Ressam's intended target was Los Angeles International Airport. Ressam was later determined to have links to bin Laden's terrorist network. In February 2000, the community obtained information that bin Laden was making plans to assassinate U.S. intelligence officials, including the director of the FBI.

In March 2000, the community obtained information regarding the types of targets that operatives in bin Laden's network might strike. The Statue of Liberty was specifically mentioned, as were skyscrapers, ports, airports and nuclear power plants. In March 2000, the intelligence community obtained information suggesting that bin Laden was planning attacks in specific West Coast areas, possibly the assassination of several public officials. In April 2001, the community obtained information from a source with terrorist connections that speculated that bin Laden was interested in commercial pilots as potential terrorists. The source warned that the United States should not focus only on embassy bombings, that terrorists sought "spectacular and traumatic" attacks and that the first World Trade Center bombing would be the type of attacks that would be appealing. The source did not mention a time frame for an attack. Because the source was offering personal speculation and not hard information, the information was not disseminated within the intelligence community.

The Joint Inquiry did not find any comprehensive intelligence community list of bin Laden-related threats to the United States that was prepared and presented to policymakers before September 11. Such a compilation might have highlighted the volume of information the community had acquired about bin Laden's intention to strike the United States. [Nonetheless, the intelligence community did not leave unnoticed bin Laden's February 1998 declaration of war and intelligence reports indicating possible terrorist attacks inside the United States. The community advised senior officials, including the Congress, of the serious nature of the threat.] America first faced major international terrorist attacks within the United States in February 1993 when a bomb was detonated in the World Trade Center and in June 1993 when the FBI arrested eight persons for plotting to bomb New York City landmarks.

In 1996, as bin Laden's involvement in directing terrorist acts became more evident, the Counterterrorist Center (C.T.C.) created a special unit which grew from ten to fifteen members to focus on him. Since 1996, the community has been actively engaged in operations with mixed success to collect intelligence on bin Laden and disrupt his network. On September 10, 2001, 35 to 40 people were assigned to the C.T.C.'s bin Laden unit. In 1999, the FBI also created a bin Laden unit at headquarters. Approximately 19 persons were working in that unit on September 10. In August 1998 after the two embassy bombings in Africa, the intelligence community quickly confirmed that the attacks had been carried out by bin Laden's network. The D.C.I. made combating the threat bin Laden posed one of the intelligence community's highest priorities, establishing it as a "Tier [Zero] priority," and he raised the status of the threat still further when he announced in December 1998 that "We are at war" with bin Laden. Whether and when the intelligence community as a whole recognized that bin Laden was waging war on the United States and that it was necessary to respond in kind was an important factor in assessing the community's response to the threat bin Laden's network posed. On August 20, 1998, in an address to the nation on military action against terrorist sites in Afghanistan and Sudan, President Clinton declared: "A few months ago, and again this week, bin Laden publicly vowed to wage a terrorist war against America." On August 22, 1998, in a radio address to the nation, President Clinton declared: "Our efforts against terrorism cannot and will not end with this strike. We should have realistic expectations about what a single action can achieve, and we must be prepared for a long battle."

In December 1998, CIA Director George Tenet elaborated on the president's statements in a memorandum to senior CIA managers, the Deputy D.C.I. for Community Management, and the Assistant D.C.I. for Military Support, declaring war on bin Laden: "We must now enter a new phase in our effort against bin Laden. We are at war. I want no resources or people spared in this effort, either inside

[the] CIA or the community. The D.C.I. stated to the Joint Inquiry that in early 1999, following his declaration, he ordered a baseline review of CIA's operational strategy against bin Laden.

According to the D.C.I.'s testimony before the Joint Inquiry, the CIA "produced a new comprehensive operational plan of attack against the bin Laden/al-Qaeda target inside and outside Afghanistan," a plan of attack that in subsequent testimony the D.C.I. simply called "the plan." The plan included a strong and focused intelligence collection program to track – and then act against – bin Laden and his associates in terrorist sanctuaries. It was a blend of aggressive human source collection, both unilateral and with foreign partners, and enhanced technical collection. To execute the plan, C.T.C. developed a program to select and train the right officers and put them in the right places. We moved talented and experienced operations officers into the [C.T.C.]. We also initiated a nationwide program to identify, vet and hire qualified personnel for counterterrorist assignments in hostile environments. We sought native fluency in the languages of the Middle East and South Asia combined with policy, military, business, technical, or academic experience. In addition, we established an eight-week Counterterrorist Operations Course to share the tradecraft we had developed and refined over the years." According to documents reviewed by the joint inquiry, the plan included covert action and technical collection aimed at capturing bin Laden and his principal lieutenants.

The Joint Inquiry has determined that the intelligence community as a whole was not on a war footing before September 11. For example, knowledge of the D.C.I.'s' declaration appears to have been limited. Some senior managers at N.S.A. and D.I.A. were aware of the statement, but many in the FBI had not heard of it. For example, the assistant director of the FBI's Counterterrorism Division testified to the Joint Inquiry that he "was not specifically aware of that declaration of war." Senior officers in other components of the government, including the Defense Department and the U.S. military, apparently were also unaware of the declaration.

When asked whether he knew that the United States had been at war with bin Laden, Deputy Secretary of State Richard Armitage responded: "I was briefed in January and February [2001], leading to my hearings in March before the U.S. Senate. The term 'at war' was, to my knowledge, not used. There was no question, though, that we were in a struggle with al-Qaeda, and al-Qaeda was the very first thing that the administration took on at the deputy's level.

[The Joint Inquiry also reviewed whether the D.C.I.'s declaration of war had any real effect in the covert action area prior to September 11. Cofer Black, former C.T.C. chief, explained in a statement to the Joint Inquiry: "After Sept. 11, the gloves came off."] While the bureau's New York office took the lead in the vast majority of counterterrorism investigations concerning bin Laden, many other FBI offices around the country were unaware of the magnitude of the threat.

Shortly after the Bush administration took office in January 2001, the National Security Council undertook a review of existing policy for dealing with al-Qaeda. In response to written Joint Inquiry questions, Deputy National Security Adviser Steve Hadley explained: "The administration took the al-Qaeda threat seriously and, from the outset, began considering a major shift in United States counterterrorism policy."

From the first days of the Bush administration through September 2001, it conducted a senior-level review of policy for dealing with al-Qaeda. The goal was to move beyond the policy containment, criminal prosecution, and limited retaliation for specific attacks, toward attempting to "roll back" al-Qaeda.

The new goal was to eliminate completely the ability of al-Qaeda and other terrorist groups of global reach to conduct terrorist attacks against the United States. Between May and the end of July 2001, four Deputies Committee meetings were held directly related to the regional issues which had to be resolved in order to adopt a more aggressive strategy for dealing with al-Qaeda. This new policy might have produced a coordinated government response to the bin Laden threat or put the nation on more of a war footing with al-Qaeda before September 11. However, as Mr. Hadley noted, "The administration finalized its review of policy on al-Qaeda at an N.S.C. principals committee meeting on September 4, 2001." President Bush had not reviewed the draft policy before September 11.

The Joint Inquiry report reveals that the intelligence community continued to be fragmented without a comprehensive strategy for combating bin Laden. The report also shows that the D.C.I. was either unable or unwilling to enforce consistent priorities and marshal resources across the community. In the spring of 1999 the D.C.I. produced a new comprehensive operational plan of attack against bin Laden and al-Qaeda inside and outside of Afghanistan. The strategy was previewed to senior CIA management by the end of July 1999. By mid-September, it had been briefed to he CIA operational level personnel, to N.S.A., to the FBI, and other partners. The CIA began to put in place the elements of this operational strategy, which structured the agency's counterterrorism activity until September 11, 2001. According to documents reviewed by the Joint Inquiry, in 1999 "the plan" consisted of a variety of CIA covert actions against bin Laden. "The plan" focused principally on CIA covert action and technical collection aimed at capturing bin Laden.

The FBI increased its focus on terrorism throughout the 1990`s and helped prevent several major attacks that would have killed many innocent people. According to Director Mueller, these schemes included a 1993 plot to attack New York City landmarks; a 1995 plot to bomb U.S. commercial aircraft; a 1997 plot to place pipe bombs in New York City subways; and a plot to bomb the Los Angeles airport in December 1999.

The FBI took several important measures to improve its ability to fight international terrorism in the United States. Former Director Freeh testified that, during the 1990s the

FBI more than doubled the number of personnel working counterterrorism, and its counterterrorism budget more than tripled. In 1998, former Assistant Director for Counterterrorism Dale Watson and other FBI leaders recognized that the bureau was reacting to terrorist attacks rather than preventing them. They initiated the "MAXCAP05" program to improve the FBI's ability to counter terrorism. In 1999, the FBI made counterterrorism a separate headquarters division, elevating its importance within the bureau, and created a separate operational unit focused on bin Laden.

Several current and past senior FBI officials also testified about bureau-initiated personnel exchanges with the CIA and the expansion of its legal attaché program (stationing FBI representatives in U.S. Embassies), both of which deepened the FBI's ability to link domestic and international threats. Finally, former Director Freeh has testified that Joint Terrorism Task Forces (JTTFs) were given increasing prominence throughout the 1990's. The JTTF model, originally created to improve coordination between the FBI and the New York City Police Department, was expanded to other cities after the first World Trade Center attack. Over time, the number of JTTFs increased, improving coordination with state and local officials and even other elements of the intelligence community, as CIA officers joined several task forces.

The Joint Inquiry record confirms that FBI officials working on terrorism faced competing priorities and the ranks of those focusing on al-Qaeda were not sufficiently augmented. Only one FBI strategic analyst focused exclusively on al-Qaeda before September 11, 2001. The former chief of the FBI's International Terrorism Section stated that he had more than 100 fewer Special Agents working on international terrorism on September 11 than he did in August 1998.

A March 24, 2004, Wall Street Journal article by Scott Paltrow and David S. Cloud stated:

An analysis indicates that after taking office in January 2001, Bush administration officials spent months considering a new strategy toward al-Qaeda and its Taliban protectors in Afghanistan but took little action before September 11. For instance, the administration didn't make any diplomatic efforts to get Saudi Arabia to help crack down on al-Qaeda during that time and applied little pressure on Pakistan, whose security forces had been big backers of the Taliban.

Secretary of State Colin Powell said the Bush administration essentially was starting from scratch because "we were not given a counter-terrorism action plan by the previous administration." Powell said, "We were not dismissive, and we did not fail to deal with the issues," including working on preparing the Predator unmanned airplane to carry weapons that could be targeted on a single individual, such as. bin Laden.

The reports stated that former President Clinton designated CIA Director George Tenet as his representative to work with the Saudis, who agreed to make an "all-out secret effort" to persuade the Taliban to expel bin Laden. The Saudi intelligence chief, Prince Turki bin Faisal, received a commitment that bin Laden would be handed over, but Taliban leader Mullah Omar balked at a September 1998 meeting with Prince Turki and Pakistan's intelligence chief.

Secretary of Defense Donald Rumsfeld said he did not recall any particular counterterrorism issue that engaged his attention before 9/11, except for development of an unmanned plane that could be used against bin Laden.

The report exonerated Clinton from charges that a cruise missile attack in 1998 on a Sudanese pharmaceutical plant – thought to be producing nerve gas for al-Qaeda – may have been launched to distract attention from Mr. Clinton's problems involving the Lewinsky scandal. The report says: "All evidence we have found points to national security considerations as the sole basis for President Clinton's decision."

In 1998 and 1999 the Clinton administration missed chances for cruise missile attacks targeting bin Laden. Seaborne Tomahawk missiles were on alert on occasions when bin Laden's location was known and he was believed vulnerable. The report says he was able to escape because of delays in the time it takes to launch the missiles, wait while intelligence officials sought to verify the reports of his location and concerns that a missile strike would cause unacceptable collateral damage.

During the 9/11 commission public hearings, except for former FBI Director Louis Freeh saying, "As FBI director, I share in that responsibility," no other White House officials have acknowledged responsibility. Richard Clarke, President Bush's former counterterrorism chief, is the only one who has apologized to the American people and the people who have lost their loved ones by saying, "Those entrusted with protecting you failed you. And I have failed you," Clarke said. Kristen Breitweiser of New Jersey, whose husband, a banker, died in the south tower said she was enormously grateful to Clarke for that.

The following is an excerpt from a June 19, 2002, CBS news broadcast:

From 1996 to 1998 when bin Laden was beginning his operation out of Afghanistan, the National Security Agency (NSA) knew his phone number and was able to listen in on phone calls he and his top lieutenants made to al-Qaeda cells around the world. But the terrorists were so careful and cryptic about what they said over the phone that the U.S.

was caught totally by surprise when in August of 1998 truck bombs detonated simultaneously outside the American embassies in Kenya and Tanzania, killing 224 people. One of the terrorists arrested after the embassy bombings gave NSA one of the first leads that might have uncovered the 9/11 plot – two men were headed to a meeting of terrorist operatives in Malaysia. NSA immediately passed the information to the CIA. The meeting took place in a high-rise apartment building on January 6, 2000. The CIA didn't have time to plant any listening devices, but it was able to get pictures of the two men, who later turned out to be two of the hijackers who flew into the Pentagon. On January 15, 2000, the two hijackers entered the U.S. Nine days later NSA suffered its computer meltdown, which lasted three days.

The NSA's nightmare is that terrorists like Osama bin Laden may use technology developed in the United States to hide their plans to attack Americans. One way they can do it is via a software program to make messages unreadable.

NSA has top-of-the-line supercomputers – some of which are capable of performing more than a trillion operations per second to help decipher unreadable jumbles of letters and numbers. They were increasingly hard-pressed to keep up with the sheer volume of traffic. As the demands grew, the system was stretched thinner and thinner until they broke down completely in the January 2000 incident.

A July 28, 2003, Newsweek article by Michael Isikoff reported:

FBI blew repeated chances to uncover the 9/11 plot because it failed to aggressively investigate evidence of al-Qaeda's presence in the United States, especially in the San Diego area, where two of the hijackers were living with one of the bureau's own informants, according to the congressional report set for release July 21, 2004.

The long-delayed 900-page report also contains potentially explosive new evidence suggesting that Omar al-Bayoumi and the hijackers, may have been Saudi government agents, sources tell Newsweek. The report documents extensive ties between al-Bayoumi and the hijackers. But the bureau never kept tabs on al-Bayoumi despite receiving prior information he was a secret Saudi agent. In January 2000, al-Bayoumi had a meeting at the Saudi Consulate in Los Angeles and then went directly to a restaurant where he met future hijackers Khalid Almihdhar and Nawaf Alhazmi, whom he took back with him to San Diego. (Al-Bayoumi later arranged for the men to get an apartment next to his and fronted them their first two months rent.)

Questions about the Saudi role arose repeatedly during the 2002 joint House-Senate intelligence-committees inquiry. But the Bush administration has refused to declassify many key passages of the committees' findings. A 28-page section of the report dealing with the Saudis and other foreign governments will be deleted. Sen. Bob Graham, D-Florida, said the Bush administration is protecting a foreign government.

The 28 missing pages of the 9/11 report is about the Saudis' relationship with the U.S. The report criticized the Pentagon for resisting military strikes against al-Qaeda camps in Afghanistan prior to 9/11, and the CIA for failing to pass along crucial information about Almihdhar and Alhazmi at a terrorist' summit in Malaysia. A few months after al-Bayoumi took them to San Diego, Almihdhar and Alhazmi moved into the house of a local professor who was a longtime FBI "asset". The professor also had earlier contact with another hijacker, Hani Hanjour. But even though the informant was in regular touch with his FBI handler, the bureau never pieced together that he was living with terrorists. The bureau also failed to pursue other leads, including a local iman who dealt with several key 9/11 figures. The report, one congressional investigator said, "is a scathing indictment of the FBI as an agency that doesn't have a clue about terrorism." But bureau officials say the report mistakes the evidence. They say the bureau checked out al-Bayoumi – now back in Saudi Arabia, and concluded he had not given the hijackers "material support." As for Almihdhar and Alhazmi, "there was nothing there that gave us any suspicion about these guys," said one FBI official.

SIX

TERRORISM

Has The Attack On Iraq Escalated Terrorism?

Many believe that the attack on Iraq by the United States and Britain has only aggravated the anger and hatred for the United States. According to reports, when the Bush administration was beating the war drum to attack Iraq, bin Laden issued a statement that if the United States attacked Iraq, al-Qaeda would attack Americans wherever they are, but if the United States did not attack Iraq, al-Qaeda would not attack Americans.

According to an October 22, 2003, Reuters article, Secretary of Defense Donald Rumsfeld, posing challenging questions to the military Joint Chiefs of Staff and others in a memo dated October 16, 2003, said the United States had no yardstick for measuring progress in the anti-terrorism war launched after September 2001. He challenged Pentagon leaders to consider and discuss troubling issues, including whether or not the United States was capturing or killing terrorists at a faster rate than they were being created by extremists. He asked, "Are we winning or losing the global war on terrorism? Does the U.S. need to fashion a broad integrated plan to stop the next generation of terrorists?

Retired Army General Wesley Clark, a Democratic presidential candidate, said, "Secretary Rumsfeld is only now acknowledging what we've known for some time – that this administration has no plan for Iraq and no long-term strategy for fighting terrorism."

In a State of the Union message, Bush said over 3,000 al-Qaeda members have been arrested and many have met a different fate. "Let's put it this way, they are no longer around." It was mentioned in the media that Bush signed an order for the CIA to use extreme methods to kill al-Qaeda terrorists.

A PBS October 16, 2003, Frontline report "Sleeper Cell"stated:

> Shortly after the September 11 attacks, President Bush secretly authorized lethal covert action to be taken against members of al-Qaeda, according to published reports.
>
> According to the report, Kamal Derwish was a recruiter of the Lakawanna cell and a casualty of the U.S. war against terrorism. In Derwish's hometown of Lakawanna, New York, on the shore of Lake Erie just south of Buffalo, there is no grave site to visit or obituary to read. His 1988 Honda Accord has been quietly sold – one of the only signs Derwish is not expected home. Officially, his death is shrouded in national security secrecy. "It's not really anything that I can confirm, I mean, whether something did happen to him or not," said Peter Ahearn, the special agent in charge of the Federal Bureau of Investigation's Buffalo, New York field office and the man once in charge of tracking down Derwish. But despite government reticence to discuss it, Derwish's demise raises moral and constitutional concerns about America's war on terror.
>
> By most accounts, Derwish was a Muslim fundamentalist. Government investigators go further, saying he was a "card-carrying member of al-Qaeda" and disciple of bin Laden. But Derwish was also an American, afforded the same due process that all citizens have under the Constitution. The war on terror, however, has changed many aspects

of America's justice system, especially for those who, like Derwish, are suspected of involvement with terrorist organizations.

Derwish was born in Buffalo, New York, in 1973. His family left their Lackawanna home to return to Yemen when he was five years old. After his father was killed in a car accident, Derwish went to live with relatives in Saudi Arabia where he was raised and educated. U.S. intelligence sources say the Saudi government deported Derwish in 1997 for alleged extremist activities. He spent a year in Yemen before returning to his hometown in Lackawanna in 1998.

Over the next three years, Derwish remained active in the Lackawanna community. He made occasional trips back to the Middle East, once in 1999 and to get married in Yemen. When he returned again to the United States in the spring of 2000, Derwish began discussing a religious pilgrimage abroad and encouraged several members of the community to consider making the trip. The journey had wide appeal, although the real destination was an al-Qaeda training camp in Afghanistan. "I was hungry for knowledge of the religion itself," said Sahim Alwan, one of Derwish's recruits awaiting sentencing of up to 10 years in prison for attending the camp. "I really was, you know, starting to learn my religion," said Sahim Alwan in an interview conducted at the Buffalo Federal Detention Center in Batavia, New York, "and I didn't see, I never really saw the mujahedeen part of it."

During April and May 2001, the Lackawanna recruits left the Buffalo suburb for Pakistan. The men, traveling in two groups, eventually made their way into Afghanistan and the Al Farooq training camp. Derwish, who had gone ahead to make arrangements, guided some of his followers to the camp himself. During the six-week training program, most of the men received weapons training and learned combat tactics. Some even met personally with Osama bin Laden. While the men were still in the camp, an anonymous letter was sent to the FBI's Buffalo field office from a member of the Lackawanna Yemen community. The letter said that "terrorists" had come to Lackawana "for recruiting the Yemenite youth" and that a group of men had gone to train with bin Laden in Afghanistan. It was then that the FBI first began to develop a rudimentary biography of Kamal Derwish.

After the 9/11 attacks, the joint task force at the FBI ballooned from one agent to 25. The men that returned from the camp denied having been in Afghanistan, and Derwish had yet to emerge as the clear leader. But after an associate of Derwish was captured in Afghanistan in the fall of 2002, sent to Camp X-Ray in Guantanamo Bay, Cuba, and interrogated, a clearer picture of the recruitment effort in Lackawanna emerged. However, in late 2002, almost two months after arresting six of his recruits, the U.S. government did locate Derwish. On November 3, Derwish, 29, was traveling through a barren stretch of Yemen's Ma'rib desert with six companions – all suspected al-Qaeda members. Tipped off by Yemeni security agents that a suspected planner of the U.S.S. Cole bombing was in the vehicle, CIA was silently trailing the group with an unmanned aircraft remotely operated from an airbase believed to be in the nearby Conroe of Djibouti. As the vehicle Derwish was riding in drove through an isolated section of highway, the Predator drone aircraft launched a Hellfire missile, destroying the vehicle and killing six of the men, including Derwish. A seventh man escaped, according to Yemen's minister of interior. A United States passport found nearby was used to identify Derwish, according to the news report.

The Bush administration has reportedly given itself the legal authority to use "extreme measures," including the targeted killing of terrorist suspects, whether Americans or foreigners. The authority rests, in part, on the premise that the United States is at war with terrorism, making terrorists "enemy combatants" and therefore lawful targets under the Hague Convention and recognized laws of war, according to legal experts.

Yasein Taher, one of the men who attended the terrorist camp, was sentenced to eight years in prison and to be supervised for three years after his release under a plea bargain arrangement, according to a December 4, 2003, Reuters article. Taher apologized to the court, his family, the Yemeni community in Lackawanna and the country for attending a military-style training camp with the radical Islamists in Afghanistan. Although Taher was not charged with the September 11, 2001, attack, he was charged with providing support to the group blamed for the attack. Taher, a 25-year-old Yemeni-American, married with a 4-year-old son, told U.S. District Court Judge William Skretny "I just want to say I was sorry for what I have done. I accept full responsibility and know it was completely wrong for me going."

And on December 3, 2003, Judge Skretny sentenced another defendant from the "Lackawanna 6," Mukhtar al-Bakri age 23, to 10 years imprisonment. al-Bakri provided FBI agents with key testimony and said he met personally with al-Qaeda leader Osama bin Laden. The others would be sentenced under plea bargains negotiated in exchange for lighter sentences. Prosecutors did not accuse any of the six of taking part in any attack or other violent crime or of knowing about plans for the September 11 attacks.

The Bush administration's statement that al-Qaeda would attack other countries has become a self-fulfilling prophecy as al-Qaeda launches attacks on a number of countries, such as the Bali, Indonesia, attack killing approximately 200 Australians. Casablanca, North Africa and Saudi Arabia have also been attacked. This is indicative of al-Qaeda's determination to launch attacks even in Muslim countries to kill Americans.

According to an October 19, 2003, Reuters article, on October 18, 2003, the Arabic television station Al Jazeera broadcast two audiotapes said to be made by Osama bin Laden, vowing more suicide attacks inside and outside the United States and demanding that the United States withdraw from Iraq. The speaker on the tapes urged Iraqis to wage a holy war against American "crusaders" in Iraq until an Islamic government is set up in Baghdad. "We, God willing, will continue to fight you and will continue martyrdom operations inside and outside the United States until you abandon your oppression and foolish acts," said the speaker, referring to suicide attacks. One tape was addressed to Americans and the other to Iraqis, said the United States had been dragged into a quagmire in Iraq and that American soldiers would be foolish to stay.

According to an August 13, 2003, New York Times report by Neil MacFarquhar, the U.S.-led invasion of Iraq is prompting a rising tide of Muslim militants to slip into Iraq to fight the foreign occupiers. Iraq could become the ultimate battlefield for Islamic militants. These fighters are using Iraq's wide open borders to enter Iraq. They shave their beards and have clean-cut hair. The U.S. is trying to guard some of the open borders, but that is a difficult task considering the number of U.S. troops in Iraq and the fact that they are stretched so thin.

According to reports, in August 2003, Egypt announced that it had arrested 23 men and was seeking two more on charges of belonging to a terrorist group. The suspects – 19 Egyptians, three Bangladeshis, a Turk, an Indonesian and a Malaysian – were planning to fight U.S. forces in Iraq, Egypt's interior minister, Habib Adli said in an interview with the magazine Al Mussawar. Kurdish forces in northern Iraq also arrested a Tunisian carrying an Italian passport and attempting to cross from Iran. Also, Syria arrested and deported an Algerian national and a German resident who organized a group of radicals to travel to Iraq from the same Hamburg mosque where Mohammed Atta, the lead hijacker in the September 11, 2001, attacks, once worshipped. German officials said the man, who is currently free but under observation, had ties to Zarqawi and had also recruited volunteers in Italy to fight in Iraq.

Up until close to the end of November 2003, the U.S. coalition forces in Iraq said they had no concrete proof that al-Qaeda was responsible for any of the attacks in Iraq. However; the following is an excerpt from a Washington Post article dated September 8, 2003, by Peter Finn and Susan Schmidt which states that al-Qaeda plans a front in Iraq:

Two years after the attack on the United States, Osama bin Laden's leadership cadre has been isolated and weakened and is increasingly reliant on the violent actions of local radicals around the world to maintain its profile. But the al-Qaeda's network is determined to open a new front in Iraq to sustain itself as the vanguard of radical Islamic groups fighting a holy war, according to European, American and Arab intelligence sources.

The turn toward Iraq was made in February 2003, as U.S. forces were preparing to attack, the sources said. Two seasoned operatives met at a safe house in eastern Iran, Mohammed Ibrahim Makawi, the military chief of al-Qaeda also known as Saif Adel, and Abu Musab Zarqawi, who had fled Iraq's Kurdish northern region in anticipation of the U.S. targeting a radical group with which he was affiliated. Zarqawi was dispatched to become al-Qaeda's man in Iraq, opening a new chapter in the history of the group and serious threat to American forces there. An Arab official familiar with the intelligence who spoke on condition that he is not identified by name or nationality said, "The monster is already near you. I don't know if you can kill it. Iraq is the new battleground. It is the perfect place. It will be the perfect place."

After the fall of the Taliban in Afghanistan, the focus of al-Qaeda's degraded leadership moved to Iran. The Iranian security services which answer to the country's powerful Islamic clerics protected the leadership, including Adel and a son of bin Laden's, Saad, as well as other senior figures, according to the intelligence officials. From guesthouses in Iran's east and south, this al-Qaeda group planned the May 12 bombing of the residential compounds in Riyadh, Saudi Arabia. The group might have hoped that a campaign of violence, including the planned assassination of leading members of the Saudi royal family, would lead to the fall of the kingdom's government, Arab officials said. One European source said the Iranians had "freeze-dried" the group. Also, Saudi Arabia then launched a major crackdown domestically. Zarqawi returned to Iraq and retreated to the Iranian side of the border with Iraq when he sensed his security was threatened, according to officials. U.S. military officials said that there were already 220 foreign fighters in U.S. custody in Iraq at that time. Thousands of potential fighters are hearing calls to go to Iraq to fight the infidel, according to European and Arab intelligence sources.

After the meeting at the safe house in February, Iranian authorities placed Zarqawi, a 42-year-old Jordanian, under house arrest. Zarqawi was the head of a cluster of Arabs who had attached themselves to Ansar al-Islam, a Kurdish fundamentalist group vowing to establish an Islamic state in northern Iraq. Ansar is believed to be closely allied with al-Qaeda, according to the U.S. government. He also believed to have a network of contacts in the Middle East and Europe. Zarqawi was wanted in connection with a planned hotel bombing in Amman on the eve of the millennium celebrations and with the assassination of U.S. diplomat Laurence M. Foley in October 2002. Jordan had requested that Iran extradite Zarqawi to Jordan, but was rebuffed by Iran.

Secretary of State Colin L. Powell said at the U.N. in February 2003 that Zarqawi was a key link between the government of Saddam Hussein and al-Qaeda. Zarqawi was released from house arrest and allowed safe passage along smuggling routes to Iraq, the source said. The U.S. had charged but never proved to the satisfaction of others on the U.N. Security Council that Zarqawi was al-Qaeda's man in Iraq.

An internal German law-enforcement report on al-Qaeda described Zarqawi as someone who has "assumed leadership responsibilities" that has been delegated "from the original center to the regional level."

According to Arab and U.S. officials who have been briefed on American interrogations, almost all of the senior figures in captivity have been cooperating with the United States, which has employed a variety of stress techniques that stop short of direct physical abuse or torture to disorient the prisoners and break their morale. In some cases, U.S. officials who are holding these senior al-Qaeda figures at secret locations have created a parallel universe to hasten their cooperation. Some of the captives, for instance, have been given magazines that are, in fact, written and printed by the CIA. Stories in these phony publications include reports that bin Laden had been killed or that the Saudi government had fallen in a coup d'etat, the Arab official said.

The operational leadership in Iran, despite some of the statements issued by bin Laden or Zarqawi, felt that another spectacular attack in the United States was operationally impossible, according to the analyses by Arab intelligence agencies. The leadership could only hope that the Taliban could regroup in Afghanistan, as it appears to be doing, and that other radicals would rally to the al-Qaeda cause of their own volition and commit atrocities in its name, according to the article. Zarqawi has since become the mastermind behind the attacks and kidnapping in Iraq according to U.S. reports.

In an attempt to round up suspected terrorists, the FBI conducted a sting operation, which could be considered entrapment, since the U.S. agent approached the suspect with the idea. Money enticement has been known to get people to do strange and bizarre things.

According to an August 13, 2003, New York Times report by Steve Trunks, a suspected arms dealer was arraigned on August 13, 2003, on federal charges that he allegedly tried to sell shoulder-fired missiles to an undercover agent posing as a Muslim terrorist bent on shooting down an airliner. Hemet Lakhani, 68, a British citizen described as a "significant international arms dealer," was ordered held without bail pending a custody hearing. He was charged with attempting to provide material support and resources to terrorists and acting as an arms broker without a license. Lakhani was arrested on August 12, 2003, at a hotel near Newark International Airport, where he had flown from London to close the deal on a sophisticated Russian SA-18 Igla missile capable of bringing down commercial airplanes. According to an FBI affidavit filed to support the charges, Larkhani also asked for a commitment from the Russian "suppliers" – actually undercover Russian agents – for 50 more missiles to be sent to the United States by August 30 and also said he was interested in purchasing a ton of C-4 plastic explosives. U.S. Attorney Christopher J. Christie described Lakhani as a "significant international arms dealer."

The Muslim extremist who wanted the missile actually was an FBI informant and the weapon was an inoperable copy brought from Russia to the United States aboard a ship to make the deal seem real, officials said. Lakhani is not believed to be connected to al-Qaeda or any other known terrorist group, federal officials said. Authorities also stressed that there was no specific, credible threat to shoot down an airliner in the United States, according to the report.

According to an August 14, 2003, World AP Asia article by Steve Gutterman, Russia's Federal Security Service said it began monitoring Lakhani once it realized he was trying to contact sellers of shoulder-fired missiles, the ITAR-Tass news agency reported. "He was taken under full control, allowing the (service) to establish the seriousness of his intentions, which he strove to realize by any means possible," said an unnamed security service official, reported ITAR-Tass. Lakhani's contacts in Russia included representatives of organized crime, the agency reported. David Lipsom, chief engineer at the factory that produces the Igla SA-18 missile, defended the plant's security, saying "like any other civilized country, our factories are guarded, all the weapons have codes, and weapons in and out of use are registered." He said there was an attempt to steal weapons the year before from another factory, but it was prevented.

Because of the potential terrorist threat of shooting down commercial planes using missiles, the Homeland Security Department has asked U.S. high-tech companies to look into developing anti-missile technology for commercial planes.

On August 13, 2003, Yahoo.com News reported that representative John Mica, Republican from Florida and chairman of the House aviation subcommittee, said the technology is available to provide a defense system "at a fairly reasonable cost and we have moved that program forward." Talking on CBS's "The Early Show," he said "we do not have to put it on every plane, but we should have a system that's converted to commercial use." He noted that a single piece of baggage screening equipment cost almost $1 million and about $800,000 to $1 million per plane for a defense system. He said it should be on all new aircraft and some selected other planes that carry large numbers of people, just like we do with air marshals.

Senator Charles Schumer, Democrat from New York, backed a bill introduced by Senator Barbara Boxer, Democrat from California that calls for outfitting all of the roughly 6,800 planes in the United States commercial fleet with anti-missile defenses. The cost is estimated at $10 billion. Schumer said that the danger of an airliner being shot down by one of these missiles is now staring the Homeland Security Department in the face. The fact that the DHS is planning to take at least two years to develop a missile defense prototype to outfit the U.S. commercials fleet verges on the dangerous. In the meantime, the United States sent experts to domestic airports as well as to airports in Iraq and major capitals in Europe and Asia to assess security. The investigators are trying to determine whether the airports can be defended against shoulder-fired missiles, according to the article.

On October 7, 2003, the Bush administration's special envoy to Afghanistan, Zalmay Khalilzad, warned that the Taliban and al-Qaeda might be planning "larger" or "more spectacular attacks" in Afghanistan as part of a campaign against the reconstruction process. He said, "We have seen a surge in activity, but we also see signs that the response has been quite effective, and I think in desperation they may try, or there are indications that they may try, to do something to get a lot of attention." At the time, Mr. Khalilzad was awaiting congressional hearings on his appointment to be ambassador to Afghanistan.

As the Bush administration stepped up the pressure on Saudi Arabia to crack down on militants, Saudi authorities announced on December 3, 2003, that they had arrested a suspect in the November 8, 2003, bombing attack that killed 18 people in the capital of Riyadh, and that they had seized a cache of weapons and explosives. Security forces arrested scores of militants in the past year, but many more remain at large. According to reports, a statement from the American embassy said the security situation is problematic, particularly in housing compounds in the Riyadh area. It said confirmation indicates that the Sedr Village housing compound in Riyadh has been under active surveillance by terrorist elements, and that the other Western compounds may also be targeted. A British embassy statement said there was a continuing high threat of terrorism in Saudi Arabia. The threats include, but are not limited to, residential compounds. On November 25, 2003, Saudi authorities intercepted a terrorist vehicle laden with explosives, killing the two suspected militants, and seizing the vehicle, which was primed for explosion.

After much criticism of the Bush administration's handling of the Guantanamo Bay detainees, by refusing to charge them and/or to let them have access to attorneys, the Bush administration gave the appearance that it was softening its position.

The following is an excerpt from a December 3, 2003, Reuters article:

> A military lawyer has been assigned to defend an Australian al-Qaeda suspect being held in Guantanamo Bay, but no charges have been filed and no trial date had been set. The assignment of a military lawyer to defend David Hicks is the first time a foreign terror suspect imprisoned at the U.S. military base in Cuba has been allowed access to a lawyer. This comes only days after the Pentagon said a U.S.- born man captured in Afghanistan would get a defense attorney. Hicks, 28, an Islamic convert from South Australia, was caught fighting for the Taliban in Afghanistan in November 2001. He has been named as one of the first six prisoners eligible for trial before a U.S. military commission.
>
> At that time, the Appointing Authority, Deputy Secretary of Defense Paul Wolfowitz, had not made the decision to approve charges and refer Hicks' case to trial. Since no charges had been approved, no trial date was set. A Pentagon spokesman said the assignment of a lawyer to Hicks did not set a precedent for other Guantanamo Bay detainees to have defense counsel, and declined to elaborate on why Hicks was chosen to be the first foreign suspect assigned a lawyer.

Also, the Pentagon said it would allow Yaser Esam Hamdi, 22, a U.S.-born man captured in Afghanistan in 2001 and held at a Navy jail in Charleston, South Carolina, to have access to a lawyer, "as a matter of discretion and military policy" because interrogators have finished collecting intelligence from him, after denying him counsel for two years and has not been charged with a crime.

The Pentagon's decision to allow Hamdi to confer with a lawyer came one day before the Justice Department filed a brief with the Supreme Court asking it to uphold a ruling by an appeals court that President Bush was within his rights as wartime president to detain Hamdi indefinitely without access to a lawyer. The United States does not recognize the detainees as prisoners of war, but as "enemy combatants." According to a report, the Pentagon's decision to allow Hamdi to have access to a lawyer is probably more a gesture to appease critics, rather than a change in its policy. The administration contends in its brief that Hamdi is not entitled to challenge his detention nor his designation as an enemy combatant.

On December 3, 2003, a federal appeals court panel ruled that crucial parts of an antiterrorism law were unconstitutional because the law, which the Bush administration relies on heavily, risks ensnaring innocent humanitarians. The ruling from the U.S. Court of Appeals for the Ninth Circuit, in San Francisco, casts doubts into the reliance of parts of a 1986 law that make it a crime to provide material support to groups designated as terrorists.

Countries whose citizens are being held indefinitely question the Bush administration policy to hold these foreign citizens without charges. For example, a November 7, 2003, Reuters article said France demanded clear information from the United States on why six French citizens are being held on the American military base in Guantanamo Bay, Cuba. The six were arrested in early 2002 held by the United States as "enemy combatants," not prisoners of war that would be granted a wide range of protections under international law. Herve Ladsous, a Foreign Minister spokesman, said "We are asking that the U.S. authorities provide us with precise information regarding why they arrested these prisoners and what they are charged with." French officials flew to Guantanamo Bay twice in 2002, soon after the arrests.

A U.N. human rights body described the detention of Frenchmen and Spaniards in Guantanamo Bay as illegal. The Bush administration has been under increased pressure from a number of countries and human rights groups since Bush invoked broad presidential powers after September 11, 2001, to detain suspected terrorists outside the civilian court system.

According to a December 11, 2003, Washington Post article, a German court ordered that the September 11, 2001, hijacker suspect, Moroccan-born Abdelghani Mzoudi, age 31, be released. This was a result of the courts being informed by fax by German federal police that they had received information, apparently from a central al-Qaeda planner now in American custody, that the defendant had no advance knowledge of the plot. Mzoudi has been imprisoned since his arrest in late 2002 on charges of membership in a terrorist organization and more than 3,000 counts of accessory to murder. The judge said Mzoudi, allegedly linked to the so-called "Hamburg cell" of al-Qaeda, will have to continue to attend the trial but is otherwise free until a verdict is reached. This decision could also affect the conviction of Mounir Motassadeq, another Moroccan, who was convicted of the same charges earlier in the year and sentenced to 15 years in prison.

Because of the December 18, 2003, San Francisco appellate court ruling that prisoners held at Guantanamo Bay have access to lawyers, the Pentagon appointed a military defense lawyer Navy Lt. Commander Charles Swift to represent another detainee, Salim Ahmed Hamdan of Yemen. Also on December 18, 2003, an appellate court in New York ruled that President Bush does not have the power to declare an American citizen seized on U.S. soil an "enemy combatant" and hold him indefinitely in military custody.

According to a report, one British detainee Moazzan Begg is among the first six prisoners cleared for possible trial. His parents said he had gone to Afghanistan to do humanitarian work – set up a school, install water pipes – and was picked up in Pakistan by American soldiers at the house where he was staying. "It is nearly a complete year since I have been in custody," he wrote to his parents. "After all this time, I still don't know what crime I am supposed to have committed. I am beginning to lose the fight against depression and hopelessness."

One has to wonder how many innocent men are incarcerated without a glimpse of hope of being released.

As the Bush administration fights to maintain its policy regarding detained suspected terrorists, the Justice Department said it would ask the Supreme Court to overturn a ruling which said that President Bush lacked the power to order an American citizen seized on U.S. soil held as enemy combatant. In its ruling, a federal appeals court in New York ordered the government to release Jose Padilla – a U.S. citizen who has been branded an "enemy combatant" – from military custody within 30 days. Padilla was in custody in the United States for 19 months as a suspect in an alleged al-Qaeda plot to detonate a radioactive "dirty bomb". According to the ruling, only the U.S. Congress – and not the president – can authorize such detentions. On November 22, 2005, Padilla was indicted on federal charge on three counts that he conspired to murder U.S. citizens, to provide material support to terrorists and providing material support to terrorists. Some believe that the U.S. decided to indict him in order to prevent his case from going to the Supreme Court.

According to a January 9, 2004, Washington Post article by Charles Lane and Fred Barbash, the Supreme Court announced that it would decide whether the Constitution authorizes President Bush's claim that he can order the indefinite detention of U.S. citizens captured abroad fighting for terrorist groups, a key element of his legal strategy in the war on terrorism. In a brief order, the justice rebuffed repeated Bush administration requests to turn down the appeal of Yaser Esam Hamdi, a U.S.-born Saudi and alleged Taliban fighter who was taken into custody by U.S. forces in Afghanistan in late 2001. A Richmond-based federal appeals court had ruled in the administration's favor, accepting the administration's view that the judicial branch should not second-guess the executive to consider military matters.

Since 9/11, the Bush administration has been arresting so-called terrorist suspects not only abroad but also in the U.S. and detaining them, some without charges. The following January 5, 2004, New York Times article by Linda Greenhouse headlined New Group Seeks to Open Secret Case, is indicative of the types of secrecy that is going on in the Bush administration in the name of terrorism:

A coalition of news and legal organizations is seeking public access to information about a post-September 11 detention case before the Supreme Court that has been handled with unusual secrecy both there and in the lower federal courts. The appeal has been filed by the federal Public Defender's office in Miami on behalf of Mohamed Kamel Bellahouel, an Algerian-born resident of South Florida and one of more than 1,000 Arab men swept up and imprisoned following the terrorist attacks of September 11, 2001. All of the lower-court records, including the actual decisions, are sealed, so there is little public information about the case. It was filed at the Supreme Court using only Bellahouel's initials, M.K.B. v. Warden, No. 03-6747.

A brief will be filed at the court on January 5, 2004, by the Reporters Committee for Freedom of the Press on behalf of 23 media organizations and other groups, including the American Immigration Lawyers Association, requesting the court's permission to intervene in the case. If granted, the request would give the organizations, which include The New York Times, The Washington Post and CNN the status of parties, with a direct stake in the outcome, rather than simply "friends of the court." They will argue that all information regarding the case should be made public except for material that is classified or truly required for national security purposes to be kept secret.

Much of the information available comes from The Miami Daily Business Review, which learned about the case in March when it was pending before the U. S. Courts of Appeals for the 11th Circuit, in Atlanta. The clerk's office of the appeals court inadvertently and briefly listed the case on a public docket. Previously, not even the existence of the case had been made public. The publicly available version of the Supreme Court petition omits many details, including even the identities of the lower courts, and includes blank pages. The Justices received complete versions. Bellahouel worked as a waiter in a restaurant in Delray Beach, Florida that the FBI says was patronized by at least two September 11 hijackers, Mohamed Atta and Marwan al-Shehhi.

During his five-month imprisonment at the Krome Detention Center in Miami, Bellahouel was taken to Alexandria, Virginia, to testify before the grand jury that was investigating Zacarias Moussaoui. The government did not charged Ballahouel with any terrorism-related crimes and apparently did not regard him as a threat. He has been free on $10,000 immigration bond since March 2002 and faces possible deportation for having overstayed the student visa on which he entered the country to attend Florida Atlantic University in 1996. His wife is a U.S. citizen.

While in custody, Bellahouel sought release through a petition for a writ of habeas corpus filed in Federal District Court in Miami. Judge Paul C. Huck closed all proceedings in the case, which was never listed on the court's public docket. The 11th Circuit then maintained the secrecy, holding an argument behind closed doors on March 5, 2003, and issuing its decision under a seal on March 31.

Furthermore, the Bush administration has been kidnapping suspected terrorists and sending them abroad to be tortured. In an April 11, 2005, interview on KPBS Washington Week with Gwen Ifell, CIA director Porter Goss confirmed that the U.S. is outsourcing torture by sending suspected terrorists to foreign countries without explanation or legal counsel to undergo mental and physical torture at the hands of unknown human rights violators. This policy is known as "Rendition."

Rendition allows the CIA to work with foreign intelligence to kidnap, and snatch suspects and take them on airplanes, usually in the dead of night to some other country without informing anyone, not even the family or the country's political leaders. Usually that person disappears. In some cases individuals pop back out and talk about their cases. Germany, Sweden and Italy said they would investigate the CIA Rendition, and are outraged. Italy is set to bring charges against U.S. agents.

Gwen asked Goss, "You take someone away from U.S. laws and rules to a country which has a more liberal understanding of what torture is and let them do the investigating?" Goss replied, "That is it. That is part of it. It started out as a way to get people off the streets who the agency believes are bad people, but there is no way they can bring them to court because they don't have the sort of evidence you would need to do that." Gwen then asked, "You would need to do that? Warehouse people somewhere where they'll never get out and never stand trial?"

But it has also become a way after 9/11 where they send people that they no longer believe they can get information out of to other countries, and by coincidence, a lot of these countries have bad human rights records, as stated in the human rights reports as using tactics that are illegal in the United States. It is illegal for the United States to send any person to a country where they believe that the person is more likely than not to be tortured, according to the KPBS report.

On January 24, 2005, BBC news reported that the U.S. picked up more than 100 people in Europe and sent them to countries to be tortured, while Europe turned a blind eye. In response, Secretary of State Condoleezza Rice said the U.S. does not condone torture.

A February 13, 2006, New York Times article reported that European Parliament set up a temporary committee to look into media reports alleging the U.S. intelligence service carried out abductions and "rendition" flights carrying prisoners and ran secret detention centers in the 25-nation bloc.

Amnesty International also reported on August 3, 2005, that two Yemeni men said they were held in solitary confinement in secret, underground U.S. detention facilities in an unknown country and interrogated by masked men for more than 18 months without being charged or allowed any contact with the outside world.

Ironically, according to an April 30, 2005, New York Times article by Don Van Natta Jr., seven months before September 11, 2001, the U.S. State Department issued a human rights report on Uzbekistan accusing them of using torture methods such as beating with blunt weapons and asphyxiation with a gas mask. However, immediately after the September 11 attacks, the Bush administration turned to Uzbekistan as a partner in fighting global terrorism by sending terror suspects to Uzbekistan for detention and interrogation.

The Bush administration, after being adamant about holding suspected terrorists indefinitely, it has rescinded its decision on a number of cases. For example, the Bush administration officials said it would return some British prisoners to England. In addition, it returned two Iranian filmmakers Saeed Aboutaleb and Soheil Karimi to their homes, after they were being held for four months by U.S.-led coalition forces in neighboring Iraq on suspicion of spying. These men work for Iran's state-run television station and were detained by U.S. troops on July 1, 2002, when they were spotted filming a U.S. military base, according to reports.

The Bush administration has also arrested an attorney for suspicion of being a part of the Madrid bombing. According to the U.S., Wakefield's fingerprints were found on a piece of bomb equipment. Wakefield was later released after being held without bail. The U.S. finally admitted that Mr. Wakefield was innocent and released him.

Since these prisoners are denied any rights to see a lawyer, to receive visitors, or to speak to their families, the mental and physical abuses are hidden from the public. And, although the Bush administration claimed that the detainees were not being abused, there were two detainees who suffered from the same injuries, according to a report. These detainees are only suspects, they have not even been charged with a crime.

A February 4, 2004, Washington Post article by Jerry Markon stated:

> A U.S. citizen, Yaser Esam Hamdi, jailed since his capture with Taliban soldiers in Afghanistan in 2001, met his attorneys for the first time on February 4, 2004. His federal public defender, Frank W. Dunham Jr., said he was pleased to finally see the man whose case he has litigated – sight unseen – for more than two years. Dunham said "seeing the client in person, being able to put a human face on this case, had an effect on me that is not measurable." He also said, "I am sure it made an impression on a client who has been looking down a lightless tunnel for 2-1/2 years, not knowing anyone is doing anything for him, and now he knows that he has a case

in the U.S. Supreme Court." The meeting however, was not private, in that military observers attended and recorded the meeting. Also, Dunham was not allowed to question his client about the conditions of his confinement. "We were not able to talk about anything substantive," Dunham said. Hamdi is the first of three people known to have been designated enemy combatants by the military to meet with an attorney.

According to a September 22, 2004, New York Times article by Eric Lichtblau, Hamdi would be free and allowed to return to Saudi Arabia. The agreement reached was driven by a Supreme Court decision in June. The court found that Mr. Hamdi and enemy combatants like him had to be given the chance to challenge their detention. The court declared that "a state of war is not a blank check for the president." The agreement requires Hamdi to renounce his American citizenship, and bars him from leaving Saudi Arabia for a time, and that he should report possible terrorist activity.

Some lawyers will not take part in representing suspected terrorists for ethical reasons. According to an August 12, 2003, CNN News report, many defense lawyers said that the Pentagon's restrictions on outside lawyers would make it unethical for them to participate alongside military defense lawyer sin a tribunal trial.

Alfred P. Carlton Jr., who left his post as ABA president on August 12, 2003, said he, for one, could not sign a list of promises the Pentagon says it will require of any lawyer who wants to participate. One point of contention is the government's ability to listen to conversations between suspects and their lawyers. The ABA may object to a requirement that tribunal lawyers get government permission before talking about the case outside the courtroom, and other rules.

The Bush administration position on terrorists is even being criticized by Judge Advocate General's Corps, (JAGs) the military's legal arm. They have attacked the tribunals as inherently unfair, contrary to international law and susceptible to political influence.

As the pressure mounts for the U.S. to either charge these suspected terrorists or release them, the Bush administration assigned an attorney to represent Salim Ahmed Handan. A March 18, 2004, Wall Street Journal article reported that Lt. Cmdr. Charles Swift, a Navy lawyer, was assigned to defend him before a military tribunal. After 15 meetings with his client, Cmdr. Swift says he's shed any misgivings he harbored about Hamdan, a 34-year-old Yemeni who has been in detention since being captured in Afghanistan in late 2001. Cmdr. Swift plans to argue that statements made by other detainees were coerced and that Hamdan was merely a poorly educated functionary desperate for a job to support his family. He has two children, ages 2 and 4. He has never seen his second child. In a brief they submitted to the Supreme Court, Cmdr. Swift wrote a section comparing the president with King George II and likening the treatment of tribunal defendants to the injustices that helped spark the American Revolution.

The JAGs plan to challenge virtually every aspect of the administration's policies on Guantanamo Bay detainees, from the denial of protections of the Geneva Conventions to the interrogation methods used in extracting statements. This may force the Bush administration either to answer in open court or risk undercutting its long-standing promise that the tribunals will be full and fair. Citing national security concerns, President Bush decreed the tribunals free from federal court review, "the principals of law and the rules of evidence" used in civilian trials and the rights afforded U.S. military defendants in court martial. That gives the tribunal members, who are military officers selected by the Pentagon, vast leeway to consider hearsay, unsworn statements and other evidence that wouldn't pass muster under normal court procedures. Defendants are entitled to a military defense lawyer and, at their own expense, a civilian lawyer who can pass security checks. But they are not guaranteed the right to see all the evidence against them.

The JAGs, including Air Force Col. Will Gun, the Harvard-trained lawyer who heads the defense office, each had to consider what effect their new job might have on their military careers. Instead of moving into a top post in the Air Force JAG Corps, as he had expected. "I am now being asked to coordinate the defense efforts of ... People who are identified as enemies of the nation," Col. Gun says. That's a fairly high-risk proposition."

After several calls for examination into President Bush's order to arrest and hold suspected terrorists indefinitely, the Supreme Court heard the first major challenge.

According to an April 21, 2004, Wall Street Journal article by Jess Bravin, a lawyer for prisoners at the American Naval base in Cuba declared that the United States wanted to create a "lawless enclave" there. John Gibbons told the justices that what is at stake is the authority of the federal courts to uphold the rule of law. But Solicitor General Theodore B. Olson, arguing on behalf of the Bush administration said the United States is at war. The administration claims that the base, which is leased from Cuba, is outside U.S. sovereignty, and therefore beyond the reach of its courts. It won the backing of lower courts before the Supreme Court agreed to review the case. The U.S. leases the land based on a 1903 agreement with the pre-Castro Cuban government. The question before the justices was whether federal courts have jurisdiction over the open-ended detention of noncitizens being held at the navy base at Guantanamo Bay, Cuba. Olson said over 10,000 American troops are in Afghanistan in response to a virtually unanimous congressional declaration of an unusual and extraordinary threat to our national security and an authorization to the president to use all necessary and appropriate force to deter and prevent acts of more attacks like those of September 11, 2001.

My concern regarding Olson's reply which should be the concern of every well-thinking American is what happens when all three houses are controlled by the same party.

Everyone knows how difficult it is to have bipartisanship. I can't imagine any meaningful checks and balances taking place under these circumstances.

And, according to an April 28, 2004, New York Times article by David Stout, lawyers for the two American citizens, Yaser Esam Hamdi and Jose Padilla, held in a Navy brig, told the Supreme Court that the treatment of their clients was contrary to America's law and heritage. The lawyer for Hamdi told the justices that "We have never authorized detention of a citizen in this country without giving him an opportunity to be heard. But Deputy Solicitor General Paul D. Clement said nothing in Hamdi's treatment is unusual or illogical. "It has been well established and long established that the government has the authority to hold both unlawful enemy combatants and lawful prisoners of war captured on the battlefield. No principal of the law or logic requires the United States to release an individual from detention so that he can rejoin the battle."

The lawyer for Padilla Jennifer Martinez argued that the detention of her client "is exactly the type of detention that our founding Fathers were concerned about, based on their experience with the British crown. She asserted that the government's argument, if upheld, would allow the president unlimited power to imprison any American anywhere at any time without trial simply by labeling him an enemy combatant. Clement said it has never been the case that prisoners of war are entitled to counsel to challenge their capture or their detention. If a prisoner of war is charged with a specific crime, then the Geneva Conventions specify that he should have counsel. But if a prisoner is simply held in a preventive detention, he is not allowed counsel.

No cameras were allowed during the Supreme Court hearings on the prisoners held as "enemy combatants." Also some parts of the hearings could be heard on tapes, but some parts were omitted, and you would see just pictures of the justices relative to the questions being asked or answered.

And, regarding Saddam Hussein's trial, the U.S. said it would turn Saddam over to the Iraqi interim government for trial. However, he will remain in the U.S. custody. In other words, this is just another example of the Bush administration's fallacy or double-talk.

According to a Wall Street Journal article by Barry E. Carter, since the U.N. Security Council recognized the U.S. and Britain as occupying powers under international law, the two countries are subject to the rules and provisions of the four Geneva Conventions of 1949. A U.S. military tribunal is one legal way to proceed against Iraqi prisoners of war or even Iraqi civilians accused of war crimes or the broader category of crimes against humanity. The Third Geneva Convention of POWs requires that these tribunals operate in the same fashion as would similar proceedings against U.S. soldiers, which include extensive due-process protections. Another approach would have the Iraqi national courts try these Iraqis. Or to use the Special Court model that was created in 2002 by the U.N. and the new Sierra Leone government, whereby the U.N. appointed five judges and Sierra Leone appointed three. However, the Bush administration has shied away from an international tribunal, because of its wide-ranging jurisdiction for various crimes. The U.N. has criticized the U.S. for not providing clear procedures for the more than 10,000 Iraqi civilians in U.S. prison in Iraq.

After numerous discussions regarding the trial of Saddam Hussein, the Iraqi leaders announced on April 19, 2004, that they have set up a tribunal to try him and other members of his Baathist regime. Salem Chalabi, the nephew of the head of the Iraqi National Congress, was named to head the tribunal of judges and prosecutors. Seven judges were assigned to the tribunal with more judges and prosecutors to be chosen. French attorney Jacques Verges, who has made a name for himself representing notorious world figures, has said he will lead a team of defense lawyers in a future trial. He said he plans to call top U.S. officials to testify about their support of Saddam during the 1980s.

The trial of Saddam Hussein started with many post-ponements. Several members of the courts were either assassinated or resigned. Prosecutors press charges against him for execution, and many Iraqis want him to get the death penalty. At the time this book went to press, Saddam's trial was still under way.

According to a December 30, 2003, Reuter's article, Defense Secretary Donald Rumsfeld named a retired Army major general, John Altenburg, as overseer of U.S. military trials for foreign terrorism suspects. Altenburg will appoint members of the panels that will hear the trials. The Pentagon also said former U.S. Attorney General Griffin Bell, former U.S. Representative Edward Biester, former Secretary of Transportation William Coleman and Chief Justice of the Rhode Island Supreme Court Frank Williams will be named major generals in the Army and will serve on a military review panel that will hear appeals to any convictions or sentences. The trials are to be held at the U.S. naval base at Guantanamo Bay, Cuba, where approximately 660 non-U.S. citizens are being held without charges at a prison base, most of whom were captured in Afghanistan.

Altenburg will oversee many aspects of the military commissions, including approving charges against suspects who President Bush deems subject to trial before these tribunals. Altenburg's other duties will include approving plea agreements. Rules created for the military trials have come under harsh criticism from some members of the legal community and human rights groups who say the procedures are heavily biased in favor of the prosecution. Rules announced stated that hearsay evidence will be permitted and the government will be permitted to monitor any communications between defendants and their lawyers.

A February 25, 2004, Wall Street Journal article said that the Defense Department announced that two alleged aides to Osama bin Laden would stand trial before U.S. military tribunals at Guantanamo Bay, resurrecting a legal proceeding last used against Axis war criminals of World War II.

The government accused Ibrahim Ahmed Mahmoud al Qosi of Sudan of joining the al-Qaeda terrorist network in 1989 and working since then to help finance and supply the group, and serving as a fighter, accountant and bodyguard for bin Laden. A second defendant, Ali Hamza Ahmed Sulayman al Bahlul of Yemen, was accused of joining al-Qaeda in 1999 and working in its "media office," preparing recruiting videos that glorified the 2000 attack on the U.S.S. Cole and collecting data on the economic impact of the September 11, 2001, terrorist attacks on the U.S. Both men captured in December 2001 and held at the U.S. Naval Base in Cuba, are charged with conspiracy.

In the meantime, members of Congress called for the U.S. to concentrate more efforts in finding bin Laden. But, the administration flip-flops on the message they send to the American people. One day the Bush administration said that it was not necessary to capture bin Laden, because he has taken himself out of the leadership position. This is after Bush made a promise to the American people to rid the world of bin Laden dead or alive. Then, during a pre-Christmas morale-boosting visit, the chairman of the U.S. Joint Chiefs of Staff, Gen. Richard Myers, made the statement to U.S. troops in Afghanistan that bin Laden is probably alive and will be caught one day "with absolute certainty."

The American people want the U.S. to go after Osama bin Laden, since he is responsible for the September 11 attacks, not Saddam Hussein, but to no avail. The Bush administration said catching Osama bin Laden would be difficult. Yet the Bush administration officials blame the Clinton administration for not getting rid of Osama bin Laden. But if we are to believe them, then we should also believe that the Clinton administration experienced similar difficulties. However, he may already be in U.S. custody somewhere in Afghanistan or Iraq. There was a rumor in

March 2004 that the U.S. has either captured or killed bin Laden and that they are waiting for an opportune time to announce either his capture or his demise.

On August 20, 1998, the Clinton administration bombed bin Laden's training camps in Afghanistan, killing dozens of his associates, but missed bin Laden by mere hours. Using Tomahawk missiles, they also blew up a pharmaceutical plant. However, his Republican critics claimed that he used the bombing to take the pressure off the Monica Lewinsky scandal. They related the bombing to the movie "Wag the Dog."

One should be reminded that it was the United States who helped al-Qaeda defeat the Russians in Afghanistan in 1989 by supplying them with ammunition. It is now believed that bin Laden has operations in over 60 countries. A November 23, 2003, Newsweek report estimated that more than 3,000 terrorists live in the United States – some as sleeper cells. The report also said that the cost of the September 11 attacks to al-Qaeda was only $400,000. How misguided the whole situation is, it is costing the U.S. hundreds of billions of dollars and tens of thousands of lives will be lost to defeat Saddam Hussein who had nothing to do with 9/11.

According to a March 7, 2004, Associated Press article, as a sign that the U.S. was planning an all-out search to capture the Talibans it prepared its usual feast for the soldiers just before the attack. The Kandahar base cafeteria dished out steak and lobster to the soldiers and stubble-faced Special Forces, perhaps in keeping with a U.S. Army tradition of laying out feasts on the eve of major operations. The next day, U.S. forces launched Mountain Storm, which would unfold across eastern and southern Afghanistan to hunt down fugitives from the al-Qaeda network and the former Taliban regime.

"There are a lot of U.S. coalition forces, and a lot of patrols – much more than the previous two years," Gen. Khan Mohammed, corps commander of Afghan government militia in the south, said. Some 70,000 Pakistani troops have moved into semiautonomous tribal regions on the Pakistan side of the frontier to take away maneuver room from al-Qaeda and Taliban fugitives believed to have taken refuge there.

At Kandahar air base, observers said modified Chinooks of the kind used by Special Forces in Iraq were among the aircraft seen landing there. One or two of the Special Forces here, ever recognizable in mirrored sunglasses and black-window four-wheel drives, admitted to being newly arrived in the country, according to the article.

On March 11, 2004, BBC News reported that Pakistan President Pervez Musharraf told the U.S. a resounding no to allowing the U.S. to enter Afghanistan from the Pakistan border to search for al-Qaeda operatives. But because a Pakistani scientist admitted to selling nuclear secrets to Iran, Libya and Syria, as a compromise Musharraf relented and let the U.S. enter Afghanistan from Pakistan to search the Afghanistan Pakistan border. The U.S. then started to send equipment and troops into Pakistan to start the manhunt.

Then on March 18, 2004, Pakistan officials said they had cornered al-Qaeda's No.2 man, Ayman al-Zawahiri and the U.S. said they were helping. However, the BBC news report was that the U.S. would be in charge of the search for al-Qaeda.

On March 19, 2004, Pakistani officials said that thousands of Pakistani soldiers backed by artillery and helicopter gunship made limited progress advancing into a 10-square-mile pocket of farming villages where 300 to 600 suspected militants have been surrounded near the border with Afghanistan. They said they believed al-Zawahiri may be trapped with the group in the South Waziristan tribal area. One report said they believe he was injured. One of their reasons to suspect that someone of importance like al-Zawahiri was there was because of the five body guards who guard only Osama bin Laden or al-Zawahiri. Of course, there was no mention that they believe Osama bin Laden was also there or that the search was intended to find him. On Monday, March 22, the announcement came that the militants escaped through a tunnel. However, The Times of London reported that a senior U.S. official said that an autopsy was being done on a body to see if it were that of al-Qaeda No. 2 man, al-Zawahiri. Of course, there was no mention that the search was for bin Laden.

A Reuters report of March 22, 2004, said that international forces found a location where fugitive al-Qaeda chief Osama bin Laden is thought to have taken refuge, according to French Defense Minister Michele Alliot-Marie. She said in an interview that French troops operating near Afghanistan's border with Pakistan had helped trace bin Laden but did not say where, how wide an area she was referring to or whether he was still there. "Our men are well established and know the terrain well. Thanks to certain information, they were recently able to make an effective contribution to locating him," Alliot-Marie told Express magazine.

Also, the Bush administration flip-flops on the "New Front on Terror." Just after Iraq was toppled, the Bush administration said Iraq was the "New Front on Terror." Then after the attacks in Turkey, speaking in England, Bush remarked "Turkey is the "New Front on Terror." What does that mean? Are we going to defend Turkey also by positioning troops there? I doubt that Turkey would want American troops controlling their military facilities. In an apparent appeasement, the Turkish government agreed that the U.S. could use its air space to fly supplies to Iraq, after refusing the U.S. access to use its airstrips to attack Iraq.

It appears that every time the Bush administration was facing criticism, regarding September 11 or the problems in Iraq, it would come out with a terrorist threat warning. The situation in Iraq deteriorated considerably in April 2004, and true to form, on April 29 the Bush administration came out with a warning that an attack could take place in a mall in Los Angeles, California. How should the American people react when these threats appear to be so convenient to take the heat off the problems and concerns facing the American people? If the U.S. should be attacked again, God forbid, the American people would again be caught by surprise. They heard so many of these purported threats that only appeared when the Bush administration thought its 2004 election may have been in jeopardy that they would probably be inclined to ignore any such future warnings.

As each holiday approached, the Bush administration warned of terrorist attacks on U.S. citizens, both at home and abroad. The warnings caused the states to spend millions of dollars to beef up security for that period. However, when the Bush administration did not provide the states with the necessary funds to defray the costs to put these extra security forces on the alert, the states decided not to take any more action when they receive these warnings. Of course, the warnings were color coded, and would be changed depending on the degree of alert. Once the states decided that they would no longer adhere to the elevated warnings, the Bush administration decided to keep the color code at "Yellow," which means there are no specific targets or specific times.

On November 22, 2003, the government warned of an increased risk of terrorist attacks on Americans at home and overseas and stressed concerns al-Qaeda could try to hijack cargo jets and crash them into targets. The government said terrorist bombings overseas and an increased volume of threats against U.S. interests at home and in foreign countries led the Homeland Security Department and FBI to issue the public warning and an advisory to law enforcement officials and private-sector security personnel.

True to form, as the Christmas holiday approached the U.S. issued another warning that American interests could be subject to attacks from al-Qaeda. There was a report that people are becoming numb to these alerts. There is really nothing the people can do to prevent any attacks. It is incumbent upon the Department of Defense, Homeland Security, the FBI and the CIA to protect the lives of the American people by working closely with other countries to cooperate in providing intelligence information so as to thwart any impending attacks before they become a reality.

Because Al-Jazeera shows tapes it receives from bin Laden or his associates, the U.S. military bombed its TV station early in the war. And a May 8, 2003, Wall Street Journal article by Yochi J. Dreazen reported that the U.S. Army issued orders for troops to seize Mosul's television station, leading an officer to raise questions about the Army's dedication to free speech in postwar Iraq. The officer refused the order and was relieved of his duty. And according to a November 22, 2005, British tabloid newspaper, The Daily Mirror, a secret memo recounted discussions between President Bush and Prime Minister Tony Blair wherein Bush wanted to launch an air strike against Al-Jazeera's headquarters in Qatar during a 2004 meeting at the White House, and that Blair talked him out of it. The Mirror reported that Bush was angered by Al-Jazeera's coverage of the April 2004 uprising in Fallujah.

It appears that al-Qaeda is succeeding in instilling fear in the American people and keep the intelligence community in a quandary, because on December 24, 2003, three days after Arabic television Al-Jazeera aired an audiotape purportedly to be al-Qaeda's second in command, Ayman al-Zawahri, saying the United States was defeated in Afghanistan and his group was chasing Americans everywhere, including the United States, the U.S. told France it would not allow flights coming into the Los Angeles airport from Paris to land because intelligence showed that terrorists are planning to hijack flights from Paris to Los Angeles. France was forced to stop all flights from Paris to Los Angeles for two days, before resuming flights. However, France said it found no evidence that terrorists were planning to hijack its flights into the United States. A name on the passenger manifest similar to that of a Tunisian pilot with possible extremist links ratcheted up concern. But officials said it turned out to be a case of mistaken identity; the name of the passenger was that of a child, a senior official said.

According to a report, the United States persuaded the French, after vigorous lobbying, to post armed marshals on the flights. One French diplomat told the Americans that he was concerned the Paris-Los Angeles flights could be disrupted for an extended period and that the public would see the issue as a result of more diplomatic friction between the two nations, according to a U.S. official who spoke with the envoy. According to a January 1, 2004, New York Times report by Rachael L. Swarns, on New Year's Eve and New Year's Day 2003, British and Mexican airlines canceled two flights into the United States, after receiving warnings from the American and British authorities that linked the flights to possible terrorist attacks. Earlier that week, U.S. officials diverted one flight from Mexico and interviewed the passengers on another flight from Britain after it landed at Dulles International Airport outside of Washington. None of the passengers was arrested on either flight.

Aeromexico's Flight 490 from Mexico City to Los Angeles was canceled on New Year's Eve after American officials advised the airline that it might be the target of terrorist attacks. British Airways Flight 223 from London to Dulles Airport was canceled on New Year's Day.

U.S. officials said American fighter jets have accompanied some flights as they landed in the United States and has required some international flights entering, leaving or passing over the United States to fly with armed air marshals. Approximately 800 to 1,000 flights come into, fly over or fly out of the U.S. every day. Also, the U.S. requires that all flights and cruise ships coming into the U.S. provide passenger lists within a certain number of hours, (I believe 72) before they arrive in the U.S. Also, among the information that must be provided include credit card numbers, itinerary, contact numbers and seat numbers. There is a fine of $6,000 for each passenger, for any company that is not in compliance with the U.S. requirement.

Other apparent "hits" from U.S. terror watch lists turned out to be an elderly Chinese woman who owns a restaurant and a Welsh insurance agent, an FBI official said.

Then, again on January 31, 2004, British Airways and Air France canceled five flights from Europe to the United States after American officials raised concerns about the possibility of terrorist attacks, including hijackings. According to February 1, 2004, New York Times article by Eric Lichtblau, the U.S. urged that armed sky marshals are placed on those routes, but the British and French airlines canceled the flights instead. British Airways canceled Flight 207 from London to Miami on Sunday and flight 223 from London to Dulles on Sunday. John Lampl, a spokesman for the airlines, said the British government told British Airways to "cancel these flights." Air France also canceled Flight 26 from Paris to Washington scheduled for that Sunday and Monday.

A Continental Airlines flight out of Europe was also canceled. U.S. officials said there was nothing on the passenger lists on those flights to arouse concerns. The intelligence pointed to an increased risk involving Air France and British Airways to the United States on Sunday and Monday.

Furthermore, according to a February 2, 2004, Associated Press report, France Transport Minister Giles de Robien said that French intelligence had no indications of its own to support U.S. warnings of a threat to transatlantic flights on Sunday and Monday, and that their decision to cancel the flights was based on the "principle of precaution when there are signals." He said when the Americans send those signals on RFO television, it is completely normal that they work with them against international terrorism.

According to reports, British airline pilots' union expressed strong reservations. An airline spokesman told Agence-France Presse "We have always said we have concerns about having armed people on aircraft. We feel it is best to have strong security on the ground and that is where the focus of attention should be." Another spokesman said "Introducing a weapon into a cabin could lead to that weapon being used against passengers. If the level of risk is so high that a sky marshal has to be deployed, then it would be easier to just not operate that particular flight." The British Airline Pilots Association complained that it was not consulted before the government announced its plan to use sky marshals. The union's general secretary, Jim McAuslan, said, "We cannot agree with the government's decision to put armed guards on aircraft, as we believe this will do more harm than good. We do not want guns on planes." A U.S. official said the cancellation of the British Airways flights was not in response to U.S. safety concerns, but rather was prompted by the refusal of British pilots to fly with armed pilots on board.

The United States has also put other nations on notice that it would not allow certain suspicious flights into its airspace without armed marshals on board.

During these alerts, some officials said they did not know if these alerts thwarted any attacks, so I was surprised when President Bush announced on February 9, 2006, that the U.S. has foiled 10 attacks, namely one at Los Angeles airport.

However, as the election campaign began to heat up, the Bush administration said U.S. and Pakistan were intensifying their search to find bin Laden, believed to be hiding along the Pakistani-Afghanistan border. Also, on January 29, 2004, the Bush administration officials said that they are sure that they will catch bin Laden this year. The Bush administration also raised the color code to "Red," the highest alert. Vice President Dick Cheney said to elect a Democrat as president would be to invite 9/11 all over again. Then, eight days after the election, the color code was changed back to "Yellow", the lowest security risk, and there was no more terrorist alert until October 2005, when Bush's rating dropped below 40, it informed New York Mayor Michael Bloomberg that terrorists were planning to bomb the subways using baby carriages or backpacks. After other countries said they could not corroborate the threat, the Bush administration said it did not expect the mayor to announce the threat.

According to a March 1, 2004, Wall Street Journal article, the Department of Homeland Security also said that it was working on a new plan to station American inspectors in foreign airports to screen passengers. The aim is to identify and catch possible terrorists before they board U.S.-bound planes. European officials said if the inspectors were limited to assisting national authorities or airport security officials by providing intelligence or access to U.S. data, the plan may meet less opposition. But if the plan is to block travelers from boarding planes and in the process possibly usurp local authorities, the idea will arouse strong objections.

Are The Bush Administration Terrorism Policies Stirring Up Conflicts Around The World?

It appears that not only are the Arab nations concerned about the Bush administration policies against them, but Latin American countries such as Brazil has expressed concerns, and has taken retaliatory measures. According to a January 2, 2004, Reuters article, on January 1, 2004, Brazilian police began fingerprinting and photographing U.S. visitors on orders of a judge who compared planned U.S. security controls on travelers from Brazil and other nations to Nazi horrors. Beginning January 5, 2004, people who need visas to enter the United States will be digitally finger-printed and photographed when they pass through immigration at major U.S. airports and seaports. A Brazilian federal judge in the state of Mato Grosso, Julier Sebastiao da Silva, said "I consider the act absolutely brutal, threatening human rights, violating human dignity, xenophobic and worthy of the worst horrors committed by the Nazis."

Will the Bush Administration Policies eradicate Terrorism or escalate it?

According to a January 5, 2004, New York Times article by Christine Hauser, the United States began fingerprinting and photographing foreigners at airports and seaports in a nationwide program that Homeland Security Secretary Tom Ridge said was intended to keep borders open and the country more secure. The new entry procedures were launched at 115 airports and at cruise ship terminals at 14 seaports, according to a news conference given by Tom Ridge in Atlanta on January 5. The program involves taking digital photographs and prints of the two index fingers of foreigners traveling to the United States on a visa. Ridge said that a test-run at Hartsfield-Jackson Atlanta International Airport since November 17, 2003, has screened 20,000 travelers, yielding "21 hits" on the FBI criminal watch list, including people with prior convictions of statutory rape, drugs and visa fraud. Ridge said "It is part of a comprehensive program to ensure that our borders remain open to visitors but closed to terrorists."

But will this program really serve as a deterrent to terrorists or will it just give them another reason to attack wherever, whenever, and whomever they can, using unsuspected subjects? Citizens from 27 mostly European countries will be exempt from the new procedure and will still be allowed to come to the United States for up to 90 days without a visa.

According to a government official on January 5, 2004, a voice heard in the Middle East urging Muslims to continue a holy war against occupiers was probably that of Osama bin Laden. Homeland Security Secretary Tom Ridge said on CBS's "Good Morning America" that a "preliminary assessment" indicated that the voice on the audiotape broadcast on the Arab satellite channel Al Jazeera was indeed that of the al-Qaeda leader. The speaker on the audiotape said that big powers were trying to gain control of the Middle East to take over its oil.

Each time that an audiotape is released purportedly from Osama bin Laden, fresh attacks occur in Iraq. And, true to form, several attacks have occurred since January 5, killing several and injuring many others. Many people believe that the attack on Iraq has only served to escalate terrorist attacks against Americans. Gen. Pervez Musharraf, Pakistan President, speaking at a conference session in Davos Switzerland on January 22, 2004, said the war in Iraq "complicated the already tense situation in which the world found itself" with many Muslims resenting the way their cause was being depicted and feeling a "deep sense of injustice and powerlessness." He said "The world became a very dangerous place to live."

And, on October 13, 2004, former chief U.N. weapons inspector Hans Blix said the U.S.-led invasion of Iraq had failed tragically in its aim of making the world a safer place and succeeded only in stimulating terrorism.

In answer to questions challenging the Bush administration's decision to detain people as "enemy combatants" with no access to lawyers or legal support, U.S. Attorney General John Ashcroft said, "We are winning the war against terrorism," insisting that despite criticism of his record, Washington was respecting the civil rights "at the highest level possible." He also alluded to the attacks of September 11, 2001, that America is at war, giving Washington the right to seize its foes.

However, the world has certainly become a very dangerous place to live, and it appears that it will only get worse before it gets better. According to CNN, on February 24, 2004, tapes attributed to Osama bin Laden's top deputy, Ayman al-Zawahiri, warned that more terror attacks are coming and criticized France's push to ban Islamic head scarves in schools. The messages which heavily criticized U.S. President George W. Bush were aired on the Al-Arabiya and Al-Jazeera Arabic-language TV networks. In the tape aired by the Qatar-based satellite Al-Jazeera, the voice said: "This Islamic nation which sent you the New York and Washington brigades has taken a firm decision to send you successive brigades to sow death and aspire to paradise."

Addressing the American people, the voice said: "whenever you receive a coffin, they should remember the U.S. crimes all over the world." The speaker described Bush as spreading false information in the United States, promoting fear and frustration in the Middle Eastern region, and appointing corrupt leaders. The speaker spoke on what he called Bush's "four claims" – that U.S. forces are trying to promote freedom and security, that U.S. forces helped Iraq to get its freedom, that the U.S. forces captured more than two-thirds of al-Qaeda leaders, and that the situation in Afghanistan is stable. He said al-Qaeda is still waging jihad and "brandishes the banner of Islam against the Zionist-crusader campaign."

In the audiotape broadcast on the Dubai-based Al-Arabiya satellite TV channel, the speaker described the French government efforts to ban head scarves in schools as "part of the West's campaign of hatred against Islam. The decision of the French president (Jacques Chirac) to issue a law to prevent Muslim girls from covering their heads in schools is another example of the Crusader and envy that the Westerners have against Muslims. Banning the head scarves in France is in line with burning villages with its inhabitants in Afghanistan, bringing houses down on the heads of sleeping Palestinians, with killing children in Iraq and robbing their oil using false pretexts...and torturing Muslims in the cells of Guantanamo Bay," the tape said. Al-Arabiya would not disclose how it received the tape purportedly from al-Qaeda's No. 2 man. The last tape believed to have come from the Egyptian-born doctor was released in December. In it, he warned that his fighters are chasing Americans in their homeland.

And, a February 10, 2004, Reuters articles said Al-Qaeda is under pressure to strike another "high-value" Western target and may be looking at attacking chemical plants or shooting down planes with surface-to-air missiles, a top German intelligence official said. "A substantial decline in activities in the next couple of years is highly improbable," Rudolf Adam, deputy head of German's BND foreign intelligence agency, told a security conference in Berlin. On the contrary, we would feel that pressure is mounting on al-Qaeda to reassert its effectiveness and its ability to strike another really big high-value target" in order to remain visible, he said.

Adam said shipping, tourist sites and supply infrastructure such as oil pipelines, power stations, electricity grids and water supplies remained potentially at risk. "We have unspecified hints that plans have been made or are still underway to target the chemical industry and chemical infrastructure," he said, without giving details. He also said that al-Qaeda might consider kidnappings – a tactic it has not previously used – as a bargaining chip to seek the release of prominent members captured during the U.S.-led war on terror. "We have some disturbing evidence that kidnappings have been planned." He said the "first generation" of al-Qaeda had been badly weakened in the war on terror, but even the capture or killing of its leader, Osama bin Laden, would leave a second generation of fighters trained in Afghan camps, and a third generation currently being recruited. "The cancer has already proliferated into innumerable metastases," he said.

Central Intelligence Agency Director George Tenet in February 2004, after his visit to Pakistan, warned that al-Qaeda has been transformed from a terrorist organization into a violent, worldwide Muslim movement that will threaten the U.S. and its allies indefinitely, even if its top leaders are captured. "The steady growth of Osama bin Laden's anti-U.S. sentiment through the wider Sunni extremist movement, and the broad dissemination of al-Qaeda's destructive expertise ensure that a serious threat will remain for the foreseeable future – with or without al-Qaeda in the picture," Tenet told the Senate Intelligence Committee in his assessment of global threats.

According to reports, many people, not just in the Muslim world, feel that the Bush administration was not doing anything to stop the bloodshed in Palestine, and the killing of Hamas leader Sheikh Ahmed Yasin by Israel adds another dimension in the war. An Islamist Web site published a statement purporting to come from an al-Qaeda-linked group vowing revenge on the United States and its allies. "We tell Palestinians that Sheikh Yassin's blood was not spilled in vain and call on all legions of Abu Hafs al-Masri Brigades to avenge him by attacking the tyrant of the age, America, and its allies. Of course, the Bush administration did not condemn Israel's killing of the Hamas leader, and said Israel must defend itself. Israel has also fired rockets on the Lebanon border, saying it was taking pre-emptive measures against attacks. Let's hope this does not bring other neighboring countries into the fray.

And on April 15, 2004, the CIA said that a tape of a man identifying himself as Osama bin Laden probably is an authentic recording of the al-Qaeda leader. The tape referenced the killing of Hamas founder Sheikh Ahmed Yassin by Israel and vows revenge against the United States for the killing. The tape also offered a truce to European countries that do not attack Muslims.

There is an old saying, "Be careful what you ask for." President Bush and his cabinet members have been saying that his pre-emptive strike in Iraq is an indication of his war on terror and that Iraq will be the central front on the war on terror. It appears that this statement has become a self-fulfilling prophecy as the insurgency expands to include a larger confluence.

Amnesty International Says World Is Not Safer.

On May 29, 2003, an Associated Press article by Jane Wardell reported:

Amnesty International reported that the U.S.-led war on terror has made the world a more dangerous and repressive place. The international human rights organization singled out the United States and Britain for detaining terror suspects without trial, under legislation introduced after September 11 attacks. "The war on terror for making the world a safer place, has made it more dangerous by curtailing human rights, undermining the rule of international law and shielding governments from scrutiny," said Irene Kjan, Amnesty International's secretary general, in launching the organization's annual report in London. "The great supporters of human rights during the Cold War now quite readily either roll them back in their own countries or encourage others to do so and turn a blind eye. What would have been unacceptable on September 10, 2001, is now becoming almost the norm," she said.

The report said most of the 1,200 foreign nationals – mostly Muslim men of Arab or South Asian origin detained in the United States during inquiries into the September 11 attacks, were either deported, released or charged with crimes unrelated to terrorism by the end of 2002. In Britain, the 11 foreign nationals still in custody at year's end were either asylum seekers or recognized refugees, the report said.

Amnesty said the detention by the United States of 600 foreign nationals at Guantanamo Bay in Cuba was a "human rights scandal" and called on America to release or charge those imprisoned there. Spokesman Rob Freer said Amnesty has repeatedly requested access to Guantanamo, as recently as the week of May 20, 2003, but received no reply.

"Children are among them, the elderly are among them and undoubtedly there are people who were picked up for being at the wrong place at the wrong time," Freer said.

Of course, the White House continues to deny that the United States is violating human rights of prisoners at Guantanamo Bay. And a spokeswoman for Britain's Home office said the powers granted by the country's new anti-terrorism and security law, which allowed the detention of some foreign nationals without charge, "are a necessary and proportionate response to the threat that we face."

According to a January 23 article in the New York Times, written by David Sanger, one senior political adviser to Bush described the president's strategy in the coming months as "a healthy mix of optimism and fear factor," tapping into what White House officials believed was a wariness among swing voters about putting the nation's security into the hands of any of the Democratic aspirants. And the Republican strategy was to meld the war in Iraq with the battle against terrorism.

But how safe are we, regardless of where you live, work, or play? But more importantly, how safe are we in general? Because no matter who is in the White House in 2005, we all will be subject to terrorism until such time that wealthy nations find better solutions to help the disenfranchised and find a balance.

The terrorists don't have to use suicide bombers all the time. They are now using cellphones to detonate explosives. Using cellphones to detonate explosives is a phenomenon that is nearly impossible to stop from a technical standpoint, according to telecom-industry and explosives experts. A Wall Street Journal article published on March 17, 2004, stated:

> The train attack in Madrid was carried out by apparently hooking up bombs to cellphones, which theoretically could have allowed them to detonate the explosives from the other side of the world. Hooking up a phone to a bomb also provides the option of using an alarm clock in the phone to detonate the explosive, which is how it appears one unexploded device was set up. A wire within a phone is connected to the detonator in a bomb. When a call is placed to the phone, an electrical circuit is completed, providing power to the detonator and setting off the explosive. "You set up your explosive device in Berlin, or wherever. Now, you decide you don't want to be anywhere near that thing when it explodes, so you fly over to San Francisco and dial the number of the cellphone," said Greg Baur, former international director of the International Association of Bomb Technicians and Investigators. "That bomb goes off, and you're halfway around the world."

Also, there is the possibility that al-Qaeda may have acquired nuclear bombs. According to a Reuters March 21, 2004, Osama bin Laden's terror network claims to have bought ready-made nuclear weapons on the black market in central Asia, the biographer of al-Qaeda's No. 2 leader was quoted as telling an Australian television station.

Pakistani journalist Hammed Mir said Ayman al-Zawahiri claimed that "smart briefcase bombs" were available on the black market. In the interview with Australian Broadcasting Corp. television, Mir recalled telling al-Zawahiri it was difficult to believe that al-Qaeda had nuclear weapons when the terror network didn't have the equipment to maintain or use them.

"Dr. Ayman al-Zawahiri laughed and said, 'Mr. Mir, if you have $30 million, go to the black market in central Asia, contact any disgruntled Soviet scientists, and a lot of ... smart briefcase bombs are available,'" Mir said in the interview. "They have contacted us, we sent our people to Moscow, to Tashkent, to other central Asian states and they negotiated, and we purchased some suitcase bombs," Mir quoted al-Zawarhiri as saying.

Shift in Rhetoric

The Bush administration shifted its rhetoric on November 21, 2003, by saying that Osama bin Laden has taken himself out of the leadership position of al-Qaeda; therefore it is no longer important to catch him. What happened to Bush's earlier remarks that he wanted Osama bin Laden dead or alive?

On the one hand, Bush and Cheney link Osama and Saddam in the same context of terrorism in just about every speech they make and that they have to be captured or killed to stop the spread of terrorism and to prevent another attack on the United States. On the other hand, before Saddam was captured, they said Saddam Hussein was no longer a threat and that Osama is no longer the leader of the al-Qaeda terrorist group. Now we do not know what to believe when U.S. government officials keep flip-flopping on statements regarding their intent to capture or kill Osama bin Laden.

A September 24, 2005, CNN news tape said Pakistan senior officials and U.S. intelligence said Osama bin Laden is crippled as a leader and his communication destroyed. Also on September 25, 2005, BBC news reported that Pakistan President Pervez Musharraf said that he would prefer if Osama bin Laden is captured outside of Pakistan and not by Pakistani police.

As dissension appeared to be mounting in the White House regarding progress on terrorism, Secretary of Defense Donald Rumsfeld sent a memo to four top defense officials questioning progress in the war on terrorism and warning that the United States faced "a long, hard slog" in Iraq and Afghanistan. This is in spite of his rhetoric all along that everything was going well in Iraq and that the troops are encountering resistance, but things were under control.

According to an October 22, 2003, Reuters report, in his memo to the Joint Chiefs of Staff and others dated October 16, 2003, Rumsfeld said the United States had no yardstick for measuring progress in the anti-terrorism war after the 9/11 attacks. "Sometimes one needs to say to a big institution: Hey, wait a minute. Let's lift our eyes up and look out across the horizon and say, Are there questions that we ought to be asking ourselves? Are there things that we ought to think about ways to do differently?"

Rumsfeld continued "My impression is that we have not yet made truly bold moves, although we have made many sensible, logical moves in the right direction, but are they enough?" He also challenged Pentagon leaders to consider and discuss troubling issues, including whether or not the United States was capturing or killing terrorists at a faster rate than they were being created.

The Iraq war is so polarized that when even a member of Congress asked similar questions, the White House and the media jumped all over them saying they are not patriotic, and that they are nitpicking.

And, the Bush administration has been secretly eavesdropping on U.S. citizens for years. It wasn't until a December 16, 2005, New York Times article reported that President Bush secretly signed an order, authorizing the

National Security Agency to eavesdrop on U.S. citizens in 2002 without procuring warrants, that the public became aware of it. The order allows the agency to monitor international telephone calls and international e-mail messages of hundreds, perhaps thousands, of people inside the United States. The Times had the information for more than a year before going public with it. According to the article, the Bush administration asked them not to publish the article at that time. Of course if the article were published at that time that might have influenced the 2004 presidential election outcome.

The Bush administration also decided to prevent the suspected terrorists from petitioning the courts to challenge their detention. On November 14, 2005, an amendment proposed by Republican Senator Lindsey Graham of South Carolina to strip Guantanamo prisoners of the right to file habeas-corpus petitions in federal court was passed by a vote of 49-42. In other words, Guantanamo Bay detainees will not be able to file petitions in the courts to argue their cases that they are being held as enemy combatants.

The Bush administration policy on terror suspects has also become the policy of Tony Blair's government as evident by the following article:

Britain Sets To Adopt New Policy on Suspected Terrorists

An Associated Press article of February 2, 2004, said that the British government was considering giving courts the power to try terrorist suspects in secret and without juries – a proposal condemned by civil liberties groups. There is also a proposal to allow judges to convict suspects on a lower standard of proof than in normal criminal trials, where guilt must be proven "beyond a reasonable doubt." The judges will be allowed to convict if they thought "on a balance of probabilities" a suspect was guilty.

Home Secretary David Blunkett said the threat of suicide terrorist attacks made it necessary to debate ways to deal with these delicate issues of proportionality and human rights on the one hand and evidential base and the threshold of evidence on the other. But Mark Littlewood, campaign director, said simply introducing more laws, greater powers and stiffer penalties will go a long way to undermining British justice and will not make the country any safer.

Baroness Kennedy, a barrister and Labour Party peer, said Blunkett was "a shameless authoritarian."

Start of the Battle
Bomb and missile strikes during the first two days of the conflict in Iraq

DAY BY DAY

WEDNESDAY

1. At about 9:15 p.m. EST, U.S. airstrikes began, including 40 cruise missiles launched from Navy vessels in the Persian Gulf and Red Sea, and bombs dropped from F-117A stealth aircraft. Throughout the day, U.S. troops moved up to, and in some cases across, the border between Iraq and Kuwait.

2. During the day, U.S. aircraft fired on Iraqi artillery capable of reaching northern Kuwait.

THURSDAY

3. Iraq fired short-range missiles at U.S. forces in northern Kuwait.

4. U.S. artillery opened fire on Iraqi troops near the Kuwaiti border; some Army and Marine units moved into southern Iraq.

5. U.S. forces launched targeted missile strikes on Baghdad for a second day.

6. Special operations units hunted for scud missiles and hidden weapon cadres in western Iraq.

7. Four American Marines and 12 British soldiers were killed in the crash of a CH-46 troop carrier. Two other U.S. helicopters went down in the region.

Sources: Defense Department; globalsecurity.org; Associated Press, Reuters

232

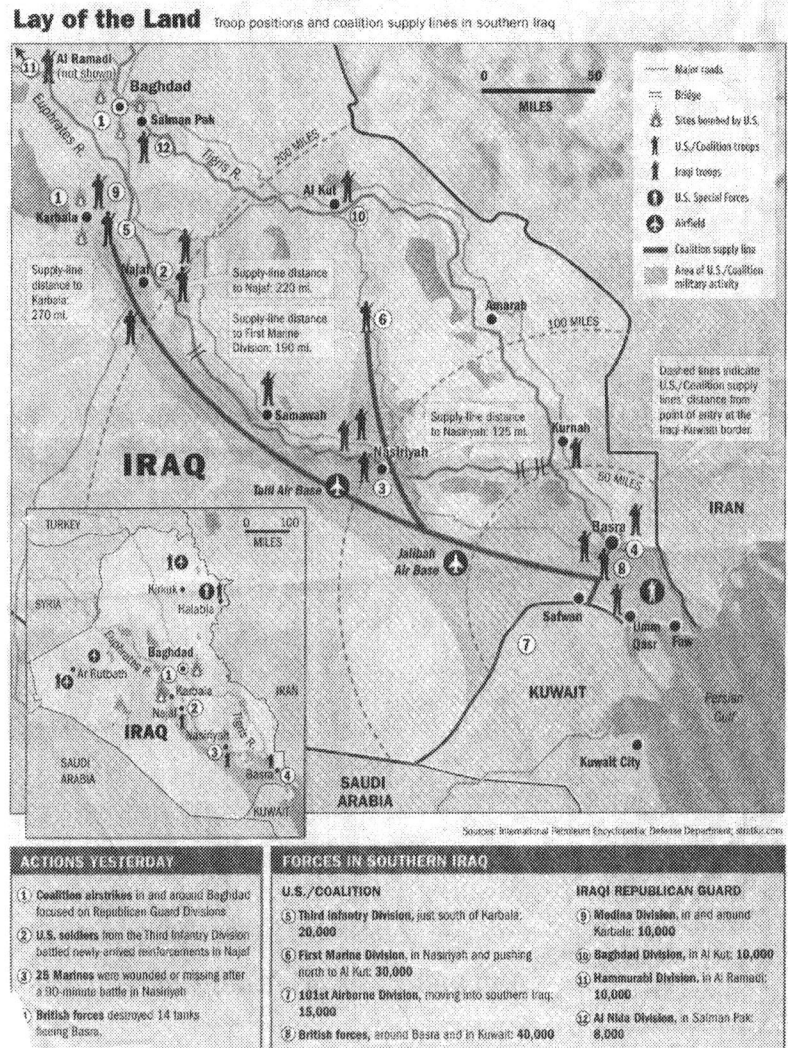

Lay of the Land
Troop positions and coalition supply lines in southern Iraq

Sources: International Petroleum Encyclopedia; Defense Department; stratfor.com

SEVEN

DEATH, DESTRUCTION AND DYSFUNCTION

What is war? War is one of the most deadly, destructive and dysfunctional aspects of the human race. Each warring faction considers the other to be the enemy, thereby creating the conditions for violence, hatred and mistrust. The soldiers are ordered by their commander-in-chief to capture and or kill the enemy. But who is the enemy – anyone the government purports it to be. While the al-Qaeda network is an enemy of the free world, Saddam Hussein was not. Yet, U.S. soldiers were ordered to attack Iraq.

These soldiers are expected to perform their duties stoically under extremely difficult conditions, while protecting themselves from being killed, captured and or mutilated. Granted the U.S. soldiers are probably the best trained soldiers in the world; however, they are only human. For some, being called upon to slaughter another human being is no easy feat regardless of their training and mindset. The constant threat of losing one's life is enough to rattle one's resolve. Also, the idea of killing another human being is not something that can be taken lightly regardless of the situation. My parents who grew up during two wars were constantly reminding us of the quote "War is Hell," because of the fact that not just the "so called enemy" will be killed and mutilated, but also the innocent civilians, the women and children who are caught up in the crossfire. But are these fighters really each other's enemy? Enemies are created when a war is created. The facts are they are ordered by their commander-in-chief, and commanding officers that these are the enemies, we want you to kill or at the very least capture them. Therefore, in order to get these soldiers in a killing mindset, they are trained so that they are able to look at another human being and think nothing of slaughtering that person, because that person is the "enemy". Therein lies the death, destruction and dysfunctionality.

The morning before the Bush administration attacked Iraq, the administration arranged for a photo-op while Bush played with his dog on the White House lawn. Was this a ploy by the administration to show the American people and the rest of the world how tough and resilient he is even in light of putting over 150,000 servicemen and women in harm's way, many of whom will never see the light of day again?

Take the Iraq war for example. Tens of thousands of people are being killed and mutilated by the United States and British bombs, missiles, grenades, etc., but who is counting? Then, there is the destruction caused by the demolition of the Iraqi infrastructure leaving the Iraqi people defenseless. Some become dysfunctional and destitute as they are left without even the basic necessities of life, namely, the sewage systems, electricity, water and not to mention the lack of life's basic sustenance – food.

The United States went into Iraq with the knowledge of the consequences of war relative to the loss of lives, the mutilation, and the human suffering. The Bush administration was very much aware of the extremely difficult conditions that the soldiers would face in Iraq. For one thing, they could have waited until the weather got a little cooler, rather than in March when the temperature exceeded 112 degrees and the sand storms gushed to more than 60 miles an hour. The soldiers were blinded by the sandstorms, insects were getting into their eyes, and their equipment kept jamming from the sand getting into them. Moreover, supply lines were stretched dangerously thin, slowing the flow of weapons, ammunition and spare parts, according to reports.

The Bush administration painted a rosy picture of what the attack on Iraq would be, namely that the war would be quick. Vice President Dick Cheney said the soldiers would be greeted with roses, and Secretary of Defense Rumsfeld told the soldiers that they would meet Saddam and his soldiers with "shock and awe." But to the soldiers' chagrin, not just the Iraqis met with "shock and awe" but they did as well. A soldier appearing on television during a report said they were really surprised of the danger that they encountered. He said he kissed his "pendant" and said "we need help from above because we can't do it alone." At times they did not know where they were going because of the sandstorms that blinded them and hampered their sense of direction.

According to an April 7, 2003, Wall Street Journal article, by Helene Cooper, the troops from the Third Infantry were in Kuwait for weeks waiting to go to war. Most of the soldiers are young kids who had no idea what to expect. However, they are brave soldiers who were told that the war would be over within days. Brig. Gen. Louis Weber told his troops in the Third Infantry Division that all he needed from them was "five good days." The Third Infantry took 17 days to reach Baghdad. The drive to Baghdad by the 20,000-member Third Infantry Division encountered fierce resistance as they fought their way to capture the airport and take over Baghdad.

The article further stated that at the center of the U.S. assault on Iraq, these soldiers often knew less about how the war was progressing than CNN viewers did. Usually, they knew only what their commanders told them about their next mission. At times, they didn't even know what direction they were going. The tale of the Third Infantry's two-week drive to Baghdad – as seen through the eyes of some of the 20,000-plus troops in its Third Brigade, known as "the Sledgehammer" – is one of bravery and arrogance, of courage and naiveté, of occasional callousness, and hope.

They faced grave danger every step of the way. However, Rumsfeld referred to it as pockets of resistance. At the same time, the Bush administration manipulated words to let the American people think that the war was going smoothly and clean. The Bush administration even went as far as to pay for positive stories in the Iraqi media. An example of the double-talk by the administration officials, in a speech to the Council on Foreign Relations, Rumsfeld gave the example of the U.S. military command in Baghdad seeking "nontraditional means" to get its message to the Iraqi people. He said, "Yet this has been portrayed as inappropriate – for example, the allegations of someone in the military hiring a contractor and the contractor allegedly paying someone to print a story – a true story – but paying to print a story," according to the Associated Press, February 22, 2006.

Also, because the Bush administration underestimated the length of the war, troops were never adequately prepared with food and water. At times, soldiers were given one meal a day while they were forced to work 24 hours a day with a few hours off in between. These young men and women are expected to work in the desert with temperatures topping 100 degrees and sandstorms of over 60 miles an hour and to perform at their peak. According to a report, originally, the troops were ordered to drink two gallons of water per day to stave off heat and exhaustion, but some of them would get only a quart and a half a day instead of the required two gallons. Two soldiers with the 101st Airborne Division collapsed from dehydration. In addition to the heat and sandstorms, the soldiers were plagued with gnats and mosquitoes. These insects were flying into the ears and mouths of the soldiers and in their food. To make matters worse, at times the soldiers had to remove their protective chemical gear that they were required to wear to protect them against the purported chemical and biological weapons because of the heat and humidity. They were also expected to be alert and successful in fighting the Iraqi soldiers who are accustomed to the harsh weather conditions, unlike the American soldiers.

Hundreds of American troops in Iraq have been infected with a parasite spread by the bite of sand flies, and the long-term consequences are unknown, an Army doctor said, according to a December 5, 2003, New York Times article,

Most of the soldiers are very young, ranging between the ages of 18 and 35. Most of them have never fought in a war before, and were really surprised by what they came upon. The American people have lost so many soldiers and so many have received severe injuries, yet both the Bush administration and the media play down the horrific massacres that occur every day in Iraq.

Among the many obstacles the soldiers faced in Iraq during the initial stages was a deadly pneumonia. According to an August 1, 2003, Yahoo News report by Will Dunham, two soldiers died and over 100 were sickened by this pneumonia, the cause of which was not known. The soldiers started to get sick on March 15, 2003, mostly Army soldiers, and at least one U.S. Marine. The troops that have been sickened by this pneumonia were geographically dispersed and came from different units. The U.S. said it had no evidence to indicate that there are chemical or biological weapons or environmental toxins involved, and that experts also have ruled out Severe Acute Respiratory Syndrome, or SARS. Moreover, a number of soldiers who returned from Iraq were tested positive for a chemical used in some of the U.S. weaponry.

U.S. soldiers in Iraq are also dying from unknown causes. For example, a 20-year-old soldier from the 1st Squadron, 10th Armored Cavalry Regiment, 4th Infantry Division died in his sleep at Camp Caldwell in Kirkush, Iraq on August 8, 2003. A fellow soldier tried to wake him and noticed he was not breathing.

And, to add insult to injury, Halliburton is providing unsafe water to U.S. troops in Iraq. At a Democratic Policy Committee Hearing on April, 7, 2006, Senator Byron Dorgan, D-North Dakota, said the Granger report issued on May 13, 2005, said that the Halliburton Company, Kellogg, Brown and Root, is providing U.S. soldiers at camp Ar Ramadi in Iraq with contaminated water. Spc. Richard Murphy, appearing at the hearing, said that KBR has been filling trucks with waste concentrate and delivering it to the troops for bathing, brushing their teeth, washing their clothes and even for making coffee. Richard Murphy served in Iraq, and is now suffering from gastrointestinal problems. Kellogg Brown & Root officials claim that the water is potable because it puts the waste water through a carbon filter. However, the water tested positive for E-Coli bacteria. Many soldiers have been affected with the bacteria, which could result in death. Dr. Jeffrey Griffiths, Associate Professor of Public Health and Family Medicine at Tuft University, said this is a chronic parasite infection. This information came to light because of whistleblowers. Mr. Dorgan has also received an e-mail from a U.S. Army surgeon serving in Iraq, describing the contaminated water at another U.S. military camp in Iraq. As of April 2006, the situation has still not been corrected. The U.S. Army paid KBR $455 million per month to deliver clean water to the troops in Iraq and Afghanistan in 2005. Spc. Murphy wants soldiers suffering from this gastrointestinal problem to contact him at www.IAVA.org so that they can get proper treatment.

In view of the constant fear of death and dismemberment, is there any wonder that a survey suggests that there is a major morale problem among the 140,000 U.S. troops in Iraq?

A Reuters article dated October 16, 2003, stated:

Air Force Gen. Richard Myers, chairman of the Joint Chiefs of Staff, told reporters he was personally worried that when he and other top officers visited troops, they were only allowed to talk to "all the happy folks." When pressed about the Stars and Stripes newspaper survey in which half of 1,939 troops responding said morale in their unit was low or very low and that they did not plan to re-enlist in the military, Myers said, "I want to see the folks that have complaints. And sometimes they won't let them near me."

The newspaper also said that a third of the survey respondents complained that their mission lacked clear definition and characterized the war in Iraq as of little or no value. Four in 10 respondents to Stars and Stripes' survey said the job they were doing had little or nothing to do with their training.

This conflicted with statements by U.S. commanders in Iraq and Bush administration officials that portray the forces there as gung-ho and well-prepared. Defense Secretary Donald Rumsfeld, in his usual rhetoric in a Pentagon briefing, said that military recruitment and enlistment figures did not appear to reflect the complaints among Reserve and National Guard troops and their families. To deflect the soldiers' concerns, the Bush administration sent the same letter signed by a number of soldiers to a number of newspapers giving the impression that everything is going well in Iraq and that they are satisfied with the conditions there. But how could they be satisfied with the conditions there when some of them cannot readily call the U.S. to talk to their family? One spouse complained that she had to send her husband money for the phone calls and then she had to wait for him to receive the money to call her. Moreover, the troops are on a longer assignment than normal. Some of the soldiers were told that they would be going home, then their orders were rescinded indefinitely. Furthermore, they are being sent to fight the insurgents without the proper body armor that could save their lives. Some soldiers were making body armor out of scrap metal. Yet the U.S. can spend billions of dollars for Iraq's restructure.

Lt. Gen. Thomas Metz, commander of the 3rd Corps, said on October 17, 2003, there could be two more yearly troop rotations until newly trained Iraqi forces are ready to take over. The U.S. said a second force of U.S. troops would replace those serving in Iraq in the spring of 2004. The size of a third rotation of U.S. troops would depend on diplomatic efforts, Metz said.

In the meantime, Washington was trying to persuade other countries to contribute troops to stabilize Iraq. But other countries were not willing to send forces to Iraq to be slaughtered in vain.

It is heart wrenching to see the cruelty that war inflicts on human beings: The U.S. soldiers that will never come home to their loved ones, and the children that will grow up without fathers or mothers. Moreover, some spouses will be left to raise their children without their counterparts, and of course, the Iraqi children who will lose one or both parents in the war will suffer the same fate. I watched on television with horror the 12-year old boy who lost both arms, lost both his parents and his brothers and sisters in the Iraq war. Then there was the little boy who lost his entire family and was suffering from shock and could not be treated at the hospital because the hospital was closed. These are horrible inflictions on human beings that should be avoided at all costs. The soldiers who survive the war will undoubtedly suffer from some kind of war syndrome, whether it is from the medication they were forced to take in case of germ warfare or other conditions.

An April 7, 2003, Time magazine article by Jim Lacey headlined, "We Are Slaughtering Them," on the Road to Death at Najaf stated:

The 2nd brigade of the 3rd Infantry Division planned to halt west of Najaf, about 100 miles south of Baghdad; it also planned on facing some resistance from local irregulars. What it didn't expect was a rush-hour-like Iraqi attack, the road dense with enemy trucks bearing down on the brigade. The headquarters had just rolled into the objective area when 10 pickup trucks loaded with men firing machine guns and RPGs come racing down the road, recalls Colonel David Perkins, commander of the 2nd Brigade. In this attack the U.S. troops estimated that they killed 1,200 Iraqi soldiers.

The fighting between the U.S. and Iraqi soldiers was analogous to the fighting between the Israelis and the Palestinians – one with smart bombs, laser-guided missiles and other sophisticated artillery, and the other with IEDs, RPGs and suicide bombers. The attacks being carried out by U.S. soldiers are fierce and bloody every step of the way, according to reports.

The first estimate when the war started was that between 3,000 and 5,000 Iraqi civilians had been killed. However, one will never know the true numbers since the administration said it will not count the number of Iraqis dead. Is that where some of the shock and awe may come in? Also, there was no mention of the number of Iraqi soldiers killed. One can just imagine that the numbers will be staggering considering that the U.S. is using sophisticated weapons to attack the Iraqis, while the Iraqis use machine guns, rocket-propelled grenades and Improvised Explosive Device (IED). Since the U.S. soldiers have been fighting the "enemies," I guess there is no need to care about the number of Iraqi soldiers killed or injured. But when you think of it, they are ordered to kill American soldiers because American soldiers are ordered to kill them. So why not put a human face to all of the dead, not just the Americans?

The Bush administration sold the American people a "bill of goods" that the war would be short. However, they played down the fierce fighting encountered by the U.S. troops. They refer to them as "pockets of resistance." Neither were the American people aware that the troops were in grave danger every step of the way. During the return of some soldiers to San Diego, the wife of a soldier, while being interviewed by a reporter, said her husband told her that for what they encountered in the Iraq war "they were not supposed to be alive."

Not only did 139 U.S. soldiers lose their lives during the major offensive, with many severe injuries, but others are dying now in greater numbers every day than during the major conflict as the war lingers.

It is understandable why many Iraqis are fighting the U.S. soldiers. For one thing, Iraqi civilians were blown up when the U.S. and Britain bombarded them with missiles and smart bombs, and they are angered over the ruination of their country, the destitution, deaths and dismemberment of even civilians. On the other hand, some may be fighting because they are disenchanted with the way the rebuilding efforts are going. Still others may be disenchanted because they are unable to provide for their families, because of lack of employment. There are so many factors that could cause ordinary citizens to turn to a life of crime, and there does not seem to be a lack of any of those factors in Iraq since the United States invaded it. For example, in one village 15 civilians were killed and more than 40 injured when a missile hit their village. The U.S. claimed it might have been Saddam Hussein attacking his own people, or, a U.S. missile may have gone astray. Yet, the U.S. claims that its guided missile is so accurate it can hit a building at a specific location and not explode for several feet below the ground.

According to reports, unexploded U.S. bombs are also a major problem in Iraq. An unexploded cluster bomb exploded and injured 160 Iraqis. Children kicked what they thought were batteries, but these exploded and injured their legs. The U.S. had said they would not use cluster bombs in residential areas, but that was not the case. Also, Iraqis said they asked the U.S. soldiers to help them defuse the unexploded cluster bombs, but were told that's not the soldiers' job. A reporter was shown an unexploded cluster bomb in the ceiling of an Iraqi home.

A June 26, 2003, Guardian Unlimited article, stated:

The group Landmine Action said Britain and the United States are attempting to weaken the provisions of an international treaty requiring belligerents to clear up unexploded cluster bombs after the end of any conflict.

Talks have been going on for ten days in Geneva to reach consensus on a protocol under United Nations convention on conventional weapons. Draft proposals would oblige countries to pay for the safe destruction of cluster bombs they had used during a war.

Richard Lloyd, the director of Landmine Action, said the U.K. had not adopted a clear position on the safe destruction of these bombs; instead they suggested that it would cooperate in addressing the problems that unexploded munitions cause.

The United States is the biggest problem and is even more resistant to call for a legal duty. They want a voluntary declaration of intent to remove cluster bombs rather than having a duty imposed on them, according to the group Landmine Action.

The Ottawa Treaty on landmines already requires states which plant mines to remove them after a conflict. The new protocol would cover unexploded cluster bombs as well as hand grenades and other explosive devices.

It is estimated that the United States and Britain used around 300,000 cluster bomb sub-munitions, or "bomblets", in the war on Iraq. Cluster bombs are usually used against troop concentrations. British aircraft dropped 66 cluster bombs, each containing 147 bomblets, and fired 2,000 artillery shells with each containing 49 bomblets. U.S. forces dropped 1,200 cluster bombs.

The United Nations' agencies have estimated that hundreds of Iraqi children have been killed or injured since the end of the fighting by picking up unexploded shells and bomblets.

Contrary to the message the Bush administration was sending the Iraqi people that once Saddam Hussein was removed they would have freedom, instead the country erupted into violence and turmoil. Because of the grave situation created by the lack of main necessities such as clean water, sanitary facilities, food, electricity, hospitals etc. Some of the Iraqis are frustrated and angry, understandably so. So, it stands to reason that they would want to take their frustration out on the U.S. troops since they are the ones that were ordered by the Bush administration to destroy their country in the first place.

Because of the lack of sanitary facilities, some Iraqis contracted diseases. According to a BBC news report, there was an outbreak of cholera and children were dying from typhoid in Iraq right after the attack due to lack of sanitary facilities causing raw sewage to run along the streets. Hospital facilities were not operating up to par, and not even the special heart unit was working.

An April 6, 2003, Associated Press article by Charles J. Hanley stated:

Baghdad's surgeons flooded with war-wounded were amputating the limbs of children and adults with too few anesthetics to block the pain and too few antibiotics to protect the patients, according to a Greek doctor. "They don't have drugs," Dr. Dimitrius Mognie said. "I saw it myself. I opened the cabinets."

Mognie's account, after a full day touring hospitals during the U.S. bombardment, was a firsthand substantiation of a report by World Health Organization officials there, who said that the Iraqi capital was running low on anesthetics, analgesics and surgical items. As the U.S. forces probed Baghdad on the ground and pounded the city intensively from the air, the International Committee of the Red Cross said its workers there reported several hundred wounded Iraqis and dozens of dead had been brought to four main city hospitals.

Mognie, 39 a general practitioner from Athens, is familiar with Baghdad's medical system, having traveled 16 times to Iraq since 1993 to research its health problems and offer support as a member of the international aid group Doctors of the World. Dr. Mognie and a colleague got one of the few aid shipments, 32 tons of blankets, food and medicine into Baghdad over a risky road from Jordan in a two-truck convoy. They could not sleep because of the sweeping view of the thunder and fire of a city under bombardment.

The next morning, at 9:45 a.m. four American bombs struck across the street. They fell to the floor as the glass windows shattered all over them. Two women were hurt. At a children's hospital, Mognie said he saw other bomb victims up close – a 7 year-old girl badly burned on her side, a child with an amputated arm, and a 9-year-old boy named Mahmoud with severe damage to his midsection. Mahmoud had picked up something that exploded, his parents said. Because they were short on critical general anesthetics, such as Pentothal and nitrous oxide, they were using Ketamine, a five-minute anesthetic, even for amputations. Surgeons were injecting child patients with Ketamine every few minutes to maintain the effect, Mognie said.

One can hardly imagine what the Iraqis went through during the major conflict and will continue to experience for years to come before this war is ended. To watch the destruction of human lives and the infrastructure on a daily basis must infuriate the families, to say the least. On the day that Saddam Hussein's statue was taken down by the U.S. soldiers and Iraqis, chaos ensued. Violence became rampant by some Iraqis against their own people and looting escalated. Soldiers fired into the crowd killing 17 Iraqis and injuring more than 70. The next day, three more Iraqis were killed when U.S. soldiers fired into the crowd again. The media learned that the U.S. soldiers were given the orders to shoot the looters on sight. However, the Bush administration later denied that such an order was given. I saw angry Iraqis on TV saying that they were not looting when they were attacked by U.S. soldiers.

An April 30, 2003, Wall Street Journal article by Yaroslav Trofimov stated:

> Rising friction between U.S. forces and Iraq's Sunni Arabs underscored America's growing problem with a fiercely nationalistic community that has controlled Iraq since its independence in 1932. Troops from the 82nd Airborne Division fired at Iraqis demonstrating near a school occupied by U.S. soldiers in the western city of Fallujah, killing 13 and wounding dozens. U.S. officials said the soldiers were responding to fire from some of the protesters, though residents disputed that claim. In the northern city of Mosul, U.S. forces scuffled with Sunni Arab protesters, killing at least a dozen civilians.
>
> While Sunni Arabs make up only about one fifth of Iraq's population, the community traditionally has dominated the officer corps and the Baghdad bureaucracy -- the backbones of the modern Iraqi state. Iraq's royal family and the military rulers who succeeded it, including Saddam Hussein, were nearly all Sunnis. Now this shell-shocked elite views the U.S. takeover of Iraq as not only destroying Hussen's regime, but also as ending their traditional dominance.
>
> The newly found prominence of Iraq's Shiites, long persecuted under Hussein but whose religious clergy is organizing itself into a political force, and its non-Arab Kurds, who are cooperating closely with the U.S., is adding to their fears. The Sunni Arabs in Musul demanded American help in reclaiming their homes from Kurdish paramilitaries. The protesters said they had fled or had been forced

out of their homes in the northwest Iraqi town of Domes during a joint U.S. Kurdish assault and their homes taken over by the Kurds.

Iraqis are divided into a number of religious and ethnic groups by estimated percentage of population. The Arab Shiites consist of 55%; the Kurdish Sunni Muslims 18%; Arab Sunni Muslims 18%; Turkmen Sunni Muslims 5%; and others 4%.

Iraqis are upset because they feel that they have been violated. For example, Iraq's holiest site of Sunni Islam, Baghdad's Abu Hanifa mosque, which houses the crypt of an eighth-century founder of the biggest of Sunni Islam's four denominations, was damaged during the fighting. Its clock tower was hit by a U.S. missile and an internal door leading to Abu Hanifa's crypt was blown off by U.S. Marines. They consider the U.S. crusaders.

I think it is apropos to give specific details on some of the deaths and injuries which occurred in Iraq during the first year of the invasion, by not just the U.S. soldiers, but others as well. This is by no means to belittle the carnage, but to emphasize and humanize the destructive nature of war and the long-term suffering attendant therein. This also gives the reader some idea of the geographical expanse that the soldiers have to cover.

Since President Bush's appearance on the U.S.S. Abraham Lincoln on May 1, 2003, declaring the Iraqi war officially over, the attacks on U.S. soldiers have increased dramatically. Every day there are several attacks sometimes as many as a dozen in one day. On May 31, 2003, 12 U.S. soldiers lost their lives. Practically every day at least one or two soldiers are killed and several wounded.

On June 6, 2003, a U.S. Navy engineer died and three others wounded when unexploded ordnance they were handling blew up near a barracks in the town of Baghdad. The sailor was killed instantly and the injured were in stable condition.

A June 9, 2003, CBS report said almost every night in Fallujah there's another ambush of U.S. soldiers patrolling the town's streets. The report quoted a soldier as saying "Instead of being the hunter, it's almost as if we're being hunted. Seems like they're waiting for us because every time you see a patrol head out, as soon as it leaves the gates, the flares go up. The lights go out so they're just kind of waiting to ambush us as soon as we get in town." The ambush starts with a rocket-propelled grenade launched at an American vehicle followed by machine gunfire from the opposite direction. In two weeks three soldiers were killed in Fallujah and more than a dozen wounded. Fallujah is a center of resistance against the U.S.-led occupation and Fallujah never really surrendered. The soldiers are of course jittery. One minute the Iraqis are waving at them and the next minute they're shooting at them. A Private First Class soldier was two weeks short of his 21st birthday when he was killed in an ambush outside of Fallujah's police station, according to the report.

On June 9, 2003, CNN news reported that U.S. soldiers were handcuffing women and children in their search to curtail violence in Iraq. Also a June 2003, CNN.com/World reported that U.S. Central Command said on June 13, 2003, that U.S. soldiers killed 27 attackers in Iraq. According to the report, an organized group of attackers ambushed a U.S. tank patrol north of Baghdad. The attackers fired rocket-propelled grenades at the 4th Infantry Division patrol in Baghdad. The tanks immediately returned fire, killing four attackers and forcing the rest to flee. Tanks and Bradley Fighting Vehicles backed by Apache helicopters pursued the attackers killing 23.

According to the article, the U.S. conducted a wide-ranging mission dubbed Operation Peninsular Strike capturing almost 400 suspected Iraqi fighters loyal to Saddam Hussein's former regime. In a separate operation, U.S. troops were battling suspected Saddam loyalists at what U.S. mili-

249

tary officials called a terrorist training camp west of Baghdad. Pentagon officials said the camp was being used by extremist or "foreign" fighters who have come from outside Iraq to try to destabilize U.S. efforts in the country. The assault began with a coordinated air strike and a firefight followed involving ground forces, including members of the 101st Airborne Division. An Apache attack helicopter was shot down, apparently by hostile fire during the mission, and an F-16 fighter plane crashed after suffering a mechanical failure. Officials said the helicopter two-man crew and the F-16's pilot were recovered safely. According to Donald Rumsfeld and other administration officials, U.S. forces have been working to wipe out pockets of resistance blamed for attacks that have been killing U.S. soldiers. The 173rd Airborne Brigade apprehended 74 suspected al-Qaeda sympathizers after a raid near the northern Iraqi city of Kirkuk. According to Central Command, U.S. forces staged the raid based on intelligence information about alleged anti-coalition elements in the area.

On June 13, 2003, the U.S. killed 17 non-Iraqis. Also on June 13 U.S. troops near the Tigers River attacked Iraqis killing 27. U.S. claims that they had reason to believe that they were planning to ambush U.S. troops. During Operation Peninsular at least 79 Iraqis were killed.

Defense Secretary Donald Rumsfeld said the Iraq operation is not a quagmire. However, if it walks like a duck and quacks like a duck, it is a duck. In other words, the war in Iraq has taken all of the attributes of a quagmire, so it is indeed a quagmire. Rumsfeld likened the situation to the United States' own lengthy and bloody transition from British rule to constitutional democracy. He drew parallels between the situation in Iraq and Afghanistan and the years immediately following the American Revolution. Rumsfeld said, "Our first attempt at a governing charter, the Articles of Confederation, failed in a sense. It took eight years before the founders finally adopted our Constitution and inaugurated our first president." He said fighting in Iraq will go on for some time with remnants of the former Baath Party that ruled Iraq for decades under Saddam Hussein, as well as Fedayeen, Saddam Hussein's paramilitary "death squads." He went on to say "We are dealing with those remnants in a forceful fashion, just as we have had to deal with the remnants of al-Qaeda and Taliban in Afghanistan and tribal areas near Pakistan."

Although Rumsfeld insisted that Iraq is not a quagmire, the administration began to rethink its strategy by going house to house trying to find those responsible for attacking the soldiers. This of course, only made matters worse as more and more Iraqis became disgusted with the constant harassment from the military. For example, according to a June 24, 2003, Washington Post article on June 23, in Qaim, Ahmed Hamad, a burly shepherd, awoke to his mother's shouts. He looked at his watch. It was 1:10 a.m., he recalled. He gazed across a horizon illuminated by destruction, where U.S. aircraft were raining fire on four trucks. About a half-hour later, he said, a missile slammed into his house. The rest of his family, 10 in all, survived. On a hot summer night in Iraq's western desert, they had been sleeping outside on cots. While the trucks were burning, about five missiles struck Hamad's house. Although everyone was sleeping outside, debris killed his sister-in-law, Hakima Khalil, and her one-year-old daughter. By the time the barrage ended, four houses were destroyed, along with two storage shops. "We're not guilty," Hamad said. "Why are they attacking families? We want to know why they're attacking families."

If the war is over, why is the U.S. using "hell fire" on the Iraqis? The claim was that they disobeyed the curfew. The Iraqi people were still not able to move about freely. Many questioned the promised freedom by the Bush administration.

A June 24, 2003, New York Times article by Douglas Jehl stated that on June 23, 2003, using Task Force 20, a secret military team, as well as American helicopters and AC130 gunship with support from predator drone aircrafts, U.S. soldiers attacked a convoy suspected of carrying fugitive Iraqi officials near the Syrian border engaging in a fight with several Syrian guards. The U.S. refused to say whether there were any fugitive Iraqi leaders in the convoy, but said that more than twenty Iraqis were detained in the combined air-ground assault in far western Iraq near the village of Qaim, but would not provide any details about their identities. A senior Defense Department official said most had been released after it was determined that they did not pose a threat. Defense Department officials also said they did not know how many vehicles had been included in the convoy or how many Iraqis had been killed in the attack. U.S. soldiers attacked the Iraqi convoy from above and then searched the wreckage for survivors.

Several senior American officials later said they had no reason to believe that Saddam Hussein or his sons were among the Iraqis killed in the strike. The official said the possibility that Hussein or his sons Uday and Qusay were traveling in the convoy had been understood to be slim from the outset. Five days after the attack, no conclusive evidence was found. When asked in a June 24, 2003, Pentagon briefing if the U.S. were in hot pursuit of Iraqis fleeing to Syria, Rumsfeld said they do not discuss rules of engagement.

In the meantime, the attacks on the military in Iraq have moved from just attacking U.S. soldiers to attacking the British troops. Up until then, the British troops received a more cordial welcome than the Americans did. However, on June 24, 2003, attackers fired on British forces in southern Iraq, killing six troops and wounding eight others in the deadliest confrontation for coalition forces since the fall of Saddam Hussein.

A CNN.com/World article reported that separately, a soldier was injured when the 1st Battalion Parachute Regiment came under fire while patrolling south of Amarah. A helicopter dispatched to assist the ground forces also came under fire as it landed, and seven people on board were wounded, three of them seriously, the prime minister's office said. The 1st Battalion has about 650 soldiers in Iraq who operated mainly around Basra and the southern oil fields during the conflict. They have been in control of Basra, Iraq's second largest city, for several weeks and have patrolled the city without helmets and flak jackets. However, the security situation in Basra has become violent. For example, a BBC news report showed a 12-year-old boy in Basra with a bullet lodged in his shoulder. Iraqis said the British are searching their homes without any respect for their privacy.

On June 24, 2003, as Baghdad went into its second day without power, U.S. forces came under fire in the town of Fallujah, near Ramadi. The troops killed five Iraqis and in two separate incidents in Ramadi west of Baghdad four Iraqis were also killed.

A June 25, 2003, article in the Guardian reads Death and Chaos in Iraq: Our soldiers should not pay the price. The death toll up to that point among British military personnel north of Basra was a fifth of the total fatalities sustained during the war to occupy Iraq. It is a sad reminder, if one were needed, that the end of the major conflict has not yet brought peace to Iraq. Up until then, it looked as if southern Iraq might be less affected than the north.

A June 25, 2003, Wall Street Journal article, "Mounting Deaths of Troops in Iraq Raises Questions," stated that armed confrontations and money problems present new obstacles to stability. Security problems in Iraq took a dramatic turn for the worse as Iraqi fighters unleashed a series of bloody attacks on British and American soldiers, raising new questions about the source of the violence and the Pentagon's ability to curb it. Six soldiers were killed and eight others wounded while training police in southern Iraq. The assaults on British forces took place in Shiite-dominated south of the country, which had been relatively calm previously.

According to the article, military confrontation and money problems both threaten to slow the reconstruction efforts in Iraq, which the U.S. needs to put the country on a more stable footing. The attacks also underscore the difficulties military leaders are having in figuring out whether they are random, or part of a coordinated campaign of resistance led by members of the once-ruling Baath Party, or even by the former Iraqi dictator himself. Gen. Myers said, "I think it's undetermined at this point how coordinated these efforts are. "We know that there are Baath Party members that don't want this country to go to a democratic form of government that they don't want."

As each month goes by, the troops in Iraq have become sitting ducks for those who are trying to get the U.S. out. Soldiers are being attacked and killed either by ambush while in their vehicles or on patrol. U.S. forces went door to door pulling residents from their homes, tying their hands behind their backs and arresting them. Many times the troops break down the doors of the residences. For example, on June 30, 2003, U.S. forces detained 180 people in raids to stamp out resistance to their occupation in Iraq. The U.S. also launched several raids, such as Operation Desert Side-winder, Operation Desert Scorpion, Apache Lightning, etc.

The Iraqis have been complaining that the invading troops have not respected them or provided basic services and security. Many see the U.S. occupation of Iraq as an invasion. They believe that now that Saddam Hussein's regime has been toppled, the U.S. should leave so that the Iraqi people can begin to take charge of their lives, according to reports.

With the constant barrage of attacks on U.S. soldiers, the president of the United States went on television to challenge the attackers. He said that the soldiers are tough enough to take anything and even said, "Bring them on!" One can only imagine how the soldiers must have felt being faced with death and disability every day and to hear their commander-in-chief using such provocative words which would no doubt urge these attackers to increase their efforts. They will have to be even more vigilant in protecting themselves from angry Iraqis.

These troops are risking their lives every day in a war that could have been prevented. How could the president who commanded these soldiers to go to war be so flippant about their well-being? One gets the impression that he is insensitive to the well-being of others. This is the same president who during the 2000 presidential campaign said he is a compassionate person. And, true to form, since Bush made the remark "Bring them on!" the attacks intensified and more soldiers are targeted.

The soldiers are not safe anywhere in Iraq. Even areas like Sadr City near Baghdad where there had not been many attacks on U.S. soldiers, and which had welcomed the U.S. soldiers initially, ambushed soldiers, killing one and wounding four. Moreover, Iraqis have become frustrated and angry over the lack of basic necessities. With the water supplies and electricity cut off, sewage system and many other services unavailable, people started to vent their anger by taking their frustration and anger out on the U.S. soldiers. On July 1, 2003, six American soldiers were wounded in Iraq. And a fatal blast at a mosque fueled Muslim anger with the occupying forces even more. According to reports, the unexplained explosion damaged a mosque in the already tense town of Fallujah, dominated by minority Sunnis. The blast killed nine people, including the imam, or prayer leader. The local U.S. commander denied allegations that a U.S. aircraft or rocket caused the damage, and the local people said the building had not been used to store explosives. Thousands of Iraqis chanted angry slogans as they buried the dead: "America is the enemy of God! Avenge the killings!"

On July 3, 2003, three soldiers were wounded near al Mustansiriyah University when a makeshift bomb exploded by their vehicle, a military spokesman said. Their Iraqi interpreter was missing. According to a Reuters report, bystanders saw troops drag four people who appeared to be badly wounded from the wreck. Shortly after the midmorning blast in central Baghdad, a U.S. vehicle and an Iraqi car were on fire. A local resident, Mohammad Owdeh said, "These explosions are a message to the Americans because they have done nothing for the Iraqi people. There will be more and more explosions." L. Paul Bremer, in charge of the

U.S.-led authority running Iraq, dismissed suggestions the violence reflected a wider discontent with U.S. rule and insisted his Provisional Authority was making great strides in restoring services and sovereignty.

On July 5, 2003, seven recruits to a U.S.-backed Iraqi police force were killed and 40 wounded in Ramadi when a remote-controlled device exploded outside a police station where they had just graduated from police training. This attack was well-coordinated for maximum results, in that the 80 police trainees were walking in formation from their training center to the police station to get their assignments as new officers when a bomb that had been placed under a sidewalk near a utility pole exploded. U.S. soldiers were guarding the police trainees with as many as 20 soldiers and two Humvees, except on their walk to the police station, according to reports.

The U.N. World Food Program was targeted in a July 6, 2003, grenade attack in Mosul, and four days later, the agency issued a release citing concern over the security situation in Iraq.

On Saturday, July 7, 2003, seven Iraqi police recruits were killed in a remote-controlled bomb blast in Ramadi. A British freelance cameraman, Richard Wild, was also shot dead at close range in central Baghdad. The killings suggested that attacks were becoming more sophisticated and targeted. According to a U.S. military statement, the U.S. started a series of operations aimed at routing out suspected attackers and saboteurs.

On July 8, 2003, a U.S. soldier was killed at Baghdad University in new and increasingly bold attacks on occupying forces in Iraq. The soldier received a "hostile" gunshot wound and later died, according to the military. According to a Reuters report, a student said he saw the soldier on the ground bleeding from a head wound. In another attack, U.S. troops in Ramadi, a volatile town about 100 km (60 miles) west of Baghdad, were ambushed with rocket-propelled grenades. A U.S. military spokesman said there were reports of casualties but did not know how many or the severity. Lt.

Gen. Ricardo Sanchez, the coalition-force commander, said that improvised explosive devices the attackers are using now show more sophistication. He said attacks on coalition averaged 13 a day in the past 45 days. "There is still a war going on." He said. "But there is no crisis. And there is no turning back."

Arrests are probably being made without good intelligence. According to a report, on July 8, 2003, the U.S. released 11 Turkish soldiers whose capture in northern Iraq had threatened to inflame tensions between the two NATO allies, Turkey's state-run Anatolian news agency reported. The U.S. did not say why the Turks were detained, but Vice President Dick Cheney spoke to Turkish Prime Minister Tayyip Erdogan by phone in an effort to calm what Erdogan had called a "totally ugly incident." Turkish newspapers ran headlines such as "Ugly American," and said the soldiers had sacks put over their heads and were treated "like al-Qaeda terrorists."

Members of the International Organization for Migration were ambushed near the southern city of Hilla when a pickup truck pulled up alongside one car and opened fire. The car collided with a bus. Personnel in a World Health Organization convoy traveling behind the International Organization for Migration vehicles treated three injured and took the Iraqi driver to a hospital, where he later died. Both convoys were clearly marked as United Nations vehicles. This is indicative of the extent of the attacks, when even the people who are helping to bring a semblance of order to Iraq are not exempt from attacks. United Nations Secretary General Kofi Annan denounced the attack. He said the United Nations is in Iraq to help the Iraqi people. They are not taking sides. He went on to say they had no way of knowing whether this was targeted at the U.N. This is a dangerous situation. Only the restoration of law and order can put an end to these attacks.

The Bush administration had insisted that the U.S. could go it alone in Iraq. Secretary of Defense Donald Rumsfeld said the United States could fight two wars at the same time, but once it became apparent that it would be difficult for the U.S. to put Iraq back together after it demolished it, it scoured the globe for nations willing to replace some of its combat-weary troops.

And as U.S. forces attempt to crack down on insurgents, they are offending many Iraqis who feel that they are being violated, targeted, attacked and killed every day, such as a 75-year-old farmer who was shot to death and his son wounded after being turned back from a coalition checkpoint west of Fallujah. And on August 10, 2003, six Iraqis were shot to death by U.S. troops as they were running home to beat the U.S. imposed curfew.

Prior to the invasion of Iraq, the U.S. was not considered an enemy of the Iraqis. By attacking Iraq and killing innocent people, many of whom are women and children, the U.S. has made many Iraqis its enemies. In other words, these enemies were cultivated by the U.S. invasion of Iraq and the treatment of the Iraqis by the U.S. soldiers, such as the indiscrimate search and seizures and, of course, the death of innocent civilians and the destruction of their homes and businesses.

An August 11, 2003, Associated Press article headlined, "Family Recalls Deadly Night in Baghdad, stated:

> The night air hung like a hot wet blanket over the north Baghdad suburb of Slaykh. At 9 p.m. an electrical transformer blew up, plunging the neighborhood into darkness. American soldiers, apparently fearing a bomb attack, went on alert. Within 45 minutes, six Iraqis trying to get home before the 11 p.m. curfew were shot and killed by U.S. forces.
>
> Anwaar Kawaz, 36, lost her husband and three of four children. "We kept shouting, we're a family! Don't shoot!" But no one listened. They kept shooting," she told the Associated Press. She is expecting another child in November, 2003. Iraqis complain

that many innocent people have died at surprise U.S. checkpoints thrown up on dark streets shortly before the curfew. Drivers hurrying home say they don't see the soldiers or hear their orders to stop.

The Kawaz family left the home of Anwar's parents on Bilal Habashi Street at 9:15 p.m. for the 10-minute drive home. They had traveled only a half-mile when they reached the intersection where they said the American bullets took their terrible toll. A few yards in front of them, two soldiers standing near two Humvees were shooting at the family's white Volkswagen, she said. Two other soldiers near a Humvee to the right of the car also fired. Witnesses told the AP that one of the soldiers fell to the ground screaming in pain, apparently a victim of friendly fire. "They killed us. There was no signal. Nothing at all. We didn't see anything but armored cars," Anwaar said, two days after the confrontation. "Our headlights were on. He (her husband) didn't have time to put his foot on the brake. They kept shooting. He was shot in the forehead. I was shouting, 'Help me! Help me!' No one came."

Witnesses said her husband, Adel Kawaz, survived for at least an hour, still sitting in the car after being shot in the head and back. Ibrahim Arsslan, whose house is on the corner where the Kawaz car came under fire, said Kawaz cried out for help. Arslan said he and a neighbor tried to remove the wounded Kawaz from the car, but the door was jammed. Then they fled when automatic rifle fire again split the air. "The next day we heard he had died," Arslan said.

Ali Taha, who lives across the street, said Haydar Kawaz, 18, was sitting up in the back of the car with a bullet wound in his head. His sister, 17-year-old Olaa, slumped dead into his arms. When the shooting stopped and the American soldiers were gone, Taha said, he and other neighbors ventured out about 11 p.m. and took the bodies of the brother and sister from the car, placed them on the pavement and covered them with a sheet. The Americans had taken the bodies of Adel, the husband, and another child, 8-year-old Mirvet. Two days later, the family still did not know where the bodies were taken. A fourth child, a 13-year-old Hadeel, survived.

"I was sitting in the middle, between my brother Haydar and sister Olaa," Hadeel said, her head bandaged. I felt blood coming down my head. I tried to drag myself out of the car. An American pulled me out. I kept telling them that my father and my brother were in the car. There was a translator with them. "My father was shouting, we are still alive!' but no one went to help him." "The Americans told me to go with them but, I was afraid they would hurt me. I didn't trust them. So I ran to my grandparents' house," Hadeel said. She told the story sitting in her grandparents' home, crying quietly, and surrounded by family. Lt. Sean McLaughlin, stationed at a base near Slaykh, could only express sympathy, although he said his unit was not involved. "No one feels worse than us. We want to build a safe Iraq. It's a difficult situation here," McLaughlin said.

A few blocks from where the car was shot up, 19-year-old Sayf Ali was shot and killed as he drove home with a cousin and a friend. He, too, didn't see the American checkpoint, survivors in the car said. Soldiers opened fire on the blue Opel station wagon, which kept moving after Ali was shot. The cousin and the friend jumped out. Soldiers kept firing until the car caught fire, incinerating Ali's body, according to one of the witnesses, Arslan. About the same time nearby, Ali Salman, 31, was driving home, also unaware of the unannounced

American checkpoints. He apparently didn't see the soldiers either and was killed.

Ghaleb Laftah, 24, who was sitting in the back of Salman's Honda, and Wisam Sabri, sitting in the front passenger seat, were wounded. "There was no light. We didn't see the Americans," said Laftah, limping from a leg injury as he walked to Salman's wake that was being held under a tent on Bilal Habashi Street. "We didn't hurt anyone. We didn't break the law," Laftah said, speaking with difficulty because of four broken teeth from the shooting. "My son …the Americans killed him," said Salman's father, Hikmat, who broke down in sobs. "He was on his way home and was caught up in the shooting. He was afraid, got out of the car and they still shot him. He was frightened, then he died. I only have one (son)," he said. Family members were also holding a wake for Sayf Ali. The men sat under a tent outside the house and the women were outdoors, according to Iraqi tradition. Sabah Azawmi, an uncle and a Sunni Muslin, said his tribe would seek revenge on the Americans.

An August 5, 2003, Associated Press article said that coalition officials cautioned that they are now facing a threat from a radical Islamist currently independent of Saddam Hussein that is both homegrown and foreign and may include Osama bin Laden's al-Qaeda network. Some senior American officials believe that violence against U.S. soldiers in Iraq is increasingly the work of foreign fighters, by implication, Osama bin Laden's al-Qaeda network. However, Iraqis and American officers on the ground said the evidence is stronger that Iraqis angry with American occupation and Saddam Hussein's loyalists are behind most attacks. U.S. officers blamed the persistent resistance on disgruntled Iraqis or officials of Saddam Hussein's Baath Party who lost out when his regime crumpled. Iraqis said American heavy-handedness in conducting searches and making arrests were recruiting local people to the insurgency.

Still, a drumbeat of comments by Bush administration officials depict the U.S.-led campaign in Iraq as part of a larger war on terrorism and seek to turn the focus away from the threat of Saddam Hussein's still unfound weapons of mass destruction. General, Richard B. Myers chairman of the U.S. Joint Chiefs of Staff, Lt. General Ricardo Sanchez, the commander of U.S. ground forces in Iraq, and Deputy Defense Secretary Paul Wolfowitz, all have made statements suggesting foreign terrorists were an increasing problem for American forces. Sanchez spoke of foreign fighters infiltrating the country, and Myers said U.S. officials were getting good intelligence in Iraq on al-Qaeda.

In Anbar Province west of Baghdad, a hotbed of resistance to the U.S. occupation, an Army spokesman, Capt. Mike Calver, said intelligence suggested that ex-regime (figures) and loyalists, who have a lot of weapons and information, were paying young men to carry out attacks on Americans. "We think Saddam's Fedayeen are operating in this area," he said, referring to a loyalist militia. "We suspect there are ex-regime loyalists – people who are much disenfranchised with the loss of the regime." Calver said the existence or depth of foreign intervention was not clear. "We suspect that this may be true, but I don't think we can quantify at this time how many attacks are carried out by al-Qaeda or Saddam Hussein's loyalists," he said. He added that captured resistance fighters "are still being processed," and that the Army is "building a profile" on them.

In interviews in Ramadi and Fallujah regions, men hinted at ties to the resistance but feared exposure if they claimed outright to be a part of the insurgency. Young men who just finished high school and University exams said they were ready to join the resistance. Of the scores interviewed, only Mohammed, a 21-year-old student in Fallujah, claimed he had heard of Afghans and Syrians linked to al-Qaeda living in his town. He had not seen any of them, he said, but had been asked by a fellow Iraqi to raise money for the fighters. He maintained that many of the town's businessmen donated money or sold weapons to the guerrillas. "It's for a good cause," he said, according to the AP article.

At that time the attacks were basically geared toward U.S. and British soldiers, since then everyone has become a target. A Jordanian embassy in Iraq was bombed, killing a number of people and injuring others. Then on August 19, the U.N. headquarters was bombed, killing 23 U.N. employees and injuring more than 100 others. The chief U.N. official, Vieira de Mello, who was nearing the end of his four-month mission, was also killed. He was in his office when the explosion ripped through the building, and was trapped in the rubble. According to eyewitnesses, a cement truck exploded at a concrete wall outside the Canal Hotel, where the U.N. was based.

After the August bombing, Secretary General Kofi Annan drastically reduced the staff in Iraq and on October 30 decided to withdraw the last 20 from Baghdad at least temporarily following a week of violence that included the bombing of the Baghdad headquarters of the International Committee of the Red Cross.

A September 3, 2003, BBC report said, U.S. soldiers mistakenly attacked the town of Hella, Iraq, killing about 60 people. They were hit by a cluster bomb. Shrapnel ripped through their houses. Hot metal tore through their skin, and one man lost his six children. The Iraqis were protesting the presence of U.S. troops and want the U.S. to leave now that Saddam Hussein's regime has been toppled. They believe that their country should be run by Iraqis, since Iraqis understand their people best. They also see the United States as occupiers rather than liberators.

It appears that since the airing of a videotape on September 10 of al-Qaeda leader Osama bin Laden, along with his top aide, urging fighters to turn Iraq into a graveyard for American troops, the attacks on U.S. soldiers intensified. Bin Laden and Ayman al-Zawahri, his right-hand man, were shown in a tape obtained by Al Jazeera Arabic television, descending a rocky mountainside as they steadied themselves with walking sticks and automatic rifles slung over their shoulders.

A September 10, 2003, Reuters article by Firouz Sedarat provides the following details:

> "To our struggling brothers in Iraq, we greet you and we pray to God to be on your side in fighting the crusaders. God is with you and the entire nation supports you. Rely on God and devour the Americans just as lions do with their prey, and bury them in the graveyard of Iraq."
>
> Zawahri said U.S. efforts to crush al-Qaeda had failed and the network had instead grown in the past two years. He promised more attacks to punish the United States.
>
> "This is the second anniversary of the New York and Washington invasions which defied America and its crusade from whose wounds it is still staggering in Afghanistan and Iraq. "We tell you (America) that what you have seen so far are only the first skirmishes and the beginning of the clash. The real battle, however, has not started yet.
>
> "We are not advocates of killing and destruction, but with the help of God, we will cut the arms of anyone that touches us or carry any aggression against us, so prepare yourself for punishment for your crimes," Zawahri said.

Since messages from al-Qaeda leaders are often seen as a signal to supporters to mount attacks, the FBI and U.S. Homeland Security officials then warned of the threat of more al-Qaeda attacks on the United States.

In the meantime, U.S. soldiers are accidentally killing civilians. For example, according to a September 12, 2003, Associated Press report, eight Fallujah policemen and a

Jordanian security guard were killed and nine others wounded when an American patrol opened fire on the police in an apparent friendly fire incident as they chased a highway bandit. It was later disclosed that the apparently friendly-fire incident in Fallujah included 25 policemen in three vehicles, two pickup trucks and a sedan, who were chasing a white BMW known to have been used by highway bandits. As the chase neared the Jordanian hospital about 1:30 a.m. on the west side of Fallujah, the police turned around after losing sight of their quarry. The American patrol at the location opened fire, said Asem Mohammed, 23, a police sergeant who was among the injured.

A September 17, 2003, New York Times article headlined: "Iraqis' Bitterness is Called Bigger Threat than Terror."

New intelligence assessments warned that the United States' most formidable foe in Iraq in the months ahead may be the resentment of ordinary Iraqis increasingly hostile to the American military occupation, Defense Department officials said. That picture, shared with American military commanders in Iraq, is very different from the public view being presented by senior Bush administration officials, including Defense Secretary Donald Rumsfeld, who once again listed only "dead-enders, foreign terrorists and criminal gangs" as opponents of the American occupation. The defense official spoke on condition of anonymity, saying they were concerned about retribution for straying from the official line. They said it was a mistake for the administration to discount the role of ordinary Iraqis who have little in common with the groups Mr. Rumsfeld cited, but whose anger over the American presence appears to be kindling some sympathy for those attacking American forces.

Other U.S. government officials said polls in Iraq had prompted some of the concerns by the State Department's intelligence branch. The findings, which remain classified, include significant levels of hostility to the American presence. The officials said indications of that hostility extended well beyond the Sunni heartland of Iraq, which has been the main setting for attacks on American forces, to include the Shiite-dominated south, whose citizens have been more supportive of the American military presence, but have also protested loudly about raids and other American actions.

As reasons for Iraqi hostility, the defense officials cited not just disaffection over a lack of electricity and other essential services in the months since the war, but cultural factors that magnify anger about the foreign military presence. "To a lot of Iraqis, we're no longer the guys who threw out Saddam, but the ones who are busting down doors and barging in on their wives and daughters," one defense official said.

However, Condoleezza Rice, President Bush's National Security Adviser, took issue with the assertion of broad Iraqi dissatisfaction with the presence of American troops, declaring that the United States was making headway in places like Baghdad and Tikrit, where much of the resistance is centered. "But there is, even in that part of the country, progress," she said in an interview. "People finished their university exams, the Iraqi symphony orchestra performed and took a tour up to the north. Kids went to school."

Some American officials said the intelligence assessments underscored that opposition to American forces in Iraq was likely to get worse before it got better. Others cautioned that it was risky to make such forecasts, and some cited what they called indicators of recent improvements in the security situation. But while President Bush and other senior administration officials have described the conflict in Iraq primarily as a battleground in the war on terrorism, the officials said, the intelligence assessments tend to cast it mainly as an insurgency in which the key variable will be the role played by ordinary Iraqis. "As time goes on, if the infrastructure doesn't improve, and American troops are still out there front and center, it's hard to see the public mood getting any better," one U.S. government official said.

A military official who acknowledged the existence of the pessimistic intelligence assessments said he took issue with some of the conclusions. He said the bounties being offered in Iraq for attacks on Americans had increased to as much as $5,000 in what he called an indication that those opposed to the American occupation were having a harder time enlisting support. The official also declared that the number of intelligence tips and other useful information provided to American forces in Iraq was generally on the increase, a sign, he said, of increasing cooperation by large segments of the Iraqi public.

To help blunt the anger directed at the American-led occupying force, Rumsfeld said again, the United States hopes to accelerate the hand-over of security responsibilities in Iraq to Iraqi police officers, border guards, civil defense forces and soldiers trained by the United States. Nearly 60,000 Iraqis are now in uniform, he told reporters at a Pentagon briefing, and the administration hopes to increase that number to about 70,000, to include more than 10,000 former Iraqi soldiers who are being trained to join the new civil defense force.

But the assassination of a high-ranking Iraqi official highlighted the difficulty involved in the effort, including the danger that Iraqis working with

American forces will become targets as collaborators, the defense official said.

Some Defense Department officials said the role played by foreign extremists, including members of the Lebanese resistance group Hezbollah, remained a source of increasing concern. The largest indication of foreign involvement came when American military forces detained some 80 foreign fighters, including Saudis, Jordanians and Sudanese, who were rounded up along with money and weapons in two separate raids conducted by the 101st Air Assault Division near the Saudi border. But they said the degree to which such fighters, along with loyalists to the former Iraqi leader, were finding support within the Iraqi population was making it difficult for American forces to track them down and root them out.

Rice said that it was "simply naïve" to believe that Iraq today was more of a haven for terrorists than it was before Saddam Hussein was ousted from power. "There is almost a sense that they were sitting someplace minding their own business – drinking tea, having meetings and then decided to come to Iraq only after the American military rolled into Baghdad. There are fighters, they are jihadists," she said. "They would be fighting someplace. Maybe they would be fighting in the Gulf. Maybe they would be fighting in Southeast Asia. Maybe they would be fighting, or trying to fight, in the United States."

For much of the summer, as attacks on American forces in Iraq continued, Rumsfeld and other Pentagon officials disputed the idea that the United States was facing a guerrilla war in Iraq. They stopped objecting to that label only after Gen. John Abizaid, the new commander of American forces in the region, publicly called the conflict a "classical guerrilla-type campaign." With American forces making up a vast majority of the coalition occupying Iraq, Rumsfeld and General Abizaid have publicly acknowledged that the overwhelmingly American flavor of the effort poses a military problem because it makes the United States the target of ordinary Iraqis' resentment. But barring a speedy withdrawal of American forces from Iraq, which the administration has ruled out, the intelligence assessments gave little reason to expect that the resistance would calm down soon, the defense officials said. "It's going to be a hard slog, and it's hard to see when or if the picture is going to get any brighter," one official said.

Although National Security Adviser Condoleezza Rice took issue with the assertion of broad Iraqi dissatisfaction with the presence of American troops, saying the United States was making headway in places like Tikrit, the attacks have stepped up. A BBC report showed an attack by Iraqis on U.S. vehicles in retaliation for the police that were killed by U.S. troops. People were running for cover. A man ran with a baby in his hand, said they have nothing but contempt for the U.S. One can appreciate their position, especially since Secretary of Defense Donald Rumsfeld and other U.S. officials said they do not do civilian body counts. But why is the Bush administration not doing civilian body counts? Is it because the numbers are astounding? As of September 13, 2003, an Iraq Body Count (IBC) estimate ranges from 6,125 to 7,843. So, one can see why U.S. soldiers are not safe anywhere in Iraq regardless of how much barbed wire and concrete surround them. Their headquarters is located in the "Green Zone," a two-mile area and is considered to be heavily fortified. It housed the American-appointed administrator, L. Paul Bremer III, his staff and thousands of troops, because on September 27, 2003, three projectiles penetrated the concrete and barbed-wire cocoon of security around the main compound for Americans in downtown Baghdad, hitting the 14th floor of the Rashid Hotel inside the compound, but causing little damage and no injuries.

On September 10, 2003, a suicide bomber killed a young boy and wounded 50 people, most of them Iraqis, when his minivan filled with explosives detonated as he sped toward a house used by American officials. A September 11, 2003, New York Times article by John Tierney stated:

> The attack was the first on the American occupiers in the capital of the Kurdish-controlled region, which had been the most peaceful and pro-American part of Iraq. The attack occurred in a quiet, affluent neighborhood shortly before 10 p.m. Witnesses said the driver accelerated the van toward a house that neighbors described as the home and office of American intelligence agents. The leader of the American military acknowledged that it was a "United States government facility," but declined to elaborate. The apparent premature explosion left an eight-foot-deep crater about 20 yards away from the American house, whose windows and façade was damaged. The bomb also caused damage to nearby houses, collapsing the roofs and facades of some homes, knocking off doors and window frames and severely cutting people with shards of glass from the shattered windows.
>
> A 4-year-old boy from Baghdad, who was visiting his grandmother, was killed by collapsing debris in the house next door to the one used by Americans. Another boy, Hunar Najmadin, 14, who was washing his bicycle in a nearby front yard, was thrown 30 feet in the air and ended up losing an eye, according to his brother, Hiwa. In all, 42 civilians were wounded, according to Colonel Schute, of the 404th Civil Affairs Battalion of the 101st Airborne. The bomb also injured six Americans and two members of the Kurdish militia who were guarding the American facility.

This attack left the Kurds to rethink their feelings about the American presence in Iraq, although they have been protected by U.S. forces and have enjoyed more than a decade of autonomy in northern Iraq. Members of the Kurdish majority in the area have their own parliament, which meets in Erbil, a city of more than a million people, 220 miles north of Baghdad. They are asking why is a CIA house in a family neighborhood, "I am very angry to think of all the children injured. Tell the Americans to take the oil and leave us in peace," said Lana Dizayai, whose windows were shattered by the explosion, more than 70 yards away.

In addition to fighting off the insurgents, the soldiers were constantly putting out fires set by Iraqis on a daily basis, making it very difficult for them to maintain any kind of semblance of order there. According to reports, relations between American troops and the people in Fallujah have been bad from the start of the American-led occupation. The attack by the U.S. Military on Friday, September 26, 2003, killing between two and five Iraqis, would lend rise to the possibility of further revenge attacks against the U.S. troops. The American soldiers are jumpy and apparently they are shooting first and asking questions later. That may have been the case when U.S. soldiers killed eight Iraqi policemen who were not in uniform.

And, despite the rising death toll, President Bush reasserted his tough stance and vowed Washington would press on with its mission. Bush said, "There is no question we have a security issue in Iraq, and we've just got to deal with it person to person. We're going to have to remain tough." But the attackers would attack and withdraw making it difficult for the soldiers to catch them. And as September draws to an end, another soldier was fatally shot when his convoy came under small-arms fire near the city of Mahmudiyah. Four hours later, one soldier was killed and another wounded when rocket-propelled grenades hit their convoy near Ba'qubah. Also, American troops battled Iraqi guerrillas in a six-hour firefight, leaving one soldier dead and another wounded. The fight began after guerrillas attacked an American convoy with roadside bomb in Habbaniya, a town 40 miles west of Baghdad, firing automatic weapons and rocket-propelled grenades.

And, of course, the British soldiers are not left unscathed. Since President Bush announced the end of the war, six British troops were shot dead in Iraq. According to a press report, the six British soldiers shot dead in Iraq pulled out family photographs in an attempt to save their lives. A June 27, 2003, CNN report said the Royal Military Police had hoped that showing their loved ones would humanize them to the gunmen. The six were the sole members of a Royal Military patrol that was training local police forces. They died following protests by civilians over weapons searches. The violence appeared to have stemmed from a misunderstanding. The townspeople expected searches for weapons to be conducted by their patrols. The actual intent was a routine joint patrol in the town working with the local militia.

Angry residents of the city of Fallujah attacked an Iraqi police station for the second straight day, slightly injuring an American soldier who joined police in trying to fight off the attackers, who were armed with rocket-propelled grenades and automatic weapons. Fallujah, in the so called "Sunni Triangle" in central Iraq is a center for anti-U.S. sentiment. Former Iraqi soldiers angry over rumors their pay would be cut off clashed with coalition troops in Baghdad and in the southern city of Basra in riots that left two Iraqis dead and dozens injured. Elsewhere, a U.S. soldier from the 4th Infantry Division was killed and another was wounded in an ambush in Sadiyah, 60 miles north of Baghdad.

According to an October 4, 2003, Associated Press article, the trouble started in Baghdad when hundreds of ex-soldiers assembled at a U.S. base at the city's former downtown airport to collect their $40 a month stipend, which the coalition has been paying since Saddam's army was disbanded in May 2003. The crowd began hurling stones at U.S. troops and Iraqi police, who fired shots to try to disperse them. Some of the rioters moved to the nearby Mansour district, where they burned and looted four liquor stores and set fire to an Iraqi police car in the upscale neighborhood. Also, in Basra, Iraq's second largest city, one protester was shot and killed by British troops when ex-soldiers rioted after hearing rumors that they would be losing their stipends.

The dismantling of Iraq's army has left hundreds of thousands of young, armed men mostly unemployed and on the streets of Iraq, rather than working with Americans to rebuild their country. Hundreds of former soldiers demonstrated outside of U.S. offices in Baghdad, and some of the rallies have turned violent. There was no place to house these soldiers because of the looting. There was no place to feed them, no place for them to take care of essential bodily functions.

Before the war, Pentagon officials expected to quickly turn a defeated Iraqi military into an army of construction workers – and possibly security guards – to help rebuild the country. Instead, most of Iraq's 300,000 to 400,000 foot soldiers went home after the American invasion, according to the AP article.

An October 21, 2003, Associated Press article stated:

Lt. Gen. William Wallace, who commanded U.S. Army forces in Iraq until June 2003, the "expectation was that they would either surrender or capitulate. What actually happened is that they just melted into the woodwork." The president of the U.S.-appointed Iraqi Governing Council called for the United States to immediately call up much of the former Iraqi military again to help keep the peace. But Pentagon officials said they couldn't do that even if they wanted to. Iraqi's American civil administrator, L. Paul Bremer, formally dissolved the country's army on May 23, 2003.

And U.S. officials said there's no way to quickly weed out supporters of deposed dictator Saddam Hussein from the ranks. Moreover, postwar looting stripped Iraqis' remaining military bases to the bare walls.

As the Bush administration continues to bring out its heavy hitters to tell the American people that the war in Iraq is going well, the soldiers continue to be bombarded with attacks from every corner of Iraq. October 7, 2003, was no exception, when three U.S. soldiers and an Iraqi interpreter were killed in two separate incidents by explosive devices near Baghdad. In one incident, a soldier with the Army's 3rd Armored Cavalry Regiment was killed west of Baghdad and another soldier wounded. In another incident, two soldiers from the 82nd Airborne Division and their Iraqi interpreter were killed south of Baghdad near Haswah and two other soldiers were wounded.

Meanwhile, a Shiite Iman and his assistant Iman Mu'ayyad Al Khazraji of the Ali Al Bayaa Mosque and Abdel Jalil Wakiya were arrested and taken into custody for storing weapons at a mosque. However, worshipers told CNN that the soldiers planted the evidence at the mosque after the iman was arrested. They told CNN that the U.S. entered the mosque to plant bombs, grenades and pistols and then photographed the cache.

On October 7, 2003, the Turkish Parliament approved the deployment of several troops to Iraq. However, because of Iraqi opposition to Turkish troops on their soil, Turkey rescinded. An October 21, 2003, Associated Press article said because of the 15-year insurgency by Kurdish rebels in Turkey that ended in 1999, the rebels now have bases in northern Iraq and the potential to resume fighting. Turkey fears that Kurds living in an autonomous area of northern Iraq could declare independence, rekindling the insurgency in Turkey. The Kurds are not likely to forget 400-year Ottoman rule in Iraq.

And as U.S. soldiers launch their offenses against the in-surgents, so too the insurgents launch their counter-attacks.

On October 9, 2003, a station wagon packed with explosives exploded inside a police station compound in one of Bagdad's biggest slums, Sadr City, killing at least eight people and wounding more than 40. According to a U.S. military officer, the blast left a crater 10 feet by 8 feet, and 4 feet deep.

An October 9, 2003, New York Times article by Raymond Bonner and Ian Fisher stated:

> Witnesses said the car rushed through the gate and into the compound at high speed, possibly running down two policemen in the process. Immediately after the bomb went off, some men went into the police compound and took weapons and money from the dead and injured, according to a police officer.
>
> At almost the same time, in one of Baghdad's richest neighborhoods, a 34-year old Spanish diplomat, Jose Antonio Bernal, was assassinated at his residence after he opened the gate to a man dressed as a Shiite Muslim cleric.
>
> In a separate attack northeast of Baghdad, an American soldier was killed when his convoy was hit with a rocket-propelled grenade in the town of Baqubah, making this the 92nd death of an American soldier in combat since President Bush declared major combat operations in Iraq over on May 1, 2003. The attacks also raise questions about how it is going to be possible to stop terror incidents, given that the country does not have an effective police force and that the Americans have concentrated on protecting themselves, living behind walls and patrolling in tanks with heavy weapons. As a result, coalition officials here said that the former regime loyalists, supported perhaps by outsiders, are turning to so-called soft targets, which include the Iraqi police, who do not even have bullet-proof vests.

The attacks also raise the question of how diplomats, the United Nations or humanitarian agencies are going to do their jobs. "It is a juggling act," said a Western official. On the one hand, he said, to be effective, one must be able to move about, to meet and talk with Iraqis, whether officials, businessmen or just ordinary Iraqis. But that is almost impossible to do these days, given the security concerns.

On October 10, 2003, The New York Times reported Shiite Outrage Heightens Fears of Danger to Americans:

Shiite anger against Americans spilled over into Friday prayers in Sadr City, the Baghdad slum where two Iraqis and two American soldiers were killed in separate incidents. The violence and subsequent public outrage raised fears of new dangers to American forces in the form of angry followers of Muqtada al Sadr, a young anti-American cleric.

A throng of perhaps 10,000 gathered to pay their respects to the two Shiites they believe were killed by American forces the night before. "No, no, to America!" they chanted as wooden coffins holding the remains of the "martyrs" were paraded along a main street. Sheik Abdul-Hadi al-Daraji, an aide to Sadr delivered the sermon and issued a defiant demand that no American soldiers be allowed inside Sadr City. He said "America, which calls itself the supporter of democracy, is nothing but a terrorist organization that is leading the world with its terrorism and arrogance."

Also in Najaf, thousands of followers of Shiite Muslim cleric Muqtada al-Sadr set out from the Imam Ali shrine on a six-mile march to U.S. headquarters shouting slogans against the new U.S.-sanctioned Iraqi Governing Council and the Americans. U.S. troops prevented the demonstrators from entering the headquarters and soldiers barricaded the building with Humvees. The crowd dispersed after clerics read an appeal by al-Sadr to go home. A statement by al-Sadr said that he wanted the coalition forces to leave Najaf and allow Iraqis to handle security for themselves.

U.S. soldiers are trained to fight the enemy. They were not trained as policemen and women to stop street violence, looting and other civilian upheavals. But they are forced to do all these things, in addition to their usual soldier duties. But as the attacks heighten in just about every place in Iraq, the U.S. soldiers are being stretched thinner and thinner. According to reports, they are called upon to quell insurgents. But as soon as they quell a group, they are ordered to another site. These 140,000 soldiers are covering a geographical area the size of California with a population of twenty-five million people.

According to an October 13, 2003, New York Times article, by Alex Berenson, on Sunday afternoon on October 12, 2003, a huge car bomb exploded outside a hotel used by members of the Iraqi Governing Council and by many Americans, killing six Iraqi security guards and wounding more than 35 others. Luckily, the bomb went off more than 50 yards away from the front of the hotel entrance, which is a highly protected building. There was no structural damage to the hotel, and only minor damage to several nearby buildings. The concrete barriers absorbed much of the force of the blast according to a military official.

According to an eyewitness, pools of blood and flesh littered the street outside the hotel in the chaos that followed the explosion. As the surviving security guards struggled to restore order, firing shots in the air, two cars burned and the wounded screamed for help. "I saw blood everywhere and people were crying for help" said Akrm Ali, a bystander. "I can't describe how I'm feeling now. I'm very shocked."

Also, on Sunday, October 12, 2003, Ibrahim Bahr al-Uloum, the Iraqi oil minister, a member of the U.S.-appointed Governing Council, survived an assassination attempt in Baghdad. He was traveling in a five-car convoy when three gunmen opened fire from a passing car. Also in the car with al-Uloum was Nabil al-Musawi, an aide to Council member Ahmed Chalabi. According to a BBC news report, U.S.-led forces are now facing an average of 20 attacks a day. The latest deaths bring the toll to 97 since May 2003.

In addition, soldiers are also dying off the battlefield. If they are not dying from accidents, they are committing suicide. For example, one soldier died when his vehicle overturned, and another drowned while attempting a rescue. One does not need to be a rocket scientist to know why so many American soldiers in Iraq commit suicide. Just listen to the daily reports coming out of Iraq. As the days go by, the death toll rises. On October 13, 2003, one U.S. soldier was killed and two others wounded in a roadside attack northeast of Baghdad. A military convoy was ambushed near the town of Jalawha, 120 kilometers (75 miles) from the capital – bringing to three the number of U.S. soldiers killed in Iraq in a 24-hour period. Two American soldiers were killed in the east of Baquba, about 40 miles north of Baghdad. A powerful bomb apparently detonated by remote control, planted just off the road was believed to be intended for an Iraqi official who some local people regarded as a spy for the Americans. The governor of Diyala Province, Abdullah Shahad al-Jaburi, was driving in a convoy from his home to his office in Baquba when the blast went off. The blast was powerful enough to flip over a Mercedes Benz traveling in the opposite direction according to an eyewitness.

An October 13, 2003, Associated Press article by Patrick Quinn stated:

In Tikrit, Spc. Moses Rodriquez suppressed a yawn as he eased himself onto a cushion and swung his machine gun into a place on the open bed of a Humvee. Sunrise was still hours away, but a buzz of activity surrounded a dusty and darkened building at an American base in Saddam Hussein's hometown. "There's times I get up for a patrol and get a weird feeling and those are the nights with RPGs or IEDs," referring to rocket-propelled grenades and improvised explosive devices – homemade bombs usually made out of artillery shells.

The soldier was going on a raid, heading for RPG alley, a street named after the numerous rockets fired at American troops. This raid was one of dozens that U.S. troops have mounted in an effort to track down resistance fighters whose attacks are killing as many as six soldiers a week in Iraq.

According to Lt. Gen. Ricardo Sanchez, the commander of U.S. forces in Iraq, the enemy has evolved – more lethal, more complex, more sophisticated, and in some cases, more tenacious. According to reports, many Iraqis feel that it is time for the U.S. to leave their country so that it can be run by someone who understands their culture. They are disheartened by the dramatic increase in the number of civilians that are being killed and injured everyday. The latest body count of civilian deaths in Iraq, by September 2003, according to the IBC Web Site, was estimated to be a minimum of 7,377 to a maximum of 9,180.

As the fighting rages on, the hospital emergency room staffs are also stretched to the limit. An October 13, 2003, BBC News article by Martin Asser, headlined "Hazards of an Iraqi Hospital," stated:

> The reporter interviewed the two young senior officers at a surgical ward of the emergency room at al-Yarmouk hospital in western Baghdad. The nights are the worst, they say, when the ward overflows with victims of the wave of lawlessness, which has swept Baghdad and its environs since the fall of Saddam Hussein's regime.
>
> The bullet injuries have become routine although staff is severely stretched to cope. The main

problem, they say, are the gangs of relatives armed with guns, knives and clubs who invariably accompany the wounded or dying patient.

"Usually by this time on Saturday morning the ward is full," says Dr. Assad, looking down the ward of 12 beds. "We have to treat people on the floor."

Dr. Assad pointed out that most of the curtains used to give patients privacy are gone. They were used during the war as burial shrouds, and they have not been able to replace them. A woman became ill during the night on Friday, but the family did not risk bringing her the 30 kilometers from Mahmoudiya at night because of the twin fears of Fedayeen attacks and jumpy American soldiers along the way. Nor did they want to take her to the hospital in Mahmoudiya because they don't have enough doctors and equipment there. The hospital does not have enough nurses or a working telephone.

Guards Need Guards

Dr. Assad said a man came in who had been shot dead. There was nothing they could do, but the people who brought him in said the doctors did nothing to help him. They threatened to kill Dr. Assad unless he brought the man back to life.

The Yarmouk does have a detachment of guards from Federal Police Security, who are meant to protect doctors and nurses from assaults, but Dr. Assad said the FPS need bodyguards themselves. The security guards carry arms and have all undergone a week's training by the U.S. Army but they are often far outnumbered by the mobs who come to berate hospital staff. Both guards and doctors told the BBC that sometimes they just hide their badges and guns or white coats and lie low.

On October 14, 2003, another suicide bomber exploded a bomb at the Turkish Embassy, which killed the suicide bomber and injured more than a dozen others. One cannot help but wonder if overthrowing Saddam Hussein by force is worth the lives of so many people? Was Saddam so out of control that the United States could not wait for the U.N. inspectors to complete their job and disarm Saddam peacefully? This was the seventh fatal vehicle bombing in Iraq in two months. Civilians are dying every day. Frustration, anger and anxiety seem to be the norm in Iraq. Of course, journalists have not escaped the wrath of war. They too are being killed or missing in Iraq. The latest count in October 2003 was that 26 journalists have been killed, and a French ITN cameraman and a Lebanese translator went missing in the ambush that killed Terry Lloyd on March 22, 2003.

The Guardian newspaper reported that ITN has accused the British and American governments of hiding the truth about the death of veteran reporter Terry Lloyd, who was killed in a "friendly fire" incident on March 22, 2003. One of the reporters' wives pleaded to the U.S. government to provide information on the death of her husband. "I am writing to beg you, and to appeal to your humanity, to break your silence and tell me what happened that day." However, her plea has been to no avail.

According to an Associated Press article, an American civilian died delivering mail to the U.S. Army on August 5, 2003, when his truck was blown apart by a remote control bomb north of Tikrit. His employer, Kellogg Brown and Root, is a subsidiary of Halliburton, a major contractor for reconstruction in both Iraq and Afghanistan.

In the meantime, the killings of U.S. soldiers went from one per week to up to four per day. As is evidenced by the deaths in Kerbala on October 17, 2003, when three U.S. military police died in an ambush in the Shiite holy city of Kerbala and another American military policeman was killed by a bomb in Baghdad. This was the deadliest single attack on U.S. forces since three soldiers died in an ambush near

Saddam Hussein's home town of Tikrit on September 18, 2003. Seven American soldiers were also wounded in the ambush in Kerbala. In addition, five U.S. soldiers were wounded when a roadside bomb exploded on a highway near the northern city of Mosul. The violence erupted when military police were investigating reports of armed men congregating on a road near the mosque after curfew.

According to an October 17, 2003, Reuters article, an Iraqi witness said U.S. troops in armored vehicles approached the house of local cleric Sayyid Mahmoud al-Hassani, a sympathizer of radical Shiite leader Moqtada al-Sadr, and ordered his followers to disarm and go home. The Americans opened fire and he saw seven dead Iraqis. One of Hassani's followers said eight of his comrades had been killed and they struck back later by firing at an American armored personnel carrier. Ali Abdullah, who lives nearby said, "What is Bush talking about democracy. The Americans are terrorists, who are choking us with their democracy."

An October 17, 2003, Reuters article by Brian Williams, said, one soldier with the 720th Military Police Battalion in Tikrit said, it's just frustrating. It's not traditional warfare. You've got no known enemy. No military target. They are surprised by the method being used to attack them. They range from mortar bombs to rocket-propelled grenades, AK47s, and the most deadly and the feared IED device which is a homemade bomb. They hung from a tree, buried by a roadside, detonated by a toy car remote control timer. Lt. Col. James Cassella, a Pentagon spokesman, said U.S. troops in Iraq face "a low-intensity conflict" that will last for "for some time." Staff Sgt. Ronnie Stewart, 35, Shreveport, Louisiana, said the mounting casualty toll and particularly the figure of 100 dead was at last bringing home to some troops that the United States was in Iraq for the long haul. He said, "I can say that the younger soldiers had their minds geared to the end of their tours in Iraq. "I think they didn't understand that this is an ongoing process. I think for a lot of soldiers it has come as a shock. Reality has just now set in for them."

And on October 18, 2003, U.S. forces in Fallujah, west of the Iraqi capital, came under attack after their ammunition truck had mechanical trouble and caught fire. They were attacked by small arms fire. A crowd of bystanders looked on, some cheering "Allahu Akhbar," or "God is great."

On October 19, 2003, there were 43 attacks on U.S. soldiers in Iraq, according to military officials. The U.S. thought that once they captured or killed Saddam Hussein's two sons, it would send a message to Saddam's loyalists and that would reduce the attacks on U.S. soldiers. However, the attacks have only escalated. According to an October 19, 2003, New York Times article by Michael R. Gordon, a snapshot of the dangers facing American forces in Iraq can be gleaned from a document on the latest threats to allied forces prepared by the occupation authority run by L. Paul Bremer III. The document is unclassified, but is marked "for official use only" and is not widely distributed. The reported incidents included an effort to shoot down C-130 transport plane with two shoulder-fired missiles, a prison break, and an attempted ambush of a local governor. The attacks involve a fair degree of coordination. An assault generally begins when an American or allied convoy is attacked by an explosive device or a salvo of rocket-propelled grenades. Then the attackers open up with AK-47s, often retreating under the cover of mortar fire. Most ambushes are initiated by a combination of RPG or IED attacks and immediately followed by small-arms fire.

The Iraqis' disdain for U.S. occupation is evidenced by an October 20, 2003, New York Times article by Ian Fisher. Crowds of young men in Fallujah danced in victory atop the smoking wreckage of a demolished American Army truck when a roadside bomb set against a monument reading "Welcome to Fallujah" exploded on a trailer hauling Hellfire missiles through the city west of Baghdad. The crowds then incinerated the truck using gasoline. When the American soldiers returned several hours later to reclaim what they could and put out the fire, they were attacked again with small-arms fire and rocket-propelled grenades, forcing them to retreat.

And on October 21, 2003, as the tension culminated in Karbala, a shootout occurred between American forces and two dozen armed guards of Hassani, leaving 11 people dead including three American military police, according to reports. American troops assisted the Iraqi police during a raid on a mosque in Karbala, arresting 32 supporters of a fundamentalist Shiite cleric who defied the United States. According to reports, Iraq's mostly moderate Shiite leadership had maintained good relations with the Americans, backing the occupation and tempering radical elements in their ranks. However; armed militias associated with Sadr and more marginal Islamist sheik, Mahmound al Hassani, have grown increasingly belligerent.

An October 22, 2003, Newsweek article by Jonathan Darman, stated:

Human Rights Watch report suggests Americans are using excessive force against Iraqi civilians. American casualties are the ugly benchmark of the occupation of Iraq. Military or political authorities who claim progress in the reconstruction risk grisly contradiction when another soldier's death is announced. Yet while many Americans think any U.S. blood is too precious to spill, Iraqi blood is a murkier topic. At the height of the war, there was little discussion of Iraqi civilian deaths – military leaders didn't always talk about them, journalists didn't always ask. But six months after George W. Bush declared major combat operations over, Iraqi civilians are still being killed. History tells us that the death of a few innocents is the inevitable price of peace. But in a discomforting new report, the humanitarian group Human Rights Watch claims that American troops often use excessive or indiscriminate force against Iraqi civilians. The group claims that coalition forces have killed 94 Iraqis in potentially unlawful circumstances since the Bush announcement in May. The Human Rights Watch used as their guideline, the Geneva Conventions. According to the rules of war, the United States, or coalition forces, as the occupying power, must use lethal force only when absolutely necessary – and when they do use it, it must be proportionate, discriminate and targeted.

Bombing in Baghdad Killed Dozens

On Monday, October 27, 2003, the increasingly violent attacks heightened as four car bombs exploded within 45 minutes of each other from the north to the south of Baghdad, killing 35 people and injuring more than 200. One of the car bombs demolished the Red Cross headquarters and the other three hit three police stations. These explosions took place on the first day of the holy month of Ramadan. According to an October 28, 2003, Associated Press article, the first blast occurred when a police car, commandeered for a suicide mission by a man in police uniform, blew up after entering the courtyard of the al-Baya's police station in Southern Baghdad, killing 15 Iraqis and one U.S. soldier. Six other Americans were also wounded. Five minutes later, a second blast struck the local headquarters of the International Committee of the Red Cross. The suicide bomber was able to approach the building because he was driving a vehicle marked as a Red Cross ambulance or the equivalent in Arab countries. The damage was minimized because the vehicle stopped 60 feet from the front of the Red Cross building at a protective line of earth-filled barrels.

As these coordinated attacks escalated, many groups decided to reduce or withdraw their staff in Iraq. The International Committee of the Red Cross said it would cut back its operations in Iraq in light of the attack on its Baghdad headquarters, which killed as many as 12 people. The Red Cross has several hundred Iraqi employees supervised by 30 to 40 international staff. Many international aid groups either left Baghdad or reduced their presence after the August 19 bombing of the United Nations building that killed 23. Doctors Without Borders said it would reduce its seven-member expatriate team in the Iraqi capital, but would continue operating clinics and supporting hospitals as much as possible. The Greek arm of Doctors of the World, which worked in Baghdad during the U.S.-led bombing, said it would probably remove two of its three staffers. The German government said it was considering whether to withdraw four water supply experts sent to Iraq in September. The World Bank and International Monetary Fund pulled out all their staff members after the U.N. bombing in August 2003. And, Paris-based Medecins Sans Frontieres said it would reduce its seven-member expatriate team in Baghdad.

The Red Cross delegates devote much of their time to visiting prisoners held by occupation forces and the Iraqi police, a main part of the agency's mandate under the Geneva Conventions on warfare and occupation. The group also offers emergency medical aid, provides water and sanitation and educates Iraqis on how to avoid land mines and other explosives.

While Wolfowitz was visiting Iraq at the Al Rasheed Hotel, a bomb blast hit the hotel, killing one U.S. soldier. Military analysts said it would be all but impossible for the Pentagon to devise a strategy to bring stability to Iraq until U.S. officials can understand the exact nature of the guerrilla forces they are fighting.

President Bush Said U.S. Progress Is Spurring Iraqi Attacks

Despite two days of deadly attacks, President Bush insisted that the United States was making progress in Iraq and said American successes were actually spurring the violence by making insurgents more desperate. He said we will hunt down the "cold-blooded killers, terrorists who are conducting the attacks. The more progress we make on the ground, the more free the Iraqis become, the more electricity is available, the more jobs are available, the more kids that are going to school, the more desperate these killers become." However, defense officials said the synchronized suicide bombings also suggested a new level of coordination by attackers. Senator John Kerry, D-Massachusetts, said, "Does the president really believe that suicide bombers are willing to strap explosives to their bodies because we're restoring electricity and creating jobs for Iraqis? Is the president arguing that the better things get in Iraq, the more dangerous it will become for American soldiers?"

According to a survey by Iraq's Center for Research and Strategic Studies released the week of October 20, 2003, 67 percent of Iraqis saw the foreign forces as occupying powers, up from 46 percent in a survey conducted shortly after the war. Fifteen percent considered the coalition as liberating forces, down from 43 percent in May. The organizer of the survey is a think tank set up by a group of Iraqi professors after Saddam's fall. They polled 1,620 Iraqis in seven cities from September 28 to October 10, 2003.

Insurgents circulated fliers telling the Iraqi people to rise up against the U.S. coalition, calling for a day of resistance. Fearing for the safety of their families, parents kept their children home from school.

Since President Bush taunted the insurgents with comments like "Bring them on!" the attacks have greatly intensified, not only against U.S. troops, but also against Iraqis that are working with the U.S.-led coalition. Moreover, the insurgents have gone one step further by attacking even the innocent, the least of which was the Red Cross attack on October 27, 2003, and anyone who cooperates with the coalition. Then, a prominent Iraqi judge, Ishmael Youssef, was gunned down outside his home on November 4. Another chief judge, Mohan Jaber al-Shoueili, was also kidnapped from his home and taken to Najaf's main cemetery where he was killed. By the beginning of October, the attacks escalated to sometimes dozens within a day. The U.S. commander, Lt. Gen. Ricardo Sanchez, said he has seen as many as 35 attacks per day during the first three weeks of October. But on November 2, 2003, the U.S. troops suffered the second deadliest attack in Iraq when insurgents shot down their giant Chinook helicopter with rocket-propelled grenades. The helicopter was taking soldiers home for a break from the battlefront when they were attacked, killing 16 and injuring 21.

According to a November 3, 2003, Associated Press article, up until around September, nightfall was the signal that sent residents scurrying behind the safety of their houses. For British military forces, which run a multinational command in the southern part of Iraq, stability is closely tied to the availability of basic services. Also, Britain treats its military forces with dignity and concerns for their well-being. The British military presence is mostly visible on foot patrol throughout the city in berets instead of helmets, and is intentionally kept low-keyed. The British forces experience as peacekeepers in Northern Ireland and other conflict zones probably makes a difference in its Iraq operation.

The Iraqi residents don't complain as much about the British forces regarding respect for their homes as they do the American forces. Captain Alan Sweeney with the Queen's Lancashire Regiment, said, "We know how to conduct a military operation in a civilian environment. The biggest lesson was knowing that the enemy is only a tiny minority of the population. If you treat everyone like the enemy, then that comes back to haunt you." Also the British troops who arrived after the end of the major combat in May received Arab language training, which has been a bridge builder. By contrast, American troops to the north often combat the language barrier by shouting louder in English or making infantry hand gestures seldom understood by Iraqis, Sweeney said, according to the article.

On Sunday, November 2, 2003, U.S. soldiers shot and killed six Iraqis traveling in a pickup truck. U.S. soldiers said the vehicle was suspected of carrying insurgents. However, the locals said the group was returning from prayers. Also, an 11-year-old Iraqi boy was killed near Fallujah after getting caught in a firefight between U.S, troops and insurgents. And the battle rages on as the insurgents set off three powerful explosions in rapid succession in an attack on the headquarters of the American Civil authorities, injuring four people. That was the fourth attack within months on the American compound, "Green Zone."

According to a November 3, 2003, Associated Press article, in President Bush's speech in Alabama on November 3, 2003, he never mentioned the 15 U.S. soldiers that have been killed, blown out of the sky by guerrilla warfare, or the 21 soldiers that were injured in the attack. Fort Carlson suffered its single heaviest combat loss since the Vietnam War with the deaths of four soldiers aboard the helicopter that was attacked on November 2, 2003. Thirteen soldiers were also wounded. Fort Carson has sent 12,000 troops to Iraq – its largest deployment since World War II.

The Bush administration does not want the American people to see the dead and dismembered bodies returning home from Afghanistan and Iraq, so they bring them home under the cover of darkness. Also, they are suppressing the media by not allowing coverage of the bodies of the soldiers returning to the U.S. military base in Dover, Delaware. According to a report, the administration's strategy is that they do not want President Bush to be seen associated with the dead or disabled U.S. servicemen and women; that is why he does not attend the funeral services for the U.S. soldiers. Under the Clinton administration and the first President Bush, the media was allowed coverage of the dead or injured soldiers. The White House played down the tragic attack on the helicopter that had taken so many lives. The Bush administration did not come out and make a statement pertaining to the downing of the helicopter. When the president was asked for his reaction to the death of 15 soldiers, he said, "I am saddened any time that there's a loss of life." One wonders what to believe since as governor of Texas he was sending people to the electric chair in record numbers. He even allowed a retarded woman to be put to death. Donald Rumsfeld, on the other hand, said, "We are going to have tragic days as this." It's easy for him to say – he does not have any loved ones fighting in Iraq.

Bush Says Iraq Attacks Don't Rise to Level of Major Combat

On November 4, 2003, President Bush said that despite the deadly attack on an American helicopter on Sunday, the United States was no longer involved in major combat in Iraq. And he insisted that Saddam Hussein was no longer a danger. The Bush administration beats the terrorist drum every time they talk about Iraq, so that the American people will continue to support the war and want the U.S. to stay the course. Bush said "A peaceful and free Iraq is essential to the security of the United States. This will help change the world in a positive way so that years from now, people will sit back and say thank goodness America stayed the course and did what was necessary to win this battle in the war on terror."

The president said that despite reports that the fugitive Saddam Hussein might be behind some of the attacks on American troops, he was no longer a menace. "He's no longer running the country. He's no longer torturing people; he's no longer developing mass graves. I mean he is no longer in power. And we'll get him. We'll get him." Bush seems to forget that those mass graves were there while the United States was supporting Saddam Hussein. These murders did not take place since September 11, 2001.

Another Black Hawk Down

On November 7, 2003, in Saddam Hussein's hometown of Tikrit, another U.S. Black Hawk helicopter went down killing all six soldiers on board. Another Black Hawk traveling with the downed helicopter and carrying a high ranking U.S. Army general was not hit. A senior U.S. official said the crash was under investigation. Local Iraqis said the helicopter was hit by ground fire. The helicopter was engulfed in flames after it crashed, according to a report from the other aircraft personnel. The aircraft were en route to Camp Ironhorse, the main U.S. military base in the north-central town of Tikrit. That was the third U.S. helicopter down in two weeks. On October 25, 2003, a rocket-propelled grenade brought down a Black Hawk helicopter near Tikrit, wounding one soldier.

On November 7, 2003, in retaliation for the downing of the helicopter, U.S. warplanes bombed targets in Iraq. The U.S. Army said the air strikes targeting suspected guerrilla hideouts in Saddam Hussein's hometown of Tikrit as a "show of force." U.S. Deputy Secretary of State Richard Armitage told a news conference in Baghdad that Iraq was still a "war zone."

According to a November 8, 2003, Reuters article by Sasa Kavic, the U.S. air strikes, named "Operation Ivy Cyclone," started on Friday night, November 7, with F-16 fighter jets dropping 500-pound bombs near the crash site. The U.S. also used armored and attack helicopters to destroy several abandoned houses which the U.S. military believed to have been used by insurgents. Also, on November 8, American forces launched "Operation Iron Hammer" using tanks, howitzers, and fighter jets in an overnight raid around the area of Tikrit.

Rumsfeld said during a speech in Washington "capturing Saddam Hussein or killing him would be very important. So we need to catch him and I think we will." According to a November 7, 2003, New York Times article by Thom Shanker and Eric Schmitt, the top American military commander for the Middle East created a covert commando force to hunt Saddam Hussein, Osama bin Laden and key terrorists throughout the region, according to Pentagon and military officials. The new Special Operations organization was designed to act with greater speed on intelligence tips about "high-level targets" and not be contained within the borders where American conventional forces are operating in Iraq and Afghanistan. Senior Bush administration officials were frustrated that Hussein was on the loose and still exerted influence in Iraq. Officials said Hussein's mere survival was inspiring attacks on American troops and Iraqi security forces; some officials believed he was playing a role in coordinating and directing the violence by his loyalists. But the Bush administration made a very costly mistake. As soon as Baghdad fell, the U.S. dismantled the Iraqi army, leaving thousands of Iraqis unemployed.

And as the violence escalated in Iraq, countries that were considering sending troops to alleviate some of the pressure and stress on the U.S. soldiers were having second thoughts. The Spanish government, one of the Bush administration's most important allies in Iraq, said that it had drastically scaled back its diplomatic staff there. Only four or five people remained in the Spanish Embassy in Baghdad. The rest of the diplomatic and administrative team was withdrawn to Jordan, according to the Spanish foreign minister, Ana Palacio. And, on November 6, 2003, the government of Turkey reversed its decision to send troops to Iraq. In a statement from Ankara, the Foreign Minister of Turkey, Abdullah Gul said he told Secretary of State Colin L. Powell of the decision in a telephone conversation. Turkey had offered to send up to 10,000 troops to Iraq. But Turkey reversed its decision due to opposition from some members of the Iraqi Council, who expressed fear that a deployment of Turkish troops inside Iraq could both incite ethnic disputes and encourage Turkish influence over its southern neighbor.

According to a November 7, 2003, New York Times article by David Stout, the announcement from Ankara regarding its decision to withhold sending troops to Iraq was a setback to the Bush administration, which had been trying to convince a number of Muslim nations to send troops to Iraq to ease the burden on the American military and to change the image of the occupation from that of a solely Western effort to one that is multiethnic as well as multinational.

A November 10, 2003, issue of Newsweek stated that on October 31, 2003, soldiers from the Bravo Company swooped down on a house in Fallujah's northern outskirts, where a Baathist named Taha and 30 comrades were holding a meeting. "Go out and grab Taha," says the company commander, Capt. Mathew Mobley. Then the battalion's chaplain asks the men to join him in a prayer. "Lord, there are bad guys out there," he says, bowing his head. "Just help us kill 'em." According to a November 11, 2003, Reuters article, the top U.S. military commander in Iraq said he was ready to unleash any weapon in his arsenal on guerrillas as the latest bombings killed at least four people and wounded 10. Lt. Gen. Ricardo Sanchez said that not a single tool that they have available would be spared if necessary to defeat the enemy.

A November 11, 2003, New York Times article by Susan Sachs said that American commanders asked tribal chieftain Sheik Khamis el-Essawi to help curb attacks against American soldiers. But Sheik Khamis said they have no control over the people that are doing the attacks. In Iraq's Shiite-dominated south, a cohesive group of Shiite Muslim clergymen quickly established themselves as the new authority figures when official hostilities ended and they urged their followers to tolerate the occupation. There has also been virtually no violence in the north, where the majority Kurds had long built up their own institutions.

On November 12, 2003, a gasoline truck crashed through a fence around an Italian military police compound in Nasiriya, followed by a car that blew up, leaving at least 18 Italians dead, including two civilians, a British military spokesman in Basra said. Nine Iraqis were also killed. Just a few days prior, a bomb attack that apparently was aimed at the British troops in Basra killed six Iraqis.

After the attack on the Italian military, Japan said it would delay sending its troops to Iraq. According to a November 13, 2003, New York Times article by Norimitsu Onishi, the government had said earlier that it would dispatch a small contingent of noncombatant self-defense forces before the end of the year, followed by a larger force the next year. This would be the first deployment of Japanese troops to a country at war since the end of World War II. The attack on the Italians, in a zone in southern Iraq that had been considered relatively safe and that the Japanese themselves had regarded as a possible destination for their troops, forced the Japanese to delay their decision. "We have consistently felt that we would like to participate in the reconstruction of Iraq as soon as possible," Yasua Fukuda, the Chief Cabinet Secretary and the government's chief spokesman, said in a press conference. "But we have to consider the changing situation and respond accordingly. We have to evaluate the situation and decide on the timing." The Japanese Parliament passed a law in July 2003, allowing the dispatch of troops to help with reconstruction and humanitarian activities. Japan's pacifist Constitution prohibits its troops from engaging in combat.

According to a November 13, 2003, Associated Press article by Slobodan Lekic, with casualties mounting in Iraq, jumpy U.S. soldiers are becoming more aggressive in their treatment of journalists covering the conflict. Media people have been detained, news equipment has been confiscated and some journalists have suffered verbal and physical abuse while trying to report on events. The incidents involving soldiers and journalists are difficult to gauge, but anecdotal evidence suggests they have risen sharply.

The president of the Associated Press Managing Editors, representing editors at AP's more than 1,700 newspapers in the United States and Canada, sent a protest letter to the Pentagon on November 12, 2003, urging officials to "immediately take steps to end such confrontations." Stuart Wilk, managing editor of The Dallas Morning News, wrote that "the effect has been to deprive the American public of crucial images from Iraq in newspapers, broadcast stations and online news operations."

In October 2003, the Belgium-based International Federation of Journalists, which includes unions representing 500,000 journalists in more than 100 countries, complained of increased harassment of reporters, including beatings of some, since the fall of Saddam Hussein's regime.

In Washington, representatives of 30 media organizations wrote to the Pentagon expressing their dismay about the harassment of journalists in Iraq. In a letter to Larry Di Rita, acting assistant secretary of defense, the Washington bureau chiefs pointed out that the Pentagon's own guidance to troops says "media products will not be confiscated or otherwise impounded."

A number of journalists, particularly Iraqis and other Arabs working for foreign media organizations, said they were routinely threatened at gunpoint if they tried to film the aftermath of guerrilla attacks. Some have been arrested and held for short periods, according to the article.

According to reports, the endless attacks on U.S. troops led the American forces once again to launch ferocious air strikes against suspected loyalists of Saddam Hussein's regime, signaling a new and more aggressive strategy to regain the initiative in the guerrilla war now raging across the country's Sunni Muslim heartland. The U.S. used an AC-130 gunship to destroy a warehouse in Southern Baghdad that was suspected of serving as a base for guerrillas planning actions against American forces. An Apache helicopter had been called in to cripple an Iraqi van suspected of carrying a mortar used to mount attacks on Americans. The AC-130 is one of the most lethal weapons in the U.S. arsenal. The AC-130 was armed with a rapid-fire 105-millimeter cannon.

According to a November 13, 2003, New York Times article by Eric Schmidt, a senior American commander in the Middle East said that the American-led occupation in Iraq faced no more than 5,000 guerrilla fighters, but that they were increasingly well-organized, well-financed and, gradually expanding their attacks to the country's relatively calm north and south. Gen. John P. Abizaid of the Army said that loyalists to Saddam Hussein – not foreign terrorists, as some Bush administration officials have asserted – posed the greatest threat to stability in Iraq. He said these Baathist groups, and other extremists, were hiring criminals and young unemployed Iraqi men to do the bulk of their "dirty work."

Thomas Korologs, senior counselor to Iraq's administrator, L. Paul Bremer, said Iraq had an unemployment rate of 60 percent, and that the insurgents are trying to break the will of the U.S. soldiers. He also said that the crime rate in Iraq was 40 percent.

One should not be surprised that violence has taken hold of Iraq. After all, the U.S. demolished its infrastructure rendering many facilities out of commission that used to provide the means for so many Iraqis to earn a living. Also, when the war was purported to be over, 100,000 prisoners were released from jail and on the streets, carrying out various attacks using rocket-propelled grenades, bombs and other weapons, for a price.

According to a November 14, 2003, New York Times article by Dexter Filkins, on the southern edge of the capital, a large building that American commanders said was a "meeting, planning, storage and rendezvous point" for the insurgents still stood, despite the military's claim that it had been destroyed in an airstrike the night before. U.S. soldiers went to the neighborhood several hours before the attack, local residents said, warning of the impending strike and making sure that everyone in the area was evacuated. Then an American AC-130 gunship strafed the building, knocking holes in the walls and wrecking much of the textile machinery arrayed inside. After the strike, U.S. soldiers went back but did not detain any suspects, and found no weapons.

The owner, Waad Dakhil Bolane, said, "Does this look like a military base to you" standing inside his factory which was still filled with textile machinery. "The Americans came here, told the guards to leave and then attacked. I don't understand." Muhammad said that too many things have gone wrong since the U.S. overthrew Saddam Hussein. "In the beginning we were all happy, but security is so bad now, we have all lost hope." "We were sending a message," an allied official said, speaking on condition of anonymity. "The message is we're coming," according to the article. But with all of the firepower that the U.S. rained down on Iraq, it would have little impact on reducing the attacks. On November 14, 2003, two American soldiers were killed and three wounded when their convoy struck an improvised explosive device about 45 miles north of Baghdad which brought the number of soldiers killed since May 1 to 158. An American civilian contractor was also killed and another was wounded. By the second week of November the average daily number of attacks against American forces had risen to 37. Also, 49 U.S. soldiers had been killed in the first two weeks of November making it one of the deadliest for the U.S. soldiers in Iraq.

It is very difficult, if not impossible for the soldiers to be able to stop the attacks. The attacks come in all forms, at different times, and in different places. The soldiers are reacting after each attack. According to reports, within minutes of an explosion, American soldiers and Iraqi police officers with searchlights began combing the desolate strip of land along the eastern side of the Tigris River near the Sheraton Hotel. Sirens wailed, and the rattle of machine gun fire cut the air in the distance. One of the many methods of attack used by the guerrillas was to place the mortars in the bed of a truck, pull over to the side of the road, launch them and drive away before the Americans have time to respond. I wonder how long it would take for Secretary of Defense Donald Rumsfeld to accept that the war in Iraq is a quagmire.

Bush said, "The enemy in Iraq believes America will run. That's why they're willing to kill innocent civilians, relief workers, and coalition troops. America will never run." Bush added, "The mission in Iraq is vital." But the triumphant postwar glow in which President Bush taunted Iraqi militants with the challenge "Bring them on!" has come home to roost. In Fallujah, villagers both young and old cheered and celebrated the downing of the Chinook helicopter. They called it the perfect present to mark the Muslim holy month of Ramadan. A taxi driver said, "We usually celebrate Ramadan at the end of the month. Now we are celebrating in the beginning after these infidel Americans were shot down."

As a Washington Post-ABC News poll showed the American people were split on whether the war with Iraq was worth fighting, the Bush administration sent out some of its officials to make statements to counter pessimism. Rumsfeld played the terrorist card by urging patience and arguing that it was better to battle "terrorists" overseas than at home. And, appearing on CNN's "Late Edition," Senate Intelligence Committee Chairman Pat Roberts said, "We do not have the security situation under control yet; we need better intelligence to prevent this kind of thing."

Isn't it ironic that when the Bush administration was making its case to attack Iraq, they relied so heavily on their intelligence and gave the impression that their intelligence was foolproof. Then when the war started to go badly they said they did not have reliable intelligence to thwart guerrilla attacks.

For months, some in Congress called for more troops to be sent to Iraq. However, Rumsfeld said no more troops were needed. The troops there are overextended, overworked and exhausted. Finally, Rumsfeld made an announcement that 80,000 reservists would be called up to go to Iraq with another 40,000 to follow so that the troops can be rotated.

President Bush jubilantly declared that major conflict was over on May 1, 2003, as he landed on the U.S.S Abraham Lincoln aircraft carrier off the coast of southern California with a banner which read "Mission Accomplished." One wonders what he meant by that, because the war had just begun. Moreover, after U.S. soldiers killed Saddam's two sons, the Bush administration gave the impression that the violence would be curtailed because the Iraqi people would not have to fear them anymore. However, the attacks have not only increased, but they became more deadly and sophisticated.

In addition to having to contend with the attacks from the insurgents, accidents continue to play a part in the loss of lives. For instance, on November 15, 2003, two American Black Hawk helicopters collided in midair and crashed, killing at least 17 U.S. soldiers and injuring five. One other soldier was reported missing. American officials said the collision occurred when one of the helicopters came under hostile fire from the ground and swerved upward to avoid it, driving its rotor into the second helicopter. It also brings the total soldiers killed in the first two weeks of November to 60. Kentucky suffered its worst casualty since the Iraqi war began. The 17 soldiers killed in the two Black Hawk helicopters were from the 101st Airborne Division, an elite unit that specializes in assaulting enemy positions by ferrying in large number of troops through the air.

Not only are we reminded every day of the continuous killing of American soldiers in Iraq and Afghanistan, but many families will have to contend with the continuous pain and suffering as they mourn the loss of their families and try to rebuild their shattered lives.

And, as the tug of war continued, U.S. forces unleashed hell fire on various targets as part of a fresh military operation against insurgents. According to a November 16, 2003, Reuters article, reporters with the 4th Infantry Division's 1-22 Battalion saw shells fired at positions from where commanders said insurgents had lobbed mortars or rockets at the division's base, inside one of Saddam's former palace complexes in Tikrit.

Reporters said the ground shook as rounds landed and flares continued to light up the night sky in an operation coordinated with other battalions in the division and backed by attack helicopters. In one attack, four M1 Abrams tanks perched on top of a desert cliff fired rounds at a position in the fields below, from where American troops said insurgents had fired a rocket earlier in the day. Exploding shells fired by other units thudded in the distance. Troops fired a 500-pound warhead satellite-guided missile from a mobile launch pad north of Baghdad for the first time since major combat was declared over. The bombardment coincided with the launch the day before of a campaign dubbed Ivy Cyclone Two, an operation aimed at insurgents in north-central Iraq, according to the article.

Lt. Gen. Ricardo Sanchez said that he believed that Iraqi police officers were providing intelligence that they got from the U.S. military to the insurgents, and that they were helping to arrange the attacks. He also believed that they were providing financing to the insurgents.

According to a November 17, 2003, Associated Press article, Calamai accused L. Paul Bremer's administration of inefficiency and failing to understand Iraq. He said the failure of the coalition to understand Iraqi society had created "delusion, social discontent and anger" among Iraqis and allowed terrorism to "easily take root." Calamai was a special counselor of the Coalition Provisional Authority in the southern province of Dhi Qar. When asked by reporters about Calamai's resignation, State Department spokesman Richard Boucher said the coalition authority has made "excellent progress" in several areas, including "the physical reconstruction of Iraq, the restoration of services to Iraqi people, the beginnings of political authority among the Iraqi ministers and an accelerated path to political authority."

Anthony Cordesman of the Center for Strategic and International Studies in Washington, who went to Iraq at the invitation of the U.S. government, said coalition authority staffers believe their headquarters is an over-centralized bureaucracy that is unrealistic about developments in Iraq. Cordesman said too many coalition authority workers are talking to Americans rather than working with Iraqis.

According to a report, an Arab language newspaper published a statement, signed by Saddam Hussein's outlawed Baath Party, declaring that armed resistance would continue despite plans by the U.S.-led coalition and chief administrator L. Paul Bremer to accelerate the transfer of power to Iraqis. The statement, which appeared on November 19,

2003, in the Web edition of the London-based newspaper Al-Hyat, said the new U.S. timetable for handing over sovereignty "will not influence the nature of the confrontation and its course set forth by the Iraqi resistance. Those who occupy Iraq, be it through multinational forces under whatever arrangements, will be treated as occupiers that should be legal targets for resistance," the statement said. Also, Russia and France criticized the U.S. timetable for handing over power to the Iraqis on July 1, 2004.

On November 17, 2003, the 4th Infantry Division soldiers killed six alleged insurgents in the Tikrit area as they searched for a former Saddam deputy, Izzat Ibrahim al Douri, who they believed to be orchestrating attacks. U.S. forces also used fighter jets to pound suspected insurgent positions. U.S. jets and Apache helicopter gunship blasted abandoned buildings, walls and trees along a road where attacks have been so common that troops nicknamed it "RPG Alley" after the rocket-propelled grenades used by insurgents. The U.S. fighter jets dropped 500-pound bombs and tanks fired their 120mm guns at suspected ambush sites. F-16 fighter aircraft dropped two bombs on insurgent targets near the town of Samara, about 60 miles north of Baghdad, according to the military. The U.S. Air Force used some of its largest weapons in its inventory to attack targets in central Iraq. A pair of 2,000-pound satellite-guided bombs were dropped near Baquoba, 30 miles northeast of Baghdad, on camps suspected to have been used for bomb-making.

In the northern city of Kirkuk, fighter jets dropped 1,000-pound bombs on terrorist targets, Maj. Gordon Tate, a spokesman for the 4th Infantry Division said. Also, the U.S. again targeted an abandoned dye factory in southern Baghdad that was hit twice the week before by artillery and air strikes. Aerial attacks were also reported on orchards and empty farmland surrounding the military base on Baghdad's western outskirts. Residents expressed bewilderment at the offensive and the choice of targets in territory fully controlled by coalition forces, and said there was no sign of any guerrilla activity in the area before the strikes. Meanwhile, gunmen assassinated a local Iraqi official in the southern town of Dowaniyah, Hmud Kadhim, the Education Minister's director general.

The insurgents have also stepped up the attacks on the Iraqi people who are helping the U.S. and other foreign forces. For example, on November 22, 2003, two suicide car bombs struck two police stations north of the capital within half an hour, killing 14 Iraqis, including two young girls, and two attackers, and injuring 50. On that same day, using donkey carts, insurgents fired a rocket which exploded in the garden of the Intercontinental Hotel, which is frequented by international media and U.S. civilian contractors. On November 19, 2003, alone there were six vehicle bombings targeting Iraqis supporting the coalition. Elsewhere, an Iraqi police colonel in charge of protecting oil installations was assassinated in northern Iraq. DHL, which has been making approximately three daily flights into Baghdad since June 2003, was attacked with a SAM-7 surface-to-air missile.

Then there was the report that three American soldiers were killed in Iraq, including two whose throats were slashed after they came under fire in the city of Mosul with rocks and gunfire. Brig. Gen. Mark T. Kimmitt, United States military's deputy director for operations in Iraq, confirmed the deaths of the two soldiers from the 101st Airborne Division, but said he would release no details about the accident. General Kimmitt said "It is our policy that we do not go into specific details on injuries sustained by soldiers."

A November 24, 2003, New York Times article by Ian Fisher and Dexter Filkins, said, in a later report, the officials recanted the statement, saying the throats were not slashed, they might have been shot in the throat, which caused the separation. Witnesses said about a dozen teenagers dragged the men from the wreckage and beat them with concrete blocks. Also, according to one witness, one of the soldiers was shot in the chin and the bullet came out of his head. He said he saw the hole in the helmet. He also said the other soldier was shot in the throat. A day after the killings, some Mosul residents were appalled at the mutilation of the bodies, believing it violated the tenets of Islam. Abdullah al Mulla, who works in a gas station, said "They kill people and barge in on families at night. If an American came to my house at night and took me away in front of my children, I would have to take revenge." Members of the Patriotic Union of Kurdistan said U.S. troops and Iraqi police raided one of their offices in Mosul about 10:00 a.m. A party member, Salem Hussein, said the Americans arrested two PUK guards and confiscated four Kalashnikov rifels, a television set, a computer, a printer, a satellite receiver and a small amount of cash.

In a speech in London, President Bush said that the United States would not retreat from "a band of thugs" in Iraq. He also called on the United Nations to "act when action is required" and to keep its word. Bush said the United States and Britain had done all in their power to prevent the United Nations from becoming irrelevant and sharing the fate of the League of Nations. "It is not enough to meet the dangers of the world with resolutions. We must meet those dangers with resolve. The coalition had not advanced into the heart of Iraq and paid a bitter cost of casualties, only to retreat before a band of thugs and assassins," Bush said.

The Bush administration tries to calm the fears of the American people regarding the attacks in Iraq, by telling them that they have the security issue under control. But if the U.S. military had security under control, why then did President Bush visit the soldiers in Iraq under the cover of darkness and in secret? According to reports, he left his Crawford, Texas, ranch disguised as a couple with his national security adviser, Condoleezza Rice with caps drawn over their faces to get out of the ranch without being noticed by the guards. Air Force One landed in Iraq with the lights off. If Iraq's security were not precarious, why then would the president keep it a secret from the world until after he returned to the safety of his ranch in Crawford, Texas? And why did the White House ask a Bloomberg reporter to swear to secrecy in order to accompany the president to Iraq? The president stayed in Iraq for 2-1/2 hours, confined to the heavily guarded airport.

Some were asking if this was a PR stunt politically motivated to appease critics and to coax the American people. Or was this to prove to the Iraqi people that despite the dangerous situation in Iraq, he was willing to visit there as a commitment that he will not cut and run? One may see this landing under the cover of darkness and the heavily fortified military installation as confirmation that the security situation in Iraq is indeed precarious. Bush's entourage was fitted with ballistic vests, and the plane landed without cabin lights and without lights on the landing strip.

Bush's message to the soldiers was that they are engaged in a difficult mission and those who attack our coalition forces and kill innocent Iraqis are testing our will. "We did not charge hundreds of miles into the heart of Iraq, pay a bitter cost in casualties, defeat a brutal dictator and liberate 25 million people only to retreat before a band of thugs and assassins," he said.

Staff Sgt. Gerrie Stokes Holloman of Baltimore said she felt "depressed" being in Iraq, but buoyed by Bush's visit. "For the most part, people are tired and want to go home. But the support and encouragement we get from our leadership builds a bond with our soldiers."

A former head of the Republican Party, Rich Bond, said "It raises the stakes. When you're playing poker and somebody is coming at you, a great way to deter them is to raise the stakes. George Bush just placed his stature in an extraordinary way to reassert his commitment to Iraq."

However, George Bush is not the first president to visit U.S. soldiers during wartime on a holiday. Bill Clinton visited Kosovo in 1999; Lyndon B. Johnson went to Vietnam for Christmas in 1967 and president-elect Dwight D. Eisenhower visited Korean battlefronts in 1952. Richard Nixon also went to Vietnam in 1969.

Just hours after Bush's visit to Iraq, another U.S. soldier was killed. And two days after his visit, seven Spanish intelligence team members were killed and one wounded south of Baghdad when rocket-propelled grenades and mortars attacked their vehicles. Earlier, Spain had lost two other military soldiers, an intelligence officer attached to the Spanish embassy and a naval officer who was among the 23 people killed in a suicide bomb attack on the U.N. building. Insurgents raised the stakes by attacking every member of the coalition troops. In November 2003 two South Korean workers were killed and two wounded when gunmen opened fire on them. Seven Spanish intelligence agents and two Japanese diplomats were killed in a separate incident. One Colombian was also killed. Australia, one of the Bush administration's staunchest allies, was considering its future in Iraq following a weekend attack on its building. Chief Executive Robert Glasser said three rocket-propelled grenades were fired at the office, causing minor damage but no injuries.

And, as the insurgents perpetrate more and more attacks in Iraq, the U.S.-led coalition tries every means at its disposal to stop the attacks. For instance, according to a November 24, 2003, Reuters article, the U.S.-led administration introduced a law in post-war Iraq banning the media from inciting hatred. In September 2003, the Governing Council announced it would temporarily limit the operations of Al Arabiya and Qaar-based Al Jazeera, accusing them of "encouraging terrorism."

I think we should also look to our backyard to people like Rush Limbaugh and others who make racial and derogatory remarks inciting bigotry and hatred. I thought one of the reasons the Bush administration took over Iraq was to make it a democratic society. What happened to free press? One doubts that closing down Arab television will stop the insurgence attacks.

On December 2, 2003, American commanders vowed that the killing of as many as 54 insurgents in the central Iraq town would serve as a lesson to those fighting the United States, but Iraqis disputed the death toll and said anger against America would only rise. And true to form, in Talafar, Iraq, suicide bombers one in a car and one on foot blew themselves up at the gates of two U.S. military bases, wounding 61 American soldiers.

The security instability in Iraq has prompted Secretary-General Kofi Annan to rule out the quick return of a U.N. presence there. On December 10, 2003, he said, "I cannot compromise the security of our international and national staff. He said he found the United Nations to be "a high-value, high-impact target for terrorists' activity in Iraq for the foreseeable future." Annan also announced the appointment of Ross Mountain, a New Zealander who heads up the Geneva-based United Nations Office for Coordination of Humanitarian Affairs, as his interim envoy to Iraq until the naming of a permanent replacement for Vieira de Mello.

Annan warned that with the United States toughening its response to Iraqi resistance fighters "first and foremost we need to act on the recognition that the mounting insecurity problem cannot be resolved through military means alone." He also said that the occupation forces have to intensify efforts to avoid civilian casualties, show restraint and guarantee detainees fully lawful treatment.

He also criticized the vague role the U.N. had been given in the past and questioned whether future duties would be worth the safety risks. He said, "In taking the difficult decisions that lie ahead, I shall be asking myself questions, such as whether the substance of the role allocated to the United Nations is proportionate to the risks we are being asked to take. Whether the political process is fully inclusive and transparent and whether the humanitarian tasks in question are truly life-saving or not." The United Nations will continue to go to Baghdad on special visits only from Nicosia, Cyprus, or a smaller office in Amman, Jordan.

2004 started off just as deadly as the previous year with four U.S. soldiers killed. One Black Hawk helicopter was shot down near Fallujah killing one soldier and injuring another. U.S. officials said insurgents posing as journalists tried to attack the soldiers who went to rescue the helicopter crew. But journalists said they were attacked by U.S. soldiers and were arrested when they arrived at the scene to cover the helicopter attack. And, in Baghdad, hundreds protested a U.S.-led raid on a mosque believed to have been an insurgent hub.

In spite of the opinion of many, including Kofi Annan, that military power alone will not resolve the insurgency problems Secretary of Defense Donald Rumsfeld said that a switch to more aggressive anti-insurgency tactic has begun to pay off. That was only a temporary reprieve, because the attacks have heated up again.

The Capture of Saddam Hussein

The Bush administration displayed Saddam's capture on a continual basis, showing his hideaway and the humiliating examination by a U.S. military officer. He looked dazed, and out of sorts. One of his daughters said he was drugged.

The U.S. said Saddam was captured on a farm near Tikrit on November 13, 2003. His hideaway looked like a squatter's residence. U.S. troops said when he was pulled out of the hole he said "My name is Saddam Hussein. I am the president of Iraq and I want to negotiate." A U.S. Special Forces soldier replied: "Regards from President Bush."

According to a December 15, 2003, Reuters article, the U.S. said the capture of Saddam is providing intelligence that has led to the arrests of key figures in the anti-U.S. insurgency. Documents found on Saddam provided information on the guerrillas' command and control network in Baghdad and confirmed the existence of rebel cells whose presence was previously only suspected, according to an Associated Press interview with Brig. Gen. Mark Hertling of the U.S. Army's 1st Armored Division.

After the capture of Saddam, President Bush said he had a simple message for the captured leader: "Good riddance, the world is better off without you." Bush said he had his own opinions about Saddam's fate, but he insisted that "my personal views aren't important in this matter." Bush has called Saddam a murderer and a torturer on several occasions. As governor of Texas, he embraced the death penalty, so there is no doubt as to what he would want for Saddam Hussein.

While Iraqi leaders want a quick trial of Saddam and to have him executed, U.N. Secretary-General Kofi Annan said the world body would not support bringing Saddam before a tribunal that might sentence him to death, and human rights groups were appalled at the rush to a trial they said was crucial to starting a healing process in this war-shattered land. Members of the U.S.-appointed Iraq Governing Council said that the trial would be televised in the interest of exposing Saddam's atrocities and beginning a process of national healing. Although President Bush said he leaves it to the Iraqi people to decide Saddam's fate, State Department spokesman Richard Boucher said the U.S. government plan to play a major role in crafting the court, according to the Reuters article.

Before Saddam Hussein was captured, the Bush administration said Iraqis were fearful that he would return, so they were not giving U.S. troops intelligence vital to curb the growing insurgency – but three months after Saddam's capture the attacks escalated even more.

So as the insurgence attacks continue, U.S. soldiers keep up the pressure. A February 2, 2004, article in Newsweek by Michael Hirsh titled "Blood and Honor," said U.S. troops kicked down doors and stomped on insurgents. It's been a long, jarring ride into Samarra, a hotbed of insurgency in the Sunni Triangle. Finally the radio crackles the order: dismount. Lt. Ben Tomlinson's platoon heads out into the chilly morning. It's 3 a.m. and quiet, except for the barking of dogs throughout the neighborhood. The soldiers quickly string out, hugging the walls of the winding ancient city to avoid roof and "keyhole" shots from snipers, listening for the "donk" of a rocket-propelled grenade. They reached the hostel, where intelligence has said the "bad guys" are hiding. Tomlinson signals and one of his men rears back and kicks the door open with several bangs of his boot. Two suspects were caught. One is flex-cuffed and shoved roughly onto the floor. Duct tape is wrapped around his head. "Tell him he is going to jail for a long time," says Tomlinson to the Iraqi translator. "Take these jackasses outside," Tomlinson orders. The soldiers keep physical abuse to a minimum, but they are not beyond twisting an ear or putting a boot to the back to get alleged insurgents to cooperate. Soon the young Iraqi is quietly weeping and is dragged off in his bare feet into the freezing night.

According to a January 9, 2004, CNN article, the U.S. has over 12,000 detainees in prison in Iraq. The U.S. said they were going to release 500 Iraqis on January 9, but after waiting for hours, the coalition administrator L. Paul Bremer said no one would be released. The Iraqis are angry and said the U.S. is playing with their emotions. Such are the "midnight raids. The lonely hours of faithful watch" that George Bush spoke of in his State of the Union Message in January, referring to the hard job of crushing the Iraqi insurgency. In his speech, Bush called the insurgents "a remnant of Saddam supporters." But the soldiers in the First Battalion of the Eighth Infantry who are doing the dirty work here in Samarra say that's often no longer whom they're fighting. After 10 months of almost nonstop combat and raids like these, the One-Eighth has seen it all. Saddam Fedayeen, Baathists, intense fire fights and organized mortar attacks. But now on December 13, a new kind of threat is emerging that comes from deep within Arab culture and has little to do with the bedraggled Iraqi tyrant. These are the "bloodline" attacks. It's the Arabic rule of five. If you do something to someone... then five of his bloodlines will try to attack you," says Captain Todd.

The One-Eighth conducts raids and patrols seven days a week with almost no R&R and even less appreciation. Though his men risk their lives every day, Brown complains he can put them in only for "peacetime" commendations; the Army is still officially pretending the war ended in May 2003. The One-Eighth's base camp is a concrete slab overhung with plastic tarp and surrounded by thick, fetid mud. Iraqis complain constantly that the U.S. troops do not respect them – they break into their homes and take them away, according to the CNN article.

The Bush administration said al-Qaeda is responsible for many of the attacks. On February 9, 2004, the Bush administration said they found evidence that Abu Musab al-Zarqawi, a Jordadian suspected of ties to al-Qaeda, was thought to have played a role in at least three major car bombings in Iraq that have killed well over 100 people. According to the Bush administration, intelligence information suggests that Zarqawi was involved in bombings, including the attacks in August on a Shiite mosque in Najaf and the United Nations headquarters in Baghdad, and the attack in November on an Italian police headquarters. But, Mustafa Alani of the Royal United Service Institute in England told the BBC on February 9 that he does not believe the document the U.S. claimed it has found to be authentic because al-Qaeda does not put its strategy on paper.

On March 24, 2004, Rumsfeld told Congress that a new round of military base closures is needed in 2006 and could yield billions of dollars in savings by 2011. The report also contained a memorandum from the chairman of the Joint Chiefs of Staff Gen. Richard Myers, saying that the chief of the Navy, Army, Air Force and Marine Corps agreed that more bases must be closed and realigned if the Pentagon is to meet the threats to America's national security. This is at a time when the U.S. is threatening so many countries with military force if they do not scrap their chemical weapons program. What is also ironic is the comment made by Bush during the 2000 campaign that the Clinton administration closed too many bases and the U.S. was not prepared for war in the event it had to go to war.

As the insurgency spread, the U.S. finds itself faced with more foes and fewer friends. According to a report, the military is faced with the problem of subduing the Sunnis of over 300,000 people and the job of neutralizing the militia of a radical Shiite cleric without alienating the rest of the Shiite population. In April 2004, the U.S. force started a campaign against both the Shiites and the Sunnis, as it appears that both are joining forces to attack and kill Americans. More than 1,200 Marines backed by attack helicopters and fighter jets battled insurgents in fierce block-by-block fighting for the fourth straight day in Fallujah. American warplanes dropped two laser-guided bombs on houses in Fallujah where Marines said insurgents had taken cover. Attack-helicopters and an AC-130 gunship strafed insurgents' positions on both sides of the Euphrates River with heavy machine guns and rockets.

April 2004 was one of the bloodiest months in Iraq, not only to U.S. soldiers, but also to Iraqis. Between April 1 and April 29, 2005, 146 U.S. soldiers were killed and more than 700 wounded. More than 1,100 Iraqis were killed and thousands wounded. Also, on April 21, 2004, some of the bloodiest violence in Iraq took the lives of 68 Iraqis, including 16 children whose bodies were charred when bombs exploded and hit their school bus on their way to school.

And as the Fallujah siege continued by U.S. forces, a rebel group threatened to target Christians and destroy churches, and called on Pope John Paul and the United Nations to stop the U.S. siege.

By April 11, 2004, U.S. and Fallujah foes agreed to a cease-fire in the Sunni town of Fallujah. It was a tentative agreement that was reached on principle that could be broken at any time according to Mahmoud Othman, a member of the American-appointed Iraqi Governing Council. But although a truce was called, U.S. troops continued to sustain attacks, in that on April 11, an AH-64 Apache helicopter was shot down killing the two crew members.

And, while the U.S. said it was honoring the cease-fire, they were attacking Fallujah with AC-130 gunship, usually at night. The soldiers were also having hand-to-hand combat in Fallajuh, kicking down doors and arresting those who were lucky enough to escape the firepower. U.N. Secretary General Kofi Annan warned the U.S. that if it attacks the holy city of Najah, it would result in unimaginable consequences.

According to reports, U.S. military officials said they would destroy Sadr's militia. The Iraqi Governing Council members proposed to the United States that it consider a deal to end a Shiite Muslim revolt by agreeing not to arrest rebel cleric Moqtada al-Sadr. An Iraqi judge issued an arrest warrant for al-Sadr in connection with the murder of another cleric in the city of Najaf in 2003. However, Sadr said he was not involved in the murder of Sayyed Abdel Majid al-Khoei, the son of the late Grand Ayatollah Abu al-Qassem al-Khoei. In the meantime, a new surge of resistance swept Iraq as thousands of Shiites and Sunnis united by overwhelming anti-Americanism. Sadr was named by the U.S. as the No.1 terrorist in Iraq and wanted him killed or captured. However, he became part of the Iraqi government. Chalabi said it was the Iraqi government that got Sadr to join the government.

Human Rights Watch, a New York-based rights group, called for a probe into U.S. action in Fallujah. Civilians who fled the fighting described the streets of Fallujah as being littered with bodies, including women and children, and Iraqi politicians have accused U.S. forces of meeting out collective punishment on the city's residents.

Hania Mufti, a senior researcher for Human Rights said, "There is enough from footage we've seen and from what has been said about what went on in Fallujah to warrant a very serious investigation. We are deeply concerned about the consistent reports we are getting about women, children and unarmed civilians being killed."

According to a November 16, 2005, CNN report, Italy's state-run RA124 news television aired a document alleging that the United States used an incendiary weapon, white phosphorous shell in a "massive and indiscriminate way" against civilians during the Fallujah offensive. Lt. Col. Barry Venable, a Pentagon spokesman, said that white phosphorous was used in Fallujah as an incendiary weapon against enemy combatants. Also, according to a CNN report with

Wolf Blitzer, white phosphorous burns the flesh off the people down to the bones. U.S. officials said that they told the civilians to leave and only the civilian sympathizers were left in Fallujah during the white phosphorous attacks. Was this one of the "shock and awes" that Rumsfeld referred to at the beginning of the war?

A New York Times article by Jeffrey Gettleman stated:

Abdul Razak al-Muaimy, a 32-year-old laborer said, "I train my son to kill Americans. That is one reason I am grateful to Saddam Hussein. They searched my house. They kicked my Koran. They speak to me so poorly in front of my children. It's not that I encourage my son to hate Americans. It's not that I make him want to join the resistance. Americans do that for me." Muaimy said his 10-year-old son did not take part in the violence against the contractors, but said: "Dad, it was exactly like what they did to us. They burned our women, they burned our children and they burned our men. This time we killed and burned four of their dead but hopefully one day we will kill and burn them all."

On a news report on April 12, 2004, a Jordanian taxi driver said people are being paid $10,000 for an American hostage and $5,000 for others.

And, on April 13, 2004, the U.S. military moved significant forces to the holy city of Najaf in preparation for a possible offensive to retake the city from the Shiite militants and capture or kill their leaders.

On April 14, an Iranian diplomat was shot and killed as he was driving to Tehran's diplomatic mission in Baghdad. The Iranian government delegation was in Iraq to try to mediate the standoff between American troops and a rebel Shiite cleric.

On Saturday, April 17, over 5,000 residents fled their homes in Fallujah and a total of one-third of the residents fled when the U.S. launched attacks in April. Approximately 300,000 Sunnis live in Fallujah and one third fled their homes when the U.S. decided to overtake Fallujah to weed out insurgence. Many were unable to return home for some time, because the solders corded off areas and closed many roads. The soldiers rounded up most of the Iraqi men in a village near Fallujah and had not been seen. The women asked the Marines where their men were, but did not get any answers.

On April 18, 2004, L. Paul Bremer spoke of the need to bring an early end to the standoffs in Najaf and Fallujah. In the end, the U.S. would bring out its firepower. Also, Secretary of Defense Donald Rumsfeld announced that 20,000 more troops would be sent to Iraq to help fight the insurgents.

The U.S. also has over 25,000 security (mercenaries) guards in Iraq. The Pentagon is relying on private security companies to perform crucial jobs once entrusted to the military. In addition to guarding reconstruction projects, private companies were asked to provide security for the chief of the Coalition Provisional Authority, L. Paul Bremer, and other senior officials. These mercenaries come from as far as South Africa's old apartheid government, to Nepal. They are from the world's elite Special Forces units and others from local SWAT teams.

Also according to a May 8, 2006, USA Today article, the U.S. is training Air Force and Navy soldiers to guard the soldiers in Iraq and to do other jobs normally carried out by the Army.

As the fighting continued, it forced the U.S. to suspend some convoys carrying supplies for the troops in Iraq until the military could provide better security for them.

In the meantime, some nations urged their citizens to quit Iraq after the abduction of three Czech journalists. France and Russia urged their citizens to leave the country or postpone traveling there. The Czech Republic called for all non-military citizens to leave. And, on April 19, 2004, Spain told its 1,300 troops to leave Iraq as soon as possible. The

European Commission President, Romano Prodi, praised Spain's new Prime Minister's decision to withdraw troops from Iraq, and suggested that other nations were likely to follow. Prodi is also a leader of the Italian opposition. A total of 40 people have been abducted. Eight Russians were released when their captors discovered that they were Russians. Among others abducted and released were seven Chines, a Briton, three Pakistanis, two Turks, an Indian, a Napalese a Filipino and three Japanese.

On May 2, 2004, an American, Thomas Hamill, 43, a Halliburton employee, was kidnapped but escaped his captors. Is it coincidental that he escaped the day that U.S. soldiers pulled back from Fallujah? Bear in mind that the captors had said they would release him if the U.S. soldiers left Fallujah. Hamill, like many other Halliburton employees, went to Iraq in order to support his family, coupled with the fact that the salaries for truck drivers in Iraq are better than those in the U.S.

A Wall Street Journal article published on May 17, 2004, said that fighting between American forces and the militia of a radical cleric is threatening a shaky calm in Shiite areas of Iraq and risks enhancing the clerics' stature at the expense of moderate leaders whom the U.S. is hoping to groom. It said that American and British forces fought a series of bloody clashes with insurgents across Iraq that left dozens of Iraqis and at least five American soldiers dead. Most of the fighting was in Shiite-controlled southern Iraq, a region that had long been friendly to the U.S. but is increasingly becoming a central battleground in the militants' campaign against the American-led occupation.

The article said that the U.S. managed to reduce tensions in Fallujah, the Sunni-dominated city that had been the main flash point of the insurgency, by withdrawing its forces from the town and turning over responsibilities from security there to a new Iraqi force commanded by a former intelligence officer. But the strategy failed in Najaf and Karbala, a pair of Shiite holy cities that erupted into open combat between coalition forces and a militia loyal to radical cleric Muqtada al Sadr. In Najaf, American tanks rumbled into an ancient cemetery on the outskirts of the city and exchanged fire with Sadr's fighters after talks on a cease-fire stalled. The golden dome atop the Imam Ali shrine, one of the holiest Shiite sites, was damaged in the fighting.

In May 2004 a reporter asked Rumsfeld how many U.S. soldiers have been killed so far in the war in Iraq. His reply was that he did not know; then, he nonchalantly said he believed it was about 400. However, a few days later on May 31, 2004, Ricardo Sanchez, the U.S. commander in Iraq, said that 893 coalition troops have been killed in Iraq so far. This is evidence of Rumsfeld's supercilious attitude regarding the lives of the men and women that they have placed in harm's way. By November 2005 more than 2,000 U.S. soldiers lost their lives in Iraq, and more than 17,000 wounded. Of course there is no mention of the soldiers who have died or have been injured in Afghanistan. On March 3, 2006, Griff White, a Washington Post foreign correspondent, said Afghanistan is looking more and more like Iraq with the constant suicide bombings.

So as the war drags on, thousands of lives are being torn apart by death and destruction. Innocent civilians, many women and children are caught in the carnage. Some of those who perpetrate wars are usually untouched by the destruction. They cannot appreciate the situations of those who are caught in these conflicts. When a soldier makes the ultimate sacrifice, it should undoubtedly be in the defense of his country or to stop or deter atrocities by dictators, or other pernicious acts against the innocent.

EIGHT

MILITARY FAMILIES

As the death toll rises into the thousands, one can surmise that U.S. soldiers are suffering both mental and physical anguish in Iraq. So it is up to the American people to put pressure on their elected officials, who in turn must put pressure on the Bush administration to bring the troops home. One can hardly imagine what these soldiers have to contend with on a daily basis, not knowing who will be killed next, or if they will ever see their families again, or be able to tuck that little girl or boy in before he or she goes to sleep at nights. Thousands will not be around to watch their children grow up, read them a story or comfort them when they feel afraid. No president should ever deny a parent that opportunity, unless it is absolutely necessary.

Very early in the war one soldier said he wished he could get wounded so that he could go home. Another said Secretary of Defense Donald Rumsfeld should resign. These soldiers are trained to fight, and they perform their duties stoically. However, when they are fighting a war that should have been prevented and to be murdered on Iraqi soil thousands of miles away from home, one would expect that it is probably more than their families can bear.

In attempting to get the support of the American people to attack Iraq, the Bush administration claimed that it had a broad coalition of more than 30 countries, when in fact the war would be carried out mostly by American and British soldiers. Australia sent troops in at the beginning of the war to demolish Iraq's defense that would be aimed at Israel, according to former New South Wales Prime Minister Bob

Carr. Speaking on UCSD TV on January 18, 2006, he referred to Australia as the undervalued ally.

French Prime Minister Chirac was berated for not joining the war frenzy to attack Iraq. Every day he was attacked in the media ranging from print media to talk show hosts and, of course many individuals who thought France betrayed the American people. Ironically, other countries such as China, Russia, and Germany also denounced the attack on Iraq, but they were not berated.

When General Eric K. Shinseki said the U.S. would need approximately 200,000 troops in Iraq after the major conflict, the Bush administration dismissed it, saying that only 60,000 would be needed. Of course, the general's assessment proved to be correct, because three years after the so called "major conflict" was over, 150,000 U.S. troops were still in Iraq fighting a quagmire, and many in Congress said the U.S. need more troops in Iraq to fight the insurgents. The American people were also misled about the length of time that the soldiers would be required to remain in Iraq after the war. When questioned, President Bush said, they will stay as long as it takes and not a day longer. The Bush administration has an uncanny way of avoiding direct questions. Secretary of Defense Donald Rumsfeld is probably the most cunning of all.

In general, soldiers cannot complain or question their assignments, so whatever they are told to do or wherever they are sent, they must obey orders. Therefore, it is up the American people to put pressure on the Bush administration to bring the troops home, who would not be there in the first place if Saddam Hussein were allowed to be contained as he had been for over 12 years through the "No Fly Zone" resolution. I would like to refer to one of my mother's teachings when we were growing up. She said always do whatever you can to prevent being in a situation where the consequences could be dire, because prevention is always better than the cure.

Finally, in November 2005, Congressman Jack Murtha, a Democrat from Pennsylvania, called for the immediate withdrawal of U.S. troops from Iraq. And, true to form, he was attacked mercilessly by the Republicans, especially, Dick Cheney. What happened to free speech? I was always under the impression that Americans are allowed to speak their minds without reprisals, as long as they are not threatening anyone with bodily harm. It is inherent in all of us to seek out the truth, and we should not have to fear retaliation. A measure was quickly put to a vote. However, the House overwhelmingly rejected a version of Murtha's resolution, including Murtha, by voting 403-3, because the GOP had crafted it without Murtha's permission to sound as antiwar as possible. This was done in order to embarrass the Democrats, who then realized that it was a trap; hence the resolution was defeated. According to a report, during the debate, an Ohio backbencher, Jean Schmidt, was given time by GOP leaders to relate a phone call from a Marine who she said wanted "to send Congressman Murtha a message: that cowards cut and run, Marines never do."

And, how long will the American people sit idly by while our young men and women are murdered, brutalized or paralyzed? What will it take before the American people take a stance to protect our young men and women? On a television talk show where two returning soldiers were present, someone called in and asked the soldiers to tell her about their experience in Iraq and would they go back. To me that is a moot question, because the soldiers swore to uphold their positions as soldiers and would not, and could not reveal their true feelings even if they disagree with their mission. When a few soldiers spoke out about the war in Iraq, the Defense Department was considering taking disciplinary action against them. And, when a soldier complained abut the stop-gap, or the backdoor draft, he was sent back to Iraq at the front lines.

Many Americans have no idea what the soldiers go through on a daily basis. For one thing, they never know who will be next to go home in a body bag or who will lose a limb or suffer other serious injuries. Since they are soldiers sworn to obey the orders of the U.S. president, the commander-in-chief, they cannot speak up against the horrific situations that they encounter, and must do their job to the best of their abilities, even under extremely difficult conditions. Despite the dangers they face every day, for some time nearly one-quarter of the 140,000 U.S. troops in Iraq had not been issued a new type of ceramic body armor strong enough to stop bullets fired from assault rifles. According to a military official, it would not be until December 2003 before all troops in Iraq would have the vests, which were introduced in 1999. But even that promise was never kept because as late as 2005, some troops did not have their body armor.

In April, 2003, Congress approved $310 million to buy 300,000 more of the bulletproof vests with 30,000 destined to complete outfitting of the troops in Iraq. Of the money, however, only about $75 million had reached the Army office responsible for overseeing the vests' manufacture and distribution, according to David Nelson, an official in that office.

Some members of Congress were angry and denounced the Pentagon. They said up to 44,000 troops lack the best vests because of the sluggish supply chain, significantly more than the Pentagon figure. According to some congressional members, relatives of some of the soldiers have resorted to buying body armor in the United States and shipping them to their troops. The military's interceptor vests, introduced in 1999, include removable ceramic plates in the front and back that can stop bullets such as the 7.62mm rounds fired by Kalashnikov rifles that are common in Iraq and Afghanistan. Older-model vests can protect against shrapnel and other low-speed projectiles but not high-velocity rifle rounds.

Each vest and its plates weigh more than 16 pounds and cost about $1,500. Are the soldiers' lives worth saving at a cost of $1,500? It does not take a brain surgeon to know that outfitting the servicemen and women with the safest equipment should be paramount. Just as in the private sector, companies will increase manufacturing facilities to meet supply and demand, so too should the U.S. Defense Department take every step necessary to ensure that suppliers have adequate facilities to provide these vests in a timely manner. There should be no excuses. If these suppliers cannot meet the need in a timely fashion, then the Defense Department should change or increase the number of suppliers who can expedite the shipment of these critically needed vests.

The Defense Department should call on the following suppliers to expedite the manufacture, and if they cannot meet the demand, they should be replaced: Armor Works LLC of Tempe, Arizona; Ceradyne Inc., Costa Mesa, California; and Simile Inc. of Phoenix, Arizona; Point Blank Body Armor, Inc., a Division of DHB Industries, Carle Place, New York; Protect Armored Products, a subsidiary of Armor Holdings, Jacksonville, Florida; and ForceOne LLC, Spruce Pine, N.C. They should not be allowed to delay the delivery time for any reason. This is a matter of life and death for the soldiers. Several soldiers serving in Iraq and Afghanistan have credited the interceptor vests for saving their lives.

Moreover, the mental and physical strain would take its toll on some of the soldiers in Iraq, as evidenced by the increasing number of suicides. Within the first seven months of the war, at least 11 soldiers and 3 Marines committed suicide in Iraq. That is an annual rate of 17 per 100,000. The Navy also investigated one possible suicide and about a dozen other Army deaths were under investigation and could include suicides. And by April 2006, 83 soldiers committed suicide.

This alarming number of suicides in Iraq raised concerns within the Army so much so that it asked a team of doctors to determine whether the stress of combat and long deployments contributed to the deaths. Yet, Secretary of Defense Donald Rumsfeld announced that he was extending the deployments of these tired, overworked soldiers for another three to four months. Bear in mind that the conventional wisdom is that soldiers should not fight longer than six months at a time in rotation. Fatigue, emotional and physical stress set in. Most of the suicides occurred since May 1, after major combat operations were declared ended. Experts said harsh and dangerous living conditions combined with a long deployment can worsen existing depression. And the accessibility of weapons in a war zone can quickly turn a passing thought into action.

As U.S. soldiers continued to commit suicide, a major Army study found that suicide-prevention teams were left behind. According to a New York Times article by Eric Schmitt, when units left their home bases to go to war in Iraq, mental-health workers left untrained to treat combat stress, and many soldiers seeking help for depression and emotional problems faced significant hurdles getting care. The study also determined that the suicide rate of soldiers in Iraq and Kuwait in 2003 was much higher than in the Army overall. A survey of 756 soldiers in the late summer of 2003 showed that 52 percent of them said their personal morale was low or very low, and 72 percent said their whole unit's morale was that bad. Most of those had been in combat.

Some U.S. soldiers committed suicide, the reason, we may never know. But according to reports, body parts are strewn all over the ground, and some body parts may not be identified since they are gathered up after an explosion by other soldiers, and then sorted out. Is there any wonder that as of April 2006, 83 U.S. soldiers committed suicide in Iraq?

President Bush had said on April 13, 2003, that he was ready to send more troops to Iraq to fight the insurgents. In the meantime, some soldiers who have been in Kuwait and Iraq as much as 18 months were told they would have to remain in Iraq for another three to four months. These soldiers have been in combat for such a long time, well past the usual 12-month assignment. Yet they are expected to perform at their peak. I think that's asking way too much of any human being. It is true that these soldiers are trained to be tough and withstand all kinds of torture, pain and suffering, but enough is enough. They are only human. What will happen to the ones who are fortunate enough to make it back home? How will they be able to rejoin their families and cope with civilian life after not knowing anything but constant fighting and killing the "enemies" and fighting for their own lives for 24 months or so? I do hope when they return they do not murder their spouses such as what happened when the first batch of soldiers returned from Afghanistan. I also hope that the U.S. government will allocate the necessary funds to prepare and retrain them so that they will not fall through the cracks and end up committing suicide and or being homeless. I sincerely hope and pray that their fighting mindset will not be carried over into their civilian lives.

According to reports, the Army sent 478 soldiers home from Iraq for mental-health issues during the first several months of the war. Officials said that in previous wars, many of those cases would have been treated in the war zone. The army does not have enough mental-health resources in Iraq to treat many of the cases. This comes back to the fact that the Bush administration took nine months to plan for the war, by some accounts, several years, but did not put enough planning in the necessary resources for the troops.

Will the soldiers who fight in this Iraq war be subjected to another Gulf War Syndrome? Will the United States do everything in its power to ensure that these soldiers are protected from another Gulf War Syndrome? It is incumbent upon the American people to make sure that the government provides the proper care for the returning soldiers. After our troops serve so valiantly in the Iraq war, we should ensure that the wealthiest nation in the world takes care of its veterans and does not allow even one soldier to fall between the cracks and become homeless, or suffer mental incapacity.

An October 6, 2003, CNN "News Night" documentary showed some of the injured soldiers at Walter Reed Hospital. A hospital spokeswoman said they had treated more than 6,600 injured. She also said the injured that are going there are now much more serious. Another spokesman said some come in with limbs that have to be amputated, while others come in with limbs blown off from the blasts.

On top of the trepidation, physical and mental anguish U.S. soldiers faced during combat in Iraq, a number of injured Army reservists and National Guards returned home to Fort Stewart for medical attention and were kept in a concrete holding room for treatment. Hopefully, the situation has been remedied. These soldiers on medical hold are either sick or suffering from injuries. Some of them had to wait as much as six weeks for orthopedic surgery and two months for eye surgery, and the same situation exists in Iraq among the Iraqis seeking help. Soldiers returning home are also advised not to give blood for at least one year to avoid contaminating the U.S. blood supplies.

Grieving Family Faced With A Double Tragedy

Sgt. Ernest Buckley was on his way home on leave from Iraq to attend his mother's funeral when the Chinook helicopter was shot down out of the sky, killing all 16 soldiers on November 2, 2003. The soldier's mother died suddenly on Friday, October 31, leaving the family to grieve over two of their beloved family members. This was such a devastating time in their lives that I do not believe there are any words of comfort that can ever alleviate the hurt that burns inside this family. According to reports, the soldier joined the Army after he was laid off from a vitamin factory. Like many that joined the Army, this soldier, a father of two children, needed a job to take care of his family and the armed forces provided that means to an end.

According to a November 4, 2003, New York Times article by Jeffery Gettleman, one grieving family member said it felt like a hole had been punched straight through them.

Another family member said Bush and some of his family members should go over there and fight for the oil, then Bush would realize what's going on. As long as they are not there they do not care.

Another family member who lost a son in the helicopter attack said the conditions under which the soldiers are living are deplorable and that they are living like dogs. Some of them are sleeping on the ground, not showering much and getting shot at all the time, according to the article.

In spite of these deplorable living conditions, they are expected to be alert at all times to fight whenever they are called upon to fight or to go out on search missions to apprehend suspected insurgents. During the initial phase of the Iraq invasion, U.S. Marines were getting only one meal a day. According to a North County Times article by Erin Walsh, at least some Marines with the Camp Pendleton-based 3rd Battalion, 1st Marine Division in central Iraq were fighting with just one meal a day in their bellies – a meal that nutritionist say wouldn't provide enough daily energy for a young girl, much less a fighting soldier.

A November 16, 2003, New York Times article by Neola Banerjee, headlined, "Rebuilding Bodies and Lives Maimed by War," reported:

Specialist Robert Acosta, of the Army's First Armored Division, was riding in the passenger seat of a Humvee toward the gates of the Baghdad airport when something entered through the window, flew by his face and hit the windshield and landed next to the driver. He grabbed the grenade with his right hand, but as he turned to throw it out the window, he dropped it between his legs. He picked it up again and the grenade exploded in his hand. "It was gone, it just disintegrated," he said of his hand. "It was just a mist of blood." Not only did he lose his right arm, it shattered his legs, the left leg now mended with a steel plate and skin grafts and the hole in his heel almost closed. In place of his right hand and part of his forearm, he wears a prosthesis that ends in a two-pronged claw. "I think I should be dead right now," the 20-year-old Specialist Acosta said. "But I feel like I failed myself. If I hadn't dropped it, I would still have my hand."

As of November 16, 2003, more than 6,800 U.S. soldiers have been evacuated from Iraq for medical reasons, including disease and "nonbattle injuries," the Army said. 58

amputees have been treated at Walter Reed Hospital so far, 47 with major single-limb removals and 11 with multiple-limb amputations.

According to a staff member at Walter Reed Hospital, the wounded from Iraq have changed the population there, from retirees with chronic ailments to young men and a few women, many under age 25, and often with missing limbs. "We have a greater demand, so we have had to hustle a bit, ramp up staff," the chief prosthetist Joseph Miller of Walter Reed Hospital said.

A soldier with the Army's 101st Airborne Division, 21-year-old Specialist Edward Platt from Pittsburgh, Pennsylvania, enlisted right after finishing high school. His parents had been in the Air Force, and he had loved living in Germany as a child. "I like the military, and it was a guaranteed paycheck twice a month," he said. "There's not that kind of guarantee anywhere else these days."

Specialist Platt entered Iraq in the spring from Afghanistan. He was sent to Mosul and while he was near the Syrian border on September 23, 2003, a rocket-propelled grenade tore away his right knee and the top of his shin, but a flap of skin and muscle along the back of his leg still attached his thigh to the lower leg and foot. Specialist Platt arrived at Walter Reed with his lower leg, but after realizing that surgical reconstruction would very likely fail, he decided in early October to have the leg removed a few inches above the knee.

Some of the injured returning from Iraq, in addition to being amputees, also suffer from secondary burns, blindness, deafness, splintered bones in an intact limb, and smashed internal organs.

When physical and occupational therapists from Walter Reed took six soldiers to a bowling alley at the Bethesda Naval Base in nearby Maryland, Specialist Platt, after trying to balance on his new prosthetic limb and bowl, experienced difficulties in controlling the ball and wobbling, so he walked away. Isatta Kanu, a physical therapist's assistant who helped Specialist Platt bowl said, "He's coming to terms with the loss of his leg. He used to be a soldier, a killer, an athlete, and now he's reduced to this."

Another soldier's sad tale happened on July 14, 2003, when a roadside bomb attacked the Humvee that Sgt. Kelley was traveling in near Baghdad. He said he was knocked backward and when he tried to use his foot to go back up it felt like there was nothing under his foot, like there was a hole in the floor of the Humvee. He pulled back his foot but he couldn't see it because of the way it was hanging. He looked at the driver Zayas, and there was blood all over his face. Sgt. Kelley told Zayas that his leg was gone, that it was out on the road back there. He switched his weapon to fire and emptied it. He said, "I was scared out of my mind and furious at the same time." His leg was dangling from a strip of skin. Finally, at the military hospital he wept. First, when the nurse pulled back the covers to show him his bandaged wound. And then, when his wife arrived.

Sgt. Kelley and his wife were both in Iraq as affairs officers with the 490th Civil Affairs Battalion, she in Baghdad and he in Ramadi. Mrs. Kelley went back to work in Baghdad, once her husband was sent to Walter Reed Medical Center. Sgt. Kelley said, "It's not losing the leg that gets me, but what people then do for you after."

Contrary to the United States, which blocked media coverage of the returning bodies, Italy allowed media coverage of its 19 soldiers who were killed in Iraq in November, 2003. The Italian government prepared the way for thousands of its citizens to show their respect by visiting the victims' coffins arrayed inside a palace that towers over the Piazza Venezia Square. The Bush administration is sanitizing the information that is presented to the American people in print, in video and in pictures on the massacre that is taking place in Iraq. On April 23, 2004, a BBC news report showed the large number of flag-draped coffins coming into the United States, and the injured being brought in under the cover of darkness.

According to a November 18, 2003, New York Times article by Frank Bruni, Italy's leaders delivered public statements, the newspapers were jammed with essays about slain heroes, and television reports were filled with crying. He said the country's response also reflects the Italians' emotionalism. Tens of thousands went to Piazza Venezia to see the coffins inside the gargantuan white monument to Victor Emmanuel II, the first king of a United Italy. The outdoor staircase was covered with flowers that they brought: hundreds of bouquets that formed a rainbow-colored carpet, so deep and dense it could be seen at least a quarter of a mile away. He also said an Italian official, Marco Calamai, resigned from the American-led administration running Iraq. Calamai was quoted by the Italian daily Corriere della Sera as saying, "The provisional authority simply doesn't work."

I guess the Bush administration did not want this kind of display in the United States, since it would have most likely affected the 2004 election. There was an outcry by the Italian public against the Italian government's decision to send several thousand Italian police officers, soldiers and civilians to Iraq. This may have prompted the Italian government to honor the fallen soldiers in such a manner. The Italian government displayed the bodies of their fallen soldiers to enable the country to honor them and show their last respects. The Bush administration, on the other hand, brings the bodies of the murdered soldiers back in secret, most likely to squash emotions and critics who say the U.S. should be working out a plan to bring the soldiers home – not sending additional troops to Iraq.

Among the injured returning from Iraq on April 10, 2004, was a Marine with a collapsed lung and a cracked shoulder. Some have lost both limbs and suffered other debilitating injuries such as facial and internal injuries, and of course the mental anguish. Considering what war entails, it should truly be the last resort. So is Bush really a compassionate president as he purported to be in his campaign rhetoric? As governor of Texas he allowed a retarded person to be executed despite requests from all over the world begging for leniency.

It is hard for many to even fathom the position that these soldiers find themselves in while fighting in Iraq, unless they have similar experiences. Yet when asked about how they feel about being in Iraq, most of them politely say that they have a job to do and they are glad to participate in over-throwing Saddam Hussein because of the September 11 attacks on the United States. Yet they live in fear every day that they are there, and I would imagine, yearn to return home to their families. They are expected to perform their duties under extremely difficult conditions, and if for any reason, they cannot fulfill their obligations, they can be brought up on charges, such as what happened to one U.S. soldier who froze when he saw an Iraqi cut in half by ammunition. Pentagon officials said they were considering charges against him for dereliction of duties.

According to a report, the U.S. has played down the fact that female soldiers are also dying in Iraq. They are taking part in major combats, taking roles that were almost inconceivable just a decade or so ago. They are flying fighter jets and attack helicopters, patrolling streets armed with machine guns and commanding units of mostly male soldiers. They have been captured as prisoners of war, killed by enemy fire and buried as heroes in Arlington National Cemetery, yet all this has gone unnoticed, except for the attention given the POW Jessica Lynch by the Pentagon to exaggerate her rescue. According to a July 10, 2003, Reuters article, the unit that included Pfc. Jessica Lynch was ambushed by Iraqi forces in March after the exhausted troops blundered into a "desperate situation" with guns that failed, according to Army investigation.

In view of the fact that female soldiers are involved in many aspects of the war in Iraq, lends itself to the participation in the prisoner abuse by female soldiers. For example, Army Pfc. Lynndie England was accused of dragging a naked prisoner on the ground with a leash around his neck and posing with a cigarette in her mouth. She was court-martialed and sentenced to three years in prison. England said she took part in the abuse to appease her boyfriend, Pvt.

329

Charles Graner Jr. England, a 22-year-old, was pregnant with Graner's child. She said that when Graner showed the pictures to his superior, his superior congratulated him and told him to keep up the good work. Graner concurred with testimony from a defense witness that officers in charge failed to control the guards at the Baghdad prison, creating stressful conditions that disoriented England and led her to take part in the mistreatment.

Another casualty of the war in Iraq are the families left at home living with fear and trepidation, not knowing if and when the doorbell will ring with the bad news that their loved ones have been killed in action. Or seeing their loved ones' decapitated bodies on television. A mother died after she saw her son's body returned from Iraq. The report was that she never stopped crying. And, of course, the ones that have returned home face a new challenge, that of coping with a different world after fighting, in many cases for over seven months, or even up to two years. The adjustment is rather difficult for them. Some of them become dysfunctional. They have to readjust to the fact that they do not have to jump at every little sound or remember that his or her family is not the enemy, but they are having difficulties readjusting. One would suspect that after being desensitized for such a long period of time, it would be extremely difficult if not impossible for some of them to become sensitized again.

Many returning troops are seeking counseling to enable them to return to a life of normalcy. It must be a stressful situation for these military families after a long separation, encountering destruction of lives to which they contribute, whether it be Iraqi soldiers, civilians or insurgents at the same time, facing life-threatening situations themselves. And, to add insult to injury, according to a CNN report, a U.S. soldier returned home after serious injuries including losing an arm, but his last paycheck was withheld because he did not bring back his equipment valued about $300. He was also told that he owed the U.S. over $2,000. This is an affront to the common decency that should be accorded to the soldiers who risk their lives for a war that did not have to take place. It is also like pouring salt into someone's wound.

The following are examples of the kinds of trepidation being endured by soldiers and their families: According to a report, Marine Lance Cpl. Chris Ruh was deployed for one year. Three months after his marriage, he went to Okinawa and then to Iraq. His wife, Peggy Ruh, 19, said she was not prepared for the days leading up to his Iraq duties. "You're kind of in denial for a long time," she said. Once they said goodbye, "it was just like somebody had died," she said.

Cpl. Ruh, on the other hand, said that once his unit breached lines at the Iraq border, he was taking fire and firing back. "It seemed like it was a movie," he said. "It seemed like a dream. This is war."

Cpl. Joshua Stickney remembers what happened to Charlie Company of the 1st Battalion, 2nd Marine Division, every time he went into his office after returning to Camp Lejeune. Empty desks greeted him. Of 14 members of his mortar section in Iraq, nine didn't make it home alive. He also lost his best friend.

Lance Cpl. Michael Williams said that Sgt. Joseph Mosner, U.S. Army, suffered a badly damaged face and broke both his legs when he entered a house that was booby-trapped. He spent nine hours in surgery in Germany while the doctors took shrapnel out of his chest and stomach. He was in an induced coma for seven days and will need two plastic surgeries on his face to restore a semblance to his former appearance.

A BBC News article reported on some of Iraq veterans' unspoken epidemic, namely that Lt. Julian Goodrun returned from the first Gulf War a hero and from the second Gulf War a suicidal wreck. Lt. Goodrun said "My nightmares are so intense I woke up one night with my hands 'round my fiancée's throat." Another night she woke him up because he was kicking and getting violent. He said, "So now I sleep on the couch until I can get my sleep, my nightmares, more under control."

Grieving Mothers

The following article, which appeared in a March 15, 2004, issue of The New York Times, is indicative of some of the views shared by grieving mothers: Nancy Hollinsaid points to her favorite photograph of her son, Lincoln Hollinsaid, wearing an Army uniform somewhere in Iraq. Even his teeth are covered in sand. Rosemarie Dietz Slovenas pulls out a photograph of her son. When people think of him, this is the one she wants them to remember. Brian Slavenas is in uniform, too, that of a Little Leaguer. These two mothers share an obvious pride in their sons. They also share the pain of losing them in Iraq. Army Staff Sgt. Hollinsaid lost his life at the Baghdad Airport and Army 1st Lt. Slavenas lost his life when his helicopter was shot down near Fallujah.

A North County Times photograph by Hayne Palmour showed a couple of Camp Pendleton Marines at a physical therapy clinic. It accompanied an article titled, "Troops wounded in Iraq recover day by day." The article reported that although their emotional and physical scars are deep, some Marines and soldiers who were wounded in Iraq say families, friends and a new physical therapy system at Camp Pendleton are helping them recover their shattered lives.

A November 28, 2005, Wall Street Journal article by Greg Jaffe, headlined, "In Iraq War Zones, Therapists Take On Soldiers Trauma." In Tal Afar, Iraq Lt. Maria Kimble, an Army mental-health worker, runs a two-person counseling team out of a small plywood office. ... One of her first patients was Sgt. Richard Parkinson. After his first tour of Iraq, which ended in the summer of 2004, he suffered nightmares and bursts of anger that grew worse once he came home. He sought counseling, but after only four sessions at his base, he was sent back to Iraq. Since returning he has had to respond to suicide bombings. One image burned into his mind, he said, is that of an Iraqi man who was missing his arm, begging him for help. Lt. Kimble said, "If I had the power, I'd stick him on a plane and send him home." One

might ask – was toppling Saddam worth the lives of so many
people?

NINE

PRISONER ABUSE

Since the attacks on the United States on September 11, 2001, the Bush administration has changed the rules of the law as it pertains to suspected terrorists. For example, the United States is holding over 660 prisoners at Guantanamo Bay from over 44 countries without being charged, without having access to lawyers, or being able to see or speak to their families. They cannot challenge their arrests or even plead their cases before a judge, and they have no contact with the outside world, which is raising great concerns among many people all over the world.

According to a December 8, 2003, Time magazine article, some prisoners try to commit suicide because there is no way out of their predicament. There were 32 suicide attempts within an eighteen-month period, which left one prisoner in a coma. Prisoners try to kill themselves by making a noose out of clothes or sheets and tried to hang themselves from the cell bars. One prisoner tried to slit his throat with a knife he had made from metal. The new mental health clinic on the base is usually close to full. Although the U.S. released some prisoners they consider harmless, new ones are always arriving. Maj. Gen. Geoffrey Miller, the officer in charge of the detention mission, said that the three youngest boys at the jail, who range from 13 to 15 would be transferred, but he did not give a date.

Relatives must be desperate and frustrated not being able to see or speak to their loved ones, some of whom I might add are probably innocent of any terrorist affiliations or crimes against humanity. I am not being sympathetic to the terrorists, I just want us to be cognizant of the fact that not all suspects are terrorists. They are labeled "enemy combatants" which means there are no rules or guidelines as to how they can be treated, so the Bush administration has given itself power and control over these detainees, many of whom have been locked away for several years.

On December 1, 2003, the U.S. announced that more than 100 prisoners, men and boys, would be released from Guantanamo Bay, and more would follow. No mention was made as to whether these released prisoners would be returned to their respective countries or be transferred to other facilities. Among the prisoners to be released were three teenagers. No specific charge was made against them.

According to reports, in February 2004, Britain and the United States negotiated a deal to send nine British detainees back home. Clive Stafford Smith, a U.S.-based British human rights lawyer, told The Observer, a British newspaper, that two of the nine British detainees, Asif Iqbal and Shafig Rasul, were likely to be released and not charged with a crime while the other seven would serve sentences in British jails after pleading guilty to unspecified charges in the United States. The British Foreign office declined to confirm the report and said that discussions with U.S. were continuing.

The following article from World – AP Australia & Antarctica dated October 8, 2003, gives a glimpse into the torture methods being used against these so-called enemy combatants by the United States:

> The U.S. military has tortured terrorist suspects held without charge at the Guantanamo Bay military prison, an Australia lawyer representing some of the suspects claimed. U.S.-based Richard Bourke, who has been working for almost two years on behalf of dozens of detainees at Guantanamo Bay, said American military officials were using old-fashioned torture techniques to force confes-

sions out of prisoners. The methods "clearly" fell under the definition of torture under international conventions, he told Australian Broadcasting Corporation Radio in an interview from the United States. "They are engaging in good old-fashion torture, as people would have understood it in the Dark Ages," he said. Earlier in 2003, U.S. officials denied using torture and said detainees are interrogated humanely, allowed to practice their religion and given good medical care. Families are denied access and can only communicate with detainees through heavily censored mail. Human rights groups and the media have been given only limited and strictly controlled access.

Bourke told ABC radio that his claims are based on reports leaked by U.S. military personnel and from descriptions by some detainees that have been released. "One of the detainees had described being taken out and tied to a post and having rubber bullets fired at them. They were being made to kneel cruciform in the sun until they collapsed," he said. Media reports that many detainees have attempted suicide and are suffering mental health problems are backed by claims of harsh treatment, he said. Bourke said governments around the world must stand up to the U.S. government and demand that the United Nations investigates the reports of torture. Almost all the detainees, from more than 40 countries, are said to be members of the al-Qaeda terrorist network or the ousted Afghan Taliban regime. They are to be tried by secret military tribunals. The U.S. government says they could be held until it declares an end to its "war on terrorism."

Guantanamo Bay a Black Hole

A December 18, 2003, Reuter's article by Grant McCool, stated: The U.S. Navy base in Guantanamo Bay,

Cuba, where suspected Taliban soldiers are being held, is a "physical and moral black hole," according to Australian lawyer Stephen Kenny, the first civilian lawyer allowed to meet a client there, David Hicks of Adelaide, Australia. By this time, the detainees have been held for two years without charges or contact with the outside world. Kenny said the United States had not issued a timetable for Hicks' case and "I don't know when, or if, David will be formally charged, or if or when he will come to trial." Hicks converted to Islam, was arrested in December 2001 while fighting with the Taliban. Kenny said Hicks, one of two Australians being held, had not killed or injured U.S. or Australian military personnel. Kenny said "he did not see any other detainees, not even in passing." The New York-based Center for Constitutional Rights will argue the detainees' case before the Supreme Court.

According to a Time magazine article, Sgt. John Campbell, a National Guardsman on a one-year deployment, when asked by a Time Magazine reporter what he misses most besides his family, talks as if he is in a detention too: "the ability to get in a car and drive somewhere else." According to the article, every week approximately half the detainees are brought in for sessions that may last anywhere from one hour to 16 hours. They are conducted by any of the 40 four-person "tiger" teams – two interrogators, a linguist and an analyst.

When you think of it, the soldiers at Guantanamo Bay are also in confinement due to the fact that they are guarding the detainees on a one-year deployment basis. The base operates on 45 square miles of property. The troops have nowhere else to go because the rest of Cuba is off limits.

According to a December 19, 2003, Washington Post article by Dan Eggen, hundreds of videotapes that federal prisoner officials had claimed were destroyed show that foreign nationals held at a New York detention facility after September 11, 2001, attacks were victims of physical and verbal abuse by guards, the Justice Department's inspector general Glen A. Fine said. Also, U.S. Bureau of Prisons improperly taped meetings between detainees and their lawyers at the Metropolitan Detention Center in Brooklyn, New York, used excessive strip searches and restraints to punish those in confinement. As many as 20 guards were involved in the abuse, which included slamming prisoners against the walls and painfully twisting their arms and hands. Some stepped on their leg restraint chains and punished them by keeping them restricted for long periods of time.

And, of course, the prisoner abuse goes well beyond Guantanamo Bay. The following which appeared in an Associated Press 2003 article, gives some insight into the kinds of abuses that are taking place in Iraq, and I am sure Afghanistan and other countries where the Bush administration is holding prisoners:

Detainees in U.S. custody in Iraq are being treated inhumanely. In Iraq's American detention camps, forbidden talks can earn a prisoner hours bound and stretched out in the sun. In these secretive islands in a scorched landscape, "they don't respect anyone, old or young" Rahad Naif said of his U.S. Army guards. He and others told of detainees in wheelchairs, and of a man carried into a stifling hot tent in his sickbed. "They humiliate everybody." Naif, 31, is one of three brothers, butchers from the east Baghdad slums, who were thrown into the three biggest detention centers by the Americans in July after a nasty quarrel with an influential neighbor.

Among the many discomforts, a prisoner said, is that 1,000 men in his section at Bucca had to share just 10 water taps. They would throw ice into the sand just to make them suffer psychologically. The common punishment, even for such lesser infractions as shouting over to the next tent or stealing food, was "The Gardens," a razor-wire enclosure where prisoners were made to lie face down on the burning sand for two or three hours, hands bound.

Amnesty International officials say they have received credible reports of shootings of prisoners. AP asked the U.S. command about deaths in the camps, but got no response.

American forces began capturing Iraqis and placing them in camps as soon as they captured Iraq. An article published in The Wall Street Journal on June 26, 2003, reports: It was nearly a month since U.S. authorities took Eman Hussain's husband away in a blue van to be interrogated about Iraq's biological weapons programs. "If he doesn't return, I'm going to kill myself," the 42-year-old mother of three said as she waited in vain for an American who had promised to try to bring word of her husband's condition. Her husband, Thamer Abdul Rahman, was a senior official in Iraq's anthrax program during the 1980s and early 1990s, according to U.S. officials and U.N. weapons experts.

Almost on a daily basis, U.S. and British forces take into custody senior officials from Saddam Hussein's regime. Among the many arrested is Gen. Abid Hamid Mahmud al-Tikriti, Saddam's personal secretary.

In January 2004, a report in the Wall Street Journal quoted several prisoners at Abu Ghraib who said they were ordered to stand upright for as long as 10 hours until they collapsed and were spat at and burned with a cigarette. One of the detainees, a small-business owner named Jajim Abdulhussein, told a Journal reporter shortly after he was released that guards at the prison told him that if he didn't confess to supporting the insurgency in Iraq that U.S. soldiers would gang rape his wife.

Similarly, Amnesty International said it has uncovered a "pattern of torture" of Iraqi prisoners by coalition troops. It has since been reported that the Pentagon knew as far back as October 2003 of the abuse, but never informed Congress. The Journal also reported that a 37-year-old shopkeeper in the Karada neighborhood of Baghdad said that "They want to fool us by saying they are here for the benefit of the Iraqis, but they are here for their own interest and treat us like animals. What goes around comes around; the Americans deserve to get killed every day. I hope more of them die."

In late April 2004, reports surfaced that confirmed the Associated Press article that the U.S. soldiers have abused the prisoners in Iraq. Photographs depicting U.S. soldiers humiliating naked Iraqi prisoners, as well as allegations leveled in an internal U.S. military report that some military intelligence officials in Iraq may have condoned or even encouraged some of the abuse have outraged the international community. Images of naked Iraqi prisoners being forced to simulate sex acts were aired repeatedly on Arab television and were splashed across the front pages of newspapers in many countries.

On May 6, 2004, new pictures surfaced, showing an Iraqi prisoner naked on the ground with a leash around his neck, being pulled by a U.S. soldier, and another shackled to a bed, with just the frames and spring, no mattress, with a ladies undergarment over his head. These abuses will no doubt fuel further outrage and attacks by Muslim radicals against the U.S. and its allies. U.S. officials knew about the allegations months before it became public. They issued letters of reprimand to the soldiers involved, but the soldiers may have been following orders, according to reports. At first the Bush administration claimed that the abuse in Iraq's Abu Ghraib prison appear to be isolated acts by low-level soldiers.

The CIA's inspector general probed several allegations, including one in which a prisoner died at Abu Ghraib in 2003. According to a May 24, 2004, Wall Street Journal article a total of 33 detainees have died in Iraq. The CIA probe would also examine allegations that a CIA case officer brandished a weapon and possibly fired it while questioning an Iraqi prisoner.

Maj. Gen. George Fay, the deputy commander of U.S. Army intelligence, led an investigation into the conduct of military intelligence officers at Abu Ghraib. A 53-page U.S. military report, completed in February, said that military police at the prison were urged by military intelligence officers and CIA agents to "set physical and mental conditions for favorable interrogation of witnesses."

Also, a May 18, 2004, Reuters article said that U.S. forces beat three Iraqis working for Reuters and subjected them to sexual and religious taunts and humiliation during their detention in January in a military camp near Fallujah. The three first told Reuters of the deal after their release but only decided to make it public when the U.S. military said there was no evidence they had been abused, and following the exposure of similar mistreatment of detainees at Abu Ghraib prison near Baghdad. They were forced to make demeaning gestures as soldiers laughed, taunted them and took photographs.

Furthermore, there was a report that Donald Rumsfeld ordered a special task force to use extraordinary measures to pry information from the captured Iraqi prisoners. And, a May 27, 2004, article in The Wall Street Journal stated that a U.S. official said that among documents regarding the Iraq-prison scandal that the Pentagon failed to give Congress is one described as a "draft update for the Secretary of Defense" on interrogation rules. The date and contents of the document referring to Defense Secretary Donald Rumsfeld are unknown. But Col. Thomas Pappas, the senior intelligence officer at Baghdad's Abu Ghraib prison, suggested in testimony to Army investigators that it discussed a set of rules to guide interrogations in Iraq and suggests that military police should "support interrogations." Congressional staffers said they hadn't received 2,000 pages of the 6,000-page Army investigation into the prison-abuse scandal.

Also, according to a June 17, 2004, New York Times article by Eric Schmitt and Thom Shanker, in November 2003, Rumsfeld, acting at the request of George Tenet, ordered military officials in Iraq to hold a man suspected of being a senior Iraqi terrorist at a high-level detention center there but not to list him on the prisoners' rolls. This prisoner and other "ghost detainees" were hidden largely to prevent the International Committee of the Red Cross from monitoring their treatment, and to avoid disclosing their location to an enemy. Maj. Gen. Antonio M. Taguba, the Army officer who in February investigated abuses at the Abu Graib prison, criticized the practice of allowing ghost detainees there and at other detention centers as deceptive, contrary to Army doctrine, and in violation of international law.

Attorney General John Ashcroft set torture methods for detainees in U.S. custody in Afghanistan, Guantanamo Bay and Iraq, and for all we know, other countries as well. The memo written by Ashcroft defining the methods including but not limited to pain that is difficult to endure, physical pain amounting to torture must be equivalent in intensity to the pain accompanying serious physical injury, such as organ failure, impairment of bodily function, or even death.

On April 30, 2005, a high-level military investigation into the prisoner abuse concluded that many prisoners were mistreated or humiliated, perhaps illegally, as a result of efforts to devise innovative methods to gain information.

A May 25, 2005, Associated Press article stated that Amnesty International said that Guantanamo Bay is "the gulag of our time," and urged Washington to shut it down. Amnesty said the U.S. administration has sanctioned interrogation techniques that violated the U.N. Geneva Convention against torture, and is shirking its responsibility to set the bar for human rights protections. The use of the term gulag refers to the extensive system of prison camps in the former Soviet Union and many remote regions of Siberia specifically designed to hold political prisoners. In mid-May 2005 the Red Cross told U.S. authorities of detainee allegations that Qurans had been desecrated. It also offered a rare public rebuke in late 2003, calling the prisoners' prolonged detentions "warring."

Declassified FBI records released on May 25, 2005 showed that prisoners at Guantanamo Bay told U.S. interrogators as early as April 2002, just four months after the first detainees arrived from Afghanistan, that U.S. military guards abused them and desecrated the Quran. Since this is the case, why did Newsweek have to withdraw its article on the burning of the Quran? Also disturbing is a June 25, 2004 memo to one of Donald Rumsfeld's top advisers that U.S. Special Forces accused of abusing prisoners in Iraq warned defense intelligence personnel not to talk about the alleged mistreatment they saw.

James J. Yee, a graduate of West Point and a former chaplain at Guatanamo Bay, was arrested in 2003 on suspicion of espionage. He said the guards would be constantly reminded of the September 11 attacks by General Miller and others and they "retaliated in whatever way they could" against the detainees. He said to extract prisoners from their cells, soldiers used a procedure known as "irfing" a team in heavy body armor, called an Immediate Reaction Force, which would physically subdue the prisoners and remove them from their cells. The charges against Mr. Yee were later dropped and Mr. Yee was given an honorable discharge.

After much criticism of the prisoner abuse, the Bush administration arranged for a controlled visit by a number of congressmen to Guntanamo Bay on June 25, 2005, who reported back that the prisoners were getting good treatment and well-fed. But a September 9, 2005, BBC news report refuted their findings. The BBC reported that they were not well-treated or well-fed and cited a case where a prisoner found a scorpion in his meal. One would have to be naïve to think that they would see anything other than an ideal situation during a pre-arranged visit. An impromptu visit on the other hand would give a more accurate picture. The BBC report also said that 20 children are being held in Solitary Five, and although not found guilty by the U.S.'s own tribunal, are still being held in solitary confinement.

Some Democratic lawmakers want an independent investigation into the prisoner abuse. However; on June 26, 2005, on NBC's "Meet the Press, Defense Secretary Donald Rumsfeld said, "I think that to go back into all of the things that's already been reviewed by everybody else doesn't make sense."

A June 26, 2005, Reuters article said that in a statement to mark U.N. International Day in Support of Victims of Torture, President Bush said "Freedom from torture is an inalienable human right, and we are committed to building a world where human rights are respected and protected by the rule of law." However; according to an October 6, 2005, New York Times article by Eric Schmitt, the White House was threatening to veto a $440 billion military spending bill if a detention amendment was tacked on, saying it would bind the president's hands in wartime. The amendment would ban the use of "cruel, inhuman or degrading treatment or punishment" against anyone in United States government custody. The amendment was endorsed by more than two dozen retired senior military officials, including Colin Powell and John M. Shalikashvili, former chairman of the Joint Chiefs of Staff. On October 5, 2005, the Senate overwhelmingly agreed to the amendment, defying the White House.

Appearing on CNN in November 2005, retired U.S. Army Col. Larry Wilkson, a former chief of staff to Colin Powell, said that Vice President Dick Cheney provided the "philosophical guidance" and "flexibility" that led to the torture of detainees in U.S. facilities. He said, "There is no question in my mind that we did. There's no question in my mind that we may be still doing it." He said Cheney's implementer in the case was Defense Secretary Donald Rumsfeld and the Defense Department.

Cheney lobbied against the measure in Congress that would outlaw "cruel, inhumane and degrading treatment."

On February 13, 2006, the U.N. Commission on Human Rights said the U.S. committed acts amounting to torture at Guantanamo Bay, including force-feeding detainees and subjecting them to prolonged solitary confinement.

TEN

IRAQ'S RECONSTRUCTION

When the Bush administration said it would go to war against Iraq with or without the United Nations or the help of its allies, apparently, it never envisioned the extent of the problems that would arise once the major conflict was over, except for the feasibility study of the oil industry conducted in the fall of 2002. For one thing, it never planned sufficiently for the needs of the Iraqis or recognized that the process of putting Iraq back together again after the demolition would be such a monumental task, not only as it relates to the financial costs, but also its stabilization. Or maybe the Bush administration had hoped that once Iraq was invaded, all the other nations would be glad to join in the rebuilding efforts. In other words, fall in line. However, the country erupted in disarray and chaos became the everyday norm.

Because of the staggering costs of rebuilding Iraq's infrastructure, the Bush administration turned to the nations that it had once berated to help with the reconstruction costs. It called on the United Nations to help allay the Iraqis' fear that the U.S. will remain an occupier for years to come. And it wants other nations to help with the rebuilding efforts by pledging funds, and to forgive billions of dollars in debt owed to them by Iraq.

Bush administration officials ridiculed France's President Jacques Chirac for insisting that it was not necessary to attack Iraq without U.N. sanction. In a very poignant statement, Chirac called on the U.S. to let the U.N. resolution take its course by completing the inspection, and if necessary give the nod for the invasion. The media also jumped on the bandwagon, ridiculing France for not participating in the invasion of Iraq, saying that the U.S. fought for France and now that the U.S. needs France they are not with us. Germany and Russia also called for the U.N. to complete the inspection, and refused to attack Iraq. However, neither the Bush administration officials nor the media attacked those countries.

The Bush administration was well aware of the problems that would be attendant to the oil industry as stated in the following October 4, 2003, New York Times article:

> A government task force secretly established in the fall of 2002 to study Iraq's oil industry gave a bleak assessment. However, early in 2003, the Bush administration said that Iraq's oil revenues would be $20 billion to $30 billion a year, which added to the impression that the aftermath of the war would place a minimal burden on the United States. Bremer estimated that Iraq's total oil revenues from the last half of 2003 to 2005 would be about $35 billion, running at a rate of $14 billion a year.
>
> Lawrence Di Rita, the Pentagon's chief spokesman said, "I think when it is all said and done, prewar estimates that may be borne out in fact are likelier to be more lucky than smart." He added that earlier estimates and statements by Wolfowitz and others "oozed with uncertainty."
>
> Amy Myers Jaffe, who heads the energy program at the James A. Baker III Institute for Public Policy at Rice University in Houston, said her group concluded in a report in December 2002 that "oil revenues would not be enough and that the expenses of reconstruction would be huge."
>
> Moreover, the United Nations reports dating back to the late 1990s documented the deterioration that occurred in Iraq's oil system as a result of trade embargoes, which curtailed Iraq's access to technology and equipment.

In September of 2002, Douglas J. Feith, the under secretary of defense for policy, asked an adviser to oversee plans for Iraq's oil industry in the event of war, according to a Pentagon official involved in the project. The result was that the Energy Infrastructure Planning Group drew on its expertise of government specialists including the Central Intelligence Agency and retired senior energy executives. It planned how to secure the oil industry during the war and afterward, restoring it to its prewar capacity. The task force's job was not to make a direct assessment of how much money the oil industry could contribute to rebuilding Iraq, but determining Iraq's actual oil production capacity. The reason for this was two-fold. First, it could help other administration officials gauge how much revenue might be generated for the reconstruction effort. Second, the administration was concerned that it did not want to be seen as profiting from invading an oil-rich nation and giving oil production levels a boost. The task force concluded that although Iraq's stated production capacity was just over 3 million barrels per day, the system was only producing 2.1 million to 2.4 million barrels.

The United Nations produced reports on Iraq regularly from 1998 to 2001. The documents painted a picture of a troubled system and cited the need for improvements, some of which are now being proposed by Bremer, such as the $125 million repair of the Qarmat Ali water plant in the south. On March 27, 2003, Mr. Wolfowitz, the deputy defense secretary, told the House Appropriations Committee that his "rough recollection" was that "The oil revenues of that country would bring between $50 billion and $100 billion over the course of the next two or three years." Also on March 27, Rumsfeld testifying before the Senate, said, "when it comes to reconstruction, before we turn to the

American taxpayers we will turn first to the resources of the Iraqi government." In April 2003 when Vice President Dick Cheney was asked about Iraq's oil during an appearance before newspaper editors, he cited higher numbers rather than the task force's findings. Cheney said, "With some investment we ought to be able to get production back up on the order of 2.5 to 3 million barrels a day, within, hopefully by the end of the year."

At the outset of the war, the administration asked Congress for $62 billion for Iraq, which included $1.7 billion for reconstruction and $489 million for oil-related repairs. In a televised interview in late April 2003, Andrew S. Natsios, head of the United States Agency for International Development, the group overseeing Iraq's reconstruction, said that amount was "it for the U.S." He said any other reconstruction money would come from elsewhere, including other countries and future "Iraqi oil revenues," which he predicted at "$20 billion a year." In an interview in early October 2003, Natsios said, he had based those comments on "the discussion in the interagency process at the time," adding, "That's what the Office of Management and Budget was telling us."

In July 2003, Wolfowitz told a group of senators that production had reached "over a million barrels per day." Although Iraq was having electrical power problems, Mr. Wolfowitz said the oil was flowing "because we brought in portable generators to provide electricity" and planned to bring in more. However, Phillip Carroll, retired petroleum executive and the senior American oil adviser in Baghdad, said that Iraqi oil production "experienced a terrible month in July because electrical problems cut us back to half of what we should have produced." Those problems, including the need to import considerable fuel, he said, led him to arrange new generator leases in late July. He also said that although gross production for the week of July 25 was a million barrels a day, 350,000 barrels had to be injected back into the ground, because of lack of storage or distribution infrastructure.

An October 5, 2003, New York Times article by Jeff Gerth, stated:

The task force, which was based at the Pentagon as part of the planning for the war, produced a book-length report describing the Iraqi oil industry as so badly damaged by a decade of trade embargoes that its production capacity had fallen by more than 25 percent. Despite those findings, Deputy Defense Secretary Paul D. Wolfowitz told Congress during the war that "we are dealing with a country that can really finance its own reconstruction, and relatively soon." Vice President Dick Cheney said in April, on the day that Baghdad fell, that Iraq's oil production could hit 3 million barrels a day by the end of the year, even though the task force had determined that Iraq was generating less than 2.4 million barrels a day before the war. Probably one of the main reasons the Bush administration requested $20.3 billion from Congress for Iraq's reconstruction is the frequency of oil field sabotage and the poor state of the oil infrastructure. In September 2003, Bremer, the American-appointed civilian administrator in Iraq said "The oil infrastructure was severely run down over the past 20 years and partly because of sanctions over the last decades."

According to the findings of United Nations missions, Iraq would need $36 billion for reconstruction for the years 2004 to 2007. The missions were undertaken by the U.N. Development Group and the World Bank Group with assistance from the International Monetary Fund (IMF) soon after the purported major combat ended. This was in addition to the $20 billion the United States-led Coalition Provisional Authority (CPA) said would be needed in critical sectors, including security and oil. According to the mission's findings, Iraq's overall reconstruction needs were vast and are a result of years of neglect and degradation of the country's infrastructure, environment and social services.

Under the U.N. Oil-for-Food program, some of the needs are covered. For instance, in 2004 about $1 billion of these needs were covered by ongoing contracts.

In August 1990 the Security Council adopted resolution 661, imposing comprehensive sanctions on Iraq following that country's invasion of Kuwait. Throughout 1991, with growing concerns over the humanitarian situation in Iraq, the United Nations and others proposed measures to enable Iraq to sell limited quantities of oil to meet its people's needs.

The Oil-for-Food program began at the end of 1996 after the United Nations and the government of Iraq agreed on the details of implementing resolution 986 (1995), which permitted Iraq to sell up to $2 billion dollars worth of oil in a 180-day period. The ceiling on oil sales was eased during 1998 and finally lifted in 1999, enabling the program to move from a focus on food and medicine to repairing essential infrastructure, including the oil industry.

The program operated against distribution plans prepared at the beginning of each phase by the government of Iraq and approved by the Secretary-General. Once approved, the distribution plan became the basis for Iraq's use of revenue raised during that phase.

Phase I of the Oil-for-Food program ran from December 10, 1996 to June 7, 1997. The first oil exported on December 15, 1996, and the first contracts financed from the sale of oil were approved in January 1997. The first shipment of food arrived in Iraq in March 1997 and the first medicine in May 1997. The Security Council continued the programme in 180-day periods called "phases." The final oil exporting period (phase XIII) authorized by Security Council resolution 1447 (2002), was in effect from December 5, 2002 through June 3, 2003.

Between March 1997 and March 2003, foodstuffs worth $13 billion and medicines and supplies worth $2 billion have been delivered to Iraq. The program helped to improve the overall socio-economic condition of the Iraqi people and prevent further degradation of public services and infrastructure. Resolution 1175 in June 1998 authorized the import of $300 million worth of oil spare parts and equipment for phase IV, and was raised to $600 million per phase from phase VI onwards. A year later, Security Council resolution 1284 (1999) removed the oil export ceiling altogether. On May 14, 2002, the Security Council (resolution 1409) introduced the Goods Review List (GRL) and a new set of procedures for the processing and approval of contracts for civilian supplies and equipment. Until that time, most contracts for humanitarian supplies were circulated to the council's 661 Sanctions committee for approval. Under the new procedures only contracts containing GRL items were to be sent to the 661 Committee for consideration.

Once Iraq came under the control of the U.S. after the invasion, the Governing Council in Iraq allows foreign companies to establish 100 percent ownership of businesses in Iraq, an unusual arrangement in the Middle East. One can see why these companies would be gearing up to doing business in Iraq. Bear in mind that on many occasions the Bush administration led almost everyone to believe that Iraq's oil wealth, not American taxpayers, would cover the cost of rebuilding Iraq.

A New York Times article published October 6, 2003, by Bernhard Zand, "Slaves of the Foreigners," stated:

> By radically opening up the Iraqi economy, America wants to attract international corporations to the banks of the Tigris. Iraqis are concerned that their country is being sold out ... Mr. Feisal al-Chudeiri's family, one of the oldest in the land of

two rivers, has seen the Ottomans, the British and Saddam Hussein come and go. Since 1772, the family has traded in dates, tea and spices, and in 1881 it founded the first steamship company on the Euphrates river. "Things don't throw us off track that easily," says the junior of the Karady Group, but I doubt that this applies to the rest of the Iraqis. Four sheets of paper bearing the sober heading "Law on the Regulation of Foreign Investment" sit on his desk. "The Americans have already made quite a few mistakes in Iraq, he says gloomily, but this law is their biggest mistake so far. It has the effect of dynamite."

Minister of Finance Kamil al-Kilani has promised that the law, put into force by the U.S. Administrator, L. Paul Bremer, will liberate Iraq from a planned economy, open the country to the global market, bring technology to the Tigris, and create jobs. In truth, the package of reforms promises foreign interests virtually unlimited access to the country's most profitable industries. Beginning in 2004, foreign nationals will be able to acquire full ownership of local firms, and even a few banks, and it will be possible to siphon off profits to other countries without restrictions. Hundreds of former state-owned businesses will be open to privatization, leaving only the oil and gas industry under government control. Scrutiny of potential investors to assess their reliability and capabilities, an absolute necessity during such changes to a system, will not be required.

Foreign companies are permitted to establish factories and local subsidiaries, the taxes they pay are capped at 15 percent, and a 5 percent duty is charged on imports. In fact, they will not be liable for payment of any taxes or duties until the end of the year. The British business publication, The Economist, praised the new law for fulfilling the "wish list of international investors," and called Bremer's creation a "capital dream." Iraqis, however, are incensed at what they fear is a sell-off of their country. Powerful interest groups previously at odds over the country's future course, suddenly find themselves joining forces in a common front opposing the economic reforms. Foreign capital is welcome, concedes moderate Sheikh Sadr al-Din al-Qubanji of the Supreme Council for Islamic Revolution in Iraq, but he is also concerned about Iraq's loss of control over investors. Radical Shiite leader Muqtada al-Sadr demands that the law be repealed, "otherwise we will act."

After being so adamant about taking unilateral action, President Bush turned to France, Germany and Russia asking them to forgive Iraq's debt of billions of dollars. I am befuddled to understand the thinking behind the Bush administration officials' decision, because while they were asking these countries for debt forgiveness of billions of dollars and pledges, at the same time, they issued a directive that excluded these countries and others from $18 billion in American-financed Iraqi construction projects. It is mind boggling how the Bush administration can slap these nations in their faces and on the other hand ask them for financial help. The explanation given by the Pentagon that the restrictions were required "for the protection of the essential security interests of the United States" should incense these nations. It appears that the U.S. was saying to these nations, you did not back us in the war, you cannot participate in the U.S.-funded rebuilding process, but if you want to be in our good graces again, then you can forgive the billions of dollars owed to you by Iraq and pledge millions of dollars to help with the rebuilding efforts.

According to reports, the National Security Council and committee deputies from a number of departments agreed, and the White House signed off on it, that the most lucrative contracts must be reserved for political or military support-ers. The United States Trade Representative's office said that contracts with the occupation authority "are not covered by international trade procurement obligations because the C.P.A. is not an entity subject to these obligations. Accord-ingly, there is no need to invoke the essential security excep-tion to our trade obligations."

A December 18, 2003, Washington Post article by Dana Milbank stated:

White House officials were steamed when An-drew S, Natsios, the administrator of the U.S. Agency for International Development, said earlier in the year that U.S. taxpayers would not have to pay more than $1.7 billion to reconstruct Iraq, which turned out to be a gross understatement of tens of billions of dollars the government now ex-pects to spend. Not long after this information ap-peared on the government Web site, it was scrubbed.

Steven Aftergood, who directs the Project on Government Secrecy at the Federation of American Scientists, said the Natsios case is particularly per-nicious. "This smells like an attempt to revise the records, not just to withhold information but to alter the historical record in a self-interested way, and that is sleazier than usual," he said.

When Ted Koppel asked Natsios on ABC's "Nightline," "You're not suggesting that the re-building of Iraq is going to be done for $1.7 bil-lion?" Natsios replied, "Well, in terms of the American taxpayers' contribution, I do. This is it for the U.S. The rest of the rebuilding of Iraq will be done by other countries that have already made pledges. Britain, Germany, Norway, Japan, Canada and Iraq oil revenues ... But the American part of this will be $1.7 billion. We have no plans for any further funding for this." USAID had put the transcript on its Web site but that also was scrubbed.

Another situation where the Bush administration backtracked is how the billions of dollars being pledged to rebuild Iraq's infrastructure would be handled. According to a report, after being under pressure from potential donors, the administration allowed a new agency to determine how to spend the billions of dollars in reconstruction assistance in Iraq. The new agency would be independent of the American occupation, and would be run by the World Bank and the United Nations. The change established some of the international control over Iraq that the United States opposed in the drafting of the United Nations Security Council resolution. Some countries were unwilling to make donations because they saw the United States as an occupying power controlling Iraq's infrastructure and self-rule.

In the meantime, a debate intensified in both houses of Congress over President Bush's $87 billion request for Iraq and Afghanistan. A bipartisan group of swing senators picked up support for a compromise proposal to rebuild Iraq with a combination of grants and loans. The compromise was intended as a way to reduce the burden on American taxpayers to rebuild Iraq, while persuading other countries to ease Iraq's debt. Lending reconstruction money to Iraq was vigorously opposed by the White House and the Republican leadership. Senators worked on a plan to give $20.3 billion as a grant only if the administration persuaded other countries to forgive most of Iraq's $200 billion debt. Sen. Evan Bayh, D-Ind., said it would give them leverage in terms of insisting the rest of the world do the right thing, which was to forgive Iraq's debt. The administration sent Secretary of State Colin Powell and Vice President Dick Cheney to Capital Hill to work against the loan proposals, according to the report.

From the offset of the war, the United States was emphatic about keeping control of Iraq and not allowing other countries to play any major role in its rebuilding. It insisted on going to war unilaterally and to unilaterally control Iraq's oil and the rebuilding of its infrastructure. When Americans started to question the logic of U.S. spending so much money to rebuild Iraq's infrastructure at a time when their own infrastructure is in need of repairs, some members in Congress said the money should be a combination of loan and grant. The Congress wanted to give Iraq a loan of $20.3 billion for its reconstruction. Sen. Susan Collins, R-Maine, said she would introduce an amendment that would require Iraq to pay back the reconstruction money once it begins making more money from its oil. However, the GOP senators said the money for Iraq must be a grant, not a loan.

According to a September 30, 2003, New York Times article by David Firestone, Sen. Ted Stevens, R-Alasca, chairman of the Senate Appropriations Committee, said Iraq was too economically fragile to bear debt, and Sen. John McCain, R-Arizona, said such a strategy would make it appear the United States was only after Iraq's oil riches. When questioned at a news conference regarding the need for an expensive aid package, Stevens said "This is an experiment, and it's risky, really risky." "But if it comes through, we will not have an army of occupation. If it comes through, we'll bring more of our people home, and there will be more people in Iraqi uniforms being policemen and providing the defense of that country sooner, if we act and give them the $20.3 billion now."

After almost a year had passed, the U.S. was no closer to bringing the troops home than when it first attacked Iraq. Republican leaders said they would make few substantive changes to President Bush's request. Committee leaders would put few restrictions on the administration's ability to spend the reconstruction money on scores of projects, many of which have been criticized by lawmakers of both parties as less than essential. An example of some of the things that were done with this money was to pay 500 consultants $100,000 to $200,000 and pay $8,000 per student to attend some kind of specialized school.

Democrats accused the Republicans of trying to rush through a bill they knew was unpopular with the public. Sen. Robert C. Byrd, the ranking Democrat on the Appropriations Committee, said the Senate was failing in its responsibility to examine closely a bill that would authorize the spending of 50 percent more than the education budget. He said, "We need a complete examination of this attempt to transform a political culture very different from our own into a democracy – a form of government never before seen in those ancient lands." "Make no mistake: this bill is the beginning of an enormous, yearlong commitment to Iraq for a mission that may well be impossible."

Many Republican lawmakers and Democrats who did not want to use American taxpayers' money to rebuild Iraq, a country that is sitting on billions of dollars in oil reserves, wanted Iraq to repay at least part of the $20.3 billion in reconstruction aid that the Bush administration requested.

Senator Mitch McConnel of Kentucky said, "The country is flat on its back, with its infrastructure destroyed, and we want to go in there and charge them for liberating their country?" To appease those who wanted Iraq to foot some of the reconstruction costs, Senate Majority Leader Bill Frist decided to postpone the vote from the week of October 1, 2003, to mid-October. Of course, this was only a ploy devised by the Senator to appease the Democrats, who urged a slower pace so that they could examine the requests much closer. However, in the end the Bush administration got what it wanted.

In Bob Woodward's book, "Plan of Attack," he wrote that President Bush left Congress in the dark when he secretly diverted $700 million worth of projects in July 2002 to prepare for the possible invasion of Iraq.

According to an October 1, 2003, New York Times article by David Firestone, Sen. Arlen Specter, R-Penn, said, "We are not asking for Iraqi oil to fund our military operations. We are asking that this Iraqi asset, the second biggest oil field in the world, be used to pay for their obligations. We shouldn't be too fast to give away $20 billion if we can find some way not to." The Bush administration sharply criticized these contentions and said that Iraq could not afford to incur any more debt. Tom Korologos, a lobbyist for the American occupation authority in Iraq said, "We're against this whole thing. It will kill us at the donor conference in Madrid." (The U.S. would ask the international communities to donate billions of dollars in aid at a conference that would be held in Madrid, Spain, in October 2003.)

But Democrats said the international community had already refused to contribute, and accused the White House of draining education and Social Security money at home to rebuild Iraq. At the committee meeting, Democrats tried to split the $87 billion spending bill in two, proposing that the $67 billion in military funds be quickly approved while the $20.3 billion in reconstruction be more closely scrutinized and debated. However, the motion failed on a 14-to-15 vote, along party lines. Another Democratic proposal, which would require the rebuilding money to be repaid to the United States using oil revenues, failed by the same margin, according to the article.

The following is an excerpt from an October, 2003, New York Times article by Paul Krugman regarding nation-building and the Marshall Plan:

> The administration that once scorned nation-building now says it's engaged in a modern version of the Marshall Plan. But Iraq isn't postwar Europe, and George W. Bush isn't Harry Truman. While Truman led this country in what Churchill called the "most unsordid act in history," the Iraqi reconstruction keeps getting more sordid. And the sordidness isn't, as some would have you believe, a minor blemish on an otherwise noble enterprise. Cronyism is an important factor in our Iraqi debacle. It's not just that reconstruction is much more expensive than it should be. The important thing is that cronyism is warping policy: By treating contracts as

prizes to be handed to friends, administration officials are delaying Iraq's recovery, with potentially catastrophic consequences. Although it's rarely mentioned nowadays, at the time of the Marshall Plan, Americans were concerned about profiteering in the name of patriotism. To get congressional approval, Truman had to provide assurances that the plan would not become a boondoggle. Funds were administered by an agency independent of the White House, and Marshall promised that Europeans, not Americans, would determine priorities.

Because of the lucrative contracts that are available for rebuilding Iraq, a group of businessmen linked by their close ties to President Bush, his family and his administration have set up a consulting firm to advise companies that want to do business in Iraq.

According to a September 30, 2003, New York Times article by Douglas Jehl, the firm, New Bridge Strategies, is headed by Joe M. Allbaugh, who was the Bush-Cheney presidential campaign manager in 2000 and the director of the Federal Emergency Management Agency until March 2003. Allbaugh was also the chief of staff to the then-Governor Bush of Texas. Allbaugh also heads his own consulting firm. Other directors include Edward M. Rogers Jr., vice chairman, and Lanny Griffith, lobbyists who were assistants to the first President George Bush and have close ties to the White House.

According to the company's Web site, newbridgestrategies.com, "the opportunities evolving in Iraq are of such an unprecedented nature and scope that no other existing firm has the necessary skills and experience to be effective both in Washington, D.C., and on the ground in Iraq." The president of the company, Howland, said the main focus would be to advise companies that seek opportunities in the private sector in Iraq, including licenses to market products there. Howland is a principal of Crest Investment in Houston, Texas, and was president of American Rice, once a major exporter to Iraq. Richard Burt was ambassador to Germany in the Reagan administration and a former secretary of state; and Lord Powell was a member of the British House of Lords and Private Secretary of defense and foreign affairs for both Prime Ministers John Majors and Margaret Thatcher. There are a total of ten principal members in the firm. Ed Rogers, the vice chairman and director, was a deputy assistant to the first President Bush and an executive assistant to the White House Chief of Staff is also vice chairman of Barbour Griffith & Rogers, a Republican lobbying firm in Washington. Rogers founded the company in 1991 with Barbour, who became chairman of the Republican National Committee.

Griffith, a director of the new company, is Chief Operating Officer of Barbour Griffith & Rogers, which he joined in 1993. He was special assistant for intergovernmental affairs to the first president Bush and later worked for him as an assistant secretary of education. Until November 2002, Rogers's wife, Edwina, was associated director of the National Economic Council at the White House.

Rep. Earl Pomeroy, D-N.D., who visited Iraq, said, "The rebuilding of Iraq will be significantly more expensive, more dangerous and take longer than the American people have been prepared for." In making its case for war, the Bush administration said the U.S. could go into Iraq unilaterally and overthrow Saddam Hussein. They never said that they would need international support to rebuild the country after the country is decimated with U.S. smart bombs. In spite of its unilateralism and confidence about putting Iraq back together, the U.S. was forced to ask other countries for money and troops to help rebuild Iraq's infrastructure and to help restore peace in the region. The Bush administration is constantly exercising the "bully pulpit" to get what it wants. The Bush administration estimated that it would need $55 billion dollars to rebuild Iraq's infrastructure. However, the international donors promised only $13 billion over a five-year period for the reconstruction of water, power, health care and other systems devastated by the American invasion.

According to an October 25, 2003, New York Times article by Steven R.Weisman, the United States, completing an extraordinary campaign for economic aid to Iraq, won commitments of at least $13 billion over five years for reconstruction of water, power, health care and other systems demolished by the American invasion. However, two-thirds of the aid will be in the form of loans rather than grants, which may affect the Bush administration's efforts to beat back Congress's drive to make a part of the money being provided by the United States to be in the form of a loan.

France and Germany would not pledge any new funds, because the U.S. had not agreed to relinquish more control and they wanted a specific timetable when Iraq would become a sovereign state.

Countries such as The United Arab Emirates offered $200 million to $250 million. Saudi Arabia offered $1 billion of which half would be in loans through 2007 and the rest would be in export credits. Prince Saud Al-Faisal said Saudi Arabia was ready to reduce some of the $24 billion it was owed by Iraq, but he did not give specifics.

Japanese Foreign Minister Yoriko Kawaguchi offered the second biggest pledge: $1.5 billion in grants for 2004 and $3.5 billion in loans for 2005-07. Kuwait, which was invaded by Iraq in what led to the 1991 Gulf War, offered $500 million in new money, on top of $1 billion already spent.

Italy added $232 million over three years – in addition to the 3,000 troops it has stationed in Iraq. China pledged $24.2 million. Poorer countries like Slovakia pledged $290,000. Bulgaria and Egypt offered technical assistance but no money. Iran, which fought Iraq from 1980-88 in a war that claimed 1 million lives, said it would let Iraq export oil through Iranian ports and supply its neighbor with electricity and gas. In other pledges announced, South Korea agreed to $200 million and Canada $230 million.

International Monetary Fund director Horts Koehler said they could loan Iraq from $2.5 billion to $4.25 billion over three years. It would be the IMF's first loan ever to the oil-rich nation. The World Bank has said it would lend Iraq $3 billion to $5 billion over the coming five years. Koehler stressed that Iraq needs economic stability and reforms, as well as debt relief, to lure private investment and lower a staggering 60 percent unemployment rate.

In all, the European Union would give $812 million in 2004, the Italian Foreign Minister Franco Frattini said, whose country holds the EU presidency. German's deputy minister for economic cooperation, Erich Stather, said Berlin might offer export credits and would play a constructive role in finding a solution to Iraq's debts.

French Trade Minister Francois Loos said his country was willing to envisage and adapt its treatment of Iraq's debt compatible with the country's finance capacity.

The IMF estimated Iraq owes about $120 billion, mainly to European and Gulf countries, plus reparations from the 1991 Gulf War. Most loans come from the World Bank and the International Money Fund, which will have to negotiate the terms of their aid along with a plan to reschedule and perhaps forgive at lease some of Iraq's existing $120 billion in debts, according to World Bank officials.

The $13 billion in loans and grants pledged will be added to the $20 billion that Congress is expected to approve for Iraq's reconstruction. However, the combined total of $33 billion falls significantly lower than the $55 billion that the World Bank and the United States assessed as Iraq's needs in the next four years.

Donor nations, the World Bank, the International Monetary Fund and other international institutions warned the United States and Iraq that they must do a better job in disclosing how the money is spent. "So far there hasn't been a good accounting of how the money was used," said Mark Malloch Brown, head of the United Nations Development Program, referring to the several billion dollars already spent in Iraq from oil revenues and seized Iraqi assets.

In the meantime, the White House threatened to veto the $87 billion package to Iraq and Afghanistan if Congress converts any money for rebuilding Iraq into loans. According to an October 21, 2003, New York Times report by David Stout, White House budget director Joshua B. Bolten told the leaders of the Senate and House appropriations committees in a letter that "the administration strongly opposes the Senate provision that would convert a portion of this assistance to a loan mechanism. If this provision is not removed, the president's senior advisers would recommend that he veto the bill." Of course, some senators were angry at this threat. Some of them said the White House would have gotten what it wanted even without the threat of a veto. Bolten argued that a demand that Iraq repay some of the money would hurt the United States' efforts in the long run partly by saddling a young government with heavy debt. He also said, by working to establish Iraq and Afghan nations that are free, prosperous, and at peace with their neighbors, we eliminate a key base of operations for terrorists and enhance the security of America and her citizens.

But, why is the United States paying so much money to Halliburton Company, Bechtel and others to get the oil operations up and running? The Bush administration said Halliburton is the most experienced firm in restoring oil refineries and putting out fires. Moreover, the oil production should be able to offset some, if not all, of the expenses that will be incurred in rebuilding Iraq. In planning to attack Iraq, the Bush administration's first priority was to secure the oil fields. Why didn't it take into account the possibility that the oil fields could become subject to saboteurs after the so-called major conflict was over, coupled with the possibility that the post-war sabotage could render the country's dependency on international financial assistance for some time to come? It made plans to protect the oil fields from being set on fire during the war, but either made no plans for after the war or underestimated the problems it would encounter after the so-called major conflict was over.

President Bush announced on December 5, 2003, that he was sending James A. Baker III, the former secretary of state, to Iraq to help the country grapple with its debt problem. This decision was based on delays in getting Iraq's oil up to a full-scale production, and the fact that the Bush administration failed to obtain the $55 billion backing for Iraq's reconstruction. Of the $55 billion requested, only $33 billion was promised by a number of countries including the U.S.'s $20 billion contribution.

According to a December 5, 2003, New York Times report by Maria Newman, "Secretary Baker would report directly to me" Bush said in a statement, "and will lead an effort to work with the world's governments at the highest levels, with international organizations and with the Iraqis, in seeking the restructuring and reduction of Iraq's official debt." Bush said, "The future of the Iraqi people should not be mortgaged to the enormous burden of debt incurred to enrich Saddam Hussein's regime. This debt endangers Iraq's long-term prospects for political health and economic prosperity." He went on to say, "the issue of Iraq's debt must be resolved in a manner that is fair and does not unjustly burden a struggling nation at its moment of hope and promise."

The Bush administration has been under increasing pressure from Democrats and others, including world leaders, for its management of post-war Iraq. The financial issues include who will pay for the country's reconstruction and how Iraq will manage its foreign debt, which totals $125 billion to $200 billion. Some legislators both in the United States and in other countries wanted to tie the discussion about how much to contribute to Iraq's reconstruction, and whether it would come in the form of loans or grants, to the questions of how war-torn Iraq will pay off its crippling foreign debt, and whether some of its debtors will forgive portions of those loans. France and Russia carry the larger share of Iraq's debt.

White House press secretary Scott McClellan said the president made the appointment to send Baker to Iraq in response to a request by the Iraqi Governing Council.

Gailani said in a statement read to reporters by United States military officials in Baghdad, "this appointment will give significant momentum to the process of resolving Iraq's external financial obligations and reflects recognition by the United States government of the importance of this process. Resolving Iraq's external financial obligations is essential for Iraq's economic development, internal stability and ability to move past the dark period of the former regime," according to the NYT article.

The invasion of Iraq will provide capital to many U.S. and foreign companies, including financial institutions. According to a December 6, 2003, Associated Press article, on December 5, 2003, sixteen nations, including the United States, Japan and some European countries, agreed to insure payment of up to $2.4 billion worth of exports to Iraq in an effort to jump-start the country's economy. Iraq's interim trade minister, Ali Adul-Amir Allawi, said the deal would do for Iraq what the Marshall Plan did for Europe after World War II. The agreement was signed in Rome by Iraq's Coalition Provisional Authority, government export banks from the 16 participating countries and the Trade Bank of Iraq. Hussein Al-Uzri, president of the Iraqi bank, said "These new and very welcome guarantees are an encouragement to firms around the world who want to do business here, that can help Iraq build and grow."

In July 2003, a consortium of about a dozen private banks led by J.P. Morgan was awarded a contract to provide letters of credit to companies looking to do business in Iraq via its newly formed trade bank, which at the time was being run by the private banks themselves. Government credit agencies such as the U.S. export-import Bank, the U.S. overseas Private Investment Corp., Italy's SACE and Australia's EFIC committed more than $2 billion to ensure the loans. The Trade Bank of Iraq will issue its first seven letters of credit to back the purchase of $7.9 million in medical supplies, part of Iraq's projected medical needs for 2004. Countries participating in the deal are: Australia, Austria,

Belgium, Britain, Czech Republic, Denmark, Germany, Italy, Japan, Luxemburg, Netherlands, Poland, Spain, Sweden, Switzerland and the United States. France did not participate.

The United States has been calling on other countries to participate in the rebuilding of Iraq by pledging funds and sending troops to help in the stabilization of Iraq. However, the U.S. continues to exercise control over the rebuilding efforts and the running of the country in general.

A December 7, 2003, New York Times article by Steven R. Weisman stated:

> Six weeks after organizers of an international donors conference in Madrid said that more than $3 billion in grants had been pledged to help Iraq with immediate needs, new World Bank tally verified grants of only $685 million for 2004. Japan changed the nature of their commitment after the conference from immediate aid to a slower, long-term help, and some countries' intentions were probably incorrectly assumed to be giving immediate aid. Furthermore, it is likely that some pledges will never materialize for one reason or another.
>
> The grant money was part of a total $13 billion that organizers said was raised at the conference. Japan and Saudi Arabia had pledged $1.5 billion each, but it turned out that half of the Saudi's $1.5 billion pledge would be in the form of credits to import goods from Saudi Arabia. Moreover, some countries changed their plan because of the growing concerns about the political stability and the security of Iraq. Some say they would donate money once the trust fund is set up. Others may wait to see a greater United Nations role in Iraq, and were reluctant to make grants during the American-led occupation. One official of a donor country says "The

problem with cash is that you don't know where it's going to end up," said an official with a donor country. "Who gets to draw this money down? The only contracts awarded have been awarded by the Pentagon." International law allows only a sovereign government to incur debt. Therefore, the United States' current plans call for a transfer of power to an Iraqi government by the middle of 2004.

But, as the United States seeks international participation in the rebuilding of Iraq, it alienates some of the very countries it tried to woo. President Bush has again angered European allies by restricting the bids for Iraq's reconstruction only to those countries that have embraced the United States' invasion of Iraq, and those that have sent troops to Iraq. This latest outrage came when Deputy Defense Secretary Paul Wolfowitz issued a decree, approved by Mr. Bush, barring any country that did not support the invasion, including France, Germany, Russia and Canada, from competing for the $18.6 billion reconstruction contracts in 2004. Since the Bush administration forbids these ally countries from participating in the reconstruction of Iraq, these countries will most likely no longer be willing to forgive Iraq's debt of the several billion dollars owed to countries like France, Russia and Germany.

According to a December 10, 2003, Associated Press article, the European Union was considering whether the ban violates world trading rules. The Russians said they would refuse to write off their $8 billion in Iraq debt. And the new Canadian government says it will reconsider its own donations and halt further aid to Iraq. Canada's Prime Minister Paul Martin said, "I find it really very difficult to fathom." He said he was "disappointed" particularly since Canada has pledged about $225 million for Iraq and has troops in Afghanistan. John Manley, Canadian's deputy prime minister said in light of the order, "It would be difficult for us to give further money for the reconstruction of Iraq." The EU executive body, the European commission, said it would study whether the order violates World Trade Organizations rules.

The union said it would examine whether the United States violated world trade rules with its decision to bar countries that opposed its war in Iraq from bidding for the $18.6 billion worth of reconstruction contracts. White House spokesman Scott McClellan said, "I think it is appropriate and reasonable that prime contracts for reconstruction funded by U.S. taxpayer dollars should go to the Iraqi people and those countries who are working with the United States on the difficult task of helping to build a free, democratic and prosperous Iraq. He went on to say that countries that want to be eligible for bidding should participate militarily, or they can donate aid.

The Bush administration said its decision to bar Iraq war opponents such as France, Germany and Russia from the $18.6 billion contracts was appropriate and a reward for U.S. supporters. The directive limited bidders for 26 lucrative contracts in Iraq to firms from the United States, Iraq, their coalition partners and other countries that sent troops to Iraq. Wolfowitz wrote that the restrictions would encourage other countries to join the coalition in Iraq. But this decision has only exasperated an already frayed relationship with the United States and its allies. Germany called the decision "unacceptable." The government spokesman Bela Anda said the decision went against "a spirit of looking to the future together and not to the past" after a deep trans-Atlantic rifts over the Iraq war.

Ludolf von Wartenberg, general manager of the Federation of German Industry said, "We suspect that in substance it contradicts the OECD principles for international tenders for public projects, although the United States in particular always calls for observing these principles." For more than a century, Germans built much of modern Iraq – from the Baghdad-Istanbul railway to the central bank building in Baghdad and the national university, along with dams, bridges, roads and canals. French telecom giant Alcatel became the first French firm to win work in Iraq, winning a subcontract to carry out a third of the two-year contract awarded to the Egyptian group Orascom to build a new mobile phone network for central Iraq, including Baghdad. U.S. firm Motorola is the other major partner in the deal, according to the article.

Wolfowitz said it was necessary to limit competition for the prime Iraq contracts "for the protection of the essential security interest of the United States." Bush defends the Iraq contract restriction, saying, "The expenditure of U.S. dollars will reflect the fact that U.S. troops and other troops risk their life...it is very simple. Our people risk their lives. Coalition- friendly coalition folks risk their lives. And therefore, the contracting is going to reflect that. And that's what the U.S. taxpayers expect." When asked by a reporter to respond to German Chancellor Gerhard Schroeder's suggestion that there might be some issues of international law involved, Bush said "International law? I better call my lawyer." In November 2003, Schroeder informed Washington that he favored restructuring Iraq's massive foreign debt to help the country recover and was open to forgiving some of the $100 billion that Iraq owes its creditors.

Sen. Joe Biden, D-Del., the ranking Democrat on the U.S. Senate Foreign Relations Committee, called it a "totally gratuitous slap" that does nothing to protect our security interest and everything to alienate countries we need with us in Iraq. It's long past time we stop treating Iraq like a prize." But for what we have seen, it is a prize. This war is being waged regardless of the cost not just monetarily, but to human lives. They cannot restore the lives lost in Iraq but they can sure restore the infrastructure, which means big bucks for many of their already rich counterparts, such as Halliburton, which has more than $12.5 billion in revenues in 2002. So it is a prize – a very huge prize at that.

Take Halliburton, for example, the Pentagon contracts awarded without competitive bidding has a potential value of $15.6 billion – note billion. Moreover, estimates put the cost of rebuilding Iraq at $200 billion. Yes, it will cost approximately $200 billion to rebuild Iraq after the United States and Britain demolished it to capture one man, the reason the Bush administration gave for invading Iraq. And, of course, Dick Cheney, being the former chief executive of Halliburton, gave preferential treatment to Halliburton. Moreover, Dick Cheney's office was involved in the awarding of the contracts to Halliburton. And, probably, the relationship between the two caused the lack of accountability.

A Pentagon investigation has found that KBR overcharged the U.S. government by as much as $61 million for fuel delivered to Iraq under a huge no-bid reconstruction contract. Halliburton said the reason it needed to charge a high price for fuel was that it must be delivered in a combat zone. Rep. Henry Waxman, D-California., and a leading critic of the contract, said the preliminary audit confirms what we've known for months, that Halliburton has been gouging taxpayers, and the White House has been letting them get away with it. Waxman's aides said, Iraq's state oil company, SOMO, pays 96 cents a gallon to bring in gas, which includes the cost of gasoline and transportation costs. The gasoline transported by SOMO and by Halliburton's subcontractor is delivered to the same depots in Iraq and often use the same military escorts.

On May 6, 2004, the Bush administration said it would ask Congress for $25 billion in additional funds for the war in Iraq and Afghanistan. Critics said the Defense Department was low-balling the figure because of the upcoming election, so that they could ask for an increase after the election, using the excuse that the violence in Iraq warrants an increase.

An article published in The Wall Street Journal on May 17, 2004, by Russell Gold and Sara Schafer Munoz cites the rising security cost in Iraq for contractors. It said the growing insurgency in Iraq is forcing contractors to spend more on employee security, recruiting and pay, creating an increasingly significant drain on funds available to rebuild the country. Reconstruction contractors say recruiting costs are rising as U.S. citizens increasingly are reluctant to work in a chaotic and dangerous war zone. Some contractors had to increase pay to get new employees. Government agencies doling out more than $18 billion appropriated by Congress for rebuilding Iraq infrastructure said the costs of providing security to workers already in Iraq rose sharply from the year before – and expect it to climb again in the weeks ahead.

...Companies that fill the most dangerous jobs, such as bodyguards, find it difficult to find staff. "Our personnel simply don't want to work there" anymore, said Kenn Kurtz, chief executive of Steele foundation, a San Francisco subcontractor with $42 million of projects and 500 bodyguards, project managers and medical personnel in Iraq. Kurtz said the problem increased since the surge of violence. He pays employees between $10,000 and $20,000 a month, up from $6,000 a month at the start of the occupation.

...Michael Billings, for one, sees the opportunity differently. Then a temporary worker in New York, the 25-year-old earlier in the year applied for several Halliburton jobs managing recreational activities on military bases that paid between $80,000 and $100,000, but didn't get hired. He was willing to consider going to Iraq, but said, "I would need a higher salary" to compensate for what he sees as heightened danger. "I understand the risks involved in going to a war zone. You have a bull's-eye on your back," he said.

According to a June 22, 2004, issue of The New Standard, Iraq's sovereign government will have little control over the oil money. A last-minute spending spree by the U.S.-led Coalition Provisional Authority and language in the U.N. Security Council resolution setting the conditions for Iraqi sovereignty appear likely to limit the interim government's ability to exercise meaningful control over the country's oil revenues.

The CPA's little-known Program Review Board (PRB) has quietly committed billions of dollars in Iraq's oil revenues to a new contract that critics say will enrich U.S. and British corporations while limiting the amount of revenue Iraq's new interim government will have at its disposal when it assumes authority from the CPA on June 30, 2004.

According to reports, when Bremer took over the American-led coalition in May of 2003, he signed a de-Baathification order denying former Saddam Baath party members from participating in any part of the new Iraqi government. He fired tens of thousands of Baathists from their government jobs, an order some experts called a big mistake. Some believe the policy converted thousands of potential allies into anti-U.S. guerrillas. He also disbanded Iraq's' 350,000-member military and barred high-ranking officers from receiving pensions, saying they were too tainted by ties to Saddam's party to have a place in Iraq's future.

An April 23, 2004, Associated Press article reported that Bremer reversed his order, allowing some Baath members (in good standing) to take part in their original profession such as teachers and professors. Also, Iraq's defense minister would recruit former high-ranking officers from Saddam's military into a new army and security services. The de-Baathification policy and the blanket disbanding of Saddam's army turned the country's best-trained military and intelligence personnel into forming the bedrock of an anti-U.S. insurgency. The United Nations' special envoy to Iraq, Lakhdar Brahimi, said banning party members from top jobs led to the dismissal of 10,000 or more surgeons, engineers and school teachers who are stewing at home instead of rebuilding society. He said they are badly needed. They should go back. Brahimi acknowledged that many may have been wrongly ousted.

A July 5, 2004, article in The New Standard, a project of Peoples Networks, stated that despite promises of over $1 billion in U.S. funding, hospital patients in Iraq continue to suffer ongoing hardship. Problems plaguing Iraqi hospitals 15 months into what has been a brutal, bloody occupation range from ongoing medicine and equipment shortages to an overall lack of proper medical infrastructure. They were getting only half the supplies received prior to the U.S.-led invasion.

Dr. Amer Al Khuzaie, Iraq's Deputy Minister of Health, is frustrated by the failure of the U.S. to allow Iraqi companies to rehabilitate the country's hospitals. The Ministry of Health does not have control over the funds. Instead, USAID, the government body responsible for allocating Iraq reconstruction funds, distributes all money through contracts to foreign corporations on behalf of Iraq. The corporations then spend the funds as they see fit. Bechtel, via USAID, has the contracts for distributing the subcontracts and money for rebuilding and rehabilitating our hospitals," Al-Khuzaie said.

The following is an excerpt from a statement by Senator Henry A. Waxman on a Democratic Policy Committee Hearing held on February 14, 2005.

Mr. Waxman said, "Over the past several months, we've heard a lot about the Oil-For-Food scandal. Several Congressional committees have launched investigations and held hearings. While I believe it is appropriate to investigate these allegations, I also think we should be investigating our own administration's conduct."

He said the United States controlled Iraq's oil proceeds from May 2003 until June 2004. Yet Congress has not held a single hearing to examine the evidence of mismanagement, overpricing, and lack of transparency in the successor to the Oil-For-Food program: the Development Fund for Iraq (DFI). The DFI was run by the Bush administration through the Coalition Provisional Authority (CPA). Under the U.S. control, it received over $20 billion in Iraqi funds and spent $14 billion. While Congress has been ignoring the DFI, a series of reports by both U.S. and international auditors have raised serious red flags about the administration stewardship of the Iraqi funds.

Mr. Waxman said the Special Inspector General for Iraq Reconstruction reported that the CPA disbursed $8.8 billion in cash to Iraqi ministries without adequate oversight. In one case, CPA transferred funds for 8,206 Iraqi guards on the payroll even though only 602 guards could actually be found. The IG concluded that, "there was no assurance that funds were not provided for ghost employees." In fact, the IG determined that the CPA's stewardship of the Iraqi funds was so poor that it did not meet the basic requirements of the U.N. Security Council Resolution that established the DFI.

An earlier IG report detected "several physical safeguard violations," including a vault key kept in an unsecured backpack. In another instance, disbursement officer left a room with the safe open.

Mr. Waxman said, "We also know that $1.5 billion in DFI funds were used to pay Halliburton's inflated fuel prices." Mr. Frank Willis, a former senior official with the CPA told Mr. Waxman's staff that Iraq was like the "wild West" awash in brand new $100 bills.

At the first congressional hearing on the Development Fund for Iraq, Rep. Waxman released a report on the U.S. mismanagement of Iraqi funds. The report details the billions in cash transferred from the Federal Reserve Bank to U.S. officials in Iraq, the lack of financial controls in Iraq, and the evidence of substantial waste, fraud, and abuse in the spending of these funds.

The following is an excerpt from A Committee on Government Reform on U.S. Management of Iraqi Funds. The report showed irregularities and corruption in disbursement to Iraqi ministers. The Coalition Provisional Authority (CPA) officials transferred $10.9 billion in DFI assets to Iraqi ministers. Of this amount, the Special Inspector General tried to audit how $8.8 billion in cash was expended. The Inspector General reported that these funds were transferred to Iraqi ministries without proper oversight or accounting controls.

Also, the CPA allocated $637 million in cash from the Iraqi funds to four regions through the CERP and RRRP programs. The Inspector General audited the cash control procedures in one of the four regions – the South-Central Region – that received CERP and RRRP funds. The audit found serious deficiencies that required "prompt attention and separate reporting."

The South-Central region disbursed $119.9 million in Iraqi funds. But the Special Inspector General found that the CPA could not account for the expenditure of $96.6 million. The Special Inspector General found evidence of fraud and referred cases to the United States Attorney for prosecution. In one of these cases, two agents who were entrusted with cash left Iraq without accounting for their balances of $777,050 and $715,000. Rather than report the missing cash, an account manager simply adjusted the accounts to remove the outstanding balances.

After the invasion of Iraq, the U.S.-run Coalition Provisional Authority took control of more than $22.4 billion in Iraqi resources and spent or disbursed $19.6 billion. While these Iraqi assets were under U.S. control, unprecedented sums were withdrawn in cash from the Federal Reserve and shipped to Iraq, where they were spent or disbursed by the CPA with virtually no financial controls. Partial audits of these expenditures have disclosed evidence of substantial waste, fraud and abuse.

Because of the lack of oversight and accounting, the extent of wasteful and corrupt spending during the period of U.S. control is not known. Additional investigation will be needed to provide a complete accounting of what happened to the Iraqi funds and to identify those responsible for excessive and fraudulent expenditures.

According to an October 10, 2005, Associated Press article, Iraq has issued arrest warrants against the defense minister and 27 other officials from the U.S. backed government of former Prime Minister Lyad Allawi over the alleged disappearance or mismanagement of $1 billion in military procurement funds.

According to a November 22, 2005, Fox News report, the U.S. money infusion into Iraq is the largest money infusion into a country since the Marshall Law. Also, a report finds that the CPA under Paul Bremer has failed to account for nearly $9 billion. The report said that billions of dollars went for corruption for reconstruction kickbacks to CPA officials.

ELEVEN

IRAQ'S TRANSFORMATION

On June 8, 2004, the Security Council voted unanimously in favor of an American and British resolution to end the formal occupation of Iraq on June 30, 2004 and to transfer full sovereignty to an interim Iraqi government. It also gives the American-led multinational force the authority to use all necessary measures in partnership with Iraqi forces to bring peace.

According to a June 9, 2004, Wall Street Journal article, the Bush administration pressed the U.N. envoy to change his proposal for a transitional Iraqi government once self-rule is returned on June 30, 2004, Iraqi and administration officials said. Instead of a government that is nonpolitical, the administration pushed for one that gives prominent roles to people with ties to political parties. With new violence flaring, Iraqi officials announced a national security law that would give the interim government the power to declare martial law and detain suspects during anti-terror sweeps.

After calling the United Nations irrelevant because it did not side with the U.S. to go to war in Iraq, the Bush administration turned to the U.N. relying on it to help stem the violence by taking an active role in the transferring of sovereignty to the Iraqi people and to assist with the proposed election in 2005. A New York Times article by Warren Hoge dated April 17, 2004, said that Edward Mortimer, a senior aide to Secretary General Kofi Annan, contrasted the call for assistance from President Bush with the disparagement he said that the United Nations had become used to from the administration. He also said that it's quite unnerving to feel you're being projected into a very violent and volatile situation where you might be regarded as an agent or faithful servant of a power that has incurred great hostility. They are fearful of taking on ill-defined responsibility and being blamed for any subsequent failure. He also said that he told members of the Security Council that he would delay sending people back in force until he had the assurance that they will have proper protection.

Now that the rebuilding of the infrastructure has commenced, the next step is creating a democratic society. That will not be an easy task since Iraq has so many different religious factions. How will the United States get Iraq to be a representative government? You have the Sunnis and the Shiites, the main tribal and religious groups. The Shiites make up 60 percent of Iraq with the Grand Ayatollah Ali al-Sistani, the most revered Shiite cleric, speaking for Iraqi Shiites as a whole. In order for the Iraqis to be unified, the Shiites will have to respect the rights and aspirations of Iraq's Kurds and Sunnis as well as other minorities.

The transfer of power to the Iraqis is also embroiled in the security instability. According to reports, when L. Paul Bremer, the American administrator in Iraq, was summoned to the White House urgently, he asserted that the pacification of Iraq was going well despite inevitable problems. But Secretary of State Colin L. Powell later acknowledged that there had been discussion at the White House about the state of security in Iraq. However, Bremer played down any suggestion that the situation in Iraq had reached a crisis point.

A September 3, 2003, Associated Press article by Barry Schweid, headlined, "U.S. Offers to Share Iraq Role with U.N.," stated:

> Shifting tactics and reaching out for help, the Bush administration offered to share with the U.N. the long-dominant U.S. role in Iraq's postwar reconstruction. Secretary of State Colin Powell de-

scribed the efforts as "essentially putting the Security Council in the game," and European governments reacted favorably to the revised U.S. approach.

France, which led opposition to the war on Iraq, said a new U.N. resolution proposed by the United States should ensure that political power will be transferred quickly to an internationally recognized Iraqi government to help restore peace. France's U.N. Ambassador Jean-Marc de La Sabliere said in New York, "The question is how to win the peace – and how to have the situation stabilized. So we will see the resolution with this in mind."

Powell said under the resolution, American commanders would remain in charge of peacekeeping operations in Iraq, but there, too, "we are asking the international community to join us even more than they have in the past."

Meanwhile, in Brussels, Belgium, the United States and other donors pushed ahead with plans to channel billions of dollars in reconstruction aid to Iraq through an international fund independent of the U.S.-led administration in Baghdad.

In Iraq, the United States handed military control over a large belt of Iraq south of Baghdad to a Polish commander. Powell said the rest of the area, around Najaf where a prominent Muslim cleric was killed in a bombing, will be turned over "once things settle down a little bit." The Polish military is leading the international force of about 9,500 that includes troops from 21 countries.

The draft U.S. resolution would:

- Transform the U.S.-led coalition force into a U.N.-authorized multinational one under a unified command, with an American officer in charge. The force would be required to submit periodic reports to the Council.

- Ask the U.S.-appointed Iraq governing Council to cooperate with the U.N. and U.S. officials in Baghdad to produce a timetable for restoring Iraq's' sovereignty.
- Ask all 191 U.N. member states and international financial institutions to provide financial and other support for Iraq's reconstruction.

German Chancellor Gerhard Schroeder, who had adamantly opposed the U.S.-led war to depose President Saddam Hussein, stressed "the necessity of giving the U.N. a significantly greater role in the political process in Iraq."

In London, a spokesman for the British Foreign Office said Britain had always seen the U.N. as playing a vital role in Iraq.

Senator Carl Levin of Michigan, the senior Democrat of the Senate Armed Services Committee, said, "We should be willing to agree to reasonable sharing of decision-making with respect to the physical and political reconstruction of Iraq. If we are willing to do so, Germany and Russia will probably go along, and France would then have little choice, I believe, but to go along as well."

Sen. Pat Roberts, R-Kansas and chairman of the Senate Intelligence Committee, said he was skeptical of "this notion on the part of some of my colleagues that all we need to do is to get greater international support, including the U.N. If you get more foreign troops in there, obviously you have a more international presence that will lead to more of a financial contribution. But if you cannot do that specific mission you're just spinning your wheels."

Powell said one of the two key goals of the resolution was to invite the Iraqi governing Council to submit a program and timetable for political evolution with a constitution and free elections. He called this effort "creating a political horizon." The second goal, he said, was to have the Security Council authorize a multinational force to which other nations might contribute troops.

U.N. authorization is perceived by the administration as a way to induce India, Pakistan, Turkey, Bangladesh and other countries to send troops. U.S. occupation is viewed negatively by many Arabs as an American effort to control an Arab country. That is one of the reasons contributors from Muslim countries are eagerly pursued by the Bush administration.

According to reports, the administration was under pressure from European and other governments, as well as from members of Congress, to share responsibility on Iraq, and even more so, as U.S. casualties mounted. By this time, more than 300 soldiers have died since the war began in March 2003. Also at stake are commercial interests. The postwar rebuilding of Iraq is likely to be lucrative, and to encourage other countries to share the dangers and the risks, the United States would also have to be willing to share some of the private contracts for the reconstruction effort. Chile's U.N. Ambassador Heraldo Munoz called the resolution a "positive step" and "better than what we have right now."

On October 16, 2003, the Security Council voted unanimously to adopt a resolution on the future of Iraq, handing the United States a major diplomatic victory in its campaign to gather wider international contributions of troops and money for the rebuilding effort.

After weeks of intensive negotiations, the United Nations Security Council unanimously adopted a new resolution outlining the roles of the United Nations, the United States-led Coalition Provisional Authority (CPA) and the Iraqi Governing Council in international efforts to bring peace and stability to Iraq. The resolution, sponsored by Cameroon, Spain, the United Kingdom and the United States, recognizes the "temporary nature" of the power exercised by the Coalition Provisional Authority and says that the 25-member Iraqi Council and its ministers "are the principal bodies of the Iraqi interim administration, which … embodies the sovereignty of the State of Iraq during the transitional period until an internationally recognized, representative government is established and assumes the responsibilities of the Authority."

The text also says that the United Nations "should strengthen its vital role in Iraq" by providing humanitarian relief and "advancing efforts to restore and establish national and local institutions for representative government." Secretary-General Kofi Annan welcomed the unanimous vote as "a clear demonstration of the will of all the members of the Security Council to place the interests of the Iraqi people above all other considerations."

An October 16, 2003, New York Times article by Felicity Barringer and Kirk Semple stated:

> Russia, France and Germany, all of which opposed the war and had been threatening to abstain from voting, agreed to back the measure, saying they were acting in the interest of Council unity.
>
> However, they made it known that they were disappointed that the resolution did not go further toward meeting their concerns, among them that there should be a quicker transfer of power from the American-led occupying force to the Iraqis. They also said they would not commit to further military and financial support for Iraq beyond the commitments they had already made.
>
> Pakistan also joined Russia, France and Germany in saying it would not contribute troops to the occupation.
>
> The resolution authorizes the creation of a multinational occupying force under the command of the United States; requests international contributions to that force and to the reconstruction; gives the United Nations an expanded but still-

subordinated role in helping the political transition; and establishes a deadline of Dec.15, 2003, for the Iraqi Governing Council to provide the Security Council with a timetable for drafting a new constitution and holding elections.

Finally, the resolution, in effect, endorses a political transition under the control of the American-led occupation authority, which had been a major point of contention between the United States and reluctant council members.

The practical impact of the resolution could become apparent at a donors conference in Madrid at which time the United States and Britain hope to receive concrete commitments of troops and money from other countries. Negroponte, the American ambassador, said that several countries had been waiting for the passage of the U.N. resolution before they would commit any resources to Iraq. The resolution, he said, "provides the framework for others to make contributions."

But the resolution papers over the fundamental differences divides the United States from many Council members, who felt that the measure should have set more restrictive deadlines for a quicker transfer of responsibilities from the oversight of Iraq during the transition.

"We miss the clear signal that the transfer of sovereignty to the Iraqis will be accelerated," Germany's ambassador to the U.N., Günter Pleuger, told the council.

In a joint statement after the vote, the ambassadors of France, Germany and Russia said, "The conditions are not created for us to envisage any military commitment and further financial contributions beyond our present engagement."

Pakistan's ambassador to the U.N., Munir Akram, said his major contention was that a United States-led multinational force created by the resolution does not have "a separate and distinct identity" from the coalition forces.

But the reluctant countries all cited the need for a united front at the Security Council to achieve progress in Iraq.

Pleuger said that the members "share the same goals in Iraq, and that is to contribute to a swift stabilization of the conditions in Iraq, to support the political and economic reconstruction process in Iraq, and to promote the restoration of sovereignty of the Iraqi people through a government democratically elected by them."

He added: "This can only succeed when the Security Council appears as unified as possible. We, therefore, did not want to stand in the way of unity of the Security Council."

Negroponte said that the final draft of the resolution included three last-minute amendments, two of which give Secretary General Kofi Annan greater freedom of action to assist Iraq's political reconstruction.

Diplomats said that as many as five countries had indicated they were likely to abstain. China agreed to support the measure, and its diplomats called their counterparts on the Security Council to seek a bridge to the final impasse. At the same time, the United States, Britain and Spain refused to include in the resolution any timetable for a transfer of power to the Iraqis, while Russia, France and Germany were insisting on just such a timetable.

China, along with several of the smaller delegations, agreed with the Europeans' proposal but also felt that unity was crucial. The Chinese ambassador, Guangyo Wang, said that he and his government tried to find a middle ground between Washington, which had almost closed the door on further negotiations, and the Europeans, who had made clear their plans to abstain.

Russia, France and Germany, which abandoned earlier demands for a quick transfer of power to an interim Iraqi authority and for U.N. control of the political transition, had submitted amendments to pin down an explicit timetable for the transition and to allow for the possibility of an earlier transfer of power to the Iraqis. Washington rebuffed the core remaining demands while making other, minor concessions.

Russia also wanted to find a formula to unify as much of the Council as possible, and offered a pared-down version of the amendments. But it also wanted to maintain the united front with France and Germany that has been a fixture throughout the Iraqi crisis.

The draft resolution, originally distributed six weeks before, has been adjusted several times after both permanent and elected members of the Council expressed grave reservations about the measure. They said that it effectively endorsed the results of a military action they had not sanctioned, and urged international contributions of troops and money – burden sharing – to occupation authorities that they said were not sharing any responsibility.

According to a November 11, 2003, New York Times article by David E. Sanger, Bush's speech on the accomplishments in Iraq appeared to be part of an effort by the White House to change American and world perceptions of the Iraqi occupation, describing it in far broader strategic terms than the ouster of a dictator. But while Bush was praising his accomplishments in Iraq, he was also struggling to create democratic institutions there as the daily casualties among American and allied soldiers led many to wonder if the United States will ever be able to transform the nation. Bush likened his remaking of Iraq to the United States effort to spread democracy in Asia and Europe after World War II. He compared what he called his administration's new "forward strategy of freedom in the Middle East" to that of President Ronald Reagan's 1982 declaration in England that soviet Communism had failed. He said that dictatorships were doomed to fail in North Korea, Myanmar, Burma, Cuba and Zimbabwe, and that "these regimes cannot hold back freedom forever." He predicted that just as Nelson Mandela emerged from captivity in South Africa to lead his nation, "one day, from prison camps and prison cells and from exile, the leaders of new democracies will arrive."

But, Imad Fawzi Shueibi, a Syrian political analyst and professor at Damascus University, suggested that Bush's message would be tainted in the Middle East by the widespread negative perception of the messenger. He said "I don't think someone who violates the human rights against people all over the world and especially the Arab world can speak about freedom and democracy. How can we believe that Mr. George Bush wants us to enter the era of democracy and the era of freedom when he remains biased toward Israel despite its violations of human rights, despite its long occupation of Arab land and its apartheid system toward the Arabs in the occupied territories?

The Bush administration's exit strategy for Iraq is that the United States would establish self-rule by June 2004, well ahead of its original schedule, and I might add, just as the American presidential election season would be getting under way. But a tug of war began between the Governing Council and Ayatollah Sistani over how an interim government should be elected. Also at stake is the ability to choose legitimate and national communal leaders. Ayatollah was insisting that the new Iraqi government be as legitimate and stable as possible. Also, there has to be a meeting of the minds regarding the relationship between religion and state, and between the clerics and the politicians.

The plan by the United States for Iraq to be a sovereign state by 2004 ran into all kinds of roadblocks.

For example, according to a November 13, 2003, New York Times article by Susan Sachs and Joel Brinkley, Iraqi

385

political leaders decided to reject a plan to write a new constitution, saying they would propose instead that they immediately assume the powers of a provisional government. Members of the Iraqi Governing Council reached a consensus that writing a constitution, and electing the drafters of a constitution demanded by the powerful Shiite clergy, Grand Ayatollah Ali al-Sistani, would be too divisive at that time. They said they would work instead on drafting what they call a "basic law" in the hope that they could win international recognition for an Iraqi government that would take over considerable authority from the American administrator of Iraq, and meet conditions laid down by the United Nations Security Council in October 2003.

The new political plan won the endorsement of most of the major players on the council, including Kurdish political leaders, the powerful Shiite Muslim parties and the minority Sunni Muslim independents, although no formal vote had been taken. Jalal Talabani, a Kurdish leader then holding the rotating president of the council, said that establishing a provisional government before drafting a constitution was both reasonable and necessary.

According to a November 16, 2003, New York Times article by Joel Brinkley and Susan Sachs, on November 15, 2003, the Iraqi Governing Council announced details of an agreement with the United States to form a democratic, pluralistic provisional government in the spring of 2004 that would provide freedom of religion and civilian control of the military. Jalal Talabani said that after the creation of the provisional government, foreign troops would stay on only by invitation. "The occupation shall end," he said. Under the plan, a transitional assembly would be selected. Members would include representatives of every geographical, religious and social group in the nation. The assembly would elect the new provisional government in June 2004. Sheik Jalal Uldin al-Saghir, the representative on the Governing Council of the Supreme Council for the Islamic Revolution in Iraq, said Iraq is moving toward a free market economy, so no laws can limit what anyone can do in the economic field. But the program for the constitution is for it to respect the Islamic identity of the Iraqi people. No law should be passed that contradicts Islamic law in its broad principles.

After the successful invasion of Iraq, the president challenged other nations such as Syria, Iran, Egypt and Saudi Arabia to begin embracing democratic traditions, and to view the fall of Saddam Hussein as "a watershed event in the global democratic revolution." Speaking at a meeting before the National Endowment for Democracy, Bush said "Sixty years of Western nations excusing and accommodating the lack of freedom in the Middle East did nothing to make us safe, because in the long run, stability cannot be purchased at the expense of liberty."

I believe it is inherently dangerous for the world's most powerful nation to taunt another nation.

A December 4, 2003, New York Times article by Joel Brinkley said that Iraqi census officials devised a detailed plan to count the country's entire population by the summer of 2004 and prepare a voter roll that would open the way to national elections in September. However, American officials rejected the idea, and the Iraqi Governing Council members said they never saw the plan to consider it. The American occupation officials rejected the plan to complete a voter roll rapidly, and at the same time tell the Governing Council that the lack of a voter roll meant national elections were impractical.

Grand Ayatollah Ali a-Sistani called for national elections in June 2004, not the indirect balloting specified in the American plan for turning over control of the country. But American officials and some Iraqis said the nation was not ready for national elections, in part because the logistics were too daunting. President Bush's national security adviser, Condoleezza Rice, acknowledged that the United States was changing course on how to form a government. She said the White House had been persuaded by the Iraqi Governing Council that writing a constitution for the country would be a lengthy, complex process that needed time – and that they could not wait that long for the transfer of civilian authority from the coalition.

The U.S.-appointed head of government council, Jalal Talabani, said this came a little too late. Rice said nothing has changed, but what is also important is that we find ways to accelerate the transfer of power to the Iraqis. She said it is important that the Iraqi people have a permanent constitution and elections for permanent government. Although Rice did not go into details, other administration officials said Bush approved in broad strokes the creation of a temporary Iraqi government, to be formed by the middle of 2004, when it plans to hold elections and turn civilian authority over to a temporary government before the new constitution was written, according to the article. However, U.S. forces will remain in Iraq for several years to come. This might be seen as a ploy to stop the attacks since the U.S. will remain a strong force in Iraq.

The Iraqis are increasingly frustrated with America's exercise of power. Iraqis favor the immediate formation of a provisional government, made up of the current Iraqi Governing Council, rather than elections. The council told Bremer that the only way the writing of a constitution would be seen as legitimate was if the delegates were elected. Grand Ayatollah Ali al-Sistani, Iraq's most influential Shiite religious leader demanded elections.

Experts assume that Shiites, who predominate in Iraq, would win a commanding majority of seats in any election. Ayatollah Sistani's demand stirred fears among some American officials that an elected constitution-writing body might write a theocratic charter that enshrined Islam as a state religion and marginalized the Sunni minority, potentially aggravating the violent rebellion of remnants loyal to Saddam Hussein. Ayatollah Sistani kept his distance from occupation forces, but administration officials said Council members tried to suggest alternatives to him, like having the convention chosen by some amalgam of elections, provincial Councils, town meetings, local caucuses and the like. But he rejected the proposals, the official said. "Sistani has enormous weight," an administration official said. "We have to heed what the Iraqis are telling us." The United Nations and many European leaders have been pushing for a more rapid transfer of power to Iraqis, and the American refusal to speed up a transfer has made it more difficult for the United States to win international support for the rebuilding of Iraq, according to the article.

A December 4, 2003, New York Times article by Joel Brinkley said census director Nuha Yousef completed a plan for the quick census in October 2003 and the election roll would be ready by September 1, 2004, and the full results would be ready in December. The U.S. led occupiers rejected the plan without offering it to the Governing Council members who announced that Shiite religious leaders opposed the indirect elections.

A December 7, 2003, New York Times article by Joel Brinkley stated:

Secular leaders worry that torn by turmoil Iraq will elect an Islamic theocracy in a popular election that is supposed to take place in June 2004. Grand Ayatollah Ali al-Sistani called for full elections instead of the caucus-style balloting envisioned in the American plan for self-rule. Most secular politicians concluded that they hoped the voters would elect a theocracy. An independent member of the Iraqi Governing Council said a lot of people are mostly afraid that the Islamists want to have direct elections because they believe clergymen will be the new government in Iraq. Abdul Aziz al-Hakin, a senior Islamic clergyman who is also on the Governing Council and is close to Ayatollah Sistani, said "We don't want at this point to have an Islamic government. We don't want a Shia government. We want a broad-based democratic government."

The Bush administration officials have also said that, seeing that Iraq's Shiites are not under the thumb of Iran's, their fears of a Shiite-dominated government have diminished. However, a number of Iraqis worry that in Iraq's present chaotic state, they fear the people may vote for the rigorous order that an Iranian-style Shiite theocracy imposes. For that reason, almost everyone except the religious leaders was determined to delay a full national election for a year or longer. The American plan calls for Iraq to choose a so-called transitional assembly of 250 people nationwide in the spring of 2004. The national Governing Council, as well as provincial and local governing Councils, would select the assembly's members. Forty percent of the nation's population consists of Sunni, Kurd and other minority, and it is unlikely that they will vote for a Shiite religious leader. Of the 60 percent Shiites, 30 percent to 35 percent is secular.

According to reports, half the Governing Council, and nearly all of the political figures in Iraq today, are former opposition leaders who lived abroad during most of Saddam Hussein's reign. Ahmad Chalabi, who was very influential in building the case against Iraq, feeding the Bush administration with purported information on weapons of mass destruction, has fallen from grace with the Bush administration because of his criticism of the Bush administration. Many, if not all of the exiled Iraqis, believe that they would be elected to the transitional assembly to be chosen in June, and ultimately to the interim government that is to be elected in 2005. However, the Governing Council decided that it would try to stay in power after the provisional government is formed in June, despite an earlier agreement to dissolve it.

Although the Coalition Provisional Authority was scheduled to go out of business by the middle of 2004, Lt. Gen. Ricardo Sanchez, the American commander in Iraq, said that their forces may have to remain in Iraq for at least a couple of years. At the same time, British Prime Minister Tony Blair said the troops would remain in Iraq for several years. Security concerns are seen as one of the biggest obstacles to holding direct elections in Iraq by June 30, 2004. Turnout for the election could be suppressed by violence. On February 5, 2004, Grand Ayatollah Ali al-Sistani escaped an assassination attempt. Furthermore, an interim constitution draft scheduled to go into effect on February 28 sparked a political debate on issues critical to the Arab nation's future – Kurdish autonomy and the role of Islam. The debate was pitting Sunni, Shiite and Kurdish politicians against one another while the U.S. blueprint for Iraq was on hold due to differences with the Shiite clergy over early elections.

Under the agreement reached on November 15, 2003, between the Council and the U.S.-led coalition, adopting the interim constitution was a first step in a two-year political blueprint that would have a transitional legislature in place by the end of May, an unelected but sovereign government a month later and allow Iraqis to vote in a general election by the end of 2005.

On December 10, 2003, United Nations Secretary General Kofi Annan announced that the United Nations international staff would operate from Cyprus because Iraq was still too dangerous for the United Nations to resume major duties in the near future. He also criticized the vague role the U.N. had been given in the past and questioned whether future duties would be worth the safety risks. However, he offered, when possible, the extensive U.N. experience in organizing elections, writing a constitution, setting up human rights bodies and continuing humanitarian aid. He also gave some political advice to the U.S.-led coalition.

As calls for the United Nations to return to Iraq came from Italian President Carlo Azeglio Ciampi, German foreign Minister Joschka fisher, French Foreign Minister Dominique de Villepin, as well as from U.S. Secretary of State Colin Powell, Annan acceded and said he would consider a new United Nations' political role in Iraq and appoint a special representative.

A January 8, 2004, New York Times article by Steven R. Weisman said the Bush administration fearful of Iraqis breaking up along ethnic lines after the American occupation ends, urged Kurdish leaders to compromise in their demand for a fully autonomous state in the north. But the Kurdish leaders rejected the request, saying that they would continue to demand nothing less than the autonomy that the Kurdish area has had since 1991, when the United States decided to protect it as a breakaway part of Iraq. The Bush administration said that the issue of Kurdish autonomy rose to the top of the list of difficulties that the United States was struggling to resolve as it returns Iraq to self-rule under a tight deadline. Kurds wish to retain not only their own armed forces, but also control over taxing power and oil revenues in Kirkuk and Khanakin, two oil-producing centers that the American occupation does not view as part of the traditional Kurdish region.

On January 27, 2004, the United Nations agreed to send a mission to Iraq to assess the feasibility of holding elections ahead of the transfer of sovereignty at the end of June, following pleas from the U.S.-led coalition and Iraq's governing council to intervene in a dispute with the country's Shia community. Speaking in Paris, Annan said he had "concluded that the United Nations can play a constructive role in helping to break the current impasse." He would send the team, once he was satisfied that the Coalition Provisional Authority would provide adequate security arrangements.

And, according to reports, on February 3, 2004, President Bush met with Kofi Annan to press him to have his aides mediate among quarreling factions in Iraq and to forge a consensus behind a plan that would allow the transfer of sovereignty to a government in Baghdad by June 30, 2004. Annan said, "We are going there to help the Iraqis, to help them establish a government that is Iraqi, a government that will work with them to assure their future, in terms of political and economic destiny." Ayatolla Sistani has refused to meet with any American mediator, including L. Paul Bremer, Iraq's civil administrator.

With the increased violence in Iraq and especially in Fallujah, Annan said the situation there is making it difficult to advise the Iraqi Governing Council on Iraqi sovereignty and elections. He said Iraq is too violent to send a large team in. However, in Bush's public conference with reporters on April 13, 2004, he said that the U.N. envoy, Lakhdar Brahimi, was working with the U.S. in the handover of June 30 to the Iraqis and is helping with the election that is to be held next year. One report said that the United Nations has a code of conduct that the U.S. soldiers do not have. So if the United Nations takes over from the U.S., the Iraqis may feel better about their country being run fairly rather than by the coalition forces.

On February 4, 2004, Kofi Annan announced that he would dispatch a team of U.N. experts to Iraq to assess whether an early vote was possible. The presidency, to consist of a Shiite, a Sunni and Kurd, would name a cabinet whose members must be confirmed by the legislators before taking office.

A February 4, 2004, Associated Press article stated that the Kurds are concerned that the U.S. may desert them as they did in the 1970s, 1980s and 1990s. The Kurds were also angry with the U.S. in October 2003 when the Bush administration pressured Turkey to send 10,000 troops to Iraq to join coalition forces in spite of the historic enmity between the Turks and the Kurds. Also in 1991 with the encouragement of the first president Bush, the Kurds rose up against Saddam Hussein after Operation Desert Storm. But the U.S. did not provide military help and many Kurds were slaughtered. Moreover, the Reagan administration ignored Saddam's brutality, opting to side with him in the Iran-Iraq war. An estimated 180,000 Kurds were killed by Saddam's forces. And, in the 1970s, the United States called off CIA support for the Iraqi Kurds to help cement a peace deal between Iran and Iraq.

Kurds want autonomy in a tripartite state that also would include Shiite and Sunni Muslim sectors. The Bush administration believes Kurds are entitled to an entity within a unified Iraq, but one that is drawn according to geographic and administrative, not ethnic lines.

Another sticking point in the transformation of Iraq is the status of U.S. troops. On February 22, 2004, Iraq's interim leaders said they could not negotiate a formal agreement with the American military on maintaining troops in Iraq, and that the task must await the next sovereign Iraqi government. Among the issues of concern is when the use of force would be allowed.

The U.S.-led Coalition Provisional Authority said direct elections for a new Iraqi government would be impossible within a few months, and a United Nations delegation indicated that it holds similar views. However, the outcome of local elections in southern Iraq, where Shiite Muslims predominate, failed to validate U.S. fears that such voting would bring about an Iran-style theocracy, and possibly incite civil war. Tobin Bradley, political adviser for the Coalition Provisional Authority, said "What we've found is that they haven't selected extremists," according to the article.

A February 18, 2004, Wall Street Journal article by Yaroslav Trofimov said the experiment with democracy in small towns around Nasiriyah led to new tensions between Shiite religious movements and occupation officials. Prominent clerics stepped up demands to hold rapid elections for the Nasiriyah-based provincial administration, whose members were appointed by the Coalition Provisional Authority. Thousands of demonstrators demanding such a poll marched toward the Coalition Provisional Authority's fortress-like compound, brandishing assault rifles and rocket-propelled grenade launchers, and chanting anti-American slogans. One of the protest organizers and regional head of the Sadr office, one of the main Shiite religious movements in Iraq, Aws al Khafaji said "The occupation forces came to this country saying they'll bring democracy – but now they have become the main obstacle to democracy."

Elections in places like Battha, a town north of Nasiriyah, have only whetted the local appetite for self-rule. Mohammed al Nassiri, a local leader of the Iraqi Hezbollah, one of many Shiite Islamic parties that sprang up after the war said they have noticed from experience that the local councils that were elected work much better than the appointed ones. The Coalition Provisional Authority resisted calls for provisional elections, fearing that such a vote here would set a precedent nationwide. Yet officials acknowledged that outcomes at the local level were encouraging. The ballot in Battha was the ninth municipal election across this province in the Shiite heartland. The election in Battha wasn't the one-person/one-vote kind that is acceptable under international standards. It was much more inclusive than the complicated system of prescreened caucuses that the Coalition Provisional Authority planed to use in the summer of 2004.

In the absence of a reliable census, the suggestion by Shiite leaders to use the oil-for-food ration list as the electoral roll was used. The list counted families, not individuals, so every family got a vote when a male member appeared with a ration card. To encourage female participation, the card allowed another vote when a woman showed up. About 1,200 families, out of 4,000 on the village's ration list, took part in the vote. They selected 10 councilmen, a doctor, three school teachers and several businessmen from a roster of 34 candidates. No violence was reported.

The United Nations' team sent to Iraq to assess the feasibility of an election or caucuses concluded that neither elections nor caucuses would be feasible during the near term. Secretary-General Kofi Annan, in his report to the U.N. Council, said elections might be possible by January 2005 if organization began soon and smoothly.

A February 20, 2004, Wall Street Journal article stated that U.S. officials and the United Nations agreed that elections in Iraq were impossible before the scheduled June 30, 2004, transfer of sovereignty. Shiite leaders, who had been calling for elections, appeared willing to accept a delay, provided that there was a clear timeframe for when they would be held. Annan said he favored establishing a 'caretaker" government to run the country until elections could be held. Such a government would be expected to eschew major policy decisions while the U.N. helps organize a national convention to draft a new constitution, with elections likely to follow by year's end. The U.N. was able to allay Sistani's fears that the Shiite majority would be marginalized in Iraq's next government. Bremer said that Washington would meet the June 30, 2004, deadline for handing over power but probably would have to make significant changes to its initial plan. U.S. officials were considering transferring sovereignty to an expanded version of the Iraqi Governing Council appointed by the U.S. in the summer of 2003. The Governing Council would take temporary control on July 1, and vesting it with sovereign powers until a legislative election could be held later in the year.

After intense negotiations, the Iraqi Council agreed on March 1, 2004, on a draft constitution on the roles of Islam and ethnic minorities, but according to a Wall Street Journal report, the document left several major issues unresolved and may be unlikely to halt the sectarian feuding. After a week-end of round-the-clock negotiations, a U.S.-appointed council agreed to compromise language on several of the most divisive provisions of the document, which will be used to govern the country when a sovereign transition government assumes power in the summer. The draft forms a litmus test for whether Iraq's new political leadership will be able to bridge the deep ethnic and religious divides. The new constitution was supposed to be in place only temporarily, but Iraq's fractious sectarian groups have worked hard to ensure that their interests are represented in it because of widespread beliefs that the document will form a blueprint for the country's permanent constitution. The constitution does a very good job of setting a general framework and deferring all sensitive issues to a later date, according to Nathan Brown, a professor of political science at George Town University.

The article also stated that Annan indicated that the United Nations would do its post-transition consulting on elections and the creation of a permanent constitution for Iraq with small teams, and the organization would not return to Iraq for the foreseeable future. Lakhdar Brahimi, United Nations envoy to Iraq, made preliminary proposals for an interim administration led by a prime minister, a president and two vice presidents to be chosen by him, a group of Iraqi judges and members of the Iraqi Governing Council and the United States-led occupying force. He also proposed the dissolution of the American-appointed council and a post-transition gathering of leaders to choose a consultative assembly to advise the interim government.

According to an April 10, 2004, New York Times article by Douglas Jehl and Warren Hoge, the U.S. appears to be relying heavily on the United Nations to win agreement from Iraqis on a transfer plan. However, the United Nations is only giving the appearance of doing the work of the allied occupiers. Brahimi will be the pivotal agent in trying to rescue the imperiled effort to forge a transitional government acceptable to the Iraqis' main political groups, a senior administration official said. The official also described an American envoy, Robert Blackwill, a deputy national security adviser coordinating Iraq policy for the administration, as "a political matchmaker" in the process.

Munir Akram, Pakistan's ambassador to the United Nations, said he believes that Brahimi is exploring three options: 1) turning over sovereignty on June 30, 2004, to the existing 25-member Iraqi Governing Council, 2) giving power to an expanded council that would add members to become more broadly representative than the present one, or 3) calling a meeting of tribal leaders like the loya jirga gathering in Kabul in 2003 when Brahimi was the U.N. envoy to Afghanistan. Brahimi was given this position when the White House urged Kofi Annan to give him that assignment, according to the article.

In the meantime, President Bush appointed John D. Negroponte as ambassador to Iraq to be effective July 1, 2004, after the transfer of power to Iraq. Bremer and the Coalition Provisional Authority would hand over responsibility for the American presence to a new mega-embassy run by Negroponte and the State Department.

According to a Wall Street Journal article, the U.S. would move its most visible U.S. offices, including the ambassador out, of Saddam Hussein's Republican Palace into a smaller palace about a mile away. The goal is to make the U.S. presence appear less imperial. There is the uncertainty over how much of a role Iraqis themselves will play. The U.S. will retain significant control in Iraq until elections are held in early 2005. In the current U.S. interpretation, a new caretaker Iraqi government won't be able to write new laws or command newly trained Iraqi forces.

The most important compromise concerns whether Islam should be the only source of Iraq law, a position espoused by the country's religious parties, or one of several sources, which is the preference of many secular and non-Muslim members of the Governing Council. The document grants freedom of speech, assembly and religion. Iraq would have a single president, assisted by a pair of deputies, who would choose the prime minister who will wield most day-to-day power in the country, according to the article.

But on March 5, 2004, the coalition was dealt another setback, when the Shiites refused to sign the document because of some wording. They believe the Kurds would have too much power that could even affect the appointment of the president.

Apparently, the U.S. did not intend to turn over sovereignty to the Iraqi people in the near future. The following March 26, 2004, New York Times article by John F. Burns and Thom Shanker gives the detail on their reasoning.

American officials say they believe they have found a legal basis for American troops to continue their military control over the security situation in Iraq. They say an existing United Nations resolution approving the presence of a multinational force in Iraq, approved by the Security Council in October 2003, gives American commanders the authority needed to maintain control after sovereignty is handed back.

Bremer issued an executive order in March 2003 specifying that the newly formed Iraqi armed forces be placed under the operational control of the American commander, Lt. Gen. Ricardo S. Sanchez, who has been named to lead American and allied forces after the transfer of political authority to the Iraqis.

Bremer and other top American officials say they believe Security Council Resolution 1511, which conferred the mandate for the American-led alliance, can be used to provide legal justification for the American military command to operate until December 31, 2005. That is the timetable agreed on by Iraqi leaders as the final transition to an elected Iraqi government.

Some Iraqi politicians maintain that the United Natios mandate was intended to lapse at the return of sovereignty. But some American officials, citing a passage in the resolution saying that the mandate would expire upon the completion of the political process, argue that it will not lapse until a permanent Iraqi government takes office.

European and United Nations diplomats said that American control would still have to be approved by the Iraqis taking office on June 30, 2004. That control, said a United Nations official, is not likely to survive the transfer of sovereignty unless the successor government approves it. The question also arises about the effects of extending the primacy of the American military.

The United Nations official said that while it would be a practical reality for American domination to continue despite Iraqi self-rule, it has to be done in a way that's not offensive to Iraqis and the international community, which emphasizes Iraqi sovereignty rather than Iraqi impotence.

However, a European diplomat said that continued American military control sends the wrong signal and gives an impression of continuing foreign occupation in Iraq.

Also, tension persists as the time drew near to choose an Iraqi president. According to a May 31, 2004, Reuters article, both the United States and the United Nations blocked the Iraqi leaders' choice of a president to replace Saddam Hussein. After a prime minister and key cabinet posts were agreed on, U.S. officials asked the Iraqi Governing Council to postpone further talks on filling the post of head of state. The U.S.-appointed Council favors its present leader, Ghazi Yawar, a prominent tribal leader with support from various ethnic and religious groups. However, Bremer and the U.N. envoy Lakhdar Brahimi were pressuring them to back Adnan Pachachi, an 81-year-old former foreign minister. However, on June 3, the U.S. and the U.N. acquiesced.

The new prime minister in Iraq in his first address to the Iraqi people warned that the departure of U.S. and Britain's forces from Iraq would amount to a "catastrophe" for the country. Ayad Alawi, appearing in a televised address three days after being chosen Prime Minister, said his countrymen, "as Iraqis, can never accept occupations," and he vowed to reclaim the country's full sovereignty on June 30, 2004. This is contrary to the views of the overwhelming majority of the Iraqis who want the U.S. and British troops to leave the country immediately. Dr. Alawi said, "Our government has decided that only the restoration of security and the safeguarding of citizens' dignity, honor and wealth will enable us to successfully proceed on the political course and achieve the transfer of full sovereignty."

Dr. Alawi is a secular Shiite who was chosen in a United Nations-sponsored selection process to lead the government that would take over when sovereignty was restored on June 30, 2004. Dr. Allawi is a neurologist who is known for his association with the Central Intelligence Agency, which supported his efforts and that of his group, the Iraqi National Accord, to topple Saddam Hussein in the 1990s, according to the Reuters article.

A June 9, 2004, Associated Press article said that Dr. Allawi was asked by a reporter after a Cabinet meeting if his Iraqi National Accord movement had ties with American intelligence during the last years of Saddam's rule. He said he was not ashamed of having worked with the CIA and other foreign intelligence services to help topple Saddam Hussein. Dr. Allawi was a member of Saddam's notorious Baath Party and served in the Iraqi intelligence services until his fallout with the regime in 1971. He went to London where he studied medicine.

A number of Iraqis agree that Allawi may not rule the country evenhandedly because of his shady past with ties to Saddam. The Kurdish leaders fear the Shiites will sideline them politically, because of the share majority of the Shiites, and the clerical hierarchy that has been cultivated by the Americans. Furthermore, the Kurds were angry because the United States and Britain refused to include an endorsement of the interim constitution in the U.N. resolution approved by the Security Council on June 8, 2004. U.N. diplomats said the decision was made to keep a reference to the interim constitution – officially the Transitional Administrative Law – out of the resolution to appease Iraq's most influential Shiite cleric, Grand Ayatollah Ali al-Husseini al-Sistani. The United Nations Security Council voted unanimously 15-0 on June 8, 2004, in favor of an American and British resolution to end the formal occupation of Iraq on June 30, 2004, and transfer full sovereignty to an interim government. This gives legitimacy to the Bush administration's role in Iraq and allows them to ask for international support to stabilize Iraq.

The Bush administration wasted no time in calling for help. It immediately called on NATO to play a larger role in Iraq once sovereignty was transferred to an interim government while attending the Group of Eight meeting on Sea Island, Georgia. The plan that was worked out by the Bush administration, the British government, the United Nations and the Iraqis in June 2004 calls for an Iraqi election in January 2005. This will be in effect a litmus test of the security stability and the political power struggle by the different factions, according to the article.

The Bush administration has a hard road ahead of it to convince the Iraqis that once the U.S.-led coalition turns over the power to the Iraqis at the end of June 2004, it will cede its powers over them. The Iraqis are especially suspicious since U.S. troops will remain there and the U.S. ambassador to Iraq, Negroponte, will have a major role there with an American staff of more than 900, assisted by 600 to 700 Iraqis. This will be the biggest American embassy in the world. Furthermore, when will the U.S. truly relinquish control of the oil and rebuilding of the infrastructure? And will it be able to assure the Iraqis of security stability, avoid civil unrest and safeguard their political rights and control.

A February 2, 2004, Associated Press article headlined, "Iraqis Set to Take Over Baghdad Security," reported: U.S. troops are preparing to hand over security patrols in Baghdad to Iraqi forces. American soldiers will gradually move to the edge of the city as more Iraqi Civil Defense Forces and police graduate from U.S. supervised training.

A Washington Post article published on January 7, 2004, reported as the Marine Corps prepares to take over occupying much of western Iraq from the U.S. Army, it is planning a fresh approach that emphasizes restraint in the force, cultural sensitivity and a public message that the new troops aren't from the Army, according to an internal Marine document and interviews with top officers. The U.S. soldiers who have been guarding Iraq's frontiers are about to leave, but the country's new border police, hastily trained and poorly armed, aren't eager to take over, according to a Newsweek article published on February 16, 2004. Armed with only a rusty pair of binoculars, an AK-47 and a half magazine of bullets, border guard Ghissa Ali Fatih leads a visitor up a rickety ladder to the roof. But he is concerned with what he cannot see. "This is a big problem for us," he says.

As of March, 2004, the job will belong to Fatih and his ragged comrades. The U.S. Army's Third Armored Cavalry Regiment, which guards 500 miles of rugged sand and desert along the Syrian, Saudi and Jordanian borders, is pulling out at the end of February 2004. Other U.S. Army troops are leaving Iraq too, including the 101st Airborne Division which controls 100 miles of the Syrian border and Iraq's frontier with Turkey. As the troops withdraw, smaller contingents of both the U.S. Army and the Marines will replace them, but the job of protecting the country's perimeter will fall mostly to a poorly equipped and hastily trained Iraqi police force. Both Iraqis and the Coalition have reason to worry. Analysts believe the most devastating attacks in the war against the occupation – the suicide bombings that have killed hundreds of Iraqis – are the work of outside infiltrators who have passed virtually at will across the unprotected borders. U.S. forces lacked the manpower to secure the borders themselves and, in the vacuum, the foreign jihads moved in.

European law enforcement officials say al-Qaeda has established a network across Europe to recruit foreign fighters, providing them with fake passports, training and cash, and guiding them along infiltration routes into Iraq. Both the Americans and the Iraqis are overextended. The Third Armored Cavalry Regiment conducts satellite surveillance and air patrols. But they remain preoccupied with battling local insurgents. For the most part, the troops have turned over responsibility for guarding the Syrian frontier to two battalions of Iraqi Border Police, or about 420 men. They are based in a few dozen observation posts that extend for only about 15 miles in either direction from the main Syrian-border crossing at Al Qaim. That leaves 70 miles of the border zone completely unguarded. The cops undergo a two-week training course and receive salaries of $160 per month. But their equipment is meager, their mobility limited and their motivation is often low. "The Coalition Provisional Authority hasn't given them anything," says Col. Antonio Aguto, who spent some of his regiment's own funds on vehicles and uniforms, according to the article.

Sen. Harry Reid of Nevada and Sen. Hillary Clinton of New York visited Afghanistan and Iraq during the Thanksgiving week. A November 29, 2003, Reuters article by Haitham Haddadin stated that Sen. Reid said the U.S. forces in Iraq and Afghanistan had critical shortages of specialized troops such as military police, civil affairs and psychological operations troops. He said, "We are beginning to see the cracks now because as these forces rotate out, and many of these troops here are reserve National Guard people who have that expertise, we don't have a second echelon of those types of troops."

Sen. Jack Reed said the United States overextended itself in Iraq, and a failure to get the Shiites' backing for the handover plan could cause huge political problems in the future. He said, "We could look back and see the decision to attack Iraq was one that ended up being very, very costly and peripheral to the real enemies that are trying to attack the United States. And, its connection with terrorist cells that attack the United States are tenuous at best, casting doubt on one of the administration's justifications for the invasion.

Sen. Hillary Clinton said that President Bush's administration was moving too fast in a planned transfer of power to the Iraqis by July. "It's going to take more than has been allotted for the process to take hold. I don't think we should be setting artificial timelines as this is a very challenging undertaking and we need to work with our Iraqi counterparts and make sure that the steps that are being taken are going to work." Clinton said more troops, preferably an international force, were needed in both Iraq and Afghanistan. She said she still thinks the administration should internationalize the military, political, and civilian presence in Iraq.

Hillary Clinton said President Bush's surprise Thanksgiving Day visit to Baghdad doesn't make up for the flaws in his strategy for dealing with the U.S. occupation and returning the government to the Iraqi people. She said she applauds Bush for visiting the troops and sending the message "that these young men and women are doing a job that is important to our country. On the other hand, it is not a substitute for a plan about how we're going to enhance security, which was the number one concern that everybody talked to me about, especially the Iraqis that I met with," she said on NBC's "Today Show." She said that Bush has also failed to say how the United States is going to create more legitimacy to move toward self-governance in Iraq.

In a November 29, 2003, U.S. News & World Report, David Gergen said the conflicting news out of Iraq is obscuring a larger reality. The United States is in an urgent race against time. Unless we bring calm there soon – in, say, three to six months – we will be forced to make exceedingly painful choices. He said the U.S. and coalition forces are making progress in Iraq. Reconstruction has started, looting is down, electricity is up, shops are reopening, hospitals expanding. Kids have returned to schools. Yet the horrific bombings in Baghdad underscore that as fast as the U.S. moves ahead, it is not moving fast enough.

The January 30, 2005, Iraqi election gave the United Iraqi Alliance a slim majority in the new National Assembly. The alliance is composed mainly of Shiite Islamist religious parties which will occupy 140 of the 275 seats in the assembly.

On May 3, 2005, Iraq's new cabinet members were sworn into office, allowing the country's first fully and freely elected government to take power. According to an August 15, 2005, New York Times article by Dexter Filkins, at least six cabinet positions including the defense ministry were contentious because political leaders failed to agree on who should fill them. Sheikh Ghazi al-Yawar, Iraq's new vice president and the only top-ranking Sunni Arab in the government, refused to appear in protest. The January 30, 2005, election was boycotted by the Sunnis. The Shiite alliance, and the Kurdish alliance who won the majority of the seats, will dominate the new Iraqi government. The Sunni Arabs are virtually without representation.

According to an August 15, 2005, New York Times article by Dexter Filkins, the deadline for Iraqi leaders to complete the country's new draft constitution ran into a roadblock. Negotiations stalled because of a number of issues. Among the issues were whether to grant the country's Shiite majority an autonomous region in the south consisting of nine provinces which is half of the provinces in the country and be allowed to form a largely self-governing region akin to the Kurdish autonomous region in the north. Also at stake is the role of Islam in the state, the rights of women and the distribution of power between central and regional governments. Leaders of the Sunni population opposed the Shiite demands. Their contention was that if the Shiites and the Kurds were granted wide powers of self-rule, there would be little left of the Iraqi state.

Some Sunni leaders said the Shiite demand for self-rule is largely a cover for hoarding the bulk of Iraq's oil revenues, since most of the oil fields are situated in the extreme south of the country. Eventually, the Shiites agreed to hold off on their demands for regional autonomy, in exchange for a mechanism in the constitution that would allow them to achieve that autonomy later. Sunni leaders rejected that proposal, saying it would only slow down, but not significantly hamper, the Shiite drive for self-rule. The Sunnis said they would insist on two-thirds majority in all the voting. Saleh Mutlak, a Sunni leader on the constitution committee, said, "If we accept federalism, the country will be finished. Also, in contention was the city of Kirkuk which is divided among three ethnic groups but claimed by the Kurdish regional government. The Kurds were pushing for a timeline to reverse decades of Saddam Hussein's "Arabization" policy that would require the repatriation of tens of thousands of people.

Also at contention is the role of Islam in the state, including a proposal by the Shiites to include a political role for the Shiite religious leadership in Najaf. The power granted to Islam in the new constitution could affect the rights of women, particularly if Islamic law is allowed to govern marriage and family disputes.

On October 4, 2005, the United Nations said that the newly adopted rules for the coming Iraqi constitution referendum appeared to violate acceptable international standards for elections. Stephane Dujarric, the spokesman for Secretary General Kofi Annan, said, "When there is a contradiction on two different interpretations within one text, that would become an issue." In the new rules, the legislators designated two different meanings for the word "voters" in a single passage where the word appears to mean the same thing.

Robert F. Worth and Kirk Semple reported in an October 5, 2005, New York Times article that Iraq's Shiite and Kurdish political leaders quietly adopted new rules for the constitution on October 2, 2005. The rules change would make it virtually impossible for the constitution to fail and has infuriated many Sunni Arab political leaders who opposed the document.

According to an October 11, 2005, Associated Press article, the Iraqi negotiators reached a breakthrough deal on the constitution and at least one Sunni Arab party said it would urge its followers to approve the charter in the October 15, 2005 referendum. Under the deal, the two sides agreed that a commission would be set up to consider amendments to the charter that would then be put to a vote in parliament and then submitted to a new referendum in 2006. The agreement would allow the Sunnis to try to amend the constitution to reduce the autonomous powers that Shiites and Kurds would have under the federal system created by the charter.

On December 15, 2005, Iraqis voted for a permanent form of government. Voters in the 18 Iraqi provinces chose among 231 parties, coalitions and candidates to select members for a 275-seat Parliament. The legislators will serve a four-year term, and they will approve a president and a prime minister. White House spokesman Scott McClellan said, "This is a historic day for the Iraqi people, for the Middle East and for the rest of the world, and it's a historic day for the advance of freedom."

However, in spite of the election, the country is embroiled in a sectarian conflict with no foreseeable resolutions. Senator Joseph R. Biden Jr., D.-Del., believes that the sectarian violence is raging and ethnic cleansing is under way. He said "The sectarian genie is out of the bottle. Ethnic militias increasingly are the law in large parts of Iraq. They have infiltrated the official security forces. Sectarian cleansing has begun in mixed areas, with tens of thousands of Iraqis fleeing their homes, and dozens of dead bodies turn up in Baghdad daily." Biden said partitioning the country into regions controlled by Shiites, Kurds and Sunnis would defuse tensions and open the way for the withdrawal of most U.S. troops by 2008.

Biden said his plan would give Iraq's main competing religious and ethnic groups administrative authority over their regions, and permit them to establish their own military forces. Each region would have a share of Iraq's oil revenue, which would be administered by a central government whose authority would be limited in scope.

THELVE

CONCLUSION

What will be the eventual outcome in Iraq, and will it become the central front in the war on terrorism as President Bush and Vice President Cheney claim, or will it become another terrorist haven, a breeding ground with warlords and new terrorist groups?

Speaking at the Heritage Foundation on October 10, 2003, Vice President Cheney said, "Our mission in Iraq is a great undertaking and part of a larger mission that the United States accepted now more than two years ago. September 11, 2001, changed everything for this country." He again reiterated the rhetoric "that to do nothing against Saddam Hussein and people like him would be to invite terrorist atrocities on a horrific scale." He said, "We came to recognize our vulnerability to the threats of the new era. We saw the harm that 19 evil men could do armed with little more than airline tickets and box cutters and driven by a philosophy of hatred."

Cheney said, "The United States would not hesitate to make another pre-emptive strike if the circumstances demand it. The strategy of deterrence, which served us so well during the decade of the cold war, will no longer do. Our terrorist enemy has no country to defend, no assets to destroy in order to discourage an attack. There is only one way to protect ourselves against catastrophic terrorist violence, and that is to destroy the terrorists before they can launch further attacks against the United States."

However, from what we have seen and heard from the al-Qaeda's network, the converse may also be true. Just as the United States is planning to attack terrorists wherever they are, so too are the terrorists planning to attack Americans wherever they may be.

However, United Nations Secretary General Kofi Annan continued to express reservations about the war in Iraq. He said it was not in conformity with the United Nations Charter and raised questions about the legitimacy of the action by the United States and Britain to go to war without specific authority from the Security Council. He said he believed the war was illegal.

According to reports, the Bush administration had long decided to attack Iraq even before the September 11, 2001, attacks. A Washington Post article dated May 13, 2005, stated that on July 23, 2002, seven months before the invasion of Iraq, the head of M-I6, Richard Dearlove, reported to Prime Minister Tony Blair at No. 10 Downing Street that President Bush wanted to topple Saddam Hussein by military action and warned that Washington's intelligence was "being fixed around the policy." According to the memo, military action was seen as inevitable. Dearlove, who had just returned from consultation in Washington with other senior British officials, said Bush wanted to remove Saddam through military action, justified by the conjunction of terrorism and WMD. Also, documents received discredited Colin Powell's information on Iraq days before he went to the U.N., according to a CNN report.

The Bush administration used deception and fear tactics to invade a foreign country. It permeated fear and paranoia in the minds of the American people, so much so that many are inclined to believe everything they are told without questions or evidentiary proof. In other words, the majority of the American people have adopted a postulated position. By telling the American people that Saddam could release biological and chemical warfare on the United States within 45 minutes of an order, the Bush administration played on their emotions. This enabled the administration to obtain a "blank check" to do as it pleases, and it has certainly taken advantage of the situation, ranging from the invasion of Iraq to the Patriot Act.

When the truth finally came out about the purported weapons of mass destruction, Bush administration officials switched their emphasis for going to war from weapons of mass destruction to Saddam's atrocities against the Iraqi people. Ironically, many of the atrocities in Iraq took place when Saddam was an ally of the United States during George Herbert Walker Bush's administration. Furthermore, Halliburton and other Bush cronies have been doing business in Iraq for years, and they all turned a blind eye regarding the suffering of the Iraqis. In fact, while Iraq was under the control of the U.S., after the 2003 invasion, insurgents were able to steal large quantities of explosives, which the Bush administration claimed were taken before it invaded Iraq. However, the IAEA had sealed the explosives and revisited the site in 2002 and 2003 before the war began.

President Bush made the decision to attack Iraq with the blessing of Congress. They put the lives of more than 150,000 U.S. soldiers at risk unnecessarily because the U.S. was not at war with Iraq and neither was there any danger of being attacked with these purported weapons of mass destruction. So many young men and women have lost their lives and so many have been incapacitated, and many families have been uprooted unnecessarily.

Many of the returning soldiers will suffer mental and physical anguish for the rest of their lives. Some families will become one-parent families, creating hardship on the surviving spouse to maintain a family on one income, or become dependent on government subsidies. Some children will never know their fathers as some soldiers were murdered in Iraq before they were born or they were too young to remember. No president should subject another human being to meet an untimely death for no good reason. No president should subject another human being to die a horrific death for no good reason. No president should allow another human being to lose an arm or a leg or both for no good reason. And no president should deny a child the love of his or her father or mother, because they were killed in an unnecessary war. One can accept, with great difficulties, the

411

loss of a soldier in defense of his country or the rights of others, but not because some warmongers wanted to invade a country because of their own selfish reasons.

It has become very clear that Saddam Hussein did not have weapons of mass destruction and the United States could not have been in danger of being attacked by Saddam Hussein. Moreover, Israel, using fighter jets provided by the United States, demolished Iraq's nuclear facilities in 1982. Also, in 1993 the Clinton administration took out Saddam's intelligence system because of Saddam's attempt to assassinate the first President Bush, and warned him if he ever attempted to hurt any American again, the consequences would be dire. Since then, Saddam never made another attempt to hurt any American.

The Bush administration deceived not only the American people when the U.S. attacked Iraq, but also the rest of the world. In many opinions, this war should not have taken place. Saddam Hussein was neither a threat to the United States nor its neighbors. If Saddam Hussein could not defend Iraq against Israel's military defense, he surely could not defend it against a superpower such as the United States.

Furthermore, it was a foregone conclusion that when Bush took over the White House he would overthrow Saddam Hussein for a number of reasons: to complete the job his father did not finish during the 1991Gulf War; because Saddam tried to kill his father, as that was one of his first remarks when he took office in 2001; plus the fact that he told a number of senators and Condoleezza Rice, his national security adviser during a meeting, "F___ Saddam. We are taking him out."

Bush has no pacificatory tendencies regarding the Iraqis. If he did, he would have disarmed Saddam peacefully. Also he would want the American people to believe that his administration is theocratic. For example, he told Bob Woodward that he gets his advice from a higher father, not his biological father, when asked if he sought advice from his father before he attacked Iraq.

412

On October 7, 2005, BBC News reported that Nabil Shaath, a Palestinian negotiator, said that in a 2003 meeting with Mr. Bush, the U.S. president said he was "driven with a mission from God. God would tell me, 'George, go and fight those terrorists in Afghanistan.' And I did, and then God would tell me, 'George, go and end the tyranny in Iraq.' And I did. And now, again, I feel God's words coming to me: 'Go get the Palestinians their state and get the Israelis their security, and get peace in the Middle East.' And by God I'm gonna do it." The allegation was scheduled to appear in a BBC documentary. White House spokesman Scott McClellan said those comments had never been made.

Rumsfeld said that when the U.S. attacked Iraq, there would be "shock and awe." And it certainly was to a great extent, since according to an August 6, 2003, Associated Press article, they dropped a number of napalm bombs on Iraqis.

"Incendiaries create burns that are difficult to treat," said Robert Musil, executive director of Physicians for Social Responsibility, a Washington group that opposes the use of weapons of mass destruction. The U.S. also used phosphorous incendiary in Iraq. According to reports, these munitions, when they come in contact with people, the flesh burns to the bone.

While the Bush administration is telling other nations to disarm their weapons of mass destruction or face the consequences, in 2003 the United States tested the most powerful nuclear bomb, referred to as the "mother of all bombs," the Aegis cruiser.

During the 2000 campaign, Bush said over and over again, "They have not led, we will." It is true the Clinton administration did not lead the U.S. into a war. As a matter of fact, it did everything to make peace around the world, and did a fantastic job of brokering peace. For example, Clinton came extremely close to ending the Israeli/Palestinian conflict, for which Republicans and the media criticized that he wanted that to be a part of his legacy.

My mother used to tell us over and over again that "You can always catch flies with honey, but you cannot catch flies with vinegar."

The Bush administration led the American people into war because that seems to have been its intention prior to taking over the White House. There wasn't anything the United Nations inspectors or Saddam Hussein could have done to prevent the invasion. As a matter of fact, on August 3, 2004, Bush said if he had known two years prior that Saddam did not have WMD, he would still have invaded Iraq.

The American people should hold Congress accountable as well because they gave Bush a carte blanche. September 11, 2001, attacks blindsided not only the Congress, but many Americans as well. The Bush administration keeps saying remember September 11 and keeps juxtaposing Osama bin Laden and Saddam Hussein until the American people believe it to be a fact that Saddam and bin Laden attacked the United States.

It would appear that the Clinton administration tried to prevent wars at all costs, while the Bush administration wanted wars at all costs. During the Clinton administration, only 35 soldiers lost their lives from terrorism. Within the first nine months of the Bush administration, 3,000 American civilians lost their lives in the September 11, 2001, attacks. And as of May 1, 2006, 2,400 soldiers have been killed in Iraq, more than 17,000 have been wounded, more than 100,000 Iraqis have been killed, and at the end of the day, one may never know the total figures of the dead and wounded from the Iraq and Afghanistan wars.

The Bush administration held a "big stick" over the heads of world leaders. Their famous words are "Either you are with us or against us." So one should not be surprised that so many countries, England no exception, caved in to its demands in the invasion of Iraq, whether in the form of supplying troops, humanitarian or financial aid.

Australian Prime Minister John Howard said he was joining the U.S.-led coalition in Iraq because Australia needs the United States. Well, apparently it has paid off for Australia, because on August 3, 2004, Bush signed a trade treaty with Australia.

It's sad that the countries that participated in the invasion could not have been steadfast in their convictions against invading another country without provocation, like France, Germany, Russia, Canada, Mexico, et al, did. Although one can understand countries that rely on the United States for aid would find it difficult to say no to the United States.

By joining the coalition in Iraq, the Spanish people paid the ultimate sacrifice when a train was attacked in March 2004 killing 200 people and wounding over 1,500 in retaliation for attacking Iraq. Spain joined the coalition against the wishes of the Spanish people. The people could not prevent the prime minister from committing troops to Iraq, but they used their votes to oust him from the government. Immediately after winning the election, Jose Luis Rodriguez Zapatero, the newly elected prime minister, said he would withdraw the 1,300 troops from Iraq by June 30, 2004, unless the United Nations takes over the peacekeeping. He called the occupation of Iraq "a fiasco" and accused Washington and London of predicating the invasion of Iraq on "lies."

One would suspect that many people around the world now see the United States as a "dictator." You do as we say or suffer the consequences, as we have heard from President Bush time and time again.

But who suffers the most in the attack on Iraq? The U.S. soldiers and their families and the Iraqi people tend to be the biggest losers in this conflict, not only in terms of death and destruction, but also the inhumane conditions under which the soldiers have to perform their sometimes impossible tasks without the proper armor that could save their lives. Some soldiers searched landfills for scrap metal to make their own armor, while the Bush administration paid Halliburton billions of dollars on no-bid plus costs contracts.

An October 28, 2004, Reuters article by Les Roberts of the Johns Hopkins Bloomberg School of Public Health reported that The Lancet Medical Journal's conservative assumptions are that about 100,000 excess deaths or more happened since the 2003 invasion of Iraq. He said, "The use of air power in areas with lots of civilians appears to be killing a lot of women and children." Also, a December 8, 2004, Reuters article said that British Prime Minister Tony Blair rejected a call from more than 40 diplomats, peers, scientists and churchmen for an independent inquiry into the civilian death toll in the U.S.-led war in Iraq.

Meanwhile, the Iraqis are living without some of the basic necessities of life. A November 30, 2004, BBC report said that the medical facilities in Iraq are in a far worse condition than before the war. On December 12, 2004, BBC reported that the Red Cross said there were unburied bodies and sewage on the streets of Fallujah and that it would be at least another month before the bulk of the refugees would be able to return home, and that some were living on the streets in the cold. Furthermore, the four purification plants damaged by the U.S. were not restored. As of October 2005, some residents were getting electricity only nine hours per day.

Because of poor planning by the U.S. prior to the invasion of Iraq, it continues to experience many difficulties in terms of bringing Iraq into the realm of democracy. First, it failed to ensure that weapons did not get into the wrong hands, failed to minimize public disorder days following the fall of Saddam Hussein in April of 2003, and failed to quickly restore basic necessities to civilians. In the height of the hot season in August, shortages of electricity and gasoline in Basra set off furious riots by frustrated residents.

A September 10, 2003, World – Canada news report by Jonathan Write stated that Canadian Prime Minister Bill Graham said that conditions in Iraq were deteriorating under U.S. occupation and without reconstruction the country risked sliding into despair, poverty, desperation and violence, to become an incredible source of terror. He said it is a threat to us all and it is why Canada committed $300 million to help with reconstruction in Iraq.

So was this war to relieve the Iraqis of a dictator, or was it truly "blood for oil?" One wonders. U.S. soldiers were told to protect the oil fields and not the hospitals and other facilities necessary for the well-being of the Iraqi people. The mainstay of the infrastructure, such as the sewage and water systems and electrical facilities were either damaged or demolished. Government buildings, i.e., police stations, department of ministries were also demolished. And, even the airport was shut down.

What did this war accomplish? Thousands of lives torn apart, the grotesque deformity, savagery and grim aftermath of war should serve as a lesson to us all of the horrors attendant with wars and that war should only be a last resort. There is no clear vision as to when the war in Iraq will end or how much it will ultimately cost the American people both in terms of lives and financial liability.

A February 24, 2004, article in the Wall Street Journal by Greg Jaffe said that with the constant deadly attacks on security forces, senior U.S. military officials are pushing to increase the amount of money going to police and regional security forces being set up to combat the insurgency there. The additional funds would be used to speed training and buy better vehicles, weapons, radios and protective gear like body armor. The money for the new initiatives could come from the Development Fund for Iraq, a newly created account that includes Iraqi oil revenues and frozen assets. Also under consideration is to slow the development of the Army, which is focusing on defending Iraq from outside threats, and funneling that money to the Iraqi Police Service and the ICDC. According to reports, as of November 2005, only one Iraqi Battalion is fully ready.

But, if the outside threat is so great, why would they see fit to reduce the army that is trying to protect Iraq from other insurgents? Furthermore, the oil money was supposed to be used to help defray the cost of rebuilding Iraq's infrastructure. After the invasion, the U.S. abandoned Iraq's army and police force. They incurred an exorbitant cost to recruit and train new army and police officers, but not quickly enough to stem the surge of attacks by insurgents. The Bush administration's hope for Iraq's transformation in January 2005 grew dim as insurgents stepped up their attacks. A U.S. classified intelligence estimate prepared for President Bush in July 2004 showed pessimism on Iraq's future. The estimate outlines three possibilities for Iraq through the end of 2005, with the worst case being developments that could lead to civil war.

According to reports, before the Bush administration invaded Iraq, it dramatically underestimated the cost and the burden of the postwar occupation. They are now spending freely, sparing no cost in both rebuilding the country's infrastructure and the security. Did Congress give President Bush too much leeway after the September 11 attacks? Many people think so, not the least of which is Omaha, Nebraska, Republican Senator Chuck Hagel who strongly criticized Congress for giving President Bush too much latitude in conducting foreign policy. Speaking at the Gallup Organization World Conference in Omaha, he said "When the security of this nation is threatened, Congress and the American people give the president great latitude. We probably have given this president more flexibility, more latitude, more range, unquestioned, than any president since Franklin Roosevelt –probably too much. The Congress, in my opinion, really abrogated much of its responsibility."

After the November 2004 election, Bush said that the American people gave him capital, and that he intends to spend it, and he certainly has, since the American people will be saddled with a $2 trillion debt because of the Iraq invasion. According to a study released on December 6, 2005, by the American Academy of Arts & Sciences, and studies by a Harvard University professor and a Colombia University professor, the Iraq war will ultimately cost America nearly $2 trillion which includes long-term care for returning soldiers, many of whom will suffer permanent brain damage. Case in point – A January 22, 2006, New York Times article by Denise Grady gives another sad tale of a returning soldier. Jason Poole, a 23-year old Marine Corporal, is learning all over again to speak and to walk. He can barely read 16 words a minute. He is blind in his left eye, deaf in his left ear, weak on his right side and is still getting used to his new face, which was rebuilt with skin and bone grafts and 75 to 100 titanium screws and plates.

War On Terror Cost Escalates

Some time ago, I believe it was in the summer of 2003, Sen. John McCain of Arizona said that the Bush administration was spending money like a drunken sailor. On January 22, 2004, President Bush said he would ask Congress for another major increase to finance domestic security, and urged Americans against taking false comfort in the absence of terrorist attacks on American soil for more than two years. Bush's warning at the New Mexico Military Institute came less than 48 hours after he used the State of the Union address to defend the invasion of Iraq. When treasury Secretary Paul O'Neal said the war would cost over $200 billion, the Bush administration dismissed the estimate and gave a much lower figure. Of course, he was later relieved of his post. There has been another estimate of $20 billion per year indefinitely, according to the Council on Foreign Relations Task Force.

According to a May 10, 2006, Wall Street Journal article, the Senate approved $109 billion in additional spending for the wars in Iraq and Afghanistan, including $1.5 billion in added Iraq reconstruction money. The administration has spent $20.9 billion to reconstruct Iraq's infrastructure and modernize its oil industry, but the effort hasn't restored the country's electricity output, water supply or sewage capabilities to prewar levels.

Maybe the reason the Bush administration did not wait to build a coalition to invade Iraq was due to the fact that the

United Nations inspectors would have completed their inspection and would not have found any weapons of mass destruction. This, of course, would have negated the administration's contention that Iraq's neighbors and the American people were in imminent danger from Saddam Hussein if he remained in power. It is sad that so many lives have been lost and continue to be lost because of a war that for the most part was unwarranted and senseless. There was no link between Saddam Hussein and Osama bin Laden. The fear and trepidation instilled in the American people were unwarranted and vagrant. There is a lesson to be learned from this war, and the hope is that both the Congress and the American people will not be so quick to give a president a blank check the next time he or she cries "wolf."

So why was Iraq attacked? An article by the Associated Press dated March 19, 2004, said that the Bush administration considered bombing Iraq in retaliation almost immediately after September 11. A former counterterrorism coordinator to the president, Richard Clarke, said that Defense Secretary Donald Rumsfeld complained on September 12 – after the administration was convinced with certainty that al-Qaeda was to blame – that "there aren't any good targets in Afghanistan and there are lots of good targets in Iraq."

Clarke told CBS news he believes the administration sought to link Iraq with the attacks because of long-standing interest in overthrowing Saddam Hussein.

And as the war lingers and so many soldiers are being killed, former Bush administration staff members have come forward to tell their story of how the Bush administration planned to invade Iraq well before September 11, the reason Bush said they attacked Iraq.

Former Treasury Secretary Paul O'Neil said Bush planned to invade Iraq two months after taking office. We also learned from Bob Woodward's book, "Plan of Attack," that Secretary of State Colin Powell warned Bush about the potential negative consequences of a war, "you break it, you own it." Powell is described as having clashed in particular with Vice President Dick Cheney, whom Woodward describes as a "powerful, steamrolling force" advocating the war, who was preoccupied with reports of links between Saddam Hussein and the al-Qaeda terrorist network. According to reports, Powell regarded Cheney's intense focus on Hussein and al-Qaeda as a "fever," and he believed that the vice president misread and exaggerated intelligence about the Iraq threat and supposed terrorist ties. And, in April 2006, six former Army generals criticized the war in Iraq.

Of the many people in the Bush administration who planned to go to war, Colin Power is the only one who knew what it would be like to fight in a war. He has been in the foxholes and has seen the destruction of lives.

In contrast, President Bush, Vice President Cheney, Donald Rumsfeld and Paul Wolfowitz have had no firsthand experience in war.

I remember as a child my parents used to quote time and time again, "War is hell!" not because they personally experienced it, but because of the human destruction attendant to wars.

The Bush administration's hypothesis was that it is liberating the Iraqis. But who stands to gain more from the destruction of Iraq? Companies who have an interest to see Saddam Hussein ousted so that they could receive lucrative contracts for the rebuilding of the infrastructure.

CNN reported on October 27, 2004, that companies working in Iraq will be allowed to bring their profits to the U.S. and pay only five percent tax instead of 35. Obviously, if a country with over 25 million people is demolished, it would cost hundreds of billions of dollars to rebuild it over a number of years. Many Iraqis are now impoverished. They lost all the major necessities of life such as electricity, water and even their daily sustenance – food is rationed.

Was it "Blood for Oil"? Did a small number of special interest groups get together and plan a war strategy so as to take over the world's second largest oil-producing country in order to have control of the oil? Was it a "power struggle?" Was the war construed to exert power around the world and to get other countries to fear the United States' financial and military might? Was this a warning to other countries – See what we did to Iraq, if you don't watch yourselves you could be next? Was this another way to hold the American people hostage by keeping the fear of terror in their thoughts and minds? If you want to remain safe from terrorism, keep the Republicans in the White House, because the Democrats are soft on terrorism and cannot protect Americans from attacks such as September 11, 2001, or is it that the U.S. wants to become hegemonic. You decide.

And as the election campaign began heating up, the mantra started all over again using the fear of terrorism to coerce the American people to keep the Republicans in the White House, the Senate and the Congress. President Bush in a speech in New Hampshire, where the Democratic primary took place on January 27, 2004, defended the military and reconstruction campaign in Iraq and said the American people will be reliving the September 11 attacks all over again. On March 4, 2004, the Bush administration launched its first election campaign portraying the attacks in order to show that it has resolve in handling the terrorist situation. And, of course, at every opportunity Dick Cheney and George Bush got, they mentioned that they are fighting the war in Iraq so that they will not have to fight it at home.

But could the September 11, 2001, attacks have been prevented and the Iraq's invasion avoided? The Bush administration blamed the September 11 attacks on the Clinton administration for not getting rid of Osama bin Laden. But the converse is true because there was a planning order called "Able Danger" set up by the Clinton administration in 1999 to target al-Qaeda offensively overseas and to stop them there before they could come to the U.S., but the Bush administration terminated the plan in the spring of 2001.

Appearing on C-Span on August 21, 2005, Lt. Anthony Schaffer said that in the spring of 2001 the Bush administration terminated the "Able Danger" program and that his file with the information on "Able Danger" is missing from where he left it. Appearing on MSNBC's Hardball with

Chris Mathews, on August 26, 2005, Schaffer said that the CIA had information on Mohamed Atta, one of the hijackers, almost a year before the 9/11 attacks. He said that these attackers live in the real world. For example, he cited the London bombings that the suicide attackers were seen together white water rafting which was their final planning before the attacks.

Congressman Curt Weldon, Republican of Pennsylvania, said the 9/11 commission botched the investigation into the "Able Program." He levied charges of massive cover-up by members of the defense intelligence community and called for a criminal investigation. He said Tony Schaeffer wanted to testify before the 9/11 commission but was refused by the commission. He also said the CIA in Florida had a meeting wherein they told employees to kill the "Able Danger" story. The "Able Danger" program consisted of 20 employees.

Although the Bush administration blamed the Clinton administration over and over for not getting rid of Osama bin Laden, the 9/11 Commission's interim report shows that Clinton declared war on Osama and his network and made it a priority and established a bin Laden unit. Moreover, the Bush team nixed Clinton's comprehensive plan to choke off al-Qaeda supplies and create an alliance with other countries to get rid of al- Qaeda, according to a Time Magazine article dated August 5, 2003.

On August 20, 1998, Clinton in an address to the nation regarding military action taken against terrorist sites in Afghanistan and Sudan said that bin Laden publicly vowed to wage a terrorist war against America. And, again on August 22, 1998, in a radio address to the nation, he said "Our efforts against terrorism cannot and will not end with this strike. We should have realistic expectations about what a single action can achieve, and we must be prepared for a long battle." In December 1998, CIA director George Tenet elaborated on the president's statement in a memorandum to senior CIA managers, the Deputy D.C.I. for Community Management, and the Assistant D.C.I. for Military Support, declaring war on bin Laden: "We must now enter a new phase in our effort against bin Laden ... We are at war ... I want no resources or people spared in this effort, either inside (the) CIA or the community." The former chief of the FBI's International Terrorism Section stated that he had fewer than 100 Special Agents working on international terrorism on September 11, 2001, than he did in August 1998.

Since al-Qaeda attacked the World Trade Center in 1993, it was never able to attack it again until the Bush administration took over. So when Cheney during the 2004 campaign assuring the American people that if the Democrats were elected, they would have another attack similar to 9/11, one should be reminded that 9/11 happened on the Republicans' watch, not the Democrats'.

During his testimony before the 9/11 commission, former New York Mayor Rudolph Giuliani said that they have an emergency program that was put in place in 1995, which worked very well in saving the lives of tens of thousands on 9/11. He said the emergency program also helped during the anthrax attack one month after 9/11 and the plane crash in Queens shortly thereafter.

During a June 2004 Senate hearing, Senator Leahy asked Attorney General John Ashcroft many questions pertaining to the Bush administration plans to fight terrorism when it took office in 2001. One of the questions to Ashcroft was that the FBI went to him and asked for an increase for the terrorism budget, but Ashcroft declined the increase. Ashcroft said he did not want to answer individual questions, but instead read a lengthy prepared statement, talking about terrorism and the threat to the United States.

On July 22, 2004, the 9/11 Commission issued its final report. The commission concluded that there were dozens of missed opportunities, clues that went undetected and crucial pieces of intelligence that America's counterterrorism investigators simply failed to share with one another. After advising his staff to go slow on the implementation of the recommendations of the 9/11 Commission, Bush reversed his position, and decided to start implementing some of the recommendations immediately, such as a national intelligence director. However, the Katrina disaster exhibits the lack of a comprehensive plan, such as that of first responders, as thousands of people on the Gulf Coast lost their lives and all of their belongings, and the state was left in ruins.

Although President Bush said we will find the people responsible for attacks on the U.S. on 9/11 and bring them to justice, as of October 2005, only Moussaoui has been put on trial for the attacks. On April 22, 2005, Moussaoui pleaded guilty for taking part in a broad al-Qaeda conspiracy that resulted in the September 11 attacks. However, he vehemently denied that he was planning to be one of the September 11 hijackers. He said bin Laden personally instructed him to fly an airplane into the White House. The U.S. is asking for the death penalty for Moussaoui, because it believes that if he had told the police about the conspiracy, when he was arrested, 9/11 would have been prevented. However, on May 3, 2006, the jurors recommended life without parole.

The Bush administration has now changed its slogan from the "global war on terror" to "a global struggle against violent extremism." Administration officials said the phrase may have outlived its usefulness, because it focused attention solely, and incorrectly, on the military campaign.

When the Bush administration attacked Iraq, it used the military capabilities left by President Clinton. They did not have to manufacture or purchase any additional weaponry. How ironic, because during the 2000 campaign Bush kept saying that the Clinton administration had run down the defense system and that the United States would be unable to fight a war with the present defense system. They claimed that the defense cuts under President Clinton had gone too far, that the armed forces had been overused badly and that readiness was poor. They said that if the United States were attacked it would not be prepared to fight a war.

However, the arsenal used in Afghanistan to defeat the Taliban's was the one left by the Clinton/Gore administration. If the defense were in such a bad condition and could not fight a war, why were they in such a rush to attack Iraq? Moreover, how could they fight two wars at the same time, one in Afghanistan and the other in Iraq? And, it is still the Clinton's military that is winning the war in Iraq and Afghanistan. It is also the same military that completed a successful action against Serbia in 1999. This shows that the Clinton administration maintained a strong and focused military able to carry out post-cold war missions. Let's give credit where credit is due. It appears that if things are going bad, Clinton gets the blame, but if things are going well, the Bush administration takes the credit.

So, was the war in Iraq Blood for Oil, lucrative contracts, revenge or superiority? From what we have seen so far, it appears that it was predicated upon a combination of all four – Blood for Oil to control the second largest oil-producing country in the world, lucrative contracts for the special interest groups who benefit from the destruction of Iraq's infrastructure, revenge against the planned assassination attempt of the first President Bush by Saddam Hussein and a power struggle among the Bush administration team to control the world.

It would certainly be a sad time in America's history, if the most powerful nation in the world invades a foreign country without the threat of being attacked by that country. The American people are suffering the consequences of this terrible unnecessary war both in terms of lives lost and the heavy financial burden. Some have lost loved ones. Some are enduring the agony of having to care for loved ones whose bodies have been dismembered. There are so many debilitating injuries being suffered by these soldiers that I, for one, shudder when I see the pain, agony and frustration on the faces of these injured soldiers and family members.

Did the Bush administration fall asleep on the job? You bet it did. Ironically, U.S. intelligence can pinpoint attacks on Saudi Arabia as to the dates and place and even warned Britain about the July 7, 2005, subway bombings, yet they could not see the potential September 11 attacks. In fact, they ignored the intelligence reports on the potential attacks on the U.S. One finds it hard to believe that with the kind of sophisticated intelligence system the U.S. has both in terms of technology and human intelligence, that the U.S. could miss such an imperative event. According to reports, President Bush had information on his desk in August 2001 that al-Qaeda was planning to hijack commercial planes and fly them into buildings in the U.S. So how is it possible that the U.S. can warn Saudi Arabia of imminent attacks, but did nothing to protect the American people when they received information of imminent attacks on the U.S.? When the Clinton administration learned that al-Qaeda was planning to attack various facilities in the United States, it did not alarm the American people; instead it worked with other countries and thwarted the attacks.

Another point that is mind-boggling is the fact that in view of the threats, the Federal Aviation Administration, which controls the nation's air traffic, was not on alert of these potential attacks. According to a December 20, 2003, New York Times article by Jim Dwyer, even after fighter jets were racing toward the city after hijackers commandeered the planes, La Guardia Airport was unaware of the hijackings, continued to send out flights until the second plane struck the World Trade Center. That was nearly an hour after the first plane had been hijacked.

Military officials have said that the Federal Aviation Administration notified them about one of the four hijackings only after that plane had crashed into the second tower at the trade center. The fourth hijacked plane took off from Newark at 8:43, after two of the earlier planes had been seized, according to the article. Moreover, when we think of NORAD (North American Aerospace Defense Command), we think of a superior defense system that is second to none that monitors the U.S. airways for possible foreign attacks. Were they not alerted of the potential attacks?

The Bush administration is trying to protect the U.S. by ordering more sophisticated weaponry. As an example, a Northrop Grumman subsidiary was awarded a $4.5 billion contract to develop a weapon that would destroy enemy missiles shortly after their launch. The eight-year contract for the defense giant's space and mission systems subsidiary covers development and testing of an interceptor to destroy a missile in its boost phase. The boost phase is the time when the missile's engines are firing, before it reaches space. The Pentagon gave Northrop Grumman and Lockheed Martin $10 million to develop a concept design for the interceptor. Does anyone believe these sophisticated weaponry systems alone will deter terrorism and keep Americans safe? Defense mechanism against terrorism will only be as good as the people in charge of the system. In addition to this sophisticated weaponry, the U.S. needs to restart its nation-building program by changing its economic and human rights policies and work with other wealthy nations to raise the standards of the less fortunate countries. When the world is at peace, it is less likely that terrorism will escalate.

As the election campaign went into full gear, the mantra started all over again using the fear of terrorism to coerce the American people to keep the Republicans in the White House, the Senate and the Congress. President Bush in a speech in New Hampshire, where the Democratic primary took place on January 27, 2004, defended the military and reconstruction campaign in Iraq and said the American people will be reliving the September 11 attacks all over again. On March 4, 2004, the Bush administration launched its first election campaign portraying the attacks in order to show that it has resolve in handling the terrorist situation. And, of course, at every opportunity Dick Cheney and George Bush mentioned that they are fighting the war in Iraq so that they will not have to fight it at home.

Given what we know about the information that the Clinton administration gave to the Bush administration regarding Osama bin Laden when they took over the White House, one can't help but wonder if the Bush administration had taken the threats of bin Laden seriously and followed up where the Clinton administration had left off, would there have been a 9/11 attack? If the Clinton administration was able to thwart the millennium attacks, why wasn't the Bush administration able to thwart the September 11 attacks? Is it because they hated Clinton so much that they did not believe him? Even so, Sandy Berger, the National Security Adviser gave them a PowerPoint presentation on the al-Qaeda network and Osama bin Laden, so why did the Bush administration ignore the warnings? And why did the Bush administration not take the threat of Osama bin Laden seriously in August 2001 when they received the report that al-Qaeda was planning to use American airplanes as weapons to attack the United States?

The report by Keane, former Republican governor of New Jersey and head of the commission who was investigating the September 11 attacks, said the attacks could have been avoided. Is that why the Bush administration stonewalled the commission and refused access to certain files and staff for months? Is that also why the Bush administration wanted to give the commission 12 months to complete a monumental task that would require several years to be thoroughly completed? If the commission was not granted an extension from the May 2004 deadline to complete the investigation, then the commission would not be able to provide a comprehensive report on the events leading up to September 11.

With the emergence of new information about the events leading up to 9/11, the Bush administration was shaken up a bit. On June 3, 2004, CIA Director George Tenet resigned from the CIA and many were asking "was he pushed or did he jump?" He retired on July 11, 2004, after seven years as CIA director, and, on June 4, 2004, James Pavitt, the head of the agency's clandestine service, and deputy director of operations also announced his resignation. This leaves one to wonder which other shoe would fall next. I believe a number of shoes should drop and that the entire truth will come to bare someday about the secret operations of the Bush administration. They have kept the American people and the Congress in the dark on many issues concerning this country.

The Bush administration is probably one of the most secretive administrations in America's history.

The Bush administration said it is fighting terrorism on all fronts, not only by killing and arresting terrorists but also by choking off their financial supplies. But a December 12, 2003, article in the New York Times written by Eric Lichtblau and Timothy L. O'Brien would indicate the converse to be true. The report said that the federal authorities do not have a clear understanding of how terrorists move their financial assets and are still struggling to prevent the flow of money to terror groups, according to a new Congress report. A report by the General Accounting Office, the investigative arm of Congress, also finds that the Internal Revenue Service did not develop a formal plan for sharing financial information with state authorities about charities under investigation. And the report says the Treasury and Justice Departments have fallen nearly a year behind in developing a plan for attacking money laundering and issues like terrorists' use of black-market gems and gold.

According to a report, prior to September 11, 2001, the view of the United States as a victim of terrorism that deserved the world's sympathy and support has given way to a widespread opinion of America as an imperial power that has defied world opinion through unjustified and unilateral use of military force.

In labeling countries such as Iran, Libya and North Korea as an axis of evil, they were put on notice that they could be next in line to be invaded by the United States. He also said, "The Iranian regime needs to know that if it stays on its present course, the international community is prepared to impose meaningful consequences."

Well, that may happen sooner that we think, because on March 7, 2006, Vice President Dick Cheney said that Iran will not be allowed to have a nuclear weapon and warned "the United States is keeping all options on the table in addressing the irresponsible conduct of the regime. And, on March 9, 2006, Ali Asghar Soltanieh, the chief Iranian delegate to the IAEA, responded by saying that

"The United States has the power to cause harm and pain, but the United States is also susceptible to harm and pain." So if that is the path that the U.S. wishes to choose, let the ball roll." And, on March 16, 2006, President Bush reaffirmed his first-strike policy against terrorists and enemy nations and said that Iran may pose the biggest challenge for America.

According to a February 13, 2006, Reuters article a British think tank, the Oxford Research Group, said that thousands of military personnel and hundreds of civilians would be killed if the United States launched an air strike to prevent Iran from developing nuclear power. The attack could lead to the closure of the Gulf at the Straits of Hormuz and would probably have a substantial impact on oil prices, as well as spurring new attacks by Muslim radicals on Western interest, the report said. On April 9, 2006, CNN reported that Seymour Hirsh said that while the Bush administration is giving the appearance that it wants to resolve the Iranian problem peacefully it is planning to attack Iran. But will the American people stand up against an Iranian invasion?

Although the Bush administration says it is going to root out terrorism and make the world safer; by taking the action to invade Iraq it has only made the world less safe. The al-Qaeda network said they would attack Americans wherever they are. This means no one is safe. By attacking Americans around the world, other nationalities will also be subject to attacks, because Americans live, work and vacation all over the world. So how is the Bush administration going to protect Americans while it attempts to root out terrorism?

How is the U.S. going to find each and every person who hates Americans in this great big wide world with billions of people? Even those who never cared for Americans one way or another could now have misgivings, not only because of the attack on Iraq, but because of the Bush administration policies and arrogance.

So how safe are Americans at home and abroad, and how will the Bush administration guarantee the safety of Americans – it's anyone's guess – but one thing is for sure, until the Bush administration stops its attitude of superiority and bullying, Americans will remain targets for terrorists. It is always best to build friendships rather than to create enemies. By that I mean, build friendships whenever possible, whether by cajoling, by tact, and/or by diplomacy. Not by browbeating, not by threats and not by bullying.

A New York Times World Opinion article dated September 11, 2003, shows the extent of resentment toward the United States as follows:

> In interviews by Times correspondents from Africa to Europe to Southeast Asia, one point emerged clearly: The war in Iraq has had a major impact on public opinion, which has moved generally from post 9/11 sympathy to post-Iraq antipathy, or at least to disappointment over what is seen as the sole superpower's inclination to act preemptively, without either persuasive reasons or United Nations approval.

> To some degree, the resentment is centered on the person of President Bush, who is seen by many of those interviewed, at best, as an ineffective spokesman for American interests and, at worst, as a gun slinging cowboy knocking over international treaties and bent on controlling the world's oil, if not the entire world.

> Foreign policy experts point to slowly developing fissures, born at the end of the cold war that exploded into view in the debate leading up to the Iraq war. "I think the turnaround was last summer, when American policy moved ever more decisively toward war against Iraq," said Josef Joffe, co-editor of the German weekly Die Zeit. "That's what triggered the counteralliance of France and Germany and the enormous wave of hatred against the United States."

> "America has taken power over the world," said Dmitri Ostalsky, 25, a literary critic and writer

in Moscow. "It's a wonderful country, but it seized power. It's ruling the world. America's attempts to rebuild the world in the image of liberalism and capitalism are fraught with the same dangers as the Nazis taking over the world."

A Frenchman, Jean-Charles Pogram, 45, a computer technician, said: "Everyone agrees on the principles of democracy and freedom, but the problem is that we don't agree with the means to achieve those ends. The United States can't see beyond the axiom that force can solve everything, but Europe, because of two world wars, knows the price of blood."

Lydia Adhiamba, a 20-yer-old student at the Institute of Advanced Technology in Nairobi, Kenya, said the United States "wants to rule the whole world, and that's why there's so much animosity to the U.S."

The major English language daily newspaper in Indonesia, The Jakarta Post, ran an article titled, "Why moderate Muslims are annoyed with America," by Sayidiman Suryohadiprojo, a prominent figure during the Suharto years. "If America wants to become a hegemonic power, it is rather difficult for other nations to prevent that," he wrote. "However, if America wants to be a hegemonic power that has the respect and trust of other nations, it must be a benign one, and not one that causes a reaction of hatred or fear among other nations."

Bush told reporters that part of his aim during the trip is "to make sure that the people who are suspicious of our country understand our motives are pure." He said, "America is following a new strategy. We are not waiting for further attacks. We are striking our enemies before they strike us again." Those are fighting words. Does that mean those who see America as their enemy will try to attack the U.S. before they are attacked? Does this mean that the U.S. will be at war for decades to come? You bet it will, unless America changes its policy and try to rebuild the harmony previously enjoyed with many nations.

No one is saying the United States should not go to war. But only if it is absolutely necessary and only after all other viable means of prevention have failed. Saddam Hussein had been under containment for over ten years. There was nothing so urgent to warrant the rush to war. The American people were not in imminent danger of being attacked by Saddam Hussein. Saddam had no weapons of mass destruction. Saddam had no link with Osama bin Laden or the al-Qaeda network. Saddam's neighbors were not in any danger of a nuclear attack by him because Israel destroyed his nuclear facilities in August 1982 with the help of United States Tomahawk missiles. The danger that Saddam posed was only to his people. In time the United Nations, Britain and United States could have disarmed Saddam and exiled him as has been done in the past in other countries. For example, President Noreaga of Panama was physically taken out of his country and brought to Miami, Florida, tried and sent to jail.

According to reports, in preparing to attack Iraq, the Bush administration bribed some of Saddam's army not to fight back when the U.S. invaded it in March 2003. It also distributed propaganda flyers and radio messages into Iraq to get their messages to the Iraqi people. So too, the Bush administration could have used the many avenues available to it to disarm and exile Saddam. Today, the world would be a lot safer without having used brute force and arrogance which has now permeated a whole new set of American haters which is now a preamble for more terrorism attacks against Americans at home and abroad. Both the Carter and Clinton administrations worked very hard to build a coalition and to build peace around the world. The cold war was over and peace was beginning to take form in many parts of the world. However, as soon as the Bush administration took over the White House, one of Bush's first remarks was that his administration would not be a nation builder. However, on September 11, 2001, after the attacks on the United States, a coalition from around the world rallied to the cause of the United States. Because they wanted to help fight terrorism and also because of the relationship that was in existence prior to the Bush administration.

The United States is less safe now than before 9/11. The more the U.S. alienates sectors of the world, the more hatred is cultivated against Americans creating even larger breeding grounds of terrorists. Under these circumstances, how can Americans be protected? I heard a report on television in early March 2004 that a plan against the United States by al-Qaeda was 90 percent completed. And in early May, New York authorities found what they called a terrorist dry run of nine empty suitcases in several trains and at FBI headquarters. Also, two tankers containing thousands of gallons of gas were stolen in New Jersey and another two full tankers were stolen in Texas over Memorial Day weekend that year. This indicates that the al-Qaeda network is always looking for ways to attack the U.S., and will stop at nothing.

One needs only to look at the Bush administration's detention policy to understand why Americans are hated all over the world. Holding "suspected terrorists" indefinitely, without due process, without the right to counsel and without the right to see their relatives, has only served to further permeate hatred, distrust and contempt for the United States. Reports that these prisoners are being tortured and placed in inhumane conditions are also indicative of the lack of concern for human beings, some of whom are innocent of any acts of terrorism.

What can be done to protect the innocent American citizens and others from the Patriot Act? It is true that those who try to do us harm should be punished, but we better make sure we are right. Because if we continue to put innocent people away indefinitely and torture them, what will happen to our society as a whole and how will the rest of the world perceive us? Then the ultimate question is: Are we any better than those dictators whom we overthrow and ridicule?

In many countries, people believe that if the Bush administration invaded Iraq, their countries could also be attacked. Some believe that because the Bush administration is building an empire, it will invade countries such as Syria and Iran. Others believe the Bush administration is fighting Israel's war by attacking Iraq. While another group believes the sole purpose of invading Iraq was to take over the Iraqi oil. Iraq is the number two oil-producing country in the world and Saudi Arabia holds the number one position. However, with the U.S. coalition at the helm, Iraq could very well become the number one oil-producing country.

The Bush administration is spending billions of dollars in Iraq, while a news report said an emergency appeal for funds to assist 16.9 million people facing starvation in the Horn of Africa went unheeded. Other countries would do well with even a small fraction of the funds that are being poured into Iraq.

According to reports, in January 2004, Iraq's Governing Council approved the creation of a new homegrown intelligence unit to crack down on infiltration and root out foreign fighters. The controversial outfit to be funded by the U.S. government and trained by the CIA will consist of hundreds of agents, including some former members of the Mukhabarat, Saddam Hussein's dreaded security apparatus. The 3rd Armored Cavalry Regiment will put another battalion of border police on the Syrian frontier before it withdraws. But troops say more is needed, including computers at official crossings to verify the identities of everyone attempting to enter Iraq legally. Although the Bush administration shies away from giving any indication as to how long U.S. troops will remain in Iraq, Britain's foreign secretary, Jack Straw, said on January 5, 2004, that British troops would stay in Iraq for years, perhaps as late as 2007.

The problems being encountered in Iraq should not surprise the Bush administration, or anyone else for that matter. According to a 2003 Washington Post article, a yearlong State Department study predicted many of the problems that have plagued the American-led occupation. Beginning in

436

April 2002, the State Department project assembled more than 200 Iraqi lawyers, engineers, business people and other experts into 17 working groups to study topics ranging from creating a new justice system to reorganizing the military to revamping the economy.

History has shown that the Middle East has survived its invaders as far back as Napoleon's invasion of Egypt through Britain's rule in Iraq in the 1920's to Israel's march into Lebanon. Time and again, countries that invade the Middle East have not adequately prepared for the difficulties they would encounter. The Bush administration is no exception. They have miscalculated support for the invasion. Before the war, Vice President Dick Cheney was telling the American people that the U.S. would be welcome with roses by the Iraqi people. Secretary of Defense Donald Rumsfeld told the soldiers that overthrowing Saddam Hussein would be a cakewalk.

Now we know differently. The American people were also told that the troops would be out within six months. Now the truth has come to bare – U.S. troops will be in Iraq indefinitely. Moreover, the United States is faced with a long drawn out battle, not from Saddam Hussein. To use President Bush's words – "Saddam is no more." But insurgents from many parts of the Middle East are killing indiscriminately. The Bush administration was warned that if it attacked Iraq, it would only incite more terrorism, not only in Iraq, but globally wherever Americans are found.

According to a North County Times Op-Ed article by Ken Schiffner, for over 200 years, the U.S. policy was not to pre-emptively strike another country, unless there was an eminent threat. Negotiations, diplomacy and restraint should be the foremost considerations to settle disputes with other nations. Pre-emptive strikes set a precedent, which means the U.S. must act in a similar manner against further threats. The U.S. could be drawn into conflicts throughout the world, none of which individually equate to an immediate threat, but combined could drain and destroy us. History has shown when the U.S. is attacked, we respond with deadly conviction, courage and purpose. The precedent of a powerful defensive posture is a positive one and a strong deterrent to future Saddams of any stripe. It engenders willing allies in the response. To pre-emptively attack a nation, however, because they might, someday, maybe attack another country can be the fuse to a power keg.

Bush claimed this invasion will be different. He broadened his war aims from removing Saddam Hussein and weapons of mass destruction to transforming Iraq into a beacon of freedom in the Middle East. In a news conference on March 6, 2003, Bush said U.S. troops would remain to help run Iraq until a new, representative government could take control. He spoke of confronting totalitarianism, of spreading "God's gift" of liberty "to each and every person," and of how Iraqi lives and freedom matter greatly to us. But as of March 2006, Iraq is on the brink of a civil war.

Who profits most from the invasion of Iraq? The companies that were also beating the war drum, not the least of which was Halliburton, whose contract as of October 2005 exceeded $10 billion and whose stock share price went from under $14 per share before the Iraq invasion to $83.90 per share in April 2006. Halliburton was also given a waiver on December 19, 2003 which would relieve it of its obligation to provide data to justify its high gasoline prices. Conoco-Phillips also profited. Its stock share price went from $42.40 in 2005 to $120 per share when it split two-for-one then traded at an intra-day high of $71.60 in October 2005. ExxonMobil's revenue in 2005 was $36.1 billion with a profit of nearly $10 billion, the biggest corporate profit in U.S. history. Also, the Chief Executive Officer received a pension of $400 million. And, the top oil companies made $25 billion in profits in the third quarter of 2005. On April 21, 2006, Oil price skyrocketed to more than $75 per barrel.

More importantly, the U.S. soldiers and their families and the Iraqi people suffer the most. According to an August 4, 2005, Reuters article, Dr. Harith Hassan, the former head of Baghdad's Psychological Research Center, said the occupation and the insurgency have turned Iraq into possibly the

438

most psychologically damaged nation in the world. He said more than 70 percent of the private clients he sees in Iraq each week are suffering from post-traumatic stress disorder (PTSD), a severe anxiety condition. According to a CNN July 27, 2005, report, one in ten U.S. soldiers returning from Iraq suffer PTSD, and that they killed more people than in the first Gulf War and handled more body parts. Notably, a soldier committed suicide after returning home from Iraq. His wife said he could not adjust to civilian life and that he slept with his gun on his bed. In spite of all this, some soldiers returned to Iraq for a third and fourth time, some said to finish the job, and some were ordered back to duty.

Because of the rising sectarian violence, on April 21, 2006, Iraqi Prime Minister al-Jaafari stepped down, removing a major obstacle to forming a new government, and resolving a stalemate. The battle over the remaining high-level posts came to an end on April 22, 2006, when Jawad al-Maliki was asked to be prime minister-designate and form a new government. Al-Maliki, a Shiite, was nominated to replace Ibrahim al-Jaafari who had been at the center of the impasse between Iraq's political parties.

According to a report, Bush's unilateralist policies have permeated fractures in the alliance that was once so eager to join the American cause to build peace and freedom around the world. The once friendly alliance has now become skeptics to a great degree. The world is now more chaotic and unfriendly. Security has now become a constant concern, not only in the United States, but also around the world.

The administration stance on security, arrest, and trials has permeated more hatred for the American people than ever before. I would surmise that many groups that were sympathetic to the American people after the September 11 attacks now have venomous feelings toward us. And it is understandable. When the most powerful nation in the world appears to be lord and master over all, then the results would be apprehension and disgust. America has become the world's dictator.

No one wants the U.S. to compromise its security, but in this age of technological expansion, it is highly likely that even the least expected country or terrorist group could develop technological warfare. Therefore, it is becoming more and more difficult for us to protect ourselves.

A February 2006 Scientific American magazine article reported that many civilian research reactors contain highly enriched uranium that terrorists could use to build nuclear bombs. The article pointed out that a terrorist organization such as al-Qaeda might acquire highly enriched uranium (HEU), build a crude gun-type detonating device and use the resulting nuclear weapons against a city.

That is why I strongly believe that the U.S. should stop focusing so much on rooting out terrorism and concentrate on rebuilding the kind of relationship it had previously. Call it nation-building if you wish, but creating peace and harmony around the world is a quicker way to reduce terrorism than trying to kill each and every suspected terrorist group, because as you kill one another comes up to take its place. That is why a peace plan is one of the most important tools available to us to stem terrorism, but who am I to give the U.S. advice on how to conduct itself, I am only an ordinary concerned American citizen.

It is my firm belief, however, that someday, because of the way in which the U.S. government is conducting its foreign policy, the U.S. would no longer remain the superpower as it is today; instead a United Europe or China may become the most powerful nation in the world. I mentioned China because in 1996, I was one of 32 Certified Financial Planners who visited China to exchange ideas on financial planning. Throughout our trip, we met with many government officials and the theme throughout the discussions was that China wants to be the number one economic country in the world. One official even said that they are striving for China's stock exchange to surpass the New York Stock

440

Exchange, and another official even used the phrase by Allan Greenspand that they are having "a soft landing."

I am not saying that the U.S. could lose its number one status within the next fifty years, but eventually it could happen.

As the Iraq invasion started to drag down President Bush's ratings, and many Republicans feared that they may lose one or more Houses in the 2006 election, the Bush administration turned to the U.N. Security Council that it once berated to help them out of their dilemma by forming a coalition in Iraq to defuse criticism of the Bush administration invasion and occupation of Iraq. The handling of Iraq contracts for rebuilding its infrastructure has caused many to believe that this was the administration goal all along, to control the oil and the rebuilding efforts.

The mistreatment of the prisoners under U.S. military control has given the Bush administration a "black eye" in the eyes of the world. The U.S. promised the Iraqi people that they would be liberated from their oppressors, but instead are being faced with some of the same degradation as under Saddam Hussein. Abu Ghraib prison, where approximately three dozen Iraqis have been killed while in U.S. custody, is the same prison used by Saddam Hussein as a torture chamber.

It appears that the Bush administration's philosophy is that since the United States of America is the most powerful nation in the world, it is not compelled to abide by any rules. It does not have to be diplomatic, it does not have to be cajoling, and it does not have to use appeasement to get what it wants or to do what it wants. In other words, it can get away with doing just about any unsavory thing and the rest of the world will just sit on their hands.

A March 19, 2003, Wall Street Journal article by Hugh Pope and Peter Waldman reminds us of the following:

> Napoleon proclaimed a similar new era of equality and respect for "true Muslims" as he

marched into Cairo, Egypt, in 1798, killing one thousand members of Egypt's ruling caste. He was accompanied by 100 French scientists, researching an encyclopedia and spreading European "enlightenment" to bemused Egyptian intellectuals. "Peoples of Egypt, you will be told that I have come to destroy your religion," said Napoleon as he entered Cairo. "Do not believe it! Reply that I have come to restore your rights!" The Bush administration also dropped leaflets of propaganda in Iraq prior to the invasion urging the Iraqis to cooperate with U.S. forces when they enter Iraq. Napoleon's real goals involved France's colonial rivalry with Britain. He sought to outflank the British and frustrate their efforts to find a new route to India. But the French committed a fatal error, repeated by nearly all Western powers since: attempting to divide and rule by appointment of minority groups to govern hostile majority populations.

Months after the French arrival, Islamic clerics stirred a mob to rebellion, killing 300 Frenchmen. The French then bombarded Cairo, killing 3,000 Cairns and ransacking the chief mosque of al-Azhar. The people of Cairo were overwhelmed with disdain at the destruction and looting of their wealth by the French. Do we see a similar pattern here?

In 1882, Britain went to Egypt and secured the Suez Canal route to its Indian Empire. This triggered a bloody revolt by nationalist Egyptians officers. For the next 40 years, British administrators ruled Egypt from behind the scenes in what was called the "veiled protectorate," fashioning themselves as liberators of Egypt's feudal peasants. Several incidents helped make Egypt a center of anti-western fervor, among them the brutal punishment of villagers when a fracas with British officers out on a pigeon hunt left an officer dead.

And in 1914, British troops landed in what is now Iraq as part of Britain's campaign against the Ottoman Turks, allies of Germany in World War I. "Britain was bursting with confidence in an easy and early victory," wrote British officer T.E. Lawrence, better known as Lawrence of Arabia, who organized the historic Arab Revolt against the Ottomans. Instead, it took four years for Britain, with vastly superior arms, to conquer all of Iraq. They too, made similar promises to Iraq: "Our armies do not come into your cities and lands as conquerors or enemies, but as liberators," said Gen. F.S. Maude, commander of the British forces in Iraq. "Your wealth has been stripped of you by unjust men. The people of Baghdad shall flourish under institutions which are in consonance with their sacred laws. The Arab race may rise once more to greatness!" But Britain retained the Ottomans' long reliance on Sunni Muslims as the governing class in Iraq, an arrangement that exacerbated conflicts with Iraq's larger Kurdish and Shia Muslim populations. British troops also launched artillery shells on the Shia city of Najaf, killing 6,000 to 10,000 Iraqis in putting down a joint revolt by Shia and Sunni Muslims in 1920.

In 1921 the British brought a leader of the Arab Revolt out of exile in London and anointed him King of Iraq – King Faisal. Years later, Hussein would make Iraq's tribes a bulwark of his own regime.

In 1982, Israel invaded Lebanon to crush Palestinian guerrillas. Shia villagers in Lebanon at first welcomed Israeli troops as liberators from Palestinian fighters who had made the border region a war zone. But as Ariel Sharon, then Israel's defense minister, pushed his forces to the outskirts of Beirut, where they killed thousands of civilians, the offensive stalled amid furious criticism in Europe, the

U.S. and Israel itself. The once grateful Shiites turned against the Israelis as occupiers, and efforts to impose a peace agreement on Lebanon through Israel's Maronite Christian allies blew up in a fury of bombings and killings. "The idea that you can change the Middle East with guns and bayonets is wrong," says Bob Dillion, U.S. ambassador to Beirut at the time.

The Bush administration expressed confidence that the U.S. with its record of democratizing defeated tyrannies in Germany and Japan, can succeed in Iraq. The administration believed it can avoid the pitfalls of the past by mounting a devastating military strike followed quickly with billions of dollars in reconstruction and humanitarian aid. The U.S. officials were also optimistic that Iraq, with its deep-rooted educational and civil-service systems, its history of secularism, its utter exhaustion after three decades of totalitarianism – and its oil wealth – is exceptionally ready to leapfrog forward.

My point of view, and I am sure the point of view of many, is that the Iraq war was unwarranted, unjustified, inhumane and extremely costly both in terms of lives lost and the financial costs. Both of which have seen inexorable increases within the first three years of the war.

The Bush administration has been running the country under such reticence so that not even the Congress has been kept abreast of certain information such as the eavesdropping and prisoner abuse. In 2001 Bush authorized the National Security Agency to monitor the international phone calls and e-mails of U.S. citizens to track people with ties to al-Qaeda without a warrant. However, Congress was not made aware of it until late 2005. And regarding the prisoner abuse, members of Congress had briefings with the Pentagon only a few days before the news broke, yet they were not informed. They learned about the abuse the same way as the general public.

When I started to write this book, I expected to complete it by the end of 2003 or early 2004. I never expected the war to last very long since the Bush administration gave the impression that it would last six months. However, as this book went to press, the battle is raging on with no end in sight, even though the Iraqis elected a Democratic government on January 30, 2005. As of April 2006, many people believe that Iraq has erupted into a civil war. My greatest wish is that something will occur very soon to end the bloodshed whether it's by divine intervention or the demands of the American people and the international community.

In these times of strife and war, how apropos are the words from a hymn by William Watkins Reid Jr.:

O God of every nation, of every, race and land, redeem the whole creation with your almighty hand; where hate and fear divide us and bitter threats are hurled, in love and mercy guide us and heal our strife-torn world.

GOD BLESS AMERICA

ACKNOWLEDGMENTS

I want to thank the many reporters whose articles and reports formed the basis for this book.

I have not personally interviewed or spoke with any of the people whose comments, experiences and suggestions appear herein, nor have I personally interviewed or spoke with any government officials. I relied solely on the information gathered from the various media, including but not limited to, daily newspaper, magazines, TV newscasts, the Internet, etc.

INDEX

London Times, 11/22/03,

Michael Moore, 2003

Middle East AP, 9/18/03,

MSNBC, 7/21/04, 8/26/05

NBC, 6/26/05

Newsweek, 10/22/03, 11/23/03, 1/24/04, 1/26/04, 1/28/04, 2/5/04,

New York Times, 1/29/03, 6/17/03, 6/24/03, 7/8/03,

7/9/03, 8/3/03, 9/9/03, 9/10/03, 9/11/03, 9/17/03, 9/29/03, 9/30/03, 10/5/03, 10/6/03, 10/10/03, 10/13/03, 10/16/03, 10/18/03, 10/21/03, 10/25/03, 10/26/03, 11/4/03, 11/7/03, 11/8/03, 11/12/03, 11/16/03, 11/17/03, 11/24/03, 11/30/03, 12/1/03, 12/4/03, 12/5/03, 12/10/03, 12/11/03, 12/29/03, 12/30/03, 1/1/04, 1/5/04, 1/23/04, 2/1/04, 2/2/04, 2/4/04, 2/5/04, 2/25/04, 3/5/04, 3/5/04, 3/24/04, 3/26/04, 4/10/04, 4/15/04, 4/17/04, 4/18/04, 4/28/04, 6/9/04, 6/17/04, 8/3/04, 9/23/04, 4/30/05, 8/15/05, 10/5/05, 2/8/06

North County Times, 5/4/03, 8/12/03, 9/8/03

KPBS, 10/16/03, 4/11/05

Reuters News, 1/31/04, 5/04, 5/18/04, 6/6/03, 6/24/03, 7/1/03, 7/3/03, 7/6/03, 7/8/03, 7/12/03, 7/21/03, 8/18/03, 8/20/03, 9/4/03, 9/16/03, 10/16/03, 10/17/03, 10/19/03, 11/2/03, 12/3/03, 12/4/03, 12/5/03, 12/10/03, 12/18/03, 12/19/03, 12/30/03, 1/2/04, 1/7/04, 2/24/04, 3/22/04, 4/11/04, 6/26/05, 8/4/05, 2/13/06

Scientific American 2/2006

The Guardian 10/13/03

The New Standard, 6/22/04,7/5/04,

Time, 4/7/03, 12/8/03, 10/05

U.N. News Center, 2/10/03, 7/4/03, 7/6/03, 8/14/03, 10/17/03, 2/15/06

USA Today, 7/11/03, 9/8/03

Wall Street Journal, 3/8/2000, 3/17/03, 3/19/03, 4/8/03, 4/11/03, 4/25/03, 4/30/03, 5/6/03, 5/8/03, 5/17/03, 6/03, 6/25/03, 7/3/03,7/7/03, 1/04, 2/2/04, 2/25/04, 3/17/04, 3/18/04, 3/24/04, 3/25/04, 4/21/04, 4/28/04, 5/24/04, 5/27/04, 11/28/2005

Washington Post, 1/7/03, 6/23/03, 9/5/03, 9/8/03, 12/11/03, 12/18/03, 12/19/03, 1/9/04, 2/4/04, 5/13/05, 11/7/05, 11/8/05.

World AFP, 8/4/03, 8/14/03, 8/20/03,

World Reuters 7/10/03

World AP, 8/4/03, 1/7/04,

Yahoo News, 8/1/03

SUPERPOWERS

The United States, with its huge arsenal, deployed over 270,000 soldiers to the Persian Gulf in March 2003. Listed below are some of the arsenal used during the invasion of Iraq:

Airborne Brigade, Airborne Division, Infantry Division, Cavalry Division, Armored Division, Armored Cavalry Regiment, Mountain Division (Light Infantry), Infantry Division (Mechanized), Army Air and Missile Defense Command, and Armed forces Central Command.

BATTLESHIPS

The USS Nimitz carried 8,000 servicemen and servicewomen, USS Kitty Hawk with 8,000 battle group, USS Harry Truman, with 6,000 air wing, USS Theodore Roosevelt 8,000, USS Abraham Lincoln 8,000, USS Constellation with a crew of 5,630 and the USNS Comfort with a crew of 1,100 Navy and civilian personnel. Six hundred 600 Coast Guard units from various parts of the United States were also deployed to Iraq. Some of these battle groups, such as the USS Kitty Hawk, were equipped with Carrier Air Wings, guided missile cruisers, guided missile destroyers, frigates, and fast-attack submarines.

The 173rd Airborne Brigade is a rapid reaction Unit of 1,800 soldiers that serve as the U.S. European Command Conventional airborne strategic response force. The 3rd Infantry Division consists of 15,000 soldiers. This unit was ordered to Kuwait in December 2002 to prepare to attack Iraq. The 101st Airborne Division, consisting of a crew of 20,000, was ordered to deploy on February 7,

2003. The 3rd Armored Cavalry Regiments consisting of a crew of 5,200 received its deployment orders on February 15th, while the 10th Mountain Division received its deployment orders February 10th in addition to other deployments.

MARINES

The 1st Marine Expeditionary Force consisting of 45,000 servicemen and servicewomen some of whom were deployed to the Persian Gulf. In addition, deployment orders went out to the 2nd Marine Expeditionary Brigade, the 15th Marine Expeditionary Unit, the 24th Marine Expeditionary Unit and the 26th Marine Expeditionary Unit.

AIR FORCE

Air Force division consist of fighter jets such as the 28th Bomb Wing with B-1B bombers, the 49th Fighter Wing with F-117A Nighthawk stealth fighters, the 1st Fighter Wing with F-15C Eagle fighters, the 60th Air Mobility Wing with KC-10 Extender refueling aircraft, the 55th Wing, which included eight squadrons of pilots, navigators, maintenance, electronic warfare officers and others. In addition, to the 116th Air Control Wing with E-8C Joint Stars ground surveillance aircraft, the 347th Rescue Wing with HC-130 combat search-and-rescue aircraft, the 43rd Airlift Wing with C-130 transports, the 4th Fighter Wing with F-15E Strike Eagle. The 6th Air Mobility Wing with KC-135 refueling tankers, the 11th Reconnaissance Squadron with Predator Unmanned aerial vehicle (UAV), the 16th Special Operations Wing with AC-30 gunships, MC-130 Combat Talons, the 52nd

Fighter Wing with F-16 Fighting Falcons, the F-16 Fighting Falcon fighter-bombers and A-10 Thunderbolts provide air support for ground forces, and the 509th Bomb Wing with B-2 Spirit stealth bombers, in addition to many other weapons including the "Shock and Awe" napalm bombs (which is kerosene and nitroglycerin) whereby when it comes in contact with human beings, it forms a human torch as was done in Vietnam and phosphorous when comes in contact with people, burns the flesh to the bone.

BRITISH ARSENAL:

Britain provided 40,000 troops and 100 fixed-wing aircraft and 27 support helicopters to fight the war in Iraq. The aircraft deployment includes Sentry AEW1 aircraft, Jaguar GR3 fighters and Tornado GR4 bombers, VC10 and Tri-Star air-to-air refueling aircraft, Hercules transport aircraft, Tornado F3 air defense aircraft with the newly integrated ASRA, Tornado GR4 bombers, Harrier GR7 jump jet fighters and 27 Puma and Chinook helicopters. Among the British forces are the 1st UK Armored Division which consists of mostly logistical and support units, Headquarters and Signal Regiment; the Queen's Dragoon Guards (reconnaissance), 28 Engineer Regiment, 1 General Support Regiment, Royal Logistic Corps, 2 Close Support Regiment, Royal Logistic Corps, 2nd Battalion, Royal Electrical & Mechanical Engineers, 1 Close Support Medical Regiment, 5 General Support Medical Regiment, 1 Regiment, Royal Military Police and 33 Explosive Ordinance Disposal Regiment, 30 Signal Regiment and 32 Regiment Royal Artillery (Phoenix UAVs).

The British also deployed their 7th Armored Brigade consisting of Headquarters and Signal Squadron, Royal

Scots Dragon Guards (Challenger 2 tanks), 2nd Royal Tank Regiment (Challenger 2 tanks), 1st Battalion The Black Watch (Warrior infantry fighting vehicles), 1st Battalion Royal Regiments of Fusiliers (Warrior infantry fighting vehicles), 3rd Regiment Royal Horse Artillery (AS90 self-propelled gun's), 32 Armored Engineer Regiment, Queens Royal lancer (Challenger 2 tanks), 1st Battalion Irish Guards (Warrior infantry fighting vehicles and 1st Battalion and the Light Infantry (Warrior infantry fighting vehicles).

In addition, the British deployed 16 Air Assault Brigade, which included Headquarters and Signal Squadron, 1st Battalion The Royal Irish Regiment, 1st Battalion Parachute Regiment, 3rd Battalion Parachute Regiment, 7 (Para) Regiment Royal Horse Artillery, (105mm Light Gun's), 23 Engineer Regiment, Household Cavalry Regiment, (1 x armored reconnaissance squadron), 3rd Regiment Army Air Corps (Lynx & Gazelle helicopters), 7 Air Assault Battalion, Royal Electrical & Mechanical Engineers, 13 Air Assault Support Regiment, Royal Logistic Corps, and 16 Close Support Medical Regiment.

Also deployed by the British was their 102 Logistic Brigade consisting of headquarters, 36 Engineer Regiment, 33 and 34 Field Hospitals, 4 General Support Medical Regiment, Elements from 11 Explosive Ordnance Disposal Regiment, etc.

ABOUT THE AUTHOR

M. M. CHANTILOUPE was educated at Adelphi University in New York. She is an emeritus Certified Financial Planner and Registered Representative.